LIFE OF CHRIST.

A CHRONOLOGICAL AND GEOGRAPHICAL

INTRODUCTION

TO THE

LIFE OF CHRIST.

BY

CH. ED. CASPARI.

From the Original German Work, Revised by the Author.

TRANSLATED, WITH ADDITIONAL NOTES, BY

MAURICE J. EVANS, B.A.

WITH MAP OF THE SCENE OF OUR LORD'S LABOURS,
AND PLAN OF JERUSALEM.

WIPF & STOCK · Eugene, Oregon

Wipf and Stock Publishers
199 W 8th Ave, Suite 3
Eugene, OR 97401

A Chronological and Geographical Introduction to the Life of Christ
From the Original German Work, Revised by the Author
By Caspari, Chretien Edouard and Evans, Maurice J.
Softcover ISBN-13: 978-1-6667-6205-1
Hardcover ISBN-13: 978-1-6667-6206-8
eBook ISBN-13: 978-1-6667-6207-5
Publication date 10/11/2022
Previously published by T. & T. Clark, 1876

This edition is a scanned facsimile of the original edition published in 1876.

AUTHOR'S PREFACE.

THE negative criticism of the Gospels, as conducted in the present day, and as it has manifested itself in a series of works treating of the life of Jesus, bases its destructive results—no doubt without always admitting it—upon philosophic presuppositions, derived from a conception of the universe hostile to the idea of a revelation. It denies the supernatural in the life of Christ, because it rejects the supernatural in general. But in connection with this, it by no means despises the external evidences derived from history and geography, so far as the testimony of these may serve as a support for those suppositions. In this manner disquiet and doubt is introduced into many a mind whose conception of the world's order is in harmony with belief in a revelation, and which would desire to remain unassailed by those philosophic doubts and presuppositions. History and chronology, geography and topography, are with great skill employed as instruments for assailing the authenticity of the Gospels, for bringing the contents of these books into mutual contradiction, and for denying the possibility of reconciling the statements of the Gospels with the facts of history and chorography.

Some years ago, therefore, I imposed upon myself the task of coming to a distinct appreciation of the value or worthlessness of these objections and attacks. I very soon became convinced that the works professedly handling these questions hitherto existing stood in need of an entire revision, and applied therefore in every case to the original sources. Since these studies proved useful to myself, and often led to results unexpected, and in my opinion not unimportant, I thought it incumbent on me to publish these results, flattering myself with the hope they might be made serviceable to others also.

It might perhaps appear strange that in studies like Biblical geography and chronology, which have been so abundantly treated of, and from so many points of view, there should yet remain important discoveries to be gleaned ; but the enigma is solved when it is considered that the exegetes have seldom drawn their chronology and geography—regarded by them as subordinate questions—from the sources themselves, but have received them at second or third hand ; that, on the other hand, professional geographers and chronologists, even the Masters among them, are no exegetes, but are often misled by inaccurate translations of the Gospels. This evil I have earnestly striven to avoid, inasmuch as in all the sources I have had recourse to the original text, and that, in addition to the sources of which my predecessors have availed themselves, I have ransacked the books of Jewish tradition—hitherto, to the great loss of the cause, too much neglected.

The literature bearing on the subject is not easily accessible ; the Patristic, archæological, and Talmudic writings, as well as the descriptions of travels, are often difficult to find. The more am I under obligations on this account to honoured friends who have been helpful to me in this respect, especially to Professor Reuss of Strassburg, as well as to the librarians of the City Library at Strassburg,[1] and of the Protestant and Catholic Seminary Libraries there, who have favoured me with advice and help.

And so may this little book, notwithstanding its defects and imperfections, go its way under the Lord's blessing.

CH. ED. CASPARI.

GEUDERTHEIM, ALSACE, 24th September 1868.

---

[1] This famous library no longer exists.

TRANSLATOR'S PREFACE.

THIS volume, as its title indicates, is designed not to set before us the Person of the Son of God in the experiences of His inner life, but to present us with a clear and well-ordered account of the various incidents in that divine-human life on earth, drawn from the narrative of the four evangelists. For this purpose it is not necessary to *prove* the inspiration of these evangelists themselves. That they wrote under the immediate impulse and control of the Holy Spirit will be believed by all who accept the testimony of Christ and His apostles; but it is with the testimony of these authoritative documents, only as that of honest and competent witnesses, that we have here to do. By the method of a keen and thorough analysis, the author renders evident the real and essential—though by no means always formal—agreement in the testimony delivered by the four separate witnesses. For our belief in the divine inspiration of the evangelists is surely not jeopardized by the admission of a certain freedom on their part in the grouping of the incidents and discourses of our Lord's life, and the more full and complete record of details on the part of one evangelist rather than another. His argument for the authenticity of the fourth Gospel is of special value in the present day, as opposed to the ever varied assaults of modern unbelief. The instances he gives of its being the work of an eye-witness might be largely increased. To these might be added the evangelist's recital of the very words rumoured throughout Judea, "Jesus maketh and baptizeth more disciples than John" (iv. 1), the minute details given by him in the history of the feeding of the five thousand, and of the storm upon the lake, and many similar traits.

The importance of the preliminary examination, with regard

to the Jewish chronology, will be at once apparent. Thus the
nobleman of Capernaum is with the Saviour at 1 P.M. (John
iv. 52). Shortly after this he returns home. After a journey
of some four hours, he is met near home by those announcing
the recovery of his son. But it is already sunset, and they
reply to his inquiry, " *Yesterday*, at the seventh hour, the
fever left him."—Mark i. 32, Luke iv. 40, with the sunset a
multitude of diseased are brought to Christ. Because with
the setting of the sun *the Sabbath was brought to a close*, and
the following day began.—In Luke xxiv. 29 the disciples
constrain their Lord to abide with them ; *because the day has
declined*. The disciples were again in Jerusalem, after a
journey of two or three hours, on the *same* day, *i.e.* before
sunset. But from p. 4 we see the day was said to *decline*
(κλίνειν) half an hour after mid-day. Similarly is the *declining
day* of Luke ix. 12 to be understood. I have added (p. 18)
a supplementary table of the Jewish calendar as compared
with the Roman, by which the date (according to the Julian
calendar) of the festivals occurring during the public ministry
of Christ will be readily found. It must be remembered,
however, that the Jewish day *begins only* on the evening of
the week day there indicated ; the *day* properly so called—τὸ
συμπλήρωμα, Acts ii. 1—falls on the following week day.
Thus 15th Nisan, A.D. 28, was properly *Wednesday*, 31st
March ; as it only *began* on the evening of Tuesday, 30th
March. So with all the other dates.

The key to the right understanding of the chronology of
the Lord's public ministry is to be sought in the determination of the date of the festival mentioned John v. 1. That
this date was the 10th Tisri (18–19th September), the day of
Atonement, A.U.C. 781, A.D. 28, may be regarded as fully
established in the following pages. The fact that this date
falls in 781 tends further to confirm the argument by which
the 15th year of Tiberius is shown to begin with the
commencement of 781. But it further follows, that since
Christ was only about (ὡσεί, *fere*) thirty years of age in the
spring of this year, He could not have been born so early as
the beginning of 750 ; otherwise He would have already
entered on His thirty-second year. His birth took place

several weeks—probably some months—before a Passover which followed the death of Herod (*Antiq.* xvii. 9, sec. 3 ; *de Bello*, ii. 1, sec. 3), either that of 750 or that of 753. The difficulties connected with our accepting the Passover of 750 as the one following our Lord's birth are : (1) that of crowding in, between the time of the lunar eclipse, March 12–13, and that of Passover, April 12, the long succession of events mentioned by Josephus (*Antiq.* xvii. 6, sec. 5—8, sec. 4), including the journey made by Herod to the baths on the eastern shore of the Dead Sea (Wâdy Zerka Maîn), and his return to Jericho ; and the procession of the funeral cortége to the mountain fort of Herodium in the Jebel Furdîs, about four miles from Bethlehem. Whiston would therefore suppose a period of thirteen months to elapse between the eclipse and the Passover, after which Archelaus went to Rome ; with how little reason, will be clear upon a moment's consideration of the relations between Archelaus and Cæsar. (2) Varus, not Quirinus, was Prefect of Syria during the greater part of 750 ; and (3) the time of Herod's death cannot be placed earlier than the beginning of the Sabbatic year, September 752.

The difficulties connected with our supposing the Passover 753 to be the one which followed our Lord's birth are : (1) the fact that this presidency of Quirinus over Syria (and probably Cilicia) is not mentioned by Josephus. But the silence of Josephus cannot invalidate the express statement of the evangelist, confirmed as it is by the testimony of Justin Martyr (himself a native of Sichem, which formed part of the former kingdom of Herod) in his *First Apology*, addressed in the first half of the second century to one so well qualified to judge of the truth of Justin's assertion as the Emperor Antoninus.[1] Justin Martyr says (*Apol.* i. 34) : " Now, there

---

[1] An abstract of the argument, by which Zumpt shows that Quirinus in all probability entered on the presidency of the conjoint provinces of Syria and Cilicia *about the close of* 750, will be found in the English translation of Wieseler, pp. 129 ff., and in Fairbairn's *Hermeneutical Manual*, p. 507. It may well have happened that, on account of the extent of his province and the wars on the frontiers (Tacitus, *Annal.* iii. 48), he should entrust the charge of the Roman interests in Judæa to Varus, acting in concert with himself. The conclusion of Zumpt is accepted by Merivale and Mommsen.

is a certain village (Bethlehem) in the land of the Jews,
distant from Jerusalem thirty-five stades, in which Jesus
Christ was born ; *as you can learn from the returns (ἀπο-
γραφῶν) made in the time of Quirinus,* who became your first
governor in Judea" (compare also chap. 46, and *Dial. cum
Tryphone,* chap. 78). (2) Josephus appears to imply that
Herod Antipas, who is known from coins to have entered on
his forty-third regnal year, was deposed in the second year of
Caligula (792). Vaillant and Galland have preserved the
inscription of a coin dating from the forty-fourth regnal year
of Antipas. This would point to the year 749, at the latest,
as the time of his accession. (3) Josephus assigns thirty-
seven full years to the reign of Philip the tetrarch. But
Philip must then have begun to reign in 749, that is to say,
during the lifetime of Herod. It is almost certain, therefore, that the princely dignity formerly (B.C. 9) conferred upon
Alexander and Aristobulus — τιμὴν βασιλείας τοῖς υἱοῖς
παραδίδωμι (*de Bello,* i. 23, secs. 1–5)—devolved about three
years before Herod's death (*i.e.* 749) upon Philip and Antipas.
There is a coin of the thirty-seventh year of Philip's reign.

As regards the commencement of John's ministry, the
reasons for believing that this coincided with the beginning
of the Sabbatic year (Sept. 780) are given in a footnote. If
this view be the correct one, Luke (iii. 2) refers not to the
commencement of his ministry, but to a later call received
by him while in the wilderness of Judea. With the time of
autumn rather than winter agrees, too, the account given us of
the food on which John lived at his first arising. The circuit
of the Jordan mentioned by Luke embraces alike Bethania
and Ænon.

In accordance with the principles laid down by the author,
the gospel narrative has been arranged in tables of parallel
columns. The order of Mark forms the basis of this arrangement, although it is not possible, within the limits of a preface,
to explain and justify every deviation from that order. The
succession of events occurring at various times in the neighbourhood of Capernaum, "the Lord's city" (ἡ ἰδία πόλις
αὐτοῦ), is naturally most difficult to determine. Sometimes
the note of time is to be found in an incident like that of

the payment of the tribute-money ; sometimes the note of place is to be found in a single expression, as in " the hem of the mantle " of Matt. xiv. 3 6, as compared with ix. 2 0.[1] The time at which the Sermon on the Mount was delivered is incidentally fixed by the Lord Himself in His allusion to the fair robes of the wild lilies, not woven with hands. The scarlet anemone was seen by Tristram in full flower in the early part of March (March 1–8); and the tuberous purple iris, supposed by Thomson to be the flower alluded to, is in bloom equally early (March 5). When Tristram saw it, it was the 18th March. The allusion to these flowers in Luke's narrative (xxii. 27) shows that he too is reporting the same discourse of the Lord as is Matthew. The author recognises only one rejection of the Lord at Nazareth. That He was not *twice* rejected there, is also the opinion of Van Oosterzee and other good expositors. To suppose that He was, would seem to involve a disregard of the Lord's own direction to His disciples for *their* guidance (Matt. x. 14). That His rejection be placed where Luke places it, is necessary to account for the Lord's withdrawal from Nazareth and taking up His abode at Capernaum. The evidence to be derived from Matt. xxiii. 37, of our Lord's having made several visits to Jerusalem, unrecorded in the first two evangelists, has already been observed by Wieseler and others. That John, in turn, was acquainted with the fact of our Lord's visible Ascension, which he does not record, is apparent from his report of the Lord's words to the disciples at Capernaum : " What, then, if ye

---

[1] From the report of the Lord's own words,—that most certain of all data,—there is good reason for believing that, alike the raising of the young man at Nain, and the raising of the daughter of Jairus at Capernaum, bear date not later than the early spring of the year 29 ; since the Lord could already say to the messengers of John, " Dead are raised ;" and Matthew records their visit to the Saviour before the events of the second-first Sabbath (April 5). It is true the Lord, in His commission to the Twelve (Matt. x. 8), conferred upon them authority to "raise dead persons ;" but His language throughout this discourse is evidently to a large extent prophetic in its application (cf. v. 18), and it is only after the day of Pentecost that the terms of His commission were fully complied with. It is certainly strange that Stier, who in other respects saw so clearly the perspective in that part of the Lord's discourse which is related Matt. x., should regard the words, "Raise dead persons,"—contained as they are in the oldest MSS.,—as a later interpolation. (According to the order of Luke, this commission was given only subsequently to the visit of John's disciples.)

should see (θεωρῆτε) the Son of man *ascending* thither, where He was before?" (vi. 62). Just as he shows his acquaintance with the fact of the Lord's baptism, by his report of the words of the Baptist relating to that event (i. 33, 34). The ground for the silence of this evangelist with regard to the Transfiguration is, perhaps, rather to be sought in the peculiar character of his Gospel itself, which sees *in the whole manifestation* of Christ the manifestation of His glory (i. 14). As far as the authenticity of Mark xvi. 9–20 is concerned, we may safely accept the verdict of Scrivener, that "the more closely it is scrutinized, the more manifestly will it be seen to form a genuine portion of the second Gospel." Whether or not the author's conclusions as to the year of the conversion of Paul, and to the presence of Judas at the institution of the Lord's Supper, be accepted, his general chronological order remains the same.

A peculiar feature of this work is the identification of Judea beyond Jordan with tho pastoral district of the Jaulan. In harmony with the pastoral character of this district is the type of parables uttered by the Lord during His ministry here, as, *e.g.*, the sheep feeding "in the wilderness" (Luke xv. 4), the lost sheep "on the mountains" (Matt. xviii. 12). See Stanley, p. 423. To the north of this district alone, Thomson saw "the pelican of the wilderness" (p. 260). Thomson, too (p. 254), places Judah of the Jordan to the north of the Sea of Galilee; but, misled by the discovery of a Seîd Yehûda immediately to the south of Tell el-Kady,—probably the Jehud of Josh. xix. 45,—he places this district to the S.E. of the ancient Dan. That a Bethania *did* exist between Bethsaida-Julias and Cæsarea-Philippi, is shown from the reading of several western codices in Mark viii. 22. That Bethsaida cannot be meant, is evident from the fact that the Evangelist Mark speaks of Bethania as a place without walls (κώμη), whereas Bethsaida is spoken of as a walled town (πόλις, Luke ix. 10 ; Josephus, *Antiq.* xviii. 2, sec. 1). Ewald accordingly, on the ground of the reading in codex D, etc., entirely endorses Caspari's view.

That the site of Eastern Bethsaida is not at Et-Tell is affirmed by Pliny (see p. 94), and is confirmed by Thomson in his text, although on his map the ordinary position is assigned to it. Thomson says (p. 360): "When I was here in 1855, the Bedawîn in the Butaiha applied the name Bethsaida to a bank on the shore of the lake, which is distinguished by a few palm trees, and in some modern maps this site is called Masadiyeh, a derivative from the same root as Bethsaida, both having reference to *fishing*. . . . It is nearly certain that it was located on the shore, and not several miles from it, at the *Tell* to which the name is now affixed." In the case of the woes pronounced upon the three cities, it would appear more natural to think the *Western* Bethsaida was present to the Lord's mind. *This* was the scene of the miracles recorded Matt. xiv. 36, and many others. Of the Eastern Bethsaida, it is difficult to say He had wrought "many" mighty works there. It is, moreover, associated by Him with the cities of Galilee. That the apostles report the Lord's words in a sense different from that in which they were accustomed to speak themselves, is only one proof the more of the strictly objective fidelity of their narration. Whether the modern Bîr Kerâzeh is the Chorazin of the age of Christ, or has only received its name from the fact of the inhabitants of the ancient Chorazin having migrated there to escape the threat of earthquakes,—which is the supposition of Canon Tristram,—may be left an open question. At any rate, it was taken for Chorazin as early as the time of Eusebius. The conclusions of the author as to the site of Capernaum have received striking corroboration from the researches of Tristram, prosecuted on the spot almost simultaneously with those of Caspari at home. "Wherever the cities stood," adds Canon Tristram, "the absence of remains and the obliteration of their very names more utterly than those of Sodom and Gomorrah, testify to a fulfilment of that prophetic woe which, though not denounced against the walls and stones, but against those who dwelt in them, is illustrated by their erasure from the face of the earth—'cast down to hell,' lost, and forgotten, though consecrated by the presence and mighty works of the divine Saviour. Capernaum in its oblivion preaches to Christendom a sermon more forcible than the columns of Tyre or the stones of Jerusalem." The general conclusions of the author are favourably discussed in an able review by Dr. Klaiber, *Jahr-bücher für Deutsche Theologie*, xiv. 1, pp. 326–336.

In the Topography of Jerusalem, it will be seen that the Pool of Bethesda is identified with the *Birket Israîn* or *Israîl*. No other reservoir in Jerusalem would seem indeed to be sufficiently large to comply with the requirements of the gospel narrative. This locality, too, would appear to be assigned to it by Eusebius, who speaks of it as *Bezatha* (*Bηζαθά*).[1] That the present Garden of Gethsemane, although greatly shorn of its former dimensions (now only 50 paces square), occupies the site of the former garden or olive-yard bearing that name, is as certain as the identity of almost any historical site can be. What other locality will equally well answer to the requirements of the history? (For some excellent observations on this point, see p. 285 of Dr. William Smith's valuable *N. T. History*.) Interesting in connection with this spot is the name *Bezetha* (*Βεζεθά*), borne by the northern quarter of the city, which, according to its *true* derivation, is from בית זיתא (= *Olive Place*), of which the name borne in the present day by one of the five wards of Gaza is the exact Arabic equivalent.[2]

The derivation assigned by the author to the name Golgotha receives confirmation from the investigations of Ritter, iv. 134, 135. For the identity of that which is known as the Holy Sepulchre with the tomb "hewn out in the rock," the testimony of Cyril, adduced in Ritter, ii. p. 33, is of great value. He speaks of "traces and remains of the garden" as still being left in his day. Of equal interest, as describing the appearance of the Sepulchre before the time of the Crusades, are the words of the venerable Bede, belonging to the first half of the eighth century. " . . . In the northern part of which monument the Sepulchre itself, that is, the place of the Lord's body, is formed from the same rock, being seven feet long, and raised to the extent of three palms' width above the rest of the pavement. Which place is open, not from above,

---

[1] That the healings wrought there were the effect of a miraculous intervention, appears to follow from the statement of John v. 7, even though the account of the angel be entirely left out.

[2] So Bædecker, p. 152, with whose view on this subject Caspari agrees.

but on the whole southern side, where the body was placed in. Now the colour of this monument and niche is said to be a mixture of red and white." This information Bede gives on the testimony of eye-witnesses. (The citation will be found in full, in the original Latin, in Macknight, ii. 542 of the fifth edition.)

The origin of the substructures under the Aksa Mosque is still a matter of discussion among scholars. For Tristram's handling of the subject, see pp. 183, 184 of his work, where a good description of these subterranean edifices is given. A general impression of their appearance is to be obtained from a woodcut on p. 689 of Thomson's *Land and the Book.*

As regards the English literature of this whole subject, I have in the notes appended made no attempt at anything like completeness in the citation of authors. My aim has been simply to supply such hints and references as may less readily be found collected in any one book. To this alone must the fact be attributed, that the admirable Handbook of Dr. Porter, for example, has been passed over in silence. The classical work of Ritter is cited, when not otherwise specified, from the English translation of Messrs. T. and T. Clark. The references to the elaborate work of Dr. Robinson are to the third and last (complete) edition of his *Researches* (1867). Bishop Ellicott is cited from the first edition of his *Lectures,*—a work which, after an interval of fifteen years, remains an unsurpassed model of critical tact and spiritual insight. The citations from Dean Stanley are from the fifth edition of his *Sinai and Palestine;* those from Canon Tristram, from his second edition (1866). For Mr. Bonar's *Narrative,* the sixteenth edition ; and for Dr. Thomson's *Land and the Book,* the English edition of 1863 is referred to. Wieseler is cited according to the scholarly translation of Mr. Venables (1864).

In conclusion, I have to acknowledge my obligation to M. Caspari for the readiness with which he has furnished me with information of great value, while the English edition of this work was being prepared for the press ; with the effect, it is hoped, of rendering this work—embodying, as it does, to a great extent the labour of the author's lifetime—fully abreast with the present stage of scientific knowledge. (For that

portion of the work included within square brackets he bears
no part of the responsibility.)   At the same time I desire to
express my thanks to the Rev. James Kennedy, M.A., of New
College, Edinburgh, for his kindness in verifying certain
references, and thus adding to the efficiency of the work ; and
to the Rev. Ellis Edwards, M.A., of the Calvinistic Methodist
College, Bala, for services of a like nature.   Every effort has
been made, on the part of the printers and myself, to secure
as great degree of accuracy as possible.   If any typographical
errors have nevertheless escaped attention, they will not, it is
believed, be found to be of such importance as to interfere
with the general trustworthiness of the volume as a book of
reference.

M. J. E.

CARNARVON, *December* 1875.

PRELIMINARY OBSERVATIONS.

It is not the portrait of Jesus Christ which is here presented, but merely the frame for that portrait.

A history of the life of Jesus, such as is on many sides aimed at in the present day, is a genetic presentation not only of that which He was, but of the reasons why He was so, and the manner in which He became so.

"In the fulness of the time" Jesus Christ came. It is therefore one of the abiding tasks of science to depict more and more clearly the then existing condition of the world, to present vividly the state of affairs, the moral conditions of society, the seeking and aspirations of the men among whom He lived. This it is necessary to do, in order to gain a background for the life of Christ, such as shall set forth that life in its full and true light. So soon, however, as this background is itself regarded as the central figure, the light to whose brightness it serves as a foil; so soon as one's efforts are directed to the end of finding in these conditions of the world and of minds the dynamic force which, so to speak, has created this life; so soon as these external agencies are accepted as the cause, by the operation of which Jesus became, and could not but become, that which He was,—the firm ground of history is at once abandoned, and—however great the efforts historically to explain and adjust the facts of His life—the memoir becomes a work of the imagination, a romance. The sources whence such a biography must be derived are the Gospels. These too, we admit, recognise a development in the life of Jesus, for they teach that He grew, and waxed strong in spirit — τὸ παιδίον ηὔξανε καὶ ἐκραταιοῦτο, Luke ii. 40. But *how* this took place, by what powers, means, and influences, is nowhere said ; on the con-

b

trary, the Gospels set Jesus before us in the completeness of
His person. It is nowhere shown when, where, and how He
formed His plan of redemption; in what way His ideas arose
and developed themselves, were modified or perfected. That
which He willed and was on the day of His crucifixion, that
He perfectly willed and was at the moment of His first
arising,—there is no trace of progress, development, or modifi-
cation. A genetic life of Jesus is an impracticable undertaking.

On the other hand, not only do we regard it as possible,
but esteem it a problem propounded to the effort of scientific
thought, to obtain such a grasp of the history of Christ as to
present Him, and render His life intelligible, not in the
process of His *becoming* what He was, but in the completeness
of that which He ultimately *was*. That, however, this work
is no easy one, of which a single thinker can fully acquit
himself, is seen from the fact that it was always, and ever
remains, the task of the whole of Christendom, and of the
Church in particular, ever more deeply, many-sidedly, and
perfectly, so to apprehend and comprehend Christ " that He
may gain a form and outline ($\mu o \rho \phi \omega \theta \hat{\eta}$)."

To the solution of this question, however, the frame and
outwork contributes more than is ordinarily recognised and
acknowledged. Frequently is the opinion expressed that the
chronological and geographical element in the life of Christ is
without significance. It is, many suppose, a matter of indifference to ascertain whether Christ's public labours extended
to several years, or only a few months; whether He was
crucified A.D. 30, or in some other year; whether the day of
His death was the preparation for Passover, or the day of the
paschal festival; whether Capernaum was situated in the
territory of Gennesar, or at the northern end of the Sea of
Tiberias; whether Sychar was identical with Sichem, or was
distinct from it; whether or not the Church of the Holy
Sepulchre marks the scene of the crucifixion and resurrection;
whether Jesus was once only, or several times, in Jerusalem:
all these outworks, it is thought, may be dispensed with, if
only the spirit, nature, and doctrine of Jesus is seized. Yet
this is a great and ruinous mistake. If Jesus Christ is thus

spiritualized, and severed from the relations of time and space, such false spiritualism receives its punishment in the result that the whole objectively historical character of the person of Jesus becomes eventually doubtful, and is subtilized into the ideal. It belongs to the very nature of history to have its roots in time and space ; the reality of the historical person is conditionated by the fact that place, relations, and time are clearly ascertained. Many of the weightiest doubts urged against the authenticity of the Gospel of John fall within this category. In this Gospel, *e.g.*, it is said that Jesus proceeded from the place where John was baptizing to Cana of Galilee in a single day. It is assumed, then, as a proved truth that this place of baptism was in the neighbourhood of Jericho—a city fully three days' journey from Cana ; from this the conclusion is drawn that it is impossible the account which represents Jesus as travelling ninety miles in one day can be the work of an eye-witness. The objection, however, disappears when it is shown that the scene of John's baptism was not near Jericho, but at the northern end of the Sea of Gennesareth, on the Upper Jordan, at a place some six or seven hours' distance from Cana of Galilee.

So, too, do we frequently read that the Synoptists teach that Jesus was crucified on the 15th Nisan ; but that the fourth Gospel, on the other hand, places this event on the preparation-day, and is thus in contradiction not only with the Synoptists, but also with the veritable Apostle John, who, according to the tradition of Asia Minor, taught that Jesus was crucified on the 15th Nisan. From this it is concluded that the same John could not be the author of that Gospel which declares precisely the opposite. This objection, however, disappears so soon as it is shown that not only the author of the fourth Gospel, but also the Synoptists and the tradition of Asia Minor give the 14th Nisan as the day of the crucifixion. Such instances prove that this outwork has its indisputable value. To prepare the frame for the portrait of Jesus is the object of the present work ; the main epochs in the life of the Lord are to be chronologically determined, His journeyings presented in their natural sequence, the localities affected by these journeys geographically fixed. In this behoof must especially a harmony of the Gospels be aimed at. The possibility or impossibility of succeeding in such an undertaking depends mainly upon the conception which one forms to himself of the Gospels. On this point, therefore, we are bound, first of all, to give an intelligible explanation.

That the three first Gospels admit of a synoptical treatment is acknowledged by all; but that the fourth Gospel can be brought within this complex is in the present day frequently and decidedly denied. This very impossibility, thus assumed, of bringing the fourth Gospel into harmony with the Synoptists is one of the main arguments urged against the authenticity of the Johannine books. The fourth Gospel, it is supposed, assigns to Jesus several years of public labour, and places the scene of His activity almost exclusively in Judea, and especially at Jerusalem; the Synoptists, on the other hand, know only of a few months of public labour on the part of Jesus, and place, with the exception of the last fatal Passover, the scene of His activity in Galilee, and especially on the shore of the Lake of Gennesareth; on this account, it is asserted, one must choose between the Logos-Gospel and the Synoptists, and the decision is, as a rule, unfavourable to the claims of the fourth Gospel. We admit that if it is true the Gospel of John places Christ in entirely different relations of time and place, the truth cannot exist on both sides, and a choice and decision becomes necessary. But, above all, the attempt at harmony must be seriously made before it is pronounced impossible. Our mode of proceeding would be censured, and certainly deservedly so, if we approached our task with a ready-formed, cut and dried opinion. Precisely because chronology and geography have to speak a decisive word in relation to the Gospel of John, it is our bounden duty, in the first place, to subject to a new test the possibility or impossibility of a harmony in this respect. We do not, indeed, approach the task free from all preconceived opinion. Christian antiquity hands down to us the fourth Gospel as a work of the Apostle John; the book itself, it is true, ascribes itself to this apostle only in its superscription; the author nowhere mentions himself by name, but refers to himself as " the other disciple," " the disciple whom Jesus loved;" but that the Apostle John is intended by these expressions is placed beyond doubt. This Gospel is avowedly the work of an eye-witness (John i. 14) ; a series of scenes bear the unmistakeable stamp of personal contemplation, inasmuch as incidental circumstances are narrated, such as a tradition would nowhere and never have preserved. To these, in the first place, belongs John i. 35–52. Observe ver. 38, " he turned himself about ; " ver. 40, " it was about the tenth hour ; " further, vers. 35, 41, iii. 1, the careful enumeration of the days, etc. These are subordinate circumstances, which in tradition get softened down ; only in the mind of a deeply-affected eye-witness do such minutiæ continue to cleave to the picture as its ineffaceable colouring. The same, too, is the case with regard to the scene, John xx. 2–10. Observe in this narrative especially ver. 4, " The two ran together ; and the other disciple ran first, quicker than Peter ; " and vers. 6, 8, " Simon Peter went in . . . and then also the other disciple." If representations of this kind are not the work of an eye-witness, they are the product of an intentionally misleading invention ; tradition, at any rate, they are not. We are therefore justified in starting with the presupposition that this Gospel proceeds from John the apostle, and in retaining this conviction until insuperable arguments convince us of the contrary.

The mission of the apostles was to testify of that which they had seen and heard. Now, if all had seen the same things, if all had been witnesses of all the Lord's acts, their accounts must necessarily accord. But the supposition that the apostles were from the very first called to the apostolate, and were all twelve from that time the Lord's companions, is an entirely baseless hypothesis. Each one of the apostles, after accompanying the Lord on a particular journey, returned to his home and calling until a fresh opportunity was presented of accompanying the Lord. Even passages like Luke v. 11 do not justify our inferring that there was a constant accompanying of Him, since it is evident that after this event Peter still continued to be a fisherman. So soon, however, as we come to the conclusion that to-day this disciple, to-morrow that, was one of the Lord's attendants, it is naturally to be expected that each one of them would especially accompany the Lord, when He was in the native land of the disciple. Nathanael in Cana, Peter on the shore of the lake, John in Judea. John was a Jerusalemite; he had in Jerusalem his acquaintances (John xviii. 15), and his house (xix. 27). No doubt there occur passages in the Synoptists, as *e.g.* Luke v. 10, which would seem to imply that John and his father Zebedee dwelt at Capernaum. Yet this apparent contradiction finds a simple solution in the following fact. Ancient Jewish tradition (*Bab. Baba Kama*, fol. 80. 2) teaches that one of the privileges of the Israelites, when dwelling in the land of Israel, was, that each one had the right of catching fish in the Sea of Gennesareth, with the single restriction of not interfering by his net with the navigation of the lake. Of this right some inhabitants of Jerusalem availed themselves, in that, during more than one month which preceded the Passover, they were wont by the Sea of Galilee to catch, dry, and perhaps salt the fish [then called τάριχος, cf. Ritter, ii. 279], in order at Jerusalem to set them before the million guests who would require provisions. Zebedee and his sons were among those inhabitants of Jerusalem who were fishermen, and were wont at this season to ply their craft, in company with Simon and Andrew, upon the lake. Hence it is we always find John at the Sea of Galilee *before the Passover* (John i. 37, vi. 1, xi. 1 ff.), but only at this season. When, therefore, Jesus was sojourning in Judea, and particularly in Jerusalem, John was His attendant, while Peter and the other Galilean disciples pursued their calling by the lake side. That which John himself witnessed on such occasions, but *only* that which he himself witnessed, did he set down in his Gospel.

It might be objected that facts like those of John iii. 1 ff., the conversation of the Lord with Nicodemus, iv. 7 ff., the conversation with the woman of Samaria, and, xviii. 33–38, the conversation with Pilate in the Prætorium, could not have been listened to by John. But why, we ask, might not John have been an ear-witness of these facts? Since in all probability Jesus, when He was in Jerusalem, dwelt in John's house, the latter might as the host be present at these conversations. In like manner John, whom there was nothing to prevent from entering into the Prætorium, may have been present at the examination of Christ before Pilate. It is conceivable, too, that John may have remained with Jesus at Jacob's Fountain, and heard the conversation. If, however, chap. iv. 8 shall be thought to contradict this supposition, it must at any rate be admitted that, immediately after his return from the city, he heard, either from the Lord Himself, or from the Samaritan woman, the substance of the conversation. This he must of necessity introduce into his Gospel; because by means of it is explained that of which he immediately afterwards gives an account, the conversion of the inhabitants of Sychar.

The earliest Christian tradition relates that Mark composed his Gospel under the direction of the Apostle Peter. This Petrine Gospel narrates, consequently, that which had been personally witnessed by Peter ; that is to say, what he had himself seen and heard when Jesus was sojourning on the shore of the lake. Under such circumstances, it is evident that but few points of contact could arise between the accounts of John and those of Mark, or, in other words, Peter ; since the former [almost] exclusively relates that which took place in Judea, the latter that which took place in Galilee.

The Gospel of Matthew has the same narrative basis as that of Mark, augmented by many discourses of Christ which are wanting in the former. The case is otherwise with Luke, whose Gospel is a collection (Luke i. 1–3), embracing not only that which was witnessed by Peter, but also much which was seen and heard by other apostles and disciples. On this account the Gospel of Luke frequently places the scene of events at Jerusalem, and thus becomes a supplementary middle link between John and Mark. That Luke supplies the connecting link, has been with more or less of clearness recognised by some, while by others this is denied. This connection is not indeed apparent on the surface ; in order to trace it out, and to avail ourselves of it for purposes of criticism, it is necessary to enter upon the question of the origin of the synoptical Gospels.

Since the mission of the apostles was to testify of that which they had seen and heard, it was incumbent on them to narrate the history of the Lord's life, so far as they themselves had witnessed it. That Peter especially took the lead in a proclamation of this kind, and was the first who imparted to these narratives their precise form, and, moreover, furnished the material of the narrative, may be inferred from the prominent position he took in the apostolic circle. Through the frequent repetition of the same accounts, the narration would gradually assume a stereotyped form. Duly qualified believers received from the apostles a fund of narrative, the same in contents and form: hence there arose a peculiar office of companions of the apostles, who narrated the words and deeds of the Lord. These appear to have been identical with the evangelists mentioned Acts xxi. 8, Eph. iv. 11. This fund of narrative was first reduced to writing by Mark, the companion of Peter. The framework of the narrative, once accepted, was (under the influence of Matthew) augmented by the addition of the discourses of the Lord, and this cyclus, too, perpetuated in writing. We thus regard the written redaction of Matthew as later than that of Mark; because, as will presently be shown more than once, the oral proclamation has already lost much in point of precision. Whether the Gospel of Matthew was composed originally in Aramaic or not, is a question into which we need not here enter. Luke has once more reduced to writing the fund of gospel narrative, which he has enriched with the fruits of his own diligent research. It is not necessary to conceive of the one author of the written Gospel as dependent on the writing of the other. The cycle of narrative, sprung originally from one and the same source, might well, in the mouth of the apostolic narrators or evangelists—so near to the source—retain a harmony sufficient to explain the frequently verbal correspondence in the three Synoptists, and at the same time their deviation the one from the other. This last feature, on the other hand, would be incomprehensible if the one evangelist were supposed to be dependent on the written narrative of the other. It is well known that popular traditions are related, often with verbal agreement, in very different districts ; how much more must this be the case with the gospel cycles, which were ever still formed under the oversight, as respects contents and form, of their founders the apostles !

But if the Gospels at first existed as stereotyped oral narratives, it is only to be expected that their definiteness, in point of time and place, should become partially softened down, and that the material belonging to one pericopè should assume the appearance of being closely connected as to time and place ; because change of time and place, as not being a matter of primary importance, was after a time no longer indicated. This blending of events in the narrative must necessarily become most apparent in the accounts of the manifestations of the Risen One. These manifestations were of brief duration, sporadic, and disconnected ; taking place now here, now there ; on one occasion in the presence of these disciples—on another, of those ; to-day this word was heard from the mouth of the Lord—to-morrow, that ; more than once was repeated the same fact of the pointing to His wounds, the breaking of the bread ; more than once was addressed to them the same salutation, Peace be unto you ! Events occurring so abruptly, so transient in their duration, so apparently disconnected, and bearing so great resemblance the one to the other as to their main features, could not in oral narration be long preserved in their distinctness as to time and place ; they blended in a single manifestation, of which the scene would appear, according to the one, to be exclusively Jerusalem—according to the other, to be Galilee. These accounts confined themselves to the testimony : *Jesus is risen from the dead, and the apostles saw the Risen One.* Only John, the eye-witness, preserved the history of the manifestations distinct as regards time and place, and only under his guidance is it possible to assign to the facts—grouped together by the Synoptists in one picture—their due place.

If Matthew and Mark have been silent as to the journeyings through Judea, it is otherwise with Luke. This latter evangelist indicates, on several occasions, a journey to Judea and Jerusalem. Luke iv. 44, according to the better codices ; ix. 51, xiii. 22, xvii. 11, xviii. 31. That from ix. 51 forward all indications that Jesus set His face towards Jerusalem

relate to the last journey, seems indeed to follow from the
language employed in this last passage, where it is said : " It
came to pass, when the days of His being taken up were
accomplished, He steadfastly set His face to go to Jerusalem."
But in the meantime we find Jesus at Bethany, x. 38 ; on
the shore of the lake, xiii. 31 ff. ; in Samaria and Galilee,
xvii. 11. If now all these declarations are to be referred to
one and the same journey, it must be assumed that Luke—in
contradiction with his promise to narrate ἀκριβῶς—has related
the events in an entirely unchronological order. Criticism is
justified in coming to such a judgment, only after the failure
of every attempt to point out a chronological order. But it
is found that John is acquainted with the same number of
journeys to Jerusalem as Luke. On this account we deem
ourselves justified in the inference, that the narratives in Luke
are given in the order of their occurrence ; while in the oral
accounts the various journeys to Jerusalem are not duly distinguished the one from the other, and to the second visit is
attached the fatal import which properly belongs exclusively
to the last. This would take place the more easily, since the
Galilean apostles, to whom we owe the fund of narrative
furnished by the Synoptists, are acquainted indeed with the
earlier journeys of Jesus to Jerusalem, but did not themselves
accompany the Lord upon these journeys ; at least not those
of them who—like Peter and Matthew—gave origin to the
gospel cycles.

After giving expression to our view touching the main
source of the history of Jesus, the Gospels, it becomes us
further to give an account of the various subsidiary works of
which we have availed ourselves. Much as has been already
done by scientific research for the right understanding of the
chronology and geography of our Lord's life, yet the present
condition of the science everywhere calls for a return to the
original sources. This duty we have strictly imposed upon
ourselves, and thus it happens that we seldom cite the works
of the said authorities, although they are known to us, and we
owe to them many an important solution. To a much greater
extent than is usually the case, we have availed ourselves of
the assistance afforded by Jewish tradition, and this certainly

to the advantage of our cause. As regards the geography of Palestine, its literature has grown during the most recent times to enormous dimensions : that any one should be acquainted with it all can no longer be required. Yet we can give the assurance that the geographical portion of our work is based upon a thorough study of the ancient authors and of those travellers of highest authority.

The material here treated arranges itself naturally in six divisions :—

The first treats of the chronological basis of the history of Christ, secs. 1–38.

The second, of the birth and childhood of our Lord, secs. 39–56.

The third, of the environs of the Lake of Gennesareth, the scene of our Lord's deeds, secs. 57–74.

The fourth, of the first year of our Lord's public ministry, secs. 75–99.

The fifth, of the second year of His ministry, secs. 100–134.

The sixth, of the third and last year, secs. 135–205.

All that concerns the topography of Jerusalem is dealt with in the Appendix.

ERRATA.

Page 166, note, line 3 from bottom, *for* Fogüé *read* Vogüé.

The following footnote refers to p. 272 :—

The presentation of the above views as to Zion-Akra first appeared in the *Studien u. Kritiken*, 1864, ii. pp. 304–328 : Caspari, " Zion und Akra die der Syrer." Since then it has made its way. Compare, *e.g.*, the *biblische Geographie* of Riess, Freiburg 1872, where it is adopted and developed. Only the writer has forgotten to mention his source. (Later note of author.)

TABLE OF CONTENTS.

THIRD DIVISION.

THE SEA OF GENNESARETH AND ITS ENVIRONS.

FOURTH DIVISION.

THE FIRST YEAR OF THE PUBLIC MINISTRY OF CHRIST.

FIFTH DIVISION.

THE SECOND YEAR OF OUR LORD'S MINISTRY.

SIXTH DIVISION.

THE THIRD AND LAST YEAR OF OUR LORD'S LABOURS.

APPENDIX.
TOPOGRAPHY OF JERUSALEM.

Scene of OUR LORD'S PUBLIC LABOURS.

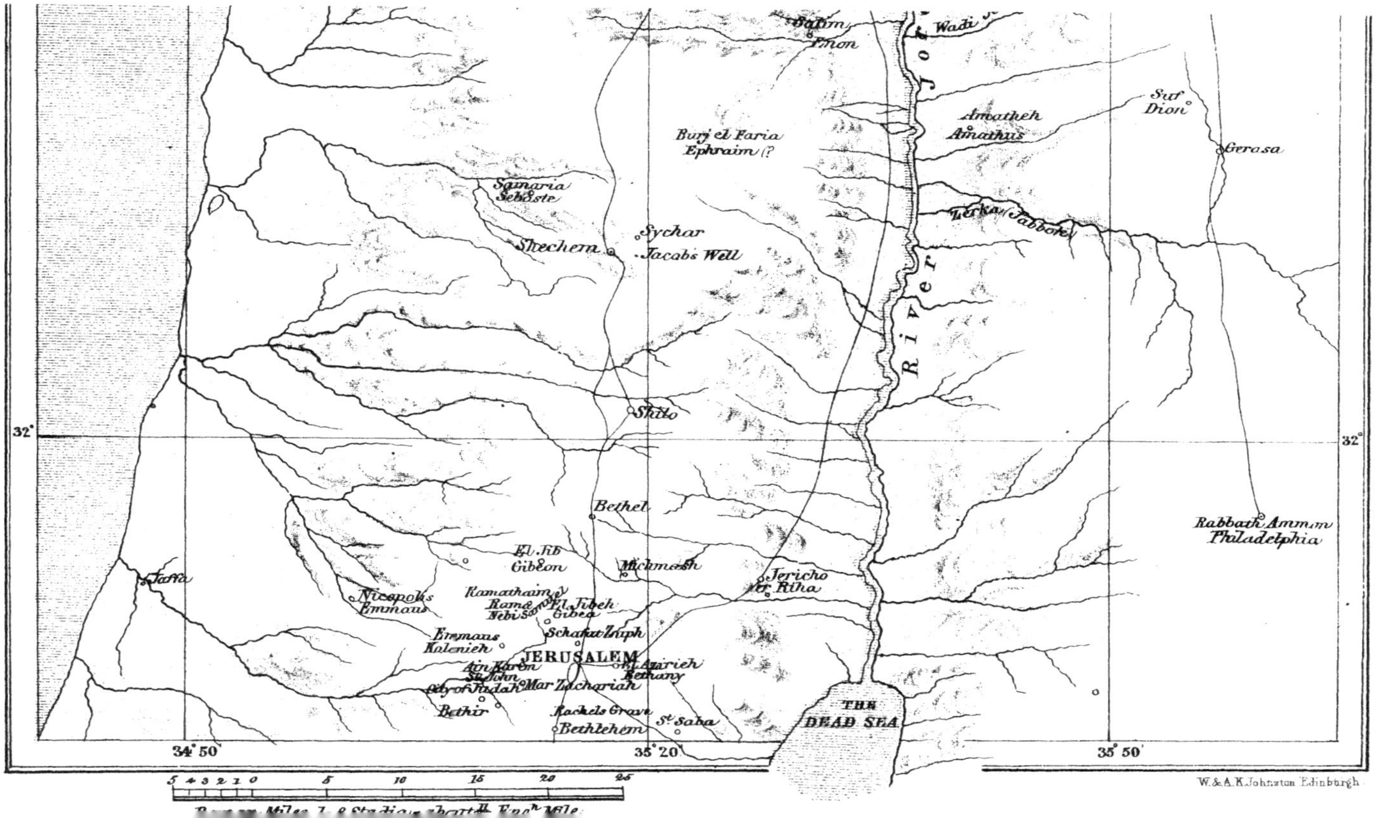

Salim
Ænon
Wadi
Jor
Sur
Dion
Amatheh
Amathus
Burj el Faria
Ephraim (?
Gerasa
Samaria
Sebaste
Zerka (Jabbok
Sychar
Shechem
Jacob's Well
River
Shilo
32°
Bethel
Rabbath Ammon
Philadelphia
El Jib
Gibeon
Michmash
Jaffa
Jericho
Er Riha
Nicopolis
Emmaus
Ramathaim
Rama
El Jibeh
Gibea
Schafat Zuph
Emmaus
Kolonieh
JERUSALEM
Ain Karem
St. John
El Azirieh
Bethany
City of Judah
Mar Zachariah
Bethir
Rachels Grave
Bethlehem
St. Saba
THE
DEAD SEA
34° 50'
35° 20'
35° 50'
5 4 3 2 1 0
5
10
15
20
25
W. & A. K. Johnston Edinburgh.

A

CHRONOLOGICAL AND GEOGRAPHICAL INTRODUCTION

TO THE

LIFE OF CHRIST.

DIVISION I.

CHRONOLOGICAL BASIS OF THE HISTORY OF JESUS CHRIST.

SEC. 1. Many earnest investigators have despaired of gaining a chronological basis for the history of Jesus. And such despairing of the possibility of the matter seems really justified, when we compare that which chronologists, each from his own standpoint, have given us as the result of their investigations. "Some fix the birth of Christ 1, 2, 3, 4, 5, 7, yea, even 19 years earlier than Dionysius did; the baptism, in the year 25, 26, 27, 28, 29, 30; His death, in the 29th or 30th, or 31st, 32d, 33d, 35th year of our era."[1] That the task we have imposed on ourselves is accompanied with great difficulties, cannot be denied; but insuperable they are not. Above all, it must not be overlooked that these difficulties have their ground, not in the Gospel narratives themselves, but in the contemporaneous profane history, of which the chronology is wrongly determined. Before we thus make the attempt to arrange the facts of the Gospels in the order of time, it is incumbent on us to determine chronologically that part of profane history which synchronizes with them.

No historic fact has ever so powerfully affected the course of the world's history as the word and work of Jesus Christ. But this influence on the course of affairs first became noticeable decades of years after the death of Jesus. During His life He came but little into contact with the great powers of this world; on which account the chronological hints are, as might

[1] Seyffarth, *Chron. Sacra*, 8. 1.

A

be expected, comparatively very few. But however limited in point of number, they are sufficient for the purpose, if examined thoroughly and without previous bias.

According to Matt. ii. 1 and Luke i. 5, Christ was born during the reign of Herod I., and, indeed, towards the end of that reign; since when this king died he was still a " child."[1] A first problem is consequently to determine the year of this king's death.

At the time of the birth of Jesus a census ordered by Augustus was made, and the star of the wise men was seen in the sky.[2]

According to Luke, the public labours of Jesus began in the 15th year of the Emperor Tiberius ;[3] and

According to John, this, His public appearing, took place in the 46th year of the rebuilding of the temple by Herod.[4]

To the determination of the year of Jesus' death belongs, in addition to the dates just referred to, Gal. i. 16–ii. 1, where it is said that the second journey of the Apostle Paul to Jerusalem took place seventeen years after his conversion.

The date of all these synchronistic facts is now to be determined. Before this, however, we must communicate so much with regard to the mode of reckoning current among the Jews at the time of Jesus, as is indispensable for the understanding of the Gospel narratives.

I.—*The Jewish Calendar.*

Sec. 2. The year of the Jews consisted of twelve lunar months, and thus contained about 354 days. But since the principal festivals were attached to definite days of the month, as well as to different seasons of the year, the lunar year was made to agree with the solar year by the intercalation of a thirteenth month every third year.

Sec. 3. **The civil day** of the Jews began with sunset, and ended with the sunset of the following day. On this account Paul, in 2 Cor. xi. 25, calls it a night-day,[5] νυχθήμερον. This

---

[1] παιδίον, Matt. ii. 20.   [2] Luke ii. 1 ; Matt. ii. 1 ff.
[3] Luke iii. 1.   [4] John ii. 20.
[5] A term which will be generally employed throughout this work, where it is necessary to remember that the day in question is a *Jewish* day.

mode of beginning the day is met with even in the history
of creation; for, Gen. i. 5, we read: "It was evening, and it
was morning, *one* day." It is well known that other ancient
nations besides Israel began the civil day with the night, as
e.g. the Germans; whence Tacitus says, that with them the
night draws after it the day.[1] In Pliny we read: "Some
looked upon the day in one way, some in another; the Baby-
lonians as between two sunrises, the Athenians between two
sunsets, the Umbrians from noon to noon," etc. Ipsum diem
alii aliter observavere: Babylonii inter duos solis ortus, *Athe-
nienses inter duos occasus*, Umbrii a meridie ad meridiem, etc.[2]
This explains the fact that the expression νυχθήμερον, used
by Paul, occurs with the Athenian Plato. That the epoch of
the Jewish day was really sunset, is confirmed by the writings
of Jewish tradition. In *Menachoth*, x. 3, the cutting of the
paschal sheaf on the 16th Nisan is described. The deputies
of the Sanhedrim repaired, at the close of the 15th Nisan, to
the field previously indicated, and waited until the reaper
said: "בא השמש, the sun is gone down." The others repeated
these words; only then was it permitted to put in the sickle,
because with the setting of the sun the 15th Nisan was
brought to an end, and the 16th began. The Karaite Elia
ben Mosheh says that the month, and thus, of course, the day
too, began with the third evening, when the sun had set, מערב
השלישי שהוא מבא השמש.[3] This period was naturally divided into
night and day; the former extended from sunset to sunrise,
the latter from sunrise to sunset.

Sec. 4. **The night** was divided by the ancient Hebrews,
with reference to the placing of the guards, into *three watches*,
אשמרות, φυλακαί; of which the first, ראש אשמרות, occurs in
Lam. ii. 19; the second or middle watch, אשמרת התיכונה,
Judg. vii. 19; and the morning watch, אשמרת הבקר, Ex. xiv.
24; 1 Sam. xi. 11. This division was retained by the Jews
in connection with the temple guards.[4] But, besides this, the
Roman division into *four night watches* was also in use. It is
met with in the New Testament, Acts xii. 3, 4, Matt. xiv. 25,
as well as in Josephus, who (*Antiq.* v. 6, sec. 5) relates that

[1] Tacitus, *Germania*, xi.   [2] Plinius, *H. N.* ii. 79.
[3] See Von Gumpach, *Ueber den altjüdischen Kalender*, p. 20.
[4] *Bab. Menachoth*, i. 1. 6.

Gideon led his company against the enemy at the fourth watch of the night, κατὰ τὴν τετάρτην φυλακήν. The four watches of the night might be indicated in Mark xiii. 35 by the appellations, evening, midnight, cock-crowing, morning.[1]

Sec. 5. **The day** was divided naturally into morning, noon, and evening; and artificially into twelve hours, of which the first began with sunrise. *Noon* embraced that time, "from half an hour before to half an hour after the sixth hour; then the sun stands still above the head of every one, casts its shadow down direct before it, and inclines to neither side; from half an hour after the sixth, however, it inclines in the sky towards evening."[2] From this it results that the *morning*, בקר, extended from the first hour to the sixth hour and a half, and the *evening*, ערב, from the sixth hour and a half to the twelfth. The Jews spoke of the period from the setting of the sun to the appearing of the stars as "the third evening," consequently the beginning of the new day.[3] The first evening corresponded to our afternoon; the second, to our evening before sunset; the third, to that from sunset to the time when the stars appear. According to Ex. xii. 6, Lev. xxiii. 5, Num. ix. 3, the paschal lamb was to be sacrificed "between the two evenings," בין הערבים, just as was prescribed in Ex. xxix. 39, 41, Num. xxviii. 4, for the daily sacrifice at even, תמיד. It lies not within our province to determine the signification of the expression, "between the two evenings," in the Old Testament sense; it suffices us to show how the Jews at the time of Jesus understood it. Now we read in the *Mishna Pesachim*, v. 1, that the *thamid* or evening sacrifice, which, as has been said, was to be presented between the two evenings, was slain at the eighth hour and a half, and presented at the ninth hour and a half; on the eve or preparation-day of the Passover it was slain at the seventh hour and a half, and presented at the eighth hour and a half; if the preparation-day fell on a Friday, *thamid* was slain at the sixth hour and a half, and offered at the seventh hour and a half, and after this the paschal lamb.

תמיד נשחט בשמונה ותחצה וקרב בתשעה ומחצה בערבי פסחים נשחט
בשבע ומחצה וקרב בשמנה ומחצה בין בחול בין בשבת הלערב פסח להיות
בערב שבת נשחט בשש ומחצה וקרב בשבע ומחצה והפסח אחריו:

---

[1] See Von Gumpach, as before, p. 47.   [2] *Bab. Pesachim*, v. 3.
[3] See sec. 3, the citation from ben Mosheh.

From this it follows that the whole afternoon, from the sixth hour and a half to sunset, was comprised under the term, "between the two evenings." In the same sense does Jarchi express himself on Ex. xii. 6 : "The time from the sixth hour is called בין הערבים, because the sun is declining towards sunset. The evening of the day begins about the seventh hour, because then the shadows begin to decline; the evening of the night, on the other hand, commences with the beginning of the night." So also Kimchi *in rad.* ערב.[1]

Sec. 6. **The week**, שבוע, ended with the Sabbath, the seventh day. The other days of the week had no special names, but were counted in order: the first day of the week, the second, and so on. This we find already to be the case in the history of the creation, Gen. i. In the New Testament mention is made only of the Sabbath and the first day of the week, *i.e.* Sunday. This latter is expressed by the following formulæ : τῇ μιᾷ τῶν σαββάτων, Mark xvi. 2, Luke xxiv. 1, Acts xx. 7 ; πρώτῃ σαββάτου, Mark xvi. 9 ; κατὰ μίαν σαββάτων, 1 Cor. xvi. 2. In Mark xv. 42 the Friday is called παρασκευή, and among the Rabbis, *errubta,* ערובתא.

Sec. 7. **The month** of the Jews was, as we have said, a lunar month, and extended from one appearing of the new moon to another. The time elapsing between one astronomical new moon and another consists of $29\frac{1}{2}$ days.[2] But since the month consisted of entire days, they counted it with pretty regular alternation as 29 or 30 days. A month of 30 days was called a full month, חדש מלא; if it had only 29 days, it was called an imperfect month, חדש חסר. The Jewish month could never have more than 30 days, and never fewer than 29. It began, not with the astronomical new moon, but with the new light; that is to say, when the first light of the renewed phase of the moon became visible. We give here the names of the months as they were current after the exile and during the age of Jesus, to which we add the Macedonian names employed by Josephus as the equivalents of the Jewish ones, and the months of our calendar more or less corresponding to these :—

---

[1] See Von Gumpach, p. 24.

[2] Properly, 29 days 12 hours 44 min. 3½ sec.

1. Nisan,	ניסן,	Xanthicus,	April.
2. Ijar,	איר,	Artemisius,	May.
3. Sivan,	סיון,	Dasius,	June.
4. Thammuz,	תמוז,	Panemus,	July.
5. Ab,	אב,	Loüs,	August.
6. Elul,	אלול,	Goripiæus,	September.
7. Tisri,	תשרי	Hyperberetæus,	October.
8. Marchesvan,	מרחשון,	Dius,	November.
9. Kisleu,	כסלו,	Apellæus,	December.
10. Tebeth,	טבת,	Audinæus,	January.
11. Shebet,	שבט,	Peritius,	February.
12. Adar,	אדר,	Dystrus,	March.

The intercalary month was always a repetition of the Adar, and was called "the second Adar," אדר שני, or Veadar, ואדר.[1]

Sec. 8. **The year** was a lunar year, consisting of twelve of these lunar months, which was brought into accord with the solar year by the intercalation of a thirteenth month, the Veadar, about every third year, so that the great festivals should always fall at the same season of the year. "The beginnings of the year (New Year's days) were four: (1) the 1st of Nisan, the same is the beginning of the year, ראש השנה, for the kings and the festivals. (2) The 1st of Elul is the beginning of the year which determines the age of the cattle for the tithes.[2] (3) The 1st of Tisri is the New Year's day for the years (from the creation?), for the Sabbath years and for the Jubilee years, as well as for the planting of trees and of vegetables. (4) The 1st of Shebet is the beginning of the year for the trees (i.e. for the tithing of the fruit trees)."[3] Of these four New Year's days, the 1st of Nisan and the 1st of Tisri are of special importance; with the former the ecclesiastical year began, and with the latter the civil. Hence the rabbinical dictum: "Nisan is the beginning of the months, and Tisri the beginning of the year," ניסן הוא ראשית לחדשי ותשרי הוא רשית השנה.

In harmony with this, Josephus says, "The flood took place in the 600th year of Noah, *in the second month*, called by the Macedonians *Dius*, but by the Hebrews *Marsuane* (Marchesvan).

---

[1] *Rosh hashanna*, vi. 2.

[2] R. Eliezer and R. Simeon, however, make this fall on the 1st of Tisri.

[3] *Mishna Rosh hashanna*, i. 1.

For so had they (the fathers) ordered the year in Egypt. Moses, on the other hand, appointed *Nisan* or Xanthicus the first month as regards their festivals, . . . yet for buying and selling and other civil affairs, he preserved the original order." [1]

Sec. 9. We have, in all that has hitherto been said, presented the Jewish calendar, in accordance with what is given in the books of Jewish tradition, on the assumption that these books are in this respect worthy of credit. But had the ancient Jews, and particularly at the time of Jesus, such lunar months and years with an intercalary month, as the Talmud asserts? The great majority of chronologists, amongst whom are Wurm, Ideler, Wieseler, v. Gumpach, and Winer, return an affirmative answer to this question. There have not been wanting, however, those who maintain the contrary, and claim for the Jews of the age of Jesus the reckoning by solar months and years. This view finds an advocate particularly in Seyffarth, in a treatise [2] which has the special object of vindicating the New Testament chronology of the Fathers. Among the assertions of the Fathers, there is one to the effect that the obscuration of the sun on the day of the crucifixion of Jesus was due to an astronomical eclipse. To maintain this position, solar months must be ascribed to the Jews; for if they reckoned by lunar months, and these months began with the new moon, the 15th Nisan must fall at the time of the full moon, in which an eclipse of the sun is impossible, since this can take place only at the time of a new moon. Seyffarth maintains that the Sanhedrim of Tiberias, which drew up the present Jewish calendar about A.D. 200, invented the lunar months and years, and got them surreptitiously introduced into the books of Jewish tradition. To this it must be objected that the Sanhedrim, if it had really practised this deception, would assuredly have represented this newly-invented calendar as handed down in the lump by tradition. But this is not the case; on the contrary, the calendar of the modern Jews introduced by the Sanhedrim is in many respects different from that described in tradition, especially in the *Mishna Rosh hashanna*, and even in con-

[1] *Antiq.* i. 3, sec. 3.　　　　[2] *Chron. sacra*, p. 43 ff.

tradiction therewith.   According to tradition, *e.g.*, the new
light defining the first day of the month was confirmed *de
visu* and by witnesses, while in the modern Jewish calendar
it is astronomically determined.   According to tradition, the
15th of Nisan, and consequently also the 1st, could fall
upon any day of the week; according to the calendar, it can
never fall on the 2d, the 4th, or the 6th day of the week.
Seyffarth seeks confirmation for his assertion mainly in the fact
that Josephus never makes mention of the intercalary month,
and infers from this silence that Josephus is not acquainted
with it, and consequently also that he knows nothing of the
lunar months and years which stand in close connection with
the intercalary month.   The silence of Josephus, however, is
no sufficient proof, and the less so, since this author distinctly
asserts that the months began with the moon's phase, and
that the festivals were attached to definite days of the month
and seasons of the year.   *Antiq.* iii. 10, sec. 5, he says that in
the month Nisan, on the 14th day, "according to the moon,"
κατὰ σελήνην (that is to say, counting from the phase), Passover began; and *Antiq.* iii. 10, sec. 3, he speaks of the 10th
day of the month Tisri, "according to the moon."   But even
if Josephus leaves the matter in part undetermined, other
trustworthy witnesses can be adduced who confirm it.

Sec. 10.   The earliest, and consequently the most important,
evidence in favour of the lunar month is found in a fragment
from the *Canon Paschalis* of the learned Anatolius, bishop of
Laodicea in the third century, which is handed down to us by
Eusebius.   Anatolius cites a commentary on the Pentateuch
attributed to the two Agathobulos, disciples of Aristobulos,
contemporary with Ptolemy Philadelphus.   "Aristobulos," it
is there said, "maintained that at the paschal festival the
sun as well as the moon must necessarily have passed the
equinoctial point; that the day of the paschal festival began
*on the 14th of Nisan after the evening, when the moon stands
diametrically opposed to the sun, as any one can see at the time
of the full moon.*   The sun then stands in the sign of the
vernal equinox."   Ὁ δὲ Ἀριστόβουλος προστίθησιν, ὡς εἴη ἐξ
ἀνάγκης τῇ τῶν διαβατηρίων ἑορτῇ μὴ μόνον τὸν ἥλιον τὸ
ἰσημερινὸν διαπορεύεσθαι, καὶ τὴν σελήνην δέ. . . . Δοθείσης

τε τῆς τῶν διαβατηρίων ἡμέρας τῇ τεσσαρες-και-δεκάτῃ τοῦ
μηνὸς μεθ᾽ ἑσπέραν, ἑστήσεται μὲν σελήνη τὴν ἐναντίαν καὶ
διάμετρον τῷ ἡλίῳ στάσιν· ὥσπερ οὖν ἔξεστιν ἐν ταῖς πανσελή-
ναις ὁρᾶν· ἔσονται δὲ ὁ μὲν κατὰ τὸ ἐαρινὸν ἰσημερινὸν ὁ ἥλιος
τμῆμα, ἡ δὲ ἐξ ἀνάγκης κατὰ τὸ φθινοπωρινὸν ἡ σελήνη.[1]
Anatolius, who lived at the period of the Sanhedrim of
Tiberias, to which we have already frequently referred, made
an excerpt from a book, probably genuine, at all events very
ancient, which describes a manner of determining the paschal
festival, in all respects agreeing with the data afforded by
Jewish tradition.   In this citation the fact is confirmed, first,
that the day began with the evening, μεθ᾽ ἑσπέραν; secondly,
that the paschal festival was always observed after the vernal
equinox; and, finally, that on the 14th Nisan the moon was
necessarily full, and in opposition with the sun; from which
follows with equal necessity, that the 1st of Nisan, and consequently the first day of each month, coincided with the new
moon; that the Jews had lunar months; and, since the
festivals were attached to definite seasons of the year, that the
intercalary month could not be wanting.

Sec. 11. Galen, born at Pergamus in Asia Minor, about
A.D. 131, says, "With those in Palestine the twelve months
together number 354 days.   But since the time from one
conjunction to another requires the addition of another half-
day to the 29 days, the two months together number 59
days, which they divide into two unequal parts, and assign to
the one month 30 days, to the other 29.   Since they
arrange the months in this manner, they are compelled to
make an intercalary month, when the deficiency of the previous
years, counted together, makes up the time of a month."
Τοῖς κατὰ Παλαιστίνην ἀριθμοῦσιν οἱ δώδεκα μῆνες ἀριθμὸς
ἡμερῶν γίγνονται τνδ᾽.   Ἐπειδὴ γὰρ ὁ ἀπὸ συνόδου τῆς πρὸς
ἥλιον αὐτῆς χρόνος ἄχρι πάσης ἄλλης συνόδου πρὸς τὰς θ᾽ καὶ
κ᾽ ἡμέρας ἔτι καὶ ἄλλο μέρος ἥμισυ προσλαμβάνει, διὰ τοῦτο καὶ
τοὺς δύο μῆνας γινομένους θ᾽ καὶ ν᾽ τέμνουσιν εἰς ἄνισα μέρη,
τὸν μὲν ἕτερον αὐτῶν λ᾽ ἡμερῶν ἐργαζόμενοι, τὸν δ᾽ ἕτερον θ᾽
καὶ κ᾽.   Ἀναγκάζονται τοιγαροῦν οἱ οὕτως ἄγοντες τοὺς μῆνας
ἐμβόλιμον τίνα ποιεῖν, ὅταν πρῶτον ἀθροισθῇ τὸ τῶν ἔμ-

[1] Euseb. *Hist. Eccl.* vii. 32.

πρόσθεν ἐνιαυτῶν ἔλλειμα, καὶ γίνηται χρόνος ἑνὸς μηνός.[1]
We have here the whole system of the ancient Jewish calendar. But since Galen, who belongs to the first half of the
second century, lived seventy years before the Sanhedrim of
Tiberias, which, according to Seyffarth, invented the lunar year,
the whole hypothesis of this chronologist falls to the ground.

Sec. 12. Clemens Alexandrinus, *Strom* vi., adduces a passage
from the writing entitled *The Preaching of Peter*, and belonging
to the second century, which reads as follows : " The Jews
render religious honour to the angels and archangels, to the
month, and to the moon ; if the moon does not shine, they do
not keep the so-called first Sabbath, nor do they observe the
new moon, nor the feast of unleavened bread, nor any feast,
nor the day of atonement." Λατρεύουσι (οἱ Ἰουδαῖοι) ἀγγελοῖς
καὶ ἀρχαγγελοῖς, μηνὶ καὶ σελήνῃ, καὶ ἐὰν μὴ σελήνη φανῇ,
σάββατον οὐκ ἄγουσι τὸ λεγόμενον πρῶτον, οὐδὲ νεομηνίαν
ἄγουσι, οὔτε ἑορτὴν, οὔτε μεγάλην ὑμέραν. This passage, at
any rate, tells us that the Jews began the month with the
moonlight.

Sec. 13. Philo, *in Decalog.*,[2] says : " The paschal festival is
observed *on the* 14*th Nisan, when the moon's disc is coming to
the full* (μέλλοντος τοῦ σεληνιακοῦ κυκλοῦ γίνεσθαι πληριφαοῦς
ἄγεται τὰ διαβατήρια)." But if the moon was full on the 14th,
it was new on the 1st. By this it is already proved that the
Jews had lunar months ; we have consequently to attach no
special weight to the more definite utterances of another work
by the same author, *De Septimanis et Festis*, of which the
authenticity is open to suspicion. In this the first of the
month is called " the new moon according to the phase," ἡ κατὰ
σελήνην νουμηνία ; and it is further said, " the beginning of this
(paschal) festival takes place on the 15th, and also for the
reason adduced, at the time of the vernal equinox, that on that
occasion, not only by day, but also during the night, the world
may be filled with the all-glorious light of the sun and the
moon." Πάλιν δὲ ταύτης τῆς ἑορτῆς ἀρχὴ πεντεκαιδεκάτῃ
μηνὸς ἐνίσταται διὰ τὴν λεχθεῖσαν καὶ ἐπὶ τῆς ἐαρινῆς ὥρας
αἰτίαν· ἵνα μὴ μεθ᾽ ἡμέραν μόνον, ἀλλὰ καὶ νύκτωρ πλήρης ὁ

---

[1] *Comment. I. in Hippocratis epidem.*, ed. Kühn, t. xvii. p. 23.
[2] T. ii. p. 206, ed. Mangey.

κόσμος ᾖ τοῦ παγκάλου φωτός ἡλίου καὶ σελήνης. The above developed Talmudic system of the Jewish calendar receives confirmation, and Seyffarth's objections their refutation, on the part of all the witnesses here adduced.

Sec. 14. It has already been said, that the beginning of the Jewish month was determined, not by the astronomic new moon or the moment of the conjunction, but by the new light, *i.e.* the appearing of the phase. This is clearly expressed in the passage cited above, sec. 12, from *The Preaching of Peter*, in which it is said, when the moon does not shine, they do not observe the new moon, ἐὰν μὴ σελήνη φανῇ. . . . οὐ νεομηνίαν ἄγουσι. The new moon must thus *shine*, its first light be visible. Yet more clearly is it said in Philo, *De Septiman. et Fest.*, " At the numenia the sun begins to irradiate the moon with perceptible splendour, and she displays to the beholders her own beauty." Νουμηνίᾳ γὰρ ἄρχεται φωτίζειν αἰσθήτῳ φεγγεῖ σελήνην ἥλιος, ἢ δὲ τὸ ἰδίον καλλὸς ἀναφαινεῖ τοῖς ὁρῶσι. The new moon and the new light, or the first of the month, were not astronomically determined, although the means of doing this were not unknown to the Jews.˙ A commission of three members, appointed by the Sanhedrim, attested the appearing of the moonlight by the evidence of eye-witnesses.[1] Yet the examination of witnesses took place only when the moon's phase was seen on the 30th of the month, in which case this 30th day was declared the first of the new month, and the old counted only 29 days; if, however, the phase was not observed on this day, it was counted as the 30th day of the old month, and the following day became of right, and without examination of witnesses, the first of the following month. In *Rosh hashanna*, ii. 7, it is said, " If the moon was not seen at its time (*i.e.* on the 30th day) it did not sanctify the month, for heaven had already sanctified it." אם לא נראה בזמנו אין מקדשין אותו שכבר קדשוהו שמים. Not only were inhabitants of Jerusalem accepted as witnesses concerning the moon, but any Jew who saw the moonlight was to come to Jerusalem to witness, and might for this end break the Sabbath. On this account it is said, *Rosh hashanna*, i. 9, " For a journey which required a night and a day they desecrated the Sabbath, to

---

[1] *Mishna Sanhedrin*, 1. 2.

attest the appearing of the moon."   על מהלך לילה ויום מהללין את
השבת ויוצאין לעדות החדש, and, *ibid.* i. 4, " At the time when the
temple was standing they broke the Sabbath every month, on
account of the preparation of the offerings, וכשהיה בית המקדש
קיים מחללין אף על כולין מפני תקנת הקרבן. In order to give the
witnesses from a distance time to arrive, the examination at
first took place in the afternoon, before *mincha* and the evening
sacrifice. If it was attested by witnesses that the moon was
seen on the previous evening, the day was sanctified, the sacrifice of the new moon was presented, and a special liturgy for
the new moon was sung before the offering of the daily evening sacrifice. At first the witnesses occupied the whole day.
Afterwards, however, these began to put off till the evening,
and the Levites were thereby thrown into perplexity as to
their singing (since they knew not whether they should keep
back the liturgy for the new moon or the daily liturgy) ; it
was resolved to receive witnesses at the latest only up to
mincha. If they came after *mincha*, this day was sanctified,
and the following day too." [1] The sacramental formula for
the declaration that the moon had appeared, and consequently
that the 30th day was the first of the new month, was the
calling out on the part of the president of the word " hallowed!"
מקדש, which cry was twice repeated by the other members
of the bench and by the people.[2]—In such wise is the matter
represented by Jewish tradition. In connection with this
view, a difficulty, we admit, presents itself. For according
to the Mosaic law the day of the new light was to be a feast
day, and to have the rank of a Sabbath; and in this sense
it is, in the passage from *The Preaching of Peter* above
cited, called σάββατον πρῶτον. But how could this day be
observed as a festival when it was only sanctified and proclaimed just before the evening sacrifice, four hours before its
end ? This difficulty, it is true, applies only to those days of
new light which followed on a month of 29 days; but of
these there were generally six in a year. Von Gumpach
therefore says,[3] " It cannot thus admit of the slightest doubt
that the first day of the month with the Jews began not with

[1] *Rosh hashanna*, iii. 4.   [2] *Ibid.* ii. 7.
[3] Von Gumpach, as before, p. 125.

the evening (of the civil day) already past, but with the evening following upon this, at sunset." Such doubt must, however, be permitted us. For if, as is clear, the examination of the witnesses took place only on the 30th of the month, and this 30th could never itself become the first of the following month, because the result of the examination was proclaimed only at the end, in the last hours of the day, so that the day following, *i.e.* the 31st, was the first day of the month,—then the Jews could never have a month of 29 days, which, on the supposition of lunar months, is simply an absurdity. The matter stands rather thus: If, on account of the delay of the witnesses, the "hallowed" could be proclaimed only after the *mincha*, yet the 30th day in question was sanctified and declared the first of the month, the Sabbath of the new moon, σάββατον πρῶτον; but because the prescribed sacrifices could not then be presented, since the day was expired, the following day also, the second of the month, was sanctified, set apart for the prescribed sacrifices, and declared the second-first Sabbath, σάββατον δευτερόπρωτον. This is taught clearly and definitely in the above cited passage from the *Rosh hashanna*, iii. 4, where it is said, if the witnesses arrived after *mincha*, then that day, *and also the following*, was sanctified. ואם באו עדים מן מנחה ולמעלה נוהגין אותו היום קדש ולמחר קדש. Now, that which took place in Jerusalem within the precincts of the temple only in this special case of the delay of the witnesses, must necessarily be the standing rule for the remainder of the land of Israel, and still more for the Jews of the dispersion, for all days of the new light which followed a month of 29 days. It could never be known whether the "hallowed" had been pronounced on the 30th day or not; they learnt that the proclamation had been made, only by beacons after the day had closed. In order, therefore, that the law might be kept, even where the case was doubtful, they regularly observed the 30th and 31st as days of the new moon, and called the former the "first Sabbath," σάββατον πρῶτον, the latter the "after Sabbath," σάββατον δευτερόπρωτον.[1]

---

[1] Cf. Joh. Seldeni *de Anno civili et calendario veteris ecclesiæ Judaicæ*, pp. 71, 77.

When, therefore, it is a question of restoring the calendar of a given year of the Jews, the new moon of each month must first be astronomically determined, and then it must be further discovered on which of the days following the new light became visible. Now, what is the difference between the time of the astronomical new moon (the conjunction) and that of the new light becoming visible ? Pliny says: " To have seen on the same day or in the same night the last light of the old moon and the first light of the new is what has happened to but few mortals ; and this can take place in no other sign than that of Aries." Novissimam vero primamque lunam eadem die vel nocte, nullo alio signo quam ariete, paucis mortalibus contigit.[1] It happened once, according to *Rosh hashanna* ii., that witnesses deposed they had seen the moon in the morning in the east, and in the evening in the west. באו שנים ואמרו ראינוהו שחרית במזרח וערבית במערב. Rabbi Johanan declared them to be false witnesses. It was thus generally regarded as impossible that the new light should be visible six hours after the conjunction. Von Gumpach[2] cites a passage from Elias ben Mosheh, according to which the smallest arc of vision for the moon contains $8° 10'$, by which is implied that the moon's disc *may* become visible under certain circumstances between $8° 10'$ and $14°$, but with a greater distance from the sun *must* become visible. According to this authority, it is possible, under given circumstances, to see the moon 14 to 23 hours after the conjunction ; with certainty, however, it is visible only after 24 hours. Wurm[3] has examined this subject with special attention. He says that the arc of vision, *i.e.* the distance of the moon from the sun, is in general difficult to determine. How soon or how late the moon's disc becomes visible after the new moon depends, in addition to the state of the weather, upon very different circumstances—the angle of the ecliptic with the western horizon at which the moon is about to set, the moon's altitude and declination, its more or less rapid movement in its orbit, and on the length of the twilight. Kepler does not doubt the possibility of seeing the moon within the first 24 hours after

---

[1] Plinius, *H. N.* ii. 14.   [2] Von Gumpach, as before, p. 119.
[3] Wurm, in *Bengel's Archiv.* 1816, ii. p. 273.

new moon; and gives us an instance that the moon was seen in Seville about mid-day, March 13, 1553, in the 23d degree of Pisces, and only 10° west from the sun, or at an arc of 10°— which requires a lapse of about 18 hours after the conjunction. Americus Vespucius in the course of his travels saw the moon on the day of the conjunction. Wurm, finally, expresses his opinion that we should not go far wrong if, in order to find the first day of the month, according to the old Jewish style, by the moon's phase, we add 24 to 48 hours to the true new moon astronomically calculated; and on p. 279 he lays down the rule *that we have on an average to add* $1\frac{1}{2}$ *days.* This principle has been accepted and carried out by Ideler, Wieseler, and most chronologists.

Sec. 15. From what has been already said, it results that the ancient Jewish year—not only the ecclesiastical, but also the civil, of which the beginning was the 1st of Tisri—was determined by the 1st of Nisan; and that the fixing of this day depended, first of all, indeed, upon astronomical facts, the new moon and the vernal equinox, but then also upon accidental circumstances, such as whether the new moon was seen or not, and upon arbitrary decision, such as whether the preceding Adar was doubled or not. The conditionating cause of the intercalation was the paschal festival, which was celebrated on the 15th. On this day the sun must have passed the vernal equinox.[1] On the 16th Nisan the paschal sheaf was gathered; respect must therefore be had, in determining the 1st Nisan, to the 16th falling when there were ripe ears. In addition to these main conditions, others also had to be taken into account. Of these we find a relation in a remarkable passage of the Talmud, *Jerus. Sanhedrin,* xvii. 4,[2] which thus reads : " Rabban Gamaliel sat upon the steps of the temple mountain and wrote to the brethren who are in Upper and Lower Daroma, in Upper and Lower Galilee, and to the brethren of the captivity in Babylon, in Media, and Greece, and to all Israel in captivity wherever they may be. We herewith do you to wit, that the young doves

---

[1] *Bab. Sanhedr.* xii. 2, xiii. 1.   Josephus, *Antiq.* iii. 10, sec. 5 : ἐν κριῷ τοῦ ἡλίου καθιστῶτος. See also above, secs. 10-12.

[2] Ugolini, *Thes.* xxv. p. 21.

and lambs are yet tender, and the time of the ripe ears is not yet come; it has seemed good to us, therefore, to add to this year 30 days." This circular letter of the elder Gamaliel, as to the authenticity of which there is no doubt, proves the existence of the intercalary system at the time of Christ, and details the arbitrary motives for the intercalation. To which, finally, we must add, that at that time the vernal equinox fell on the 23d of March. The 1st Nisan could not thus at the earliest fall before the 8th of March.

Sec. 16. For the New Testament history the determining of the 1st Nisan is of special importance; because it can and must contribute to the settling of the day of Jesus' death, and, by means of the day, also of the year. To this end Wurm has calculated and arranged in a table the new moons in question from the years 28 to 36.[1] In this table he has defined the moment of the new moon, and from this, by the application of his principles, as above given, gained the date of the 1st Nisan according to the phase, and finally registered the 15th Nisan, with the day of the week on which it falls, first according to the true new moon, and then according to the phase. We excerpt only so much of this table as concerns the new moon, adding the day of the week, which is the same for the 15th Nisan as for the 1st:—

A.D.	Time of the New Moon.	Day of the Week.	1st Nisan according to the Moon's Phase.	Day of the Week.
28	15th March, 2 h. 16 m. A.M.	2	16th March.	3
28	13th April, 4 h. 10 m. P.M.	3	15th April.	5
29	2d April, 7 h. 42 m. P.M.	7	4th April.	2
30	22d March, 8 h. 8 m. P.M.	4	24th March.	6
31	12th March, 12 h. 56 m. A.M.	2	13th March.	3
31	10th April, 2 h. 0 m. P.M.	3	12th April.	5
32	29th March, 10 h. 57 m. P.M.	7	31st March.	2
33	19th March, 1 h. 16 m. P.M.	5	21st March.	7
33	17th April, 9 h. 30 m. P.M.	6	19th April.	1
34	9th March, 9 h. 2 m. A.M.	3	11th March.	5
34	7th April, 6 h. 42 m. P.M.	4	9th April.	6
35	28th March, 6 h. 19 m. A.M.	2	30th March.	4
36	16th March, 5 h. 53 m. P.M.	6	18th March.	1
36	15th April, 5 h. 15 m. A.M.	1	16th April.	2

[1] Wurm, as before, p. 293.

For the right understanding of this table as to the day of the week, a remark is necessary with regard to a fact unfortunately overlooked by Wurm, Von Gumpach, and most chronologists. Wurm's day of the week has reference to the Julian day, which extends from midnight to midnight, and does not apply to the Jewish day of the week, which consists of a night-day, of which the epoch is sunset. Let us explain ourselves by an example. In the year 28 the new moon fell on the 15th March, feria 2, a Monday; the 1st Nisan, according to the phase, was thus the 16th March, feria 3, a Tuesday. But on this Tuesday the 1st Nisan began only about six in the evening; with this hour, however, the Jewish feria 3 had ceased, and feria 4 had begun. If the Jewish feria 3 had been meant here, the date of the 15th March, on which the Jewish third day of the week fell at six in the evening, must have been given; but this Wurm could not intend, since it is in formal contradiction with his established rule. If we would thus translate the Julian days of the week, given by Wurm, into the Jewish,—in those cases where they indicate the 1st and 15th Nisan according to the phase,—we must always take a day of the week one stage later.

In order to become convinced of the correctness of Wurm's calculation, we compare here a calculation made entirely independently of that of Wurm, by Z. Oudemans, Professor of Astronomy in Utrecht :[1]—

Year of Christ.			Time of Conjunction.
28	.	.	Monday, 15th March, 2 h. 25 m. morning.
28	.	.	Tuesday, 13th April, 3 h. 52 m. evening.
29	.	.	Saturday, 2d April, 7 h. 28 m. evening.
30	.	.	Wednesday, 22d March, 8 h. 2 m. evening.
31	.	.	Sunday, 11th March, 11 h. 47 m. evening.
31	.	.	Tuesday, 10th April, 1 h. 51 m. evening.

The difference in the results amounts only to minutes. Even in the year 31, where Wurm gives 12th March, and Oudemans 11th, there is between 11 h. 47 m. evening, and 12 h. 56 m. morning, a difference only of 69 minutes.

Sec. 17. We must yet further show by an example how the 1st Nisan according to the phase, and consequently also

[1] It is to be found in a *Mémoire* by Chavannes in the Strasburg *Revue de Théologie*, 1863, p. 221.

the 15th Nisan, is to be determined by means of this table. We shall later show that the year of the death of Jesus is the 30th of the Dionysian era, A.D. 30, and that the crucifixion took place on the 14th Nisan, at the preparation for the Pass-over.   We take thus this year 30 as an example.

The conjunction took place Wednesday, 22d March, at about 8 h. 8 m. in the evening.   At 6 P.M. on this 22d March the Jewish fifth day of the week (Thursday) had begun ; but this could not possibly be the 1st Nisan, because the moon at the beginning of this night-day was the old decreasing one. Just as little could the Jewish sixth day of the week, beginning 23d March at 6 P.M., be the 1st Nisan, because at this hour the moon was only 22 hours old, and thus as a rule not yet visible.   At that time, consequently, the 1st Nisan fell on Friday, 24th March, as Wurm also gives it.   Only we must here repeat that this 1st Nisan was the night-day beginning on the said Friday at 6 P.M., consequently for the Jews the seventh day, or Sabbath.   At the beginning of this night day the moon was 46 hours old.   The 15th Nisan was always on the same day of the week as the 1st.   From this it follows that the great day of Passover, the 15th Nisan, fell in the year 30 on Friday the 7th April,—7 April, feria 6, as Wurm gives it,—and began on this day at 6 P.M., with the beginning of the Sabbath.

Below is appended, for convenience of reference, a brief calendar of the Jewish year, from the beginning of January A.D. 28, to the third Pentecost, Saturday, 27th May, A.D. 30, nine days after the Lord's ascension.

Date in Julian Year.	A.D. 28.	A.D. 29.	A.D. 30.
Jan. 1	15th Thebet, Friday.	26th Thebet, Saturday.	7th Thebet, Sunday.
Feb. 1	17th Shebet, Monday.	28th Shebet, Tuesday.	9th Shebet, Wed.
March 1	15th Adar, Monday.	26th Adar, Tuesday.	7th Adar, Wednesday.
April 1	17th Nisan, Thursday.	27th Veadar, Friday.	9th Nisan, Saturday.
May 1	17th Ijar, Saturday.	28th Nisan, Sunday.	9th Ijar, Monday.
June 1	19th Sivan, Tuesday.	29th Ijar, Wednesday.	11th Sivan, Thursday.
July 1	19th Thammuz, Thurs.	30th Sivan, Friday.	
Aug. 1	21st Ab, Sunday.	2d Ab, Monday.	
Sept. 1	22d Elul, Wednesday.	3d Elul, Thursday.	
Oct. 1	23d Tisri, Friday.	4th Tisri, Saturday.	
Nov. 1	24th Marchesvan, Mon.	5th Marchesvan, Tues.	
Dec. 1	25th Kisleu, Wed.	6th Kisleu, Thursday.	

In the year A.D. 30 the 1st Nisan began on the 24th March, a Friday, at 6 P.M., with the opening Sabbath ; the 15th Nisan fell on Friday, 7th April, and began at 6 P.M. with the Sabbath. The 14th Nisan, or preparation of the Passover, began on Thursday, 6th April, at 6 P.M., and continued till Friday at 6 P.M.

II.—*The Principal Epochs in the Life of King Herod.*

Sec. 18. Josephus [1] says that Herod died 34 years after the execution of Antigonus, and 37 years after his own appointment as king by the Roman senate. We have thus here the three main epochs in the life of Herod which mutually determine each other—his appointment as king; his actual occupation of the throne, in consequence of the capture of Jerusalem and the death of the Asmonæan Antigonus ; and, lastly, his own death.

Sec. 19. According to *Antiq.* xiv. 14, sec. 5, Herod obtained from the senate at Rome the title of king in the 184th Olympiad, during the consulate of Caius Domitius Calvinus, consul the second time, and of Caius Asinius Pollio. After the sitting of the senate Anthony and Augustus went out, taking Herod between them, μέσον ἔχοντες Ἡρώδην Ἀντώνιος καὶ Καῖσαρ, in order to present the offering in the Capitol. This took place, consequently, after the reconciliation between Anthony and Augustus, which took place after the peace of Brundusium, towards the end of the year U.C. 714, B.C. 40. The appointment of Herod, however, took place in the following year ; because it is said, *Antiq.* xiv. 14, sec. 2, that Herod had entered upon his journey to Rome, which led him to this high dignity, during the winter season, χειμῶνος τε ὄντος, from which it is to be inferred that he reached Rome either during the winter or in early spring. At this season of the year 40 Anthony was not in Rome, and was still in hostility towards Augustus. The chronologists who place the appointment of Herod by the senate in the year B.C. 40, thus come into collision with the patent facts of history. This appointment took place in the spring of the year U.C. 715, B.C. 39.

[1] *Antiq.* xviii. 8, sec. 1.

With this agrees the 184th Olympiad, which embraces the years 715–718.

Sec. 20. Herod had by this recognition obtained only the title of king, and the reversionary right to the throne, the actual possession of which he must first obtain by force of arms. To this possession he attained by the conquest of Jerusalem and the murder of Antigonus, by which this event was quickly followed. According to Josephus, *Antiq.* xiv. 6, sec. 4, Herod took Jerusalem under the consulate of Marcus Agrippa and Caninius Gallus, in the 185th Olympiad. The 185th Olympiad embraced the years U.C. 719–722. But, since the epoch of the Olympiads was in the time of autumn, the latter part of the year of Rome 718, from about August, counted as part of the 185th Olympiad. The consulate mentioned was the third after that under which the appointment had been made. In the *Chronicon* of Cassiodorus we read of the following succession of the consulates :—

> Gn. Domitius and C. Asinius,
> L. Censorinus and C. Norbanus,
> App. Claudius and C. Norbanus,
> *M. Agrippa and L. Caninius.*

If now, of which there can be no doubt, the date of the appointment was U.C. 715, the capture of the city must have taken place in the year 718 ; and the more so, since Josephus, *Antiq.* xiv. 15, sec. 14, expressly says that the two events were separated by an interval of three years. The occupation of the city, however, must fall at the end of the year 718, since it belongs not to the 184th, but to the 185th Olympiad. The correctness of the particular last determined will presently become evident. It is incumbent on us first of all to discover by another method the date of the capture. Josephus, *Antiq.* xiv. 16, sec. 4, says that "this capture took place in the third month, on the fast of the Atonement, as though it were a periodical return of the calamity inflicted upon the Jews by Pompey ; for by the man before referred to (Herod) was their city taken on the same day, after an interval of 27 years : τῷ τρίτῳ μηνὶ, τῇ ἑορτῇ τῆς νηστείας, ὥσπερ ἐκ περιτροπῆς τῆς γενομένης ἐπὶ Πομπηΐου τοῖς Ἰουδαίοις συμφορᾶς· καὶ γὰρ ὑπ' ἐκείνου τῇ αὐτῇ ἑάλωσαν ἡμέρᾳ μετὰ ἔτη εἰκοσικαιεπτά." Now, according to *Antiq.* xiv. 4, sec. 3, the capture of Jerusalem by Pompey took place "in the third month, on the day of the Atonement, during the 179th Olympiad, under the consuls C. Antonius and Marcus Tullius Cicero." The 179th Olympiad comprises the years U.C. 691–694. The consulate mentioned belongs certainly to the year U.C. 691, or B.C. 63. According to Cassiodorus, the consulate of M. Agrippa and L. Caninius is really the 27th after that of Antonius and Cicero. Twenty-seven years after 691 is 718. When Josephus says that the capture of Jerusalem took place "in the third month," not the third month of the year (Sivan) is to be understood thereby, as Wieseler and others suppose, but the third month of the siege; the capture took place not in Sivan, but in Tisri, at the fast of Atonement, which was celebrated on the 10th Tisri. Ἡ ἡμέρα τῆς νηστείας is the constant expression for the fast of the Atonement,[1] and does not designate "any fast day whatever." Von Gumpach thinks the Jews must certainly have instituted a fast in commemoration of the capture of Jerusalem by Pompey, and that this fast—naturally in the month of Sivan —is intended by Josephus in the account of the capture by Herod on the same day of the year. But, unfortunately, not only does history and the Jewish calendar of fasts and festivals know nothing of such appointment, but Josephus says of Pompey himself that he took the city τῇ τῆς νηστείας ἡμέρᾳ. This fast-day thus existed even before the capture by Pompey. What has been already said before receives elucidation from the following comparison of texts:—

CAPTURE OF JERUSALEM.

BY POMPEY.		BY HEROD.
Bell. i. 7, sec. 4: Τρίτῳ γὰρ μηνὶ τῆς πολιορκίας εἰσέπιπτον εἰς τὸ ἱερόν.	*Antiq.* xiv. 4, sec. 3: Καὶ γὰρ ἁλούσης τῆς πόλεως, περὶ τὸν τρίτον μῆνα τῇ τῆς νηστείας ἡμέρᾳ.	*Antiq.* xiv. 16, sec. 4: Τοῦτο τὸ πάθος συνέβη τῇ Ἱεροσολυμιτῶν πόλει τῷ τρίτῳ μηνὶ, τῇ ἑορτῇ τῆς νηστείας, ὥσπερ ἐκ περιτροπῆς τῆς γενομένης ἐπὶ Πομπηΐου τοῖς Ἰουδαίοις συμφοράς.

---

[1] [Cf. Acts xxvii. 9.]

When Josephus, *de Bello,* says that Pompey captured the temple in the third month of the siege, it follows that in the same history, in the *Antiq.,* " the third month " is also to be counted from the beginning of the siege ; and since the occupation by Herod is described as a remarkable repetition of the same incidents, so must in that case also the words " in the third month " have reference to the time of the siege. Once this is admitted, and there is in no case seen a reference to the day of the year, it follows as a matter of course that the words ἡ ἑορτή or ἡ ἡμέρα τῆς νηστείας must be taken in the sense we have assumed, of " fast of the Atonement." The parallel instituted by Josephus, the περιτροπή, has either no meaning at all, or it says that Jerusalem with its temple was twice captured within the space of 27 years, on each occasion on the fast of the Atonement, and each time after a siege of three months.

The main objection to our explanation of the matter is, according to Wieseler, the statement of Josephus,[1] that the Jews had endured a siege of five months before Herod took the city : πέντε μησὶ διήνεγκαν τὴν πολιορκίαν ; from which it is supposed to follow that " the third month " could not be that of the siege. But the difficulty entirely disappears so soon as one considers that in *de Bello* Josephus reckons also the blockade begun before Herod's wedding, but in the *Antiquities* counts from the time of the siege properly so called, which began with the arrival of Sosius and the Roman allied troops. In the former case the siege lasted five months, in the latter three. *Antiq.* xiv. 15, sec. 14, we read that after the winter was past, λήξαντος δὲ τοῦ χειμῶνος—thus about the beginning of March—in the third year after his elevation to the dignity of king, Herod pitched his camp in the neighbourhood of Jerusalem ; afterwards he broke up this camp, approached close to the walls, and began the blockade. Now if the festival of Passover had been disturbed by this blockade or the siege following it, Josephus would, as is his wont, have made mention of this not unimportant circumstance. Since he does not do so, it may be assumed as certain that Herod had remained quiet in his first camp

---

[1] Josephus, *de Bello,* i. 18, sec. 2.

during the whole time of the Passover, in order not to rouse the body of the Jews against him by the interruption of the festival. He thus began the blockade after the season of Passover, at the end of Nisan. Then he repaired to Samaria, where he celebrated his wedding with Mariamne. After this wedding there now began, according to *Antiq.* xiv. 16, sec. 1, the siege properly so called, in conjunction with Sosius, who had now arrived. But the siege began in summer,—θέρος τε γὰρ ἦν,[1]—how then could it be assumed that, after a lapse of five months, it was already at an end in Sivan, *i.e.* June, at the beginning of summer? The first wall was stormed 40 days after the beginning of the actual siege, 15 days later the second wall fell; this makes together 55 days, not quite two full months. The siege of the temple and out-buildings lasted, finally, until the 10th Tisri, thus one full month. These results are to be chronologically arranged as follows :—

With the first spring Herod takes up a camp in the neighbourhood of Jerusalem, and waits in this until the Passover guests have withdrawn.

After Passover, at the beginning of Ijar, five months before the fast of Atonement, he sits down before the city and invests it, and then goes to the wedding in Samaria.

At the beginning of Thammuz, three months before the fast of the Atonement, he begins, in conjunction with Sosius, the actual siege; storms the first (outermost) wall after 40 days, *i.e.* in the middle of Ab; and the second 15 days later, end of Ab or beginning of Elul; lays siege to the temple for about a month, and occupies it on the 10th Tisri, the fast of the Atonement, all in the year U.C. 718, B.C. 36.

Sec. 21. In connection with the siege of Jerusalem by Herod, Josephus makes mention[2] of yet another circumstance of great chronological importance. He says that the besieged were distressed by famine on account of its being a Sabbatic year at the time, τὸ γὰρ ἑβδοματικὸν ἐνιαυτὸν συνέβη κατὰ ταυτὸν εἶναι; and later,[3] the distress following the surrender of the city is partly explained by the fact that a Sabbath year was

---

[1] *Antiq.* xiv. 16, sec. 2.   [2] *Antiq.* xiv. 16, sec. 2.

[3] *Antiq.* xv. 1, sec. 2.

still running its course, ἐνειστήκει γὰρ τότε τὸ ἑβδοματικὸν ἔτος. But, according to Jewish tradition, the year of the destruction of the temple by Titus was also a Sabbatic year. Now, Jerusalem was destroyed A.D. 70, U.C. 823 ; and in reality the year Tisri 822 to Tisri 823 is the 15 - times - 7th from the year 717–718. It would lead us too far to enter upon the proof—in opposition to those chronologists who accept the year 71 as that of the destruction of Jerusalem—that the year 70 is the true date. On this question we refer the reader to Von Gumpach's thorough handling of this difficult subject.[1] We believe that the proof for the year 70 may be satisfactorily derived from the statements of Jewish tradition. In *Seder Olam Rabba* xxx. we read a saying of R. Jose, often repeated in the Talmud,[2] " In like manner as the first temple was destroyed at the end of the Sabbath, and at the end of the Sabbath-year, when the order of Jehoiarib was ministering, on the 9th of the month *Ab*, so was it with the second temple." כשהריב הבית בראשונה אותו היום מוצאי שבת היה ומוצאי שביעית היתה ומשמרתו של יהויריב היתה ותשעה באב היה וכן שניית. Here we at once encounter a first difficulty. Many chronologists translate מוצאי שביעית " in the year after the Sabbath-year," and not " at the end of the Sabbath-year." They appeal to the fact that it is said, *Bab. Sanhedrin*, i. 2, " The intercalary month is not made on the Sabbath-year, not even at the end of it;" and in the scholium to this passage, " at the end" is explained by " in the eighth year." From this, then, it is concluded that " in the end of the Sabbath-year" means " in the year following the Sabbath-year." But this conclusion is incorrect, and is based on a misunderstanding of the nature of the Jewish calendar. The Jewish year began with Nisan : in the seventh year, which opened with this month, there began with the seventh month, Tisri, the Sabbath-year, to which were accordingly counted the first six months of the eighth year, with which the new cycle began. The first half of the eighth year was accordingly an integral part of the Sabbatic year. The temple was destroyed in Ab, the eleventh month of the seventh year, beginning with Tisri, and the fifth month of the eighth year, beginning with

---

[1] Von Gumpach, as before, p. 283 ff.

[2] Cf. *B. Bab. Erachin*, fol. 11, 2 ; *Bab. Taanith*, fol. 29, 1.

Nisan, and belonged thus to the end of the Sabbath-year, and at the same time to the eighth Nisan year. The scholium thus does not say that "the end of the Sabbath-year" is the year following the Sabbatic year, but that it is the Sabbatic year itself. The month Ab which follows the Sabbath-year belongs not to the eighth, but to the ninth year, the second of the new cycle. We have thus to understand the saying of R. Jose to mean, that the temple was destroyed in the month Ab, the eleventh month of the Sabbath-year itself. His statement, so far as concerns the first temple, is not in accordance with history. The first temple was not destroyed in the Sabbath-year,—which institution, moreover, was not observed before the captivity,[1]—and the destruction took place not on the 9th, but on the 10th Ab.[2] Neither does the statement of R. Jose entirely accord with the history of the destruction of the second temple. Josephus says, *de Bello*, vi. 4, secs. 1–5, that on the 8th Loüs (Ab) the porticos of the inner court were set on fire. On the 9th, the Jews, overwhelmed with dismay, were quiet, and Titus gave orders to get the fire under; on the 10th, about the fifth hour, the Jews made a sortie upon the Romans engaged in subduing the flames, but were repulsed. On this occasion the Romans penetrated as far as the temple itself, into which one of them now cast a firebrand. This took place, Josephus expressly tells us, on the 10th Ab, the day of the destruction of the first temple. The fire now raged throughout that day and the night which followed it. According to Jewish notions, fire was thus set to the temple on the 8th Ab, since the inner courts were an integral part of the sacred buildings. In order to commemorate on one fast-day the two destructions, that of the first and that of the second temple, one of which temples was set on fire on the 10th, and the other on the 8th Ab, the Jews selected the intervening 9th Ab, and justified themselves by artificial explanations, about which much is to be read in *Tosaphta Taanith*, iii. 7, and *Jerus. Taanith*, iii. 7.[3] It still remains for us to examine how the matter stands as regards the Sabbath, on which day the temple is said to have been

---

[1] 2 Chron. xxxvi. 21.   [2] Jer. lii. 12.
[3] Ugolini, *Thes.* xviii. pp. 669, 809.

destroyed.   In the year 70, the astronomical new moon determining the month Ab fell on the evening of the 26th July ;
the phase became visible on the 27th, perhaps not before the
28th, at any rate not on the 26th July.   If the 27th was the
1st Ab, the 8th Ab, the night-day beginning on the evening
of August 3, was a Sabbath.[1]   If the 1st Ab fell on 28th
July, then the 8th fell on the evening of 4th August, on the
first day of the week.   The 9th Ab was thus either on the first
or second day of the week, but not possibly on a Sabbath.
But, since the 8th was a Sabbath, and on this 8th, according
to Josephus, the fire broke out in the sacred buildings, the
whole matter is explained on the presupposition that the Jews
had designedly transposed the date to the 9th, in order to
commemorate at the same time the destruction of the former
temple on one anniversary day.   Let us now test the result
of the supposition that the temple was destroyed A.D. 71.   In
this year the 1st Nisan corresponded with the 20th March :
tho 9th Ab was either the 126th or 127th day after this
date—consequently 24th or 25th July, Wednesday or Thursday ; but in no case Sabbath.   And just as little could the
8th be a Sabbath.   The year 71, consequently, cannot be the
year of the destruction.   The sanctuary was set in flames in
the year 70, on the [evening of the] 3d of August, in a
Sabbatic year.

    Sec. 22.   We have seen that the Sabbath-years 717–718
and 822–823 mutually determine and confirm each other.
The same is the case with two other Sabbath-years, of which
we read in the history after the captivity.   In 1 Macc.
vi. 20, 49, 53, 57, mention is made of the great dearth which
was occasioned in the 150th year of the Seleucidan era by
the intervention of a Sabbath-year.   The epoch of this era is
Tisri, B.C. 312, U.C. 442 ; the 150th year of this era is Tisri
592–593.   The events recorded manifestly fall in the winter.
According to 2 Macc. xiii. 1, 2, it came to the knowledge of
the Jews that Antiochus Eupater was marching against Judea.
There is no improbability in the supposition that this was at
the end of the year 149, about the month *Ab*.   Induced

---

[1] [That is to say, the 4th of August in the year 70, according to the Julian
calendar, fell on a Saturday.]

most likely by such reports, Judas sought to make himself master of the Acra in Jerusalem before the arrival of the Syrians; he laid siege to it in the year 150,[1] in the beginning of the year, about the month of Tisri.   In the meantime the Syrians had laid siege to Bethsura.   The place was obliged to capitulate on account of the dearth of provisions occasioned by the Sabbath-year.   That must evidently mean, because there was no harvest on the previous Nisan.   The previous Nisan, however, belonged to the 149th year.   The Sabbath-year was consequently the year of Rome 591–592.   This year actually precedes that of the taking of Jerusalem by Herod by 18 times 7 years, and that of the destruction of the temple by 33 times 7 years.   They were thus each and all of them Sabbatic years.—1 Macc. xvi. 14–16, it is related that Simon was murdered in the month of Shebet, in the year 177; and Josephus, *Antiq.* xiii. 7, secs. 4–8, tells us that it was then a Sabbatic year.   The year 177 ær. Seleuc. is the year of Rome, Tisri 619–620.   This year is the 14-times-7th from the taking of Jerusalem by Herod, and the 29-times-7th from the destruction of the temple.   From this it follows that 591–592, 619–620, 717–718, 822–823, were Sabbatic years, and that the taking of Jerusalem by Herod really belongs to the year 718.   This date may be looked upon as the most certain of any given in the history of Herod.

Sec. 23. Josephus says, *de Bello,* i. 19, sec. 3, that an earthquake took place in the 7th year of the reign of Herod, when that king was at war with the Arabians, and the war around Actium was coming to a point, *i.e.* was beginning, at the commencement of the spring, κατ' ἔτος τῆς βασιλείας ἕβδομον, ἀκμάζοντος δὲ τοῦ περὶ Ἄκτιον πολέμου, κατὰ γὰρ ἀρχομένου ἔαρος.   The Actic war began in the year of Rome 722, by the declaration of war against Cleopatra, and ended with the battle of Actium, 2d September, in the year of Rome 723.   If, at the beginning of the spring of the year 722, in which the war in question began, Herod had been king for seven years, he must have obtained this dignity in the year 715, which, as we have already seen,[2] was the case.

---

[1] 1 Macc. vi. 20.   [2] Cf. sec. 19.

From this passage is to be explained the parallel passage, *Antiq.* xv. 5, sec. 2, which, according to our view, must be translated : " In the meantime, while the battle at Actium between Octavius Cæsar and Anthony was impending,—τῆς ἐπ' 'Ακτίῳ μάχης συνεσταμένης, — in the 7th year of the rule of Herod, was an earthquake." [1]

Sec. 24. *Antiq.* xv. 11, sec. 1, Josephus says that Herod had begun the construction of the temple in the 18th year of his reign ; *de Bello,* i. 21, sec. 1, it stands in the 15th year. Since, however, Josephus counts the years of Herod sometimes from the appointment by the senate, sometimes from the taking of Jerusalem, which happened three years later, it appears that the fifteen years have reference to this latter fact, and the eighteen to the former. The year of the temple-building was, consequently, 715 plus 18, equal to 718 plus 15, *i.e.* U.C. 733. We have, however, another method whereby to arrive at the date of the temple-building. We are told, *Antiq.* xv. 10, sec. 3, immediately before the mention of the temple-building, that when the 17th year of Herod was at an end — ἤδη δὲ αὐτοῦ τῆς βασιλείας ἐπτεκαιδεκάτου παρελθόντος (not παρερχομένου) ἔτους—Cæsar (Augustus) came into Syria. Now, the journey of Augustus falls in the spring of the year of Rome 734, B.C. 20. But because the 17th year was past, the 18th, which is presently given as the year of the temple - building, had begun. The rebuilding of the temple thus belongs to the year 734, the year of Augustus' journey to Syria : it is really the 15th plus a few months after the taking of Jerusalem, which happened in Tisri ; but the 19th, and not the 18th, after the appointment by the senate.

Sec. 25. **Year of Herod's Death.**—*Antiq.* xvii. 8, sec. 1, Josephus tells us that Herod's reign, counted from the death of Antigonus, lasted 34 years, from his appointment by the Romans 37 years : 715 plus 37 equals 718 plus 34, *i.e.* U.C.

---

[1] [If, as seems to be implied by the words of Josephus, the battle of Actium was actually fought *in the 7th year* of Herod's reign, the historian must date from the latter part of the year 717, before "the depth of the winter" (*Antiq.* xiv. 15, sec. 12), at which time Herod had entered on the campaign for the final subjugation of Judea.]

752. But since Herod died at the beginning of the year, before Passover, and took Jerusalem in the autumn, it is possible that the year of Herod's death was 753. *Antiq.* xvii. 6, sec. 1, and *de Bello,* i. 33, sec. 1, it is said that Herod at the time of his death was about seventy years of age. According to *Antiq.* xiv. 9, sec. 2, as compared with xiv. 8, sec. 5, Herod was fifteen years old in the ninth year of the reign of Hyrkanus, *i.e.* nine years after the taking of Jerusalem by Pompey; he was therefore born about 684, and would have been fully 70 years old in 754, and was thus almost 70 years old (σχεδόν) in 753.

In the 15th year of Tiberius, Jesus was about 30 years of age.[1] The 15th year of Tiberius is U.C. 781 ; if thus the birth of Jesus was in the year 751, it seems the time of Herod's death—which was after the birth of Christ—could not have been, at the earliest, before 752.

All these accounts place the death of Herod, at the earliest, in the year 752.

Sec. 26. As opposed to these, there is another series of texts, which make the year 750 the year of Herod's death.

In *Antiq.* xvii. 13, sec. 2, it is stated that Archelaus the son of Herod was banished by Augustus in the 10th—*Bell.* ii. 7, sec. 3, says in the 9th—year of his ethnarchy. According to *Antiq.* xviii. 2, sec. 1, Quirinus had already, in the 37th year after the battle of Actium, confiscated the property of the banished Archelaus. This 37th year ended with the 2d September U.C. 760. The banishment must thus have taken place at the latest in the year 760 ; if Herod died ten or even nine years earlier, his death must have been in the year 750 or 751. [If, however, the 9th year of his reign was reckoned from the completion of *eight* full years, Herod's death might most naturally be supposed to fall in the year 752.]

According to *Antiq.* xviii. 6, sec. 1 ; 7, secs. 1, 2, Agrippa received from Caligula, who had succeeded Tiberius on the 16th March, year of Rome 790, permission to enter upon his kingdom. Upon this Herod the tetrarch repaired to Rome, at the same time to solicit the title of king; but was sent into exile. This banishment fell in the year of Rome 792 or 793.

[1] Luke iii. 1, 23. [ὡσεί, about, towards, cf. John xix. 14.]

Now, according to Eckhel,[1] coins of Herod the tetrarch, belonging to the 43d year of his reign, are still in existence. Reckoning back these years from 792–793, we get the year of Herod's death as U.C. 750 or 751.

According to *Antiq.* xviii. 4, sec. 6, Philip the tetrarch died in the 20th year of the reign of Tiberius, after a rule of 37 years. The 20th year of Tiberius ended in August 787 ; reckoning 37 years backwards from this, gives the year of Rome 750 as the year of Herod's death.

Sec. 27. The calculation from above downwards gives uniformly U.C. 752 or 753 as the year of Herod's death ; the calculation from below upwards gives, on the other hand, 750, or, at most, 751 [in one case 752] as the possible year. It is self-evident that Josephus has somewhere reckoned two years two many; probably because he counted certain consulates, which lasted only a short time, as embracing full years. That he has in reality counted two years too much is clear from *Antiq* xx 10, sec. 1, where it is said that the office of the high priest, from the death of Antigonus to the destruction of the temple, had continued 107 years. But from 718 to 823 there are only 105 years ! Both dates were, as we have seen, Sabbatic years ; these could not be 107 years from each other, because that number is not divisible by seven.

Chronologists have sought in various ways to explain this contradiction. Wieseler [p. 48 of English translation] seeks to remove the difficulty by the application of the rabbinical principle, that Nisan is the beginning of the year for the kings, and that a single day over the year counts as another year ;[2] but he forgets that it is expressly said this rule applies only *to the kings of Israel.*[3] The rule was an expedient for resolving the chronological difficulties connected with the duration of the reign of the kings before the captivity, who alone with the Rabbis bear the name of " kings of Israel ;" and cannot be applied to the history after the captivity, since neither the Asmonæans nor the Herodians were

---

[1] *Doct. Num. Vet.* iii. p. 486.

[2] Wieseler, *Synopsis* [p. 48 of English translation].

[3] לא שנו אלא למלכי ישראל, *Rosh hashanna,* i.

kings of Israel. Seyffarth, on the other hand,[1] gets out of the difficulty by maintaining — not that Josephus counts two years too much, but—that modern chronologists count two years too little, between the accession of Herod and the destruction of Jerusalem. We cannot enter here into his elaborate argumentation; we confess ourselves, however, unconvinced by his reasoning.

It remains thus admitted that Josephus somewhere counts two years too much. But where does the error lurk ? In the history of Herod ? or in the history after his death ? Here, unfortunately, all certain data are wanting. We cannot afford to leave unexhausted any means which may contribute to the deciding of this question.

Sec. 28. Josephus relates that some time before the death of Herod an eclipse of the moon took place. Let us see if we can avail ourselves of this circumstance to determine the year of this king's death. With a view to this result, Wurm[2] has calculated the eclipses occurring from B.C. 6 to B.C. 1, which were visible at Jerusalem.

In the year B.C. 6 there was no lunar eclipse.

In the year B.C. 5 there were two, total, the one on the 23d March, the other on the 15th September.

In the year B.C. 4 there was a partial one, of 5 inches, on the 13th March, at 3 h. 4 m. A.M.

In the years B.C. 3 and 2, none.

In the year B.C. 1, a total eclipse on the 10th January, at 1 h. 54 m. A.M.

The years 6, 3, and 2 before Christ are thus inadmissible, because they are without any lunar eclipse. The choice consequently lies between the years B.C. 5, 4, and 1, or U.C. 749, 750, 753, the very years between which sections 25 and 26 had already left us a choice, without casting into either scale a decisive weight. Let us now more closely examine the history of this eclipse. Josephus relates[3] that Herod caused a certain Judas Sariphæi and one Matthias Margolothi to be burned alive. On the same night there occurred an eclipse of the moon. From that time forward the sickness of Herod increased. When the sufferings became unendurable, he

---

[1] *Chron. Sacra*, pp. 11, 92 ff.   [2] Wurm, as before, p. 26 ff.

[3] *Antiq.* xvii. 6, secs. 2-4.

betook himself to Callirhoë, beyond Jordan, where he used the warm baths. There his physicans thought it advisable to warm him by a bath of oil; in this, however, he was near dying. Coming to consciousness again, and having no hopes of his recovery, he divided large sums of money amongst his soldiers, officers, and friends, and returned to Jericho. In a paroxysm of melancholy he gave orders for summoning together the leading men among the Jews from every part (ὁπούποτε). Their number was great, because they were collected together out of the whole nation. These he caused to be shut up in the hippodrome, and ordered his sister Salome after his death to have them all put to death, that the Jews might not rejoice over his decease.[1] After he had issued this command, letters reached him from Rome, announcing that the emperor authorized him to banish or execute his son. This news revived him. When, however, the pains again got the upper hand, he sought to kill himself, but was prevented. The outcry raised on account of this attempt led Antipater in his prison to suppose his father was dead, and he sought to bribe his jailor. When Herod heard of this, he caused Antipater to be put to death, and five days afterwards himself expired.[2] Salome then set at liberty the members of the Jewish leading families shut up in the hippodrome.[3] Archelaus honoured his father with a royal funeral, mourned seven days, gave a banquet to the populace, and after laying aside his mourning, repaired to the temple, where he was well received by the populace.[4] Soon, however, a hostile reaction set in, which became the more perilous, inasmuch as the festival of Passover was near at hand.[5] Now, how many days do all these events require for their occurrence? That they might occupy three months, no one will be inclined to doubt; neither can it be denied that they might have happened within thirty days even. The eclipse does not thus decide our question. The eclipses of the years 5 and 4 occurring just thirty days before Passover are possible, that of the year 1 before Christ occurring three months before Passover is equally so. There

---

[1] *Antiq.* xvii. 6, secs. 5, 6.   [2] *Antiq.* xvii. 7, xviii. 8, sec. 1.
[3] *Antiq.* xvii. 8, sec. 2.   [4] *Antiq.* xvii. 8, secs. 3, 4.
[5] *Antiq.* xvii. 9, secs. 1–3.

remains to us, considering the multitude of intervening events, only a presumption against the years 5 and 4, and in favour of the year 1. Let us see now what Jewish tradition has to say to us on this intricate question.

Sec. 29. Particularly fortunate or unfortunate events are yearly celebrated by the Jews on the anniversary of their occurrence by days of rejoicing or mourning. These days are designated in the old calendar of festivals, the *Megillath-Taanith*. In this book two days are spoken of as the days of Herod's death. In chap. ix. it says: " The 7th Kisleu is a fortunate day (יום טוב), because on that day Herod died, who was an enemy to the sages." Chronologists have rightly rejected this date, since it is five months from the Passover. In chap. xi., however, of the same book we read—what has hitherto been overlooked by the chronologists—" The first Shebet is a doubly fortunate day, as the day of the death of Herod and Jannai ; for there is joy before God when the wicked are taken out of this world. The sages relate that King Jannai, when he came to die, shut up the seventy elders of Israel, and gave orders to the jailor to put them to death when he (Jannai) should die ; that the Israelites, instead of rejoicing over his death, might have to bewail their sages. Now," it goes on to say, " King Jannai had an intelligent wife, Salome (שלמינת). When the king was dead, she took the signet off his finger, and sent it to the jailor with the message, ' Your sick master gives the elders their liberty.' He set them at liberty, and each one went to his house. Only after their deliverance was the king's death made known." This account does not at all tally with the account of King Alexander Jannæus ; for he did not wait until his death to accomplish the slaughter of the Rabbis and Sanhedrists, but had banished and executed them long before. If we substitute for the name of Jannai the name of Herod, we have almost word for word that which Josephus relates: the shutting up of the leading Jews in the hippodrome, the order for their execution and the motive for it, the liberation of them by Salome. Tradition has, as is often the case, interchanged the names, but preserved the facts and the date. The 1st of Shebet is thus the day of Herod's death, while, perhaps, the 7th of

C

Kisleu is to be assigned to Jannai. If Herod died on the 1st Shebet, the lunar eclipse occurring before his death can be neither the first of the year 5, nor that of the year 4; because both occurred on the 15th Adar, *i.e.* six weeks later. In the year 753, anno 1 before Christ, the 10th January, the day of the lunar eclipse, was on the 15th Tebeth; when, 14 days later, on the 1st Shebet, Herod died, it was the 24th January. Jewish tradition may in this way be right, and would thus be a confirmation of the year 753, or 752 plus 24 days. We confess, nevertheless, that the time of 14 days is a very short one for all that is related between the eclipse and the death of Herod; and that, on the other hand, two and a half months is very long for that which occurred between this death and Passover. But must not the royal interment of Herod at Herodium have occupied several weeks in its accomplishment?

III.—*Principal Epochs in the Life of Christ.*

Sec. 30. **The Census.**—Joseph and Mary dwelt at Nazareth; if, this notwithstanding, Jesus was born at Bethlehem, the occasion is to be found in the census, on account of which Joseph must repair to his ancestral city. It is said in Luke ii. 1–4, " It came to pass in those days (in which John was born), that there went out a decree from Augustus Cæsar, that all the world should be enrolled. This enrolment was $\left\{\begin{array}{c}\text{before that made}\\\text{or}\\\text{the first made}\end{array}\right\}$ by Quirinus, governor of Syria [or, better: *as* governor of Syria]. And every one, in order to be enrolled, went into his own city. And Joseph also went up from Galilee, out of the city of Nazareth, into Judea, to the city of David, which is called Bethlehem, because he was of the house and lineage of David, to be enrolled, with Mary, who was espoused to him." The main point is, consequently, to know what is meant by the words Αὕτη ἡ ἀπογραφὴ πρώτη ἐγένετο ἡγεμονεύοντος τῆς Συρίας Κυρηνίου. The common translation is: This census was the first, and was made under Quirinus. We prefer the other: This census was that immediately preceding the census of Quirinus. Grammatically, this rendering is justified by the πρῶτός μου, "He was before me," of John i. 15, while the historical difficulties are removed by it.[1] Quirinus, who as præses of Syria held a census in the year of Rome 759 or 760,[2] obtained this office about the year 758. That Luke does not by an anachronism transfer this census of the year 759 to the time of Christ's birth, but intends an earlier one, is shown even by the word πρώτη, "the first," taken in the ordinary sense. It is not impossible, indeed, that Quirinus—before that well-known census—may have conducted an earlier one in some subordinate capacity under C. Sentius Saturninus or P. Quintilius Varus; but then the expression ἡγεμονεύοντος would be misleading, because it must be taken by every reader in the sense of "when he was *hegemon*, president." Luke characterizes the census which was contemporaneous with Jesus' birth as a general census of the empire, not as one affecting only Syria and Palestine. The fact of the existence of a Roman census embracing the land of Judea, before the well-known census of Quirinus in A.D. 6, has been doubted: (1) because Judea was not then an immediately Roman province; and (2) because neither Josephus nor any other historian makes mention of such a census. As concerns this last objection, it may suffice here, as in many other cases, that Luke—who is an historian as well as Josephus, and proves himself thoroughly conversant with the history—testifies to the actual fact of this ἀπογραφή. The silence of profane authors is to be explained by the fact that the work of Dio Cassius, the principal historical work relating to that period, is defective precisely in the epoch at which the birth of Christ must be placed.[3] But Josephus

---

[1] [Zumpt, however, has sought to show that Quirinus was in all probability *twice* pro-prætor of Syria—once, as successor of Quintilius Varus, from about the end of B.C. 4 to the end of B.C. 1; and again, as successor of Volusius Saturninus, from A.D. 6 to A.D. 11. See note to the English translation of Wieseler, pp. 129–135; and comp. A. W. Zumpt, *Das Geburtsjahr Christi*, Leipzig 1870; cf. Ellicott, *Life of our Lord*, pp. 58, 59, and note to p. 58.]

[2] Josephus, *Antiq.* xviii. 1, sec. 1; Acts v. 37.

[3] [Josephus also, who passes over the entire interval between the accession of Archelaus and his deposition, makes no mention of the first presidency of Quirinus. He ascribes to Varus the merit of quelling the disturbances which arose after the death of Herod, and next speaks of the (second) well-known

might pass over this census, just because it was a measure affecting not only Palestine, but also the whole Roman empire, the execution of which was completed in Judea without tumult. As regards the first objection, it rests in the first place upon a misconception, since the expression ἀπογραφή is taken in the strict sense of a census, or valuation for purposes of assessment of property, for which the more exact Greek term is ἀποτί-μησις. Ἀπογραφή may designate the census in the narrower sense, but may equally well denote an enrolment or return of the population. The Emperor Augustus possessed a *breviarium totius imperii*, in which also was contained *quantum sociorum in armis:*[1] in this, Judea could certainly not be wanting. This " breviarium " necessarily presupposes one if not more registrations, although the historians tell us nothing of them. That the vassal-Prince Herod was not so independent of Rome as some would assume, is manifest from the fact that, even under Pompey, Judea was tributary ;[2] which requires us to presuppose a census in the strict sense of the term, although Josephus is equally silent about this also.   It is, besides, incorrect to say that Luke alone is acquainted with a census preceding that of Quirinus in A.D. 6 ; Tertullian[3] speaks of such a census as taking place under Sentius Saturninus, between 744 and 748 ; and Eusebius, of another belonging to the 42d year of the reign of Augustus.   The supposition that these two Christian writers derived their statement only from the account of Luke, is entirely baseless; and even though this were the case with Eusebius' *Chronicon*, it cannot be said of Tertullian, who places the birth of Christ in the 41st year of the reign of Augustus, when Saturninus had long ceased to be

presidency of Quirinus. If, however, Herod died between the close of B.C. 4 and of B.C. 1, all that is related concerning the period of Herod's death belongs, according to the dates fixed by Zumpt, to the administration of Quirinus. If, on the other hand, Herod died in the year of Rome 750, the census preceding or contemporaneous with Herod's death could not have been carried out by Quirinus, on the assumption that Zumpt's argument is well founded. The testimony of the evangelist as to this census would therefore seem to point to the later year as the true date of Herod's death.]

[1] Sueton. *Octav.* 101 ; Tacit. *Ann.* i. 11.

[2] *Antiq.* xiv. 4, sec. 4, ὑποτιλῆς φόρου. Pompejus captis Hierosolymis tributarios Judæos fecit : *Chron.* Euseb. ad Olymp. 179.

[3] *Adv. Marcionem,* iv. 6.

præses of Syria. The historians speak expressly of three censuses under Augustus; these took place in the years of Rome 726, 746, 767. If, now, we suppose that of 726 was delayed a year owing to some political obstacle or other, then the years 725, 746, 767 are regularly separated from each other by an interval of seven years, and its multiple. But since these censuses are called *lustra*, we may infer that during the age of Augustus the *lustra* were septennial. If, as is probable from the nature of the case, the assessment of those lands of the οἰκουμένη in any way dependent on Rome was simultaneous with these *lustra*, it becomes in the highest degree probable that the census at the close of Herod's reign would be carried into effect as part of a more general measure of state. Seyffarth is perfectly justified in calling attention to the fact that the censuses under Augustus, above referred to, all fell on Sabbatic years of the Jews. Sabbatic years were: 725, 732, 739, 746, 753, 760, 767. The census of 725 was, as we have said, owing to some cause, postponed till 726; that of 746 includes the registration made by Saturninus, for which Tertullian vouches; the census for which Luke vouches must have coincided with the year 753; that of 767 falls in the year of Augustus' death. With regard to the Sabbatic years above noticed, it must be premised that their point of beginning is always the month of Tisri in the preceding year. It is evident that the result of this combination renders probable the year 753 as that of the death of Herod, at least by the proof that this king cannot have died before Tisri 752–753.—Objection has been further raised that, according to Luke, every one, in order to be enrolled, was under obligation to proceed to the city of his tribe and family, and that even the women were compelled to do so. In opposition to this, we remark that this last particular is not adduced, as required by a general rule: Mary might accompany Joseph of free choice, and the more so since Joseph probably intended to take up his permanent abode in Bethlehem, the city of David, " where Christ should be born." And if he afterwards turned aside to Nazareth, this took place under divine direction.[1] Such a journeying of multitudes,

[1] Matt. ii. 23.

each to his own city, must certainly cause great confusion and loss of time. But, since the assessments fell in Sabbatic years, these inconveniences lost a great part of their significance.[1]

Sec. 31. **The Star of the Wise Men.**—In Matt. ii. 1–4, 9, we read, " When Jesus was born . . . there came magi out of the east to Jerusalem, saying, Where is He that is born King of the Jews ? for we have His star ($a\dot{v}\tau o\hat{v}\ \tau \dot{o}\nu\ \dot{a}\sigma\tau\acute{e}\rho a$) in the east, and are come to worship Him. . . . And, lo, the star which they saw in the east went before them, till it came and stood over where the child was." Is there any chronological datum to be derived from this account ? Abarbanel says that three years before the birth of Moses a conjunction of Jupiter and Saturn was witnessed in the sign of Israel, to wit, " Pisces," and that the recurrence of this phenomenon, in the year A.D. 1463, would introduce the birth of the Messiah. Other Jewish traditions, of a like kind, bearing on this question, have been collected by Seyffarth [2] To some such supposition Josephus also would seem to allude.[3] The conjunction of the said two planets was consequently looked upon by the Jews as the constellation of Moses and Messias. Kepler was the first to calculate for chronological purposes the time of this conjunction in " Pisces," and showed that it took place in the year of Rome 747. Ideler [4] subjected the matter to a new test, and found that in the year 747 U.C., Jupiter and Saturn first entered into conjunction on the 20th May, in the 20th degree of " Pisces." They then appeared, before sunrise, in the eastern sky, and were only one degree distant from each other. On the 20th October there was a second conjunction in the 16th degree of Pisces, and, on the 2d November, a third in the 15th degree of the same sign. In the two last conjunctions, too, the difference of declination amounted only to about one degree. Two years later, in the year of Rome 749, there was a conjunction of all the planets; this assumed the form of a child, the form which Jewish tradition gives to

[1] On the question of the census here discussed, comp. Winer, artt. "Quirinus, Schatzung, Abgaben;" Wieseler, as before, p. 65 ff. of Engl. tr.; Seyffarth, as before, p. 87 ff.

[2] Seyffarth, as before, p. 89 ff. [3] *Antiq.* ii. 9, secs. 2, 7.

[4] Ideler, *Chron.* ii. p. 405.

the constellation of Messiah. Was, then, this last conjunction, or one of the others, the star of the wise men ? The Gospel narrative speaks of a star (ἀστήρ), and not of a constellation or combination of stars (ἄστρον); although, it is true, the usage of the Greek writers would seem not to distinguish very sharply between the significations of these two words. This would thus be a possible explanation. The latest moment at which the conjunction of the planets could point out to the magi the place where the child was, was the year of Rome 749. If we were then to assume this to be the year of Jesus' birth, he would have been, in the 15th year of Tiberius, not about 30, but fully 33 years of age. But this conjunction, which assumed the form of a child, did not appear in " Pisces," the sign of Israel, and could not therefore be the constellation of Messiah. This we should rather have to seek in the conjunctions of 747; but by this means the difficulty is only increased, since Jesus would then have been 35 years of age in the 15th year of Tiberius. According to Jewish tradition, Moses was not born during the time of the conjunction, but only three or four years after it; this conjunction was thus not an indication of the birth of Moses, as an event which had already taken place, but a pre-indication of it in the future. In this sense the same conjunction was now to be regarded as the star of the Messiah; it was to precede His birth by several years. But in this way the matter loses its definite character, and ceases to serve as an element in the chronology. Wieseler sees the star of the wise men in another star, a new one, probably a comet, appearing in the year B.C. 4, of which the Chinese astronomical tables give an account, which was visible in February and March.[1] But how could the magi know that a comet—usually the sign of misfortune—was the star of the Messiah ? It will be apparent that facts of this kind can afford no certain basis for the determination of the year of Jesus' birth; and we can follow neither Ideler and Sanclemente nor Wieseler when, on such astronomical grounds, they declare in favour of the year 747 or 750 as that of the Lord's birth.

From the Fathers, too, nothing which greatly avails us is to

[1] Wieseler, as before, p. 61 of Engl. tr.

be gleaned. Tertullian, as we have said, places the birth of Christ in the 41st year of Augustus, that is, the year of Rome 752. The *Chronicon paschale* places the birth of Jesus in the 41st year of Augustus, the death of Herod in the 44th year, thus U.C. 754. Eusebius, in his *Chronicon*, places the birth of Jesus in the year 42 of Augustus, and the death of Herod in the year 47 of this prince, thus in the year of Rome 758. Others, *e.g.* Cassiodorus, *Chronicon*, state that Jesus was born during the consulate of C. Lentulus and M. Messala, which falls in the 41st year of Augustus. The consulates are the most certain means of determining the chronology of this period. Unfortunately, however, it must here be observed that, according to the assertion of Augustine, no original tradition has preserved the consulate either of the year of the Lord's birth or of His death: per Olympiades et consulum nomina multa sæpe quæruntur a nobis, et *ignorantia consulatus quo natus est Dominus et quo passus, nonnullos coegit errare.*[1] Thus much remains as the result of the declarations of the Fathers, that they all, without exception, were of opinion that Herod was alive at any rate in the 41st year of Augustus, that is to say, in the year of Rome 752. This confirms our view that Herod died at the beginning of the year 753.

Sec. 32. **The year of Jesus' entering on His public work.** —That the appearing of Jesus at the feast of Passover, related in the 2d chapter of John, belongs to the year in which the public ministry of Jesus began, and, indeed, to the first months of this year, is perfectly clear. Now during that festival the Jews demanded of Jesus a sign.[2] He answered, " Destroy this temple, and in three days I will raise it up." The Jews replied, " Forty and six years was this temple (ὁ ναός) in building."[3] In the language of the New Testament, a strict distinction is, as a rule, maintained between τὸ ἱερόν, the sanctuary in general, without the holy house, and ὁ ναός, the holy house, in distinction from the rest of the sanctuary. But since there is no expression covering at the same time both ideas, here, in consequence of this expression being just before used by Jesus, the term ναός is

---

[1] Augustinus, *De Doctrina Christiana,* ii. 28.
[2] John ii. 19.　　　　　　　　　　　　[3] John ii. 20.

employed for the sanctuary, inclusive of the temple proper. The objection of the Jews has consequently the following sense : During 46 years have workmen been employed on these sacred buildings,—temple and porticos,—and wilt Thou accomplish this in three days ?   Josephus says, indeed, that the holy house was completed in a year and a half, and the outer courts in 8 years.[1] He cannot, however, here be speaking of an absolute completion ; for the works were continued until shortly before the outbreak of the Jewish war, since, according to *Antiq.* xx. 9, sec. 7, the sanctuary was completed only under the Procurator Albinus—ἤδη τότε καὶ τὸ ἱερὸν ἐτετέλεστο.   From Mark xiii. 1, 2, it is to be inferred that this work of building was still being urgently pressed forward in the year of Jesus' death ; for, in the mouth of persons who came yearly to Jerusalem, the exclamation, " Behold, what stones, what a building !" could not have reference to buildings completed now thirty years, and already often seen before ; but to a structure rising before their eyes.   According to what has been said in sec. 24, Herod began the building in the year 734 ; 46 years added to this gives the year 780, which, according to the Jewish mode of calculation, expired with 1st Nisan of the year 781.   Since the Jews held their conversation with Jesus at the beginning of the Jewish year, they would not count in the year 781, on which they had scarcely entered.

Sec. 33. **The 15th year of the reign of the Emperor Tiberius.**—In Luke iii. 1, 2 we read : " In the 15th year of the reign of Tiberius Cæsar, Pontius Pilate being governor of Judea, and Herod being tetrarch of Galilee, and his brother Philip tetrarch of Ituræa and of the region of Trachonitis, and Lysanias the tetrarch of Abilene, Annas and Caiaphas being the high priests, the word of God came unto John, the son of Zacharias, in the wilderness." Since Luke is writing the history of Jesus, and not that of John, this wealth of chronological data must refer primarily to Jesus, and only incidentally to the Baptist.   The time of John's activity is involved in the nearer definition of the time of Jesus' appearing, since his arising was simultaneous with that of the Lord,

[1] *Antiq.* xv. 11, secs. 5, 6.

in the sense that the baptism of Jesus coincided with the early part of the ministry of John. Since the great mission of John was to make known the person of Him who should come, after he had himself recognised Him, the beginning of John's labours is only to be placed at such an interval before the baptism of Jesus as might be necessary in order for him to gather the multitude around him, for which the space of a month might very well suffice. The year 15 of Tiberius is thus the year in which Jesus and John alike began their labours.[1]

The further notes of time in Luke do not more nearly define the date. Pontius Pilate was procurator from U.C. 779 to 789, when he was deposed shortly before the Passover.[2] Herod Antipas reigned from the death of Herod I. until [the second year of Caligula] 792. Philip was also tetrarch from Herod's death until the 20th year of Tiberius, *i.e.* 786–787. Of Lysanias of Abilene nothing further is known.[3] The greatest difficulty is occasioned by the mention of Annas as high priest, ἀρχιερεύς. This man, according to *Antiq.* xviii. 2, sec. 1, became high priest at the time of the census under Quirinus, about 759, and was deposed at the beginning of the reign of Tiberius, towards 767 of Rome. Caiaphas attained to this dignity in the year 770, and lost it in the year 789.[4] How could Luke, then, advance the statement that Annas was high priest in the 15th year of Tiberius? We are greatly inclined to share Wieseler's view,[5] that Luke calls not alone the high priest, strictly speaking, by the name of ἀρχιερεύς, but applies this name also to the Nasi, or president of the Sanhedrim. In Matt. xxvii. 1, Mark xv. 1, Luke xxii. 66, and often elsewhere, the high priests, οἱ ἀρχιερεῖς, are spoken of in the plural, and in connection with the members of the Great Council, from which it necessarily follows that other offices, or, better, another office was honoured

---

[1] [This conclusion is inevitable, if we suppose the *beginning* of John's ministry to be included under this reference. If, however, we suppose a *later* stage to be intended (cf. Acts xiii. 24, 25), nothing prevents our placing the beginning of John's ministry anywhere after the early part of September in the previous year, at which time a Sabbatic year commenced.]

[2] Josephus, *Antiq.* xviii. 4, sec. 2.

[3] See, on the subject of this tetrarch, Wieseler, as before, p. 160 of Engl. tr.

[4] *Antiq.* xviii. 2, sec. 2 ; 4, sec. 3.   [5] *Synopsis*, p. 169.

with this title. This usage might arise from the fact that Annas, when he was high priest, was also at the same time Nasi of the Sanhedrim, and that, after being deprived of the office of high priest, he continued to retain the dignity of Nasi, and at the same time the old title of high priest, which is still bestowed upon him in Acts iv. 6. Jewish tradition indeed says[1] that Hillel and his descendants, Simeon ben Hillel and Gamaliel ben Simeon, filled the office of Nasi for a hundred years in succession, until the destruction of the temple. But there is here an intervening domination of the Sadducees passed over,[2] during which the family of the Hillels, who belonged to the Pharisaic party, assuredly did not hold the presidential chair. Throughout the whole of this interval of Sadducean domination, then, Annas was probably the Nasi —say from 759 to 784.

Sec. 34. Dio Cassius says, lvi. 29, " Augustus died on the 19th August of the year of Rome 767," *i.e.* A.D. 14 of the Dionysian era. Since it is ordinarily assumed that the years of Tiberius' reign are to be counted from the death of his predecessor, the 15th year of Tiberius is fixed as from the 19th August 781 to the same date 782, A.D. 28–29, ær. Dionys. According to the results obtained, sec. 32, Jesus began His public labours with the opening of the year 781 ; according to the datum of Luke, however, it could begin at the earliest only on the 19th August of this year. Are we to suppose this statement of the evangelist is a blunder ? Since the whole history of the labours of Jesus detailed in the Gospel of Mark does not require us to suppose a full year, and since Luke seems to have taken Mark's Gospel as a framework for his own, the thought occurs that Luke, who knew the year of Jesus' death,—which is the 16th of Tiberius, reckoning from August to August,—had ascribed to the Lord only one year of public labour, and on that account placed the beginning of it in the 15th year of Tiberius. This hypothesis, however, does not hold good, because it pre-supposes that Luke derived this year 15 not from certain testimony, but from a computation. The memorable year of the arising of the Baptist and of Jesus was certainly fixed

[1] *Bab. Sanhedrin*, f. 15.   [2] Comp. on this point sec. 145.

in the recollection of the αὐτόπται and contemporaries of the evangelist, from whom (Luke i. 2) he derived his account. But if the date received by tradition was the year 15, then the whole year 781, reckoned from January, and not merely from the 19th August, must have been intended. Seyffarth makes a remark, in our view well-founded, which the more deserves notice, inasmuch as the author himself had not specially the 15th year of Tiberius before his mind. He says:[1] " Primarily, we must suppose the first year of an emperor's reign was counted from the time at which his predecessor died. . . . In the course of a few years, however, the first year of the new prince was extended to the new year's day of the year in the course of which the preceding ruler died." According to this principle, the entire year 781 was comprised under the 15th year of Tiberius. Without, however, leaning upon this, which is after all only an hypothesis, we will seek rather to obtain an immediate historic support for our position. Augustus died, as has been said, on the 19th August, U.C. 767. Tiberius died 16th March 790 ; the regnal period of the latter was consequently 22 years, 6 months, 27 days. (Josephus[2] has 22 years, 6 months, 3 days, because, by an oversight, he has subtracted 16 days from 19, instead of 19 from 16.) Now Suetonius says, Obiit (Tiberius) anno tertio et vigesimo imperii, decimo septimo Kalend. Aprilis, Cn. Acerronio Proculo, C. Pontio Nigro, coss. : he thus ascribes to Tiberius 23 full years.[3] Now, it is not the wont of this historian to express the regnal period of the emperors by round numbers of years, but by years, months, and days. Thus he says of Caligula that he reigned 3 years, 10 months, and 8 days. And so with the other emperors. The same is true in the case of other historians, as Cassiodorus, Eusebius in his *Chronicon*, etc.,

---

[1] Seyffarth, as before, p. 10.   [2] Josephus, *de Bello*, ii. 9, sec. 5.

[3] [Suetonius, in speaking of the death of Tiberius *in the 23d year* of his reign, would seem, however, only to mean that he had completed his 22d. That Luke reckons Tiberius' reign from the beginning of the year is self-evident, from the fact that the baptism, which took place in the beginning of February (sec. 84), must otherwise have fallen in the 14th year. The mode of computation of the regnal years of Tiberius from the time of his *joint* sovereignty is now adopted by Wieseler, art. "Neutest. Zeitrechnung," in Herzog's *R. E.*]

who usually give months and days, and yet, like Suetonius, ascribe to Tiberius 23 years, instead of 22 years, 7 months. All these count Tiberius' years from the beginning of the year—at the latest from the month of March — u.c. 767. Now, Suetonius says[1] that Tiberius celebrated his triumph, falling in the beginning of the year 767, " ac, non multo post, *lege per consules lata ut provincias cum Augusto communiter administraret*, simulque censum ageret. Condito lustro in Illyricum profectus est. Et statim ex itinere revocatus ; jamquidem affectum sed tamen spirantem Augustum reperit." To this corresponds that which Tacitus says, *Ann.* i. 3, *Filius, collega imperii*, consors tribunitiæ potestatis adsumitur (Tiberius) omnisque per exercitus ostentatur. Suetonius and the other historians consequently reckon the years of Tiberius not from the death of Augustus, but from the day in which he became collega imperii, *i.e.* from February, the month of the *lustra*. In the same manner Luke reckons. The 15th regnal year of Tiberius is thus the whole year 781 ; and in this way the notes of time in Luke perfectly agree with those of John.

Sec. 35. **Year of the Conversion of the Apostle Paul.—** The apostle says, Gal. i. 18, ii. 1, 2, that 3 years after his conversion he came for the first time into contact with the apostles at Jerusalem ; and then, 14 years later, a second time, in consequence of a revelation. To these two journeys to Jerusalem unquestionably correspond that first journey of Acts ix. 26, at the same time related as being his first journey ; and the other, narrated in Acts xi. 30, which likewise was occasioned by a revelation,[2] and followed by a return to Antioch.[3] To what year, then, does this second journey belong ? Acts xi. 27–30 we read, " In those days came prophets from Jerusalem to Antioch. One of them, Agabus by name, stood up, and testified by the Spirit that there should be presently a great dearth throughout all the world. This actually took place in the time of Claudius. Each, then, of the disciples determined, every one according to his means, to send ministration to the brethren dwelling in Judea. This they did, sending it to the elders by the hand of Barna-

---

[1] Sueton. *Tiber.* 21.   [2] Acts xi. 27.
[3] Acts xii. 25, xiii. 1 ; Gal. ii. 11.

bas and Saul." And, xii. 25, it is said, "Now Barnabas and Saul returned from Jerusalem (to Antioch), after having completed the ministration." Between these accounts—narrating the arrival in Jerusalem and the departure from the city—the account is inserted of the acts of Herod (Agrippa I.) in persecuting the church at Jerusalem, putting to death James the brother of John, and imprisoning Peter, who was, nevertheless, miraculously delivered; and the further history of Herod, in that he was praised as a god, and on that account eaten up of worms.[1] Manifestly not all that is related, chap. xii. 1–24, can have taken place during Paul's stay in Jerusalem. The first point, then, is to explain why this account is inserted at this precise stage of the history. After Luke, Acts i.–viii., had detailed the events connected with the rise and early vicissitudes of the congregation at Jerusalem, he relates, chap. ix., the conversion of Paul, an event, thus, which—according to Gal. i. 18 ff.—took place 17 years before the second journey. In the same chapter, ix. 26, mention is made of the first journey of the converted Saul to Jerusalem. That which is recorded, Acts ix. 31 to xiii. 1, consequently occupies, according to Gal. ii. 2, a space of 14 years. Acts ix. 31–xi. 18 we have the history of the *Palestinian Christian congregations*, grouping themselves around Jerusalem; then, xi. 19, the account is resumed of the persecution which followed the death of Stephen, and the rise and development of the congregations *among the Gentiles* is described, up to the period when Paul brought the contribution to Jerusalem, and in this way effected a union between the Gentile congregations and the mother church. Acts xi. 19–30 embraces thus a period of 17 years. Having reached this point of the history, Luke had to take up into his narrative that which had in the meantime happened in Jerusalem, between the conversion of Cornelius and the arrival of the deputation from Antioch. This is done, chap. xii. 1–24. When was Cornelius converted? According to Acts x. 1, he was centurio of the *cohors Italica*. The presence of a Roman garrison at Cæsarea shows that the town was then under the immediate supremacy of Rome. This town, together with

[1] Acts xii. 1–24.

Samaria and Judea, came under the sway of Herod Agrippa I. in the year A.D. 41 or 42, and became the capital of his kingdom.[1] The conversion of Cornelius falls thus at the latest in the year 41, and the parenthesis, Acts xii., embraces all that happened under Agrippa at Jerusalem during three years ; and extends even beyond the death of Agrippa, since it is said, xii. 24, that after his death the word grew and multiplied, up to the time at which, by the coming of Paul, the Gentile Christians were brought into closer connection with Jerusalem.   How far beyond the death of Agrippa these words lead us, must be further shown below.   First of all, we have to determine the time of Agrippa's death.   *Antiq.* xix. 8, sec. 2, we read that Agrippa reigned four years under Caius Cæsar (Caligula), and three years under Claudius.   The reign of Claudius began in the January of the year 41.[2]   The death of Agrippa consequently fell in the year 44.   His kingdom was then, on account of the minority of his son, Agrippa II., administered by the procurators Cuspius Fadus, Tiberius Alexander, and Cumanus. This last entered into office in the beginning of the year 49 ; the two former held it from 44 to the end of 48.   It was, according to Josephus,[3] under these two that the famine broke out which is referred to in Acts xi. 28.   Since this raged under both procurators, Fadus and Alexander, it belongs to the last year of the former and to the beginning of the governorship of the latter.   The year of the change of procurators is unfortunately unknown.   When, however, we compare what took place under the government of the one and of the other,[4] we must suppose Fadus to have remained at the helm of affairs considerably longer than Alexander.   The mutation of procurators cannot be placed earlier, but also not later, than the year 47.   This is consequently the year of the famine, in which Paul brought the contribution of the Antiochian Christians to Jerusalem.   The conversion of this apostle, having taken place 3 plus 14 = 17 years earlier, belongs to the year 30.   Since Paul counts in round numbers of years, by the sum of 3 plus 14 it is possible something more or less than

---

[1] *Antiq.* xix. 4, 5, sec. 1 ; 6, sec. 1 ; *de Bello*, ii. 11 ; 12, sec. 6.
[2] Sueton. *Calig.* 58.   [3] *Antiq.* xx. 5, sec. 2.
[4] *Antiq.* xix. 9, sec. 2–xx. 2, sec. 3.

17 full years may be meant, thus from the end of 29 to the end of 30. The year 29 is *à priori* impossible; because the crucifixion of Christ must be placed in the 17th year of Tiberius. Paul's conversion took place after Pentecost; thus towards the end of the year 30, but not later. When we take into account the intense excitement awakened by the earlier activity of the apostles, and the rapid succession of events thereby occasioned, we feel no difficulty in supposing that all that is recorded in Acts iii. 1–ix. 3 took place in a space of from two to three months; and the more so, inasmuch as we are justified by viii. 1 in regarding that which is related viii. 4–40 as being synchronous with the conversion of Paul, described chap. ix. 1 ff. If the raging of the young Pharisaic zealot continued only for a month after the stoning of Stephen, this may have sufficed to inflict incalculable injury. Paul's conversion belongs thus to the autumn of the year 30.

Sec. 36. Our note of time, as concerns the conversion of the apostle, differs very considerably from the views generally prevalent. This conversion is made much later by all chronologists. Pearson and Süskind place it in the year 35, Hug in the year 36, Eichhorn and Schott in the year 37, Anger in the year 38, Schrader in the year 39, and Wurm in the year 41. But thus the second journey of the apostle, which took place 17 years later, comes out as late as from 52 to 58. The chronologists have felt this difficulty, indeed, and sought to evade it, either by regarding the second journey of the apostle, Gal. ii. 1, as not identical with the second in Acts, chap. xii. 25, but with the third, chap. xv.— or, by not counting together the years 3 and 14, but assuming the *terminus a quo* of the 14 years is not the first journey, but again the conversion of the apostle. As regards this last expedient, it is contrary to the ordinary mode of speaking. Every unprejudiced reader will understand the words (of ver. 1) ἔπειτα διὰ δεκατεσσάρων ἐτῶν πάλιν ἀνέβην εἰς Ἰ. as meaning that the *terminus a quo* was the first journey just related. Let us test the other expedient, which consists in regarding the second journey, of which the account is given in Gal. ii. 1, as the journey of the apostle to the Apostolic Council, Acts xv. It must thus be assumed, either that Luke, contrary to the truth, invented one or other of the journeys recounted, Acts ix. 26, xi. 30 ; or else, that Paul, notwithstanding the asseveration of Gal. i. 20 : Behold, before God, I lie not ! nevertheless, did not speak the truth, but intentionally passed over in silence one or other of his journeys ; for that he should forget one of them is impossible. If we are not to call in question the trustworthiness either of Paul or of Luke, then the second journey of Paul, that of Acts xi. 30, must be the one meant in Gal. ii. 1. It must be so, even on account of the subordinate circumstances. The journey of Gal. ii. 1 was occasioned by a revelation, κατὰ ἀποκάλυψιν ; a revelation, Acts xi. 28, was the occasion of the journey in Acts xi. 30, but not of that to the Apostolic Council. In both cases Barnabas was the companion of the apostle ;[1] no mention is made, in either case in the Acts, of Titus as accompanying him.[2] That Paul, during his second visit to Jerusalem, both could and *must* give an account of the progress of the gospel among the Gentiles—such as that referred to in Gal. ii. 2—although such account is passed over by Luke, is a necessary consequence of the first contact of the Pauline Gentile Christians with the assembly at Jerusalem. The recommendation of the contribution made to the apostle, Gal. ii. 10, most naturally attaches itself to the contribution of which Paul had been the messenger, Acts xi. 30. It need not awaken surprise that Paul, in his Epistle to the Galatians, makes no mention of his third journey, that to the Apostolic Council. His object is to prove that he derived his apostolic office not from the twelve, but from the Lord. Had he received it from the apostles, this must have taken place on the occasion of the first journey, or at the latest of the second ; since it was precisely in his character as an apostle that he came to the Apostolic Council. It sufficed, therefore, that Paul assured the Galatians such had not been the case, either on his first or second meeting with the twelve : the third he could safely leave out of the question. Besides, it is possible that the Epistle to the Galatians was written before the Apostolic Council was held.

[1] Acts xi. 30, xv. 2 ; Gal. ii. 1.　　　　　[2] Cf. Gal. ii. 2.

IV.—*The Year of our Lord's Death.*

Sec. 37. Jesus entered upon His public labours 46 years after the beginning of the temple reconstruction; that is to say, at the beginning of the year U.C. 781, A.D. 28, æra Dionys. (sec. 33). His labours began shortly before the Passover of this year;[1] at the time of the Passover festival in the following year He was staying by the Sea of Gennesareth;[2] on the Passover of the year of Rome 783, A.D. 30, He was crucified. Earlier than the second year after the 15th of Tiberius, thus before the year A.D. 30, the crucifixion cannot have taken place; but also not later, since the conversion of the Apostle Paul cannot be placed later than the autumn of the year A.D. 30 (sec. 35). We shall show that Jesus was crucified on a Friday, which was the preparation for the Passover, the 14th Nisan. On that year the 15th Nisan consequently fell on a Sabbath. The ordinary supposition is, that that Friday, the day of the crucifixion, was the 15th Nisan. Since this point of difference cannot here be decided, we state the requirement that, on the year of the Lord's death, the 15th Nisan must fall on a Saturday or a Friday. We would refer here to Wurm's table, communicated sec. 16, with the single observation that the 15th Nisan always falls on the same day of the week as the 1st Nisan; the feria given for this last is also the feria of the 15th. But in order to avoid mistake, we will give the days of the week marked in Wurm's table as those on which the 15th Nisan fell:—

DAY on which the 15TH NISAN fell, according to the LUNAR PHASE, in the Years 28–36.

YEAR.				MONTH.				DAY OF WEEK.
28	.	.	.	30th March	.	.	.	3, or
28	.	.	.	29th April	.	.	.	5.
29	.	.	.	18th April	.	.	.	2.
30	.	.	.	7th April	.	.	.	6.
31	.	.	.	27th March	.	.	.	3, or
31	.	.	.	26th April	.	.	.	5.
32	.	.	.	14th April	.	.	.	2.
33	.	.	.	4th April	.	.	.	7.

---

[1] John ii. 1–13. [2] John vi. 4.

YEAR.				MONTH.				DAY OF WEEK.
34	.	.	.	25th March	.	.	.	5, or
34	.	.	.	23d April	.	.	.	6.
35	.	.	.	13th April	.	.	.	4.
36	.	.	.	1st April	.	.	.	1, or
36	.	.	.	30th April	.	.	.	2.

[The second date in the years 28, 31, 34, 36 is owing to the intervention of the Veadar, sec. 8.]

We have already shown, sec. 16, that the week-day of the 15th Nisan began about six on the previous evening; so that the Jewish feria is always to be taken one stage later than ours. In the year 28, *e.g.*, the 15th Nisan was on the evening of the 30th March, feria 3, that is, Tuesday; but with it began the Jewish fourth day. Wurm's table accordingly teaches us that the 15th Nisan fell on Friday evening, feria 6, thus the Sabbath of the Jews—in the years 30, 33, 34. The year 33, however, is to be struck out; since in this year the 15th Nisan, properly speaking, fell on the Jewish first day of the week. If we were to ask in what years the 15th Nisan fell on feria 6 of the Jews (feria 5, Thursday, of the Christians), the year 30 is no doubt possible;[1] and in addition, the years 31 and 34. We have already by another method established the fact that the year 30 was that of the Lord's crucifixion; the calculation of the 15th Nisan confirms this result. For in the year 30 the 15th Nisan fell on the Jewish Sabbath, which began on Friday, 7th April, at six o'clock in the evening. The years 28, 29, 31, 32 are already excluded by the fact that in them the 15th Nisan did not fall on a Sabbath. The year 33 is impossible on account of the epoch of Paul's conversion [and of the length of ministry it would require us to presuppose]. The same is the case with the years 34–36.

We can therefore say, with perfect certainty, that Jesus was crucified in the year 30, æra Dionys., 783 of Rome, on the preparation of the Passover, Friday, 7th April.

If we had not been assured by the statement of Augustine, above cited (sec. 32), that the consulate of the year of Christ's death is not made known with the documentary evidence of certain tradition, the assertion of many Fathers, Tertullian

[1] Cf. sec. 17.

especially, would cause us perplexity.   These maintain that
Jesus was crucified under the consulate of the Gemini.   Now
this consulate coincides with the 15th year of Tiberius' reign,
U.C. 781.   Since, however, this consulate is not adduced on
the authority of any documents, Tertullian could only have
arrived at it by a calculation.   This miscalculation was
based on the fact that Luke, after mentioning the 15th year
of Tiberius,[1] affords no further chronological datum.   Tertullian, like many who in modern times have made research
into the matter, supposed that the whole history of Jesus, as
related by the Synoptists, was completed in a few months—
that consequently Jesus was crucified in the very year in
which He began His public labours.   It is to be remarked
that Tertullian and most of those Fathers who place the death
of Jesus under the consulate of the Gemini, expressly add
that it was the 15th year of Tiberius.   This year they have
manifestly derived from Luke iii. 1.

Soo. 38.   We present below in a tabulated form the collected
results of our chronological investigations hitherto made :—

U.C.	A.C.	
441	313	Tisri. Epoch of Seleucidan era, sec. 22.
591–592	163–162	Tisri–Tisri. Sabbatic year, 1 Macc. vi. 49, 53, sec. 22.
619–620	135–134	Tisri–Tisri. Sabbatic year, 1 Macc. xvi. 14; *Antiq.* xiii. 8. 1, sec. 22.
685	69	Year of Herod's birth, sec. 27.
691	63	Capture of Jerusalem by Titus on the day of Atonement, 10th Tisri, sec. 20.
715	39	Herod receives from the Senate at Rome the title of king, sec. 19.
718	36	Herod takes Jerusalem (27 years after Pompey had captured it) in the third year of his appointment, during a Sabbatic year, which began Tisri 717, secs. 20, 21.
734	20	In the spring, after the expiration of the 17th year of Herod's reign, Augustus came to Syria. During this year, summer 734, the building of the temple began, sec. 24.
752	2	Jesus is born. Census and Sabbatic year from Tisri 752–753.

---

[1] Luke iii. 1.

U.C.	A.D.	
753		Lunar eclipse, 10th January. Herod died 24th January, at an age of about 70 years—37 years after his appointment as king, 34 after the taking of Jerusalem, secs. 25–29.
781	28	Jesus, about 30 years of age, is baptized in the beginning of the year, 15th Tiberius. He was in Jerusalem at the Passover 30th March, 46 years from the beginning of the temple restoration, secs. 32, 33.[1]
783	30	Jesus crucified—on Friday, 7th April, which was the 14th Nisan, sec. 37. Conversion of Paul towards the close of the year, sec. 35.
786	33	First journey of the Apostle Paul to Jerusalem, three years after his conversion, sec. 35.
797	44	Death of Agrippa I., sec. 35.
800	47	Second journey of the Apostle Paul to Jerusalem, 17 years after his conversion, and 14 years after his first journey, sec. 35.
823	70	Destruction of Jerusalem by Titus, at the end of the Sabbatic year, which extended from Tisri 822 to Tisri 823, sec. 21.

[1] [The work of the temple-restoration properly so called, after being pushed forward during nine and a half years, was brought to a close on the anniversary of Herod's accession, the festival of which was observed at the same time with that of the temple-restoration (*Antiq.* xv. 11, secs. 5, 6). As the anniversary of the storming of Jerusalem can hardly be intended here, the reference must be to the time of Herod's becoming king *de jure*, which event—as is shown above, sec. 19 —took place in the spring. The work of rebuilding must therefore have begun in the latter part of summer or in autumn, but not in the winter-month of Kisleu.]

DIVISION II.

BIRTH AND CHILDHOOD OF JESUS.

SEC. 39. Since the evangelists Mark and John begin the history of Jesus with His baptism by John, we are limited, as regards the history of the birth and childhood of the Lord, to the account given by Matthew and Luke. This last evangelist first gives an account of the birth of the Lord's forerunner, John the Baptist, whose history from beginning to end is most closely interwoven with the history of Jesus Christ. This birth is treated of in the first chapter of the present division. In the second chapter we shall speak of the birth of Jesus; in the third, of the history of His childhood; and in the fourth, of the history of His youth.

I.—*The Birth of John the Baptist.*

Sec. 40. John was born in the city Juda,[1] in the days of King Herod.[2] His father was Zacharias, a priest of the course of Abia, and his mother Elizabeth, of the family of Aaron.[3] The birth of John took place six months before that of Jesus Christ.[4]

Sec. 41. **The city of Juda,** the birthplace of John the Baptist.—Luke i. 39, 40 we read: " Mary arose in those days (when it had been proclaimed to her she should become the mother of the promised Son of David), and went (from Nazareth) into the hill country with haste, into a city of Juda, and entered into the house of Zacharias, and saluted Elizabeth." It is ordinarily assumed that the words εἰς τὴν ὀρεινὴν . . . εἰς πόλιν ʼΙούδα are to be taken in such wise that ʼΙούδα shall apply equally to the hill country and to the city,

---

[1] Luke i. 39.   [2] Luke i. 5.
[3] Luke i. 5.   [4] Luke i. 39, 40 ; cf. i. 31, 36.

so that it is equivalent to saying, εἰς τὴν ὀρεινὴν Ἰούδα . . . εἰς πόλιν Ἰούδα. This view fails to commend itself to us ; because the two members of the sentence are separated by the words μετὰ σπουδῆς, beyond which the attraction cannot be supposed to pass. There was in the land of Judea a district known as ἡ ὀρεινή.[1] Now Pliny calls the neighbourhood of Jerusalem Orine—*Orine, in qua fuere Hierosolyma.*[2] This affords an important clue. What, then, is the city of Juda, πόλις Ἰούδα ? It cannot by any means be admitted that the evangelist is speaking in general terms, and means only that Mary repaired to some city or other of Judah. There can be no question but Luke, at a time so little removed from the events of which he gives the narrative, was in a position to learn—whether through the disciples of John or through Christians—in what city of Judea John was born, and whither Mary repaired to Elizabeth. His words are to be taken as meaning that Mary went to a place which is called the city of Juda. The great majority of Biblical geographers espouse the view of Reland, that the city of Juda is identical with Jutta, יוטה, the Levitical city in the mountains of Judah.[3] Certainly it is not impossible that a hard T should in the later dialect assume the softer sound of D ; but that such was not the case with the word in question, is shown by the existing name, which is still pronounced Jutta.[4] The place lies to the south of Hebron, and thus deep in the territory occupied from the time of the Captivity by the Idumæans, to which even Hebron belonged, since Josephus speaks of this as a city of Idumæa.[5] In such a place assuredly no families of the priestly order would make their abode.—It is true we meet with a city of Juda or Judah, עיר יהודה, in the Old Testament. In 2 Chron. xxv. 28 it is stated that Amaziah was buried in the city of Judah. Now since, according to 2 Kings xiv. 20, Amaziah was buried in the city of David, the city of Judah must be synonymous with the city of David, and must denote that part of Jerusalem belonging to the tribe of Judah. But the supposition that John was born at Jerusalem cannot be reconciled with the statement of Luke i. 65. In the neighbourhood of Jerusalem,

---

[1] Luke i. 39, 65.   [2] Plin. *H. N.* v. 15.   [3] Josh. xv. 55, xxi. 16.
[4] Robinson, *Palest.* i. 494, ii. 206.   [5] Josephus, *de Bello,* iv. 9, sec. 7.

however, in the Wâdy Bettîr, there exists a place known as Khirbet el-Jehud, a name which is identical with עיר יהודה, πόλις 'Ιούδα. It is supposed, indeed, that this name signifies " ruins of the Jews ; " but a hundred ruins in Palestine would be as much entitled as this place to bear the name of " ruins of the Jews," which yet are not called so. Whence, then, does this ruin in the Wâdy Bettîr derive the exclusive right to this appellation ? When we consider the tenacity with which the names of places are clung to in the East, it becomes apparent that we have here to do with an ancient name retained until now, and that Khirbet el-Jehud is no other than the city of Juda, the birthplace of John the Baptist. The fact must not, moreover, be entirely overlooked, that in the immediate vicinity of Khirbet el-Jehud tradition points out spots intimately connected with the childhood of the Baptist. We need only remind of " the wilderness of John," of " Mar Zacharia," the monastery of John at En-Kârim,[1] etc. Similarly is the position of this town defined in the *Chronicon paschale*, Olymp. 184, where it is said the city of Juda is distant from Jerusalem twelve miles — εἰς πόλιν 'Ιούδα, οὖσαν ἀπὸ μιλίων ιβ'.[2]

Sec. 42. **The time of the birth of John the Baptist** is not more nearly defined by Luke. We learn only that his birth took place in the days of Herod, and preceded that of Jesus by an interval of six months. There is, however, another statement, of which some have sought to avail themselves as affording a chronological datum. Zacharias, the father of the Baptist, was, according to Luke i. 5, of the course of Abia. During his ministration in the temple a son was promised to him. Upon the expiration of the days of his ministering he returned home. After these days Elizabeth his wife conceived (i. 24). From this it follows that the promised son was born after nine months, and Jesus after fifteen months. Is, then, anything to be determined concerning these dates from the time

---

[1] [Where, indeed, Thomson (*Land and Book*, p. 664) would, in accordance with tradition, fix the actual birthplace of John.]

[2] On Khirbet el-Jehûd, cf. Ritter, *Erdkunde*, xvi. pp. 428, 515 ; Robinson, iii. 266, 267. [It lies a good six miles W.N.W. of Bethlehem, from which it is difficult of approach.]

of ministration of the class of Abia ? Since this period of service may be calculated for each year, it follows that the month and day of the birth of John, and consequently of Christ, could be deduced from it, if we were only sure of the year ; this, however, is not the case, so that a calculation as to the time of service of Abia can help us but little. Yet, since the question is an interesting one in itself, we will proceed to state it. According to 1 Chron. xxiv. the priests were divided into twenty-four classes, of which the class of Jehoiarib was the first, the class of Abia the eighth. Each class accomplished a ministry of one week, always from the first day of the week to the end of the Sabbath. This order, too, was observed after the Captivity,[1] so that if we learnt what particular class was ministering on any occasion after the Captivity, we could calculate the time of service of the class of Abia in a given year. Wieseler assumes that the temple service restored by Judas Maccabæus began with the order of Jehoiarib. Seyffarth supposes that Zerubbabel began with the course of Abia. But these are only hypotheses, wanting in any confirmatory text, and consequently cannot serve as the foundation of a calculation. Jewish tradition affords us a more certain basis. When the temple was destroyed, it affirms[2] that the course of Jehoiarib was ministering. The day of the destruction of the temple was a Sabbath, 3d August. The class of Abia would thus, according to our rule, have been entering on its ministration on the 14th September, and have closed it on the 21st September, in the year 823 (A.D. 70). A very simple calculation shows that the course of Abia would come out of office in the year 748, on the 10th April and the 1st October ; in the year 749, on the 18th March and the 2d September ; in the year 750, the 17th February and the 4th August ; in the year 751, the 1st February, the 18th July, and the 2d December. If, thus, we presuppose—what is most probable—that Jesus was born in the year 752, towards the end of the year, then the son was promised to Zacharias during the ministering of his class, which went out of office in the year 751, on the 18th July. Nine months later, consequently about the 18th April 752,

[1] Josephus, *Antiq.* vii. 14, sec. 7.   [2] Cf. sec. 21.

took place the birth of John the Baptist, and yet six months
later—consequently, about the 18th October 752—that of
Jesus Christ. But how little reliance is to be placed upon
conclusions of this kind will be evident to all.

II.—*The Birth of Jesus Christ.*

Sec. 43. The Messiah, the Son of David, was, according to
the prophecy of Micah, v. 2, to be born at Bethlehem of
Judah. Joseph and Mary, however, dwelt at Nazareth in
Galilee. The census of the empire enjoined by Augustus
became, under the divine guidance, the occasion of a transitory
settlement on their part in Bethlehem, the city of David, because
Joseph was of the house and lineage of David. Thus was Jesus
born at Bethlehem, six months after the birth of the Baptist.

Sec. 44. **Nazareth.**—In this town dwelt the parents of
Jesus before His birth; there was the promise given to Mary,
that the Messiah should be born of her;[1] thither did they
return, and there did they dwell, after the birth of Jesus at
Bethlehem, and the flight to Egypt.[2] Because Jesus was
brought up in this place, and there passed His youth, He is
also called the Nazaræan,[3] or Nazarene.[4] Palestine, on the
west side of the Jordan, is divided by nature into two hilly
table-lands, of which the southern bore the name of Judea,
the northern that of Galilee. These table-lands are divided
by a fruitful plain, which rises a little above the level of the
sea, and was formerly known as Jezreel or Esdrelon,[5] but now
bears the name of Merj Ibn 'Aamir. The mountain-wall
forming the northern boundary of this plain, and at the same
time the southern dip in the Galilean table-land, is pierced,
at about mid distance between its eastern and western
extremities, by a narrow valley. Through this passes the
ordinary pilgrims' route from Jerusalem to Galilee, which
leads, after a journey of about three miles, to en-Nâsira. This
is the present name of the ancient Nazareth. The place lies in
a natural amphitheatre, formed by white chalky hills, in the

---

[1] Luke i. 26.   [2] Luke ii. 39 ; Matt. ii. 22 ; Luke ii. 51, iv. 16.
[3] Ναζωραῖος, Matt. ii. 23.   [4] Ναζαρηνός, Mark i. 24.
[5] Written also Ἐσδρηλώμ, Judith i. 8.

midst of which some travellers have thought they recognised the crater of an extinct volcano. Eusebius writes in the *Onomasticon*, " Nazareth . . . in Galilee, opposite Legio (now Ledjûn) towards the east (read N.E.), fifteen miles distant therefrom, near to Mount Tabor." [1] The name Nazareth does not occur in the O. T. It is nevertheless in the highest degree probable that this name is only a later dialectic transformation of Sared, שָׂרִיד, the border city of Zebulon.[2] The initial N of the modern name is probably derived from the Ain of En-Sered. The ancient Sared must at all events have occupied the site of the present Nazareth ; for the boundaries of Zebulon on its north side are marked out east and west from Sared. There is named as the nearest town on the east, Chisloth-Tabor,[3] a place which is confessedly to be identified with Iksal, an hour's journey east of Nazareth. From Sared towards the west the frontier ran through Maralah, now Malûl, an hour's journey west of Nazareth. Nazareth, the former Sared, thus belonged to the tribe of Zebulon. Nazareth lies on the western side of the lovely amphitheatre-like hollow, which, narrow and somewhat oval in form, extends from S.S.W. to N.N.E., with a length of about a mile, and a width of from a third to half a mile. Its houses stand upon the lower part of the declivity of the western mountain, which rises abrupt and high above them. Upon the summit of this mountain, which is richly adorned with sweet-smelling herbs and flowers, lies a Wely called Neby Ismail, situated about 500 feet higher than the Latin convent, which itself rises 1182 feet above the level of the sea.[4] To the south-east the basin of the valley contracts itself, and ends in this direction towards the plain of Esdrelon. From the mountain of the foresaid Wely opens up the magnificent panorama described by so many travellers. The town of Nazareth consists of stone houses with flat roofs, among which towers especially the fortress-like Latin convent, well walled round,

---

[1] Ναζαρέθ . . . ἐν Γαλιλαίᾳ, ἀντικρὺ τῆς Λεγεῶνος, ὡς ἀπὸ σημείων ιε πρὸς ἀνατολῆς, πλησίον τοῦ ὄρους Θαβώρ.

[2] Josh. xix. 10, 12. Iksal-Chesulloth.   [3] Josh. xix. 12.

[4] [Ritter, ii. 379, gives the height of Neby Ismail as 1790 feet above the Mediterranean ; Baedecker, p. 378, gives it 545 mètres, which amounts to nearly the same.]

which is the principal building of the place. Its little church of the Annunciation is said by tradition to stand on the site of the house of the Virgin Mary, which is supposed to have been carried by angels to Loretto. The pilgrims' hospice belonging to the convent, and called Casa nuova, is said to be one of the pleasantest in the East. The Maronites have a little church in the south-western part of the town, lying under a rocky mountain wall which falls precipitously a distance of 40 or 50 feet. Several such cliffs are to be found in the western mountains about the town. One of these may well have been the place from which they sought to cast Jesus down.[1] That, on the other hand, which passes for it with the monks, lies two English miles south-east of the town. The church of the Greeks is situated in the south-eastern part of Nazareth, and claims equally with that of the Latins to stand on the spot which became the scene of the Annunciation. Beneath this church rises the fountain of the Virgin.[2] The legendary sites are of later origin; Jerome and Antoninus Martyr know nothing of them. This latter pilgrim,

---

[1] Luke iv. 28, 29. [Stanley identifies *the* cliff with this very one over the Maronite convent. He says : Nazareth "is built 'upon,' *i.e.* on the side of, 'a mountain,' but the 'brow' is not beneath but over the town, and such a cliff ($\chi\rho\eta\mu\nu\delta\varsigma$) as is here implied is to be found, as all modern travellers describe, in the abrupt face of the limestone rock, about 30 or 40 feet high, overhanging the Maronite convent at the south-west corner of the town."—*Sin. and Pal.* p. 367. *Ancient* Nazareth was, however, according to Tristram, *on* the "brow" of the hill. See *Land of Israel*, p. 122 ff., where, moreover, the character of the Christian inhabitants is fairly vindicated.]

[2] ["Hither, doubtless, went Mary daily for water, just as we saw the mothers of Nazareth to-day . . ." "We took a long ramble afterwards over those hills where our Lord must often have wandered when a child. Bare and featureless, singularly unattractive in its landscape, with scarcely a tree to relieve the monotony of its brown and dreary hills (I speak, of course, of their *winter* character), without ruins or remains, without one precisely identified locality, there is yet a reality in the associations of Nazareth which stirs the soul of the Christian to its very depths. It was not the place where the sublimity of the scenery, the depth of the gorges, or the solitude of the forest, could have filled a boyish mind with wild dreams or enthusiastic visions—there was nothing here to suggest deeds of heroism or feed the reveries of romance ; it was the nursery of One whose mission was to meet man and man's deepest needs on the platform of commonplace daily life."—(Tristram, p. 122.) . . . "The one locality in Nazareth of which there is no doubt that it has remained unchanged from the days of our Lord. Often must He in childhood have trodden the path down to that fountain with His blessed mother."—(*Ibid.* p. 419.)]

however, speaks with enthusiasm of the beauty of the women and the marvellous fertility of the district around the town. " In civitate (Nazareth) tanta est gratia mulierum Hebræorum ut inter Hebræos pulchriores non inveniantur, et hoc a S. Maria sibi concessum dicunt, nam et parentem suam dicunt eam. Et dum nulla sit caritas Hebræis erga Christianos, illæ sunt omni caritate plenæ. Provincia paradiso similis: in tritico, in frugibus similis Ægypto, sed præcellit in vino et oleo, pomis et melle." [1]

Sec. 45. **Bethlehem.**—In this town was Jesus born.[2] In Matthew it was called Bethlehem of Judea, Βηθλεὲμ τῆς 'Ιουδαίας, in contradistinction from Bethlehem of Galilee,[3] of which without the addition the reader might think, and the more so since Joseph and Mary came from Nazareth in Galilee to Bethlehem. The place, now called *Beit-Lahm,* lies six miles to the south of Jerusalem, near to the road leading from Jerusalem to Hebron, upon the ridge of the mountains of Judah, on a hill stretching from east to west. At the eastern end of the little town, upon an eminence, stands the strongly-built convent, in which is found the cave (transformed into a church) which tradition reveres as the birthplace of Jesus.[4] In Luke ii. 7 it is said, " She (Mary) brought forth her first-born son, and wrapped him in swaddling-clothes, and laid him in a manger, because there was no room for them in the khân " —διότι οὐκ ἦν αὐτοῖς τόπος ἐν τῷ καταλύματι. The stable in which Jesus was born might well be a cave. Tradition has the Gospel narrative neither for nor against it. It is noteworthy that, according to Jewish tradition,[5] the Messiah should be born in Birath-Arba of Bethlehem Judah, בבירת ערבא דבית לחם יהודה. Birah denotes a citadel. The " castle of Arba," belonging to Bethlehem, could not have existed anywhere else

---

[1] On Nazareth, cf. Robinson, *Palestine,* ii. pp. 333–343 ; Ritter, *Palestine,* iv. 368–375 ; and the monograph of Tobler, *Nazareth in Palestina.*

[2] Matt. ii. 1 ; Luke ii. 4.   [3] Josh. xix. 15.

[4] [The authority on which this tradition rests is specified in Ellicott (p. 62, note 1), who considers the tradition itself a far from improbable one. Tristram (p. 73) believes that the φάτνη was in the lower room of some humble dwelling, whither the holy family had repaired for hospitality on being shut out from the already overcrowded khân.]

[5] *Echa Rabbati,* fol. 72. 1.

than on the site of the fortress-like convent, in which the
sacred cave is found. In any case the Christian tradition
dates from a very early period; for even Justin Martyr, who
was a native of Sichem, and lived at the beginning of the
second century, says, in his *Dialogue with Trypho*, that Christ
was born in a cave; so also Origen, *Contra Celsum*, l. 1, and
Jerome, in *Epitaph. Paulæ*, where he says of this pilgrim, "In
Bethlehem ingressa et *in specum* Salvatoris introiens, postquam
vidit sacrum virginis diversorium et stabulum . . ." The
church Mariæ de præsepio, above the hewn-out cave, is the
oldest in Palestine, and is built in Grecian style in the form
of a cross. Whether it is the same which, according to the
account of the Pilgrim of Bordeaux (A.D. 333), in the *Itiner.
hierosol.*, was built by Constantine, we must leave undecided.
Two flights of stairs, one on each side the altar, lead down by
fifteen steps into the rocky cavern, which is 39 feet long, 11
feet broad, and 9 feet high. A white marble slab, with a
wreath of silver rays, marks the place of the birth; it bears
the inscription, *Hic de virgine Maria Jesus Christus natus est.*[1]
Bethlehem is called in Luke ii. 4, 11, as well as in 1 Sam.
xx. 6, " the city of David," because David was born there.[2]
Thither repaired Joseph, Luke ii. 4, because he was of the
house and lineage of David.

Sec. 46. Too much is inferred when, from Luke ii. 4, it is
concluded that every Israelite must on the occasion of the
census repair to the city of his tribe and family, in order to
be enrolled. It is quite possible that the journey to Bethlehem was an act of free choice on Joseph's part, having as its
object the availing himself of the opportunity afforded of thus
confirming his descent from King David, and of having
registered in his name the ancestral possessions which should
come to him. His intention seems at the same time to have
been, henceforth to dwell in Bethlehem; since after the flight
into Egypt he returned thither, and was only led by a divine
admonition to turn aside to Nazareth.[3] We know unfortunately very little concerning the way in which the Mosaic
precepts affecting family registers and hereditary possessions

[1] Von Raumer, *Palestina*, p. 315. [Stanley, 438, 439 ; Ritter, iii. 339–350.]
[2] 1 Sam. xvi.   [3] Matt. ii. 22, 23.

were carried out after the Captivity, and particularly at the time of Christ. But if we take into account the scrupulous endeavour peculiar to the Judaism after the Exile, to comply as far as possible with the requirements of the law, we may be certain that in both respects all that was possible was accomplished. That registers of descent were kept, is vouched for by Ezra ii. 1–57, and especially ii. 59–63 ; and that they were preserved in the case of those performing the functions of the priesthood, and particularly in that of descendants of the house of David, is confirmed by the books of Jewish tradition. Thus we read in *Jerus. Taanith*, fol. 68. 1, that a genealogical table existed in Jerusalem, which showed that Hillel was descended from David through Abital; and in *Jerus. Kidushin*, iv. 5, that in the archives of Jeshana at Zippori (Sepphoris), עַרְכֵי הַיְשָׁנָה שֶׁל צִפּוֹרִים, trustworthy records of the descent of the priests were to be found. This place, called Jeshana, was the seat of the Sanhedrim under R. Jehuda hakkadosh. The ordinary Jew did not indeed cling with great tenacity to such registers of his family, any more than to his family inheritance ; but every one went where he thought he could attain to a prosperity which had only too narrow a basis in his ancestral heritage. But David's descendants might well cleave to their inheritance, especially if they were without fortune. Not all Israelites absent from the place whence they sprung were consequently in a position to repair at the census to their ancestral city ; but only those who, like the descendants of David and of Aaron, had hereditary rights and an ancestral heritage to confirm. How many of these there were, and how great was the stir caused by the taxing, cannot now be ascertained. At any rate, it could be carried out without occasioning great material loss, since, as we have seen (sec. 30), it fell on a Sabbatic year.

Sec. 47. **The Field of the Shepherds.**—The birth of Messiah was proclaimed by an angel of the Lord to the shepherds, who in that same district, ἐν τῇ χώρᾳ τῇ αὐτῇ, were in the field, and kept watch by night over their sheep.[1] The place where the shepherds received the heavenly message was thus close to Bethlehem. It was early pointed out by Christian tradition

[1] Luke ii. 8.

to the devout pilgrim.   In the *Onomasticon*, art. " Bethlehem," it is said : " About a thousand paces distant (from Bethlehem) is the tower of *Eder*, the Tower of the Flock, which name foretokened the revelation of the birth of the Lord given to the shepherds." At the distance indicated, east from Bethlehem, on the road leading from Jerusalem to Hebron, are to be found the ruins of a church erected by Helena, mother of Constantine, at the place which was the scene of the heavenly appearing.[1] That this occupied the site of the former Tower of the Flock is beyond doubt.   Jewish tradition, too, is acquainted with a tower of this name.   In *Jerus. Shekalim*, viii. 8, and *Jerus. Kidushin*, ii. 9, it is said that flocks which are met with between Jerusalem and Migdal-Eder, מגדל עדר, are to be considered sheep for sacrifice.   A keeping watch of the shepherds by night can be looked for nowhere else in the neighbourhood of Bethlehem than at this tower.

III.—*History of the Childhood of Jesus.*

Sec. 48. **The Slaughter of the Children at Bethlehem.—** Matt. ii. 1–8.   When Herod saw himself deceived by the magi, who were to bring him intelligence concerning the new-born King of the Jews, he, in his wrath, issued the command that all children of two years and under in Bethlehem and its neighbourhood should be slain.   The child Jesus escaped this slaughter, which aimed at Him alone, by the flight into Egypt, enjoined upon Joseph by a revelation in dream.

The truth of this history has been doubted by many, on the ground that Josephus does not relate it.   Mention, however, is made of it by a heathen historian, Macrobius, who says, *Saturnalia*, ii. 4 : " When Augustus heard that Herod, king of the Jews, had, with the children under two years of age, which he caused to be put to death, caused his own son to be slain, he said : ' It is better to be Herod's swine than his son.' "[2]

---

[1] The place is now called Er-Rawâl, and lies near to Bêt-Sahur.   Tobler, *Denkblätter aus Jerusalem*, p. 693.

[2] Cum enim audisset (Augustus), inter pueros, quos in Syria Herodes, Rex Judæorum, infra biennium jussit interfici, filium quoque ejus occisum, ait : Melius est Herodis porcum (ὗν) esse, quam filium (υἱόν).

The massacre by Herod of the children under two years of age is consequently a proved fact, the evidence for which cannot be shaken by the silence of Josephus. What else could move the tyrant to a slaughter of children, save the dread of a family which might imperil his throne and succession ? and what family could inspire him with terror, save that of the Asmonæans, dethroned by him, or the house of David, dear to the nation ?

According to Macrobius, the slaughter of the children was connected, not indeed in point of fact, but in point of time, with the execution of his son Antipater, which took place five days before Herod's death. The murder of the children was thus one of the last atrocities of the raving and raging tyrant, impelled by painful disease, while he had not as yet repaired to Jericho, but was still in Jerusalem, Matt. ii. 3—synchronous thus with the execution of Matthias and the eclipse of the moon.

Sec. 49. **Rachel's Grave.**—In reference to this slaughter of the children, Matthew says, ii. 17, 18 : " Then was fulfilled that which was spoken by Jeremy the prophet,[1] saying, In Rama was a voice heard, lamentation, and weeping, and great mourning, Rachel weeping for her children, and would not be comforted, because they are not." The writer had manifestly before his mind the grave of Rachel, which lies about a mile and a half north of Bethlehem, on the road leading to Jerusalem. The position of this grave corresponds exactly to the requirements of the text in Gen. xxxv. 19, 20 : " And Rachel died, and was buried in the way to Ephrath, that is, Bethlehem. And Jacob set up a pillar over her grave ; that is the pillar of Rachel's grave unto this day." The distance of the place from Ephrath, given in the text, xxxv. 16, כברת הארץ, can no longer be determined ; but it was at all events, judging from 2 Kings v. 19, but a short distance. This grave of the mother of Benjamin lay in the domain of Judah. It was only what might be expected, that the Benjamites should erect a cenotaph on their own domain. That the Israelites were wont to erect empty tombs of this sort is evident, e.g., from the statement of the *Onomasticon*, art. " Beth-

[1] Jer. xxxi. 15.

E

lehem," where it is said that in this town was shown also the grave of Jesse and that of David. The pilgrim of Bordeaux also says that, not far from the basilica erected by Constantine at Bethlehem, there are to be found in a cave the monuments of Ezekiel, Asaph, Job, Jesse, David, and Solomon, with a Hebrew inscription, containing these names: inde non longe est monumentum Ezekiel, Job, et Jesse, David, Solomon, et habet in ipsa cripta, ad latus deorsum descendentibus hebraice scriptum nomina supra scripta. Now it is well known that Ezekiel was buried at Babylon, David and Solomon at Jerusalem. At Bethlehem there could thus only be their cenotaphs. Such cenotaph had Rachel, as we learn from 1 Sam. x. 2. Samuel, in dismissing Saul at Rama or Ramathaim Zophim, to return to Gibeah, said to him : "When thou art departed from me to-day, thou shalt find two men by Rachel's sepulchre in the border of Benjamin at Zelzah (עם קבורת רחל בגבול בנימן בצלצח)." Here the grave of Rachel at Bethlehem cannot be meant, because this lies neither within nor on the confines of Benjamin, but four miles and a half distant from it, in the tribe of Judah ; and because the way pointed out to Saul led to Gibeah. Samuel had his house and his high place at Ramah, dwelt there during the whole time of his judgeship,[1] and was buried there in his house.[2] Therefore it is called Ramah, "his city," i.e. Ramah-Samuel.[3] In 1 Sam. i. 1 it is called Ramathaim Zophim of Mount Ephraim, רמתים צופים מהר אפרים, and at the same time it is said that an ancestor was then called Zuph-Ephrathi, צוף אפרתי. But since, according to 1 Chron. vi. 1, 33, Samuel was descended from Levi, the word Ephrathi in this place cannot have the meaning "descendant of Ephraim," but is to be derived from the name of the mountain, Ephraim or Ephrem. The position of this mountain is to be learnt from the appellation of Ramah-" Zophim." According to 1 Sam. ix. 5, 6, Ramah lay in the land of Zuph ; and for this reason Josephus[4] renders the words, "when they came into the land of Zuph," by the words, "when they were come to the town of Ramah"—ὡς ἐγένοντο κατὰ τὴν Ῥαμαθὰν πόλιν. Now mention is often made in the books of Jewish

[1] 1 Sam. vii. 17, viii. 4, xix. 18.   [2] 1 Sam. xxv. 1.
[3] 1 Sam. xxviii. 3.   [4] Antiq. vi. 4, sec. 2.

tradition of a place Zophim, צוֹפִים, from which those coming from the north first obtain a view of Jerusalem. " When any one at Zophim catches sight of Jerusalem (the desolate), he is to rend his garments."[1] The space between Jerusalem and Zophim shares, in some respects, in the sanctity of that city.[2] The place is thus the Scopus of Josephus.[3] Now at the spot where alone the Scopus can be looked for, all the maps indicate the existence of a hamlet, Shafât, in which is to be recognised the old name Zuph, Zophim. The land of Zuph is thus the upland plain of Benjamin, extending northward from Jerusalem. On this spot was to be found Rama, now En Nebi Samwîl. For it is usual with the present inhabitants of Palestine to give to a place the name of a distinguished man belonging to it. Thus, in the present day, Bethany is called El-Azirîeh, or better, El-Lazirîeh, i.e. Lazarus ; Hebron is called El-Khalîl, the Friend (sc. of God), i.e. Abraham. En Nebi Samwîl lies on the aforesaid plain, upon a mountain rising 500 feet above the surrounding country, five or six miles northwest of Jerusalem. In this place there exists, built upon the ruins of an ancient church, a mosque with Samuel's grave. The position corresponds to the data furnished by the Onomasticon, " Rama, civitas Saulis (read Samuelis) in 6° milliario ab Ælia, ad septentrionalem plagam contra Bethel ;" and that of Josephus : " Ramathon, distant 40 stadia from Jerusalem."[4] This position becomes perfectly clear from the history of the concubine, Judg. xix. 11–15. The Levite, coming from Bethlehem, passed (on the western route) by Jebus, when the day was fast declining,[5] and thought of passing the night in Gibeah or Ramah :[6] the sun set when they came to Gibeah.[7] The two places were thus adjacent, and were the first one met with after passing Jebus. Where then did Gibeah lie ? According to Josephus,[8] it was distant 20 stadia from Jerusalem ; and Jerome, in Epitaph. Paulæ, says of this pilgrim, that she came through Ajalon and Gibeon (El-Jîb), and

---

[1] Jerus. Moëd Katon, iii.
[2] Bab. Berachoth, fol. 13. 2 ; Pesachim, iii. 8.
[3] De Bello, v. 2, sec. 3.   [4] Antiq. viii. 12, sec. 3.
[5] Chap. ix. 11.   [6] Chap. ix. 13.
[7] Chap. ix. 14.   [8] Antiq. v. 2, sec. 8.

then to Gibeah, the town of the concubine; and then leaving
the monument of Helena on the left, came to Jerusalem.[1] The
monument of Helena lay north-west of Jerusalem, near to the
Psephinus tower;[2] and, in order to leave this to the left,
Paula must come from the west-north-west : in this direction,
accordingly, was Gibeah to be found, where also the name is preserved to this day. Tobler says[3] that down where the Wady
Nebi Samwîl debouches, in the vicinity of Nebi Samwîl, into the
Wady Bêt-Hanîna, he saw a cave-sepulchre, Moghâret ed Jîbeh.
Ed-Jîbeh is Gibeah; the place lies at the foot of the Nebi
Samwîl. Consequently Ramah and Gibeah were near to each
other. The Levite preferred Gibeah, because there was not,
as at Ramah, a mountain to climb. This full examination of
the ground was necessary, because Robinson has too hastily
identified En-Nebi Samwîl with Mizpah, and placed Gibeah and
Ramah on the route to Sichem. When, then, we consider how
uncertain is the orthography of names in the Old Testament,
it must greatly strike us that, precisely In the neighbourhood
of our En-Nebi Samwîl, we meet with a Mount Ephron,[4] and a
town Hophra.[5] Must not Mount Ephraim, Ephrati, Ephron,
Hophra, be one and the same ? Of Ephrath-Bethlehem we
cannot at any rate think in this connection. Where, then, did
Rachel's cenotaph lie ? In any case near Nebi Samwîl, *i.e.*
Ramah, "before one comes to Zelzah," which latter place seems
to us to be preserved in Bîr el-'Ozeiz, upon the way from El-Jîb
to Nebi Samwîl.[6] This cenotaph in Benjamin was before the
mind of Jeremiah in connection with the words cited : the
Evangelist, however, applies these words to the sepulchre near
Bethlehem.

Sec. 50. **The Flight to Egypt.**—When the Magi had left
Bethlehem, Joseph received a command in a dream to arise,
and, taking the child and His mother, to flee into Egypt,
because Herod sought the child's life. Upon the death of
Herod, Joseph, who was supernaturally informed of this event

---

[1] In Gabaa urbe usque ad solum diruto paululum substitit, recordato peccato
ejus et concubinæ in frustra divisæ . . . Quid diu moror ? ad lævam mausolæo
Helenæ derelicto . . . ingressa est Jerusalem.

[2] Josephus, *de Bello*, v. 4, sec. 2.　　　　[3] *Denkblätter*, p. 367.

[4] Josh. xv. 9.　　　[5] Josh. xviii. 23.　　　[6] Robinson, ii. p. 256.

in a dream, returned with the child and His mother to the land of Israel. But when he heard that Archelaus was king in Judea in Herod's stead, he feared to enter this land, and, repairing to Galilee, went and dwelt at Nazareth.[1] The journey from Bethlehem to the north of Egypt is one of about seven days. The sojourn in Egypt was in any case of brief duration, since Jesus is called a young child after as before.[2] The return took place when Archelaus was king;[3] but the title of king was borne only for a short time by this prince, when it was changed by Augustus into that of Ethnarch.[4] If Herod died on the 24th January U.C. 753, and the departure of Archelaus for Rome took place immediately after the Passover, then the return from Egypt would fall somewhere between these two events—perhaps about the time of the Passover.

Sec. 51. Before we venture on the attempt more precisely to define the date of all these events, we have to harmonize Matthew's account of the birth of Jesus with that given by Luke. Both Evangelists represent Christ as being born in Bethlehem. If, however, the Gospel of Matthew were our only source of knowledge on this point, the impression would be left upon us that Bethlehem had been up to that time the dwelling-place of Joseph and Mary, because no mention is made of a journey thither, and afterwards Galilee and Nazareth become the new dwelling-place only in consequence of a divine command.[5] Luke, on the other hand [taken alone], would lead us to suppose that Nazareth was the original dwelling-place of Joseph and Mary, and that some two months after the birth of the child they returned to Nazareth.[6] Yet it does not follow that Matthew is in contradiction with Luke, from the fact of his not mentioning the earlier dwelling in Nazareth; he might well pass over this circumstance as not pertaining to the subject of his history. It is remarkable that only Matthew gives an account of the star of the wise men, of the

---

[1] Matt. ii. 13–23.   [2] παιδίον, Matt. ii. 20.   [3] Matt. ii. 22.

[4] Josephus, *Antiq.* xvii. 8, secs. 1–4; 11, sec. 4.

[5] Matt. ii. 22.

[6] Luke ii. 39. The offering for purification of Luke ii. 22 was, according to Lev. xii. 4, 6, presented forty days after the birth.

slaughter of the children, and the flight into Egypt; and, on the other hand, only Luke of the presentation in the temple ; but even with regard to these facts the narratives do not contradict, but complement each other. Nothing prevents our supposing that the Magi arrived in Bethlehem only a few days after the birth of Christ, and that Herod instantly, after finding himself deceived, issued his command of blood, the effect of which was frustrated by the flight into Egypt. The sojourn there, with the journey to and fro, calls for no more than three or four weeks; because Joseph had learnt the facts of Herod's death not by rumour, but by a divine revelation.   On the other hand, the fact that Archelaus was made king, or rather had made himself so, he learnt not from revelation, but from the report of the people ;[1] he may well thus have returned to Bethlehem, have offered the offering of purification for Mary,[2] and only then have returned by divine direction to Nazareth.[3]   On the supposition of a rapid succession of ovents in the order here given, the two accounts may be harmonized, but only in this order. For if, with many exegetes, we should assume that the presentation in the sanctuary took place before the flight, we should have to choose between the statement of the one Evangelist concerning this flight, and that of the other concerning the return to Nazareth ; side by side these two accounts could not exist.[4]

Sec. 52. If now we combine all the chronological elements which relate to the birth of Jesus, the following results are obtained therefrom :—

(1.) Jesus was born at Bethlehem in the year of Rome 752. His birth took place during the lifetime of Herod, consequently before the 24th January 753. Long before the death of this king it cannot be placed, because Matt. ii. gives to every reader the impression of an intimate connection

---

[1] Matt. ii. 22.   [2] Luke ii. 22.   [3] Matt. ii. 22 ; Luke ii. 39.

[4] [If no other considerations entered into the question than those derived from chronological data, this conclusion would be warranted. On psychological grounds, however, the scene of Luke ii. 25-35 becomes, after the flight into Egypt and the death of Herod, impossible. On the other hand, it falls most naturally *before the visit of the Magi.* We cannot, therefore, from Luke ii. 39, insist upon the *immediate* sequence of the return to Nazareth upon the presentation in the temple.]

between the facts related, and also that of their rapid succession. It is true, it is assumed by many that Jesus must have been born about two years before the arrival of the Magi, because Herod caused the children of two years and under to be put to death. That he included children even of two years is to be explained as a measure of precaution on the part of the tyrant, who could not from the words of the Magi alone discover with certainty the age of the child. The star is evidently spoken of as something miraculous, which did not proclaim to the Magi the birth of the child after an interval of about two years, but immediately revealed to them that event ; so that they could be in Bethlehem in about fourteen days after it. If we were required to suppose that Jesus had been born about two years earlier, we should have to surrender the account of Luke, which represents the sojourn at Bethlehem as something passing, brought about incidentally by the census, and terminating with that event and the birth of the Lord, which was contemporaneous with it.

Sec. 53. (2.) Jesus cannot have been born before the month of October 752. We have already, sec. 30, drawn attention to the great degree of probability there is that the census in Judea was always held on the Sabbatic year. If such census took place in the year 752, this probability becomes a certainty. For since Tisri 752 to Tisri 753 was a Sabbatic year, the simplest statecraft required that an operation, in any case tedious and disturbing, should not be entered on before the beginning of the year of rest. In the year 752, the 1st Tisri, consequently the beginning of the Sabbatic year, probably fell on the 24th August. Before this date Joseph did not enter upon his journey. The calculation of the service of the course of Abia, sec. 42, also points actually to the middle of the month of October, so that the birth cannot well be placed earlier, although it may fairly be placed later. We thus remain not very far removed from the ancient Christian tradition, which gives 25th December as the date of the birth of Jesus Christ. We cannot, nevertheless, regard this date as one handed down from the beginning, but must trace its origin to an astrological consideration. In the first Christian centuries the 25th December was looked upon as the day of the winter solstice.   The Church Fathers disposed of the four cardinal days of the year as follows :—

1. Vernal equinox. Annunciation, 25th March.
2. Summer solstice. Birth of John the Baptist, 24th June.
3. Autumnal equinox. Conception of John, 24th September.
4. Winter solstice. Birth of Jesus, 25th December.

It is not for a moment to be supposed that Providence would, by such an arrangement, give countenance to the dicta of astrological reveries.   If the presentation in the temple coincided with the return from Egypt, consequent upon the death of Herod, then it belongs to a date subsequent to the 24th January ; but since it took place forty days after the birth, the birth of Jesus can at the earliest have taken place 14th December 752, and at the latest towards the 10th January, after which Herod left Jerusalem.

We have thought we ought to present the possible deductions from the given premises; but, as some of these premises are very uncertain, we must not attach too great a value to these deductions.   As a certain result we obtain the fact that Jesus was born after the 1st Tisri 752, in the first half of the Sabbatic year.

Sec. 54. The year of Rome 752 is the second before A.D. 1 of the era of Dionysius.   But since Dionysius placed the birth of Christ on the 25th December, he may not have taken into account the six remaining days of the year, and have looked upon the year 753 as the year Null, and the year 754 as the year A.D. 1.   In this way the reckoning of the Dionysian era is perfectly correct.   The unmathematical, confusing disorder in our chronology, through which the name of B.C. 1 is given to the year before A.D. 1, cannot be laid to the charge of Dionysius, who probably placed a year Null between B.C. 1 and A.D. 1, and began the year A.D. 1 a year (and those six days) after the day of the birth.

IV.—*History of the Youth of Jesus.*

Sec. 55. The Evangelists relate nothing concerning the youth of Jesus, beyond the visit to the Paschal festival, when

He was twelve years of age.[1]   In the law all the males in
Israel are required to appear before the presence of Jehovah
thrice every year,[2] namely, at the feast of Passover, of Pentecost, and of the Ingathering in the end of the year.   As
concerns the women and children, nothing is prescribed in the
law.   According to Hillel's school, the women were to attend
the feast once, namely, at Passover.   The fathers were to take
with them their sons as soon as they were twelve years of
age, with which age they became "sons of the law," בני התורה.
With this custom the account of the Evangelist Luke corresponds.   How great the number of the Passover guests at
that time was, may be inferred from the following report
of Josephus, who says:[3] "The paschal lambs were slain (on
the 14th Nisan) between the ninth hour and the eleventh.
Around every lamb there are gathered at least ten, often as
many as twenty, guests; and the number of the lambs slain
was 25,600."   From this it follows that the number of
persons taking part in the festival was something like two
millions and a half.   If the population of Jerusalem be rated
ever so highly, and a considerable number be set down to the
account of exaggeration, there still remains a million of guests
coming from elsewhere.   These all left Jerusalem pretty
much on the same day.   That in such a sea of human beings,
a child, who, moreover, purposely remained behind, might be
lost, without the parents on that account being chargeable
with negligence or indifference, ought to have been evident to
the exegetes.   The festival guests of the same place and the
same house could not possibly, under such circumstances,
muster in Jerusalem itself; they would, on the contrary, meet
in the evening at a resting-place previously agreed upon.
When Joseph and Mary did not find the child there, they
returned and sought Him for three days.   Neither this seeking, nor the maternal remonstrance, "Son, why hast thou thus
dealt with us?   Behold, thy father and I have sought thee
sorrowing," justifies the supposition of indifference or negligence.   They found the child in the sanctuary;[4] there He was

---

[1] Luke ii. 41–52.   [2] Ex. xxiii. 14–17.   [3] *De Bello*, vi. 9, sec. 3.
[4] ἐν τῷ ἱερῷ, that is to say, in the courts of the temple, not in the temple
itself.

sitting in the midst of the doctors.   Sitting was not permitted
in the court of Israel; consequently the court of the women,
or the outer court, the so-called court of the Gentiles, must be
meant.   Not even one of the synagogues is to be thought of,
of which several were to be found on the temple mountain;
but rather one of the gates, which, for the purpose of such
assemblies, were made in the form of an exedra.—The history
teaches that Jesus as a child had the consciousness of being
the Son of God;[1] but at the same time that He passed naturally
through all the stages of human development, and was not as
a child already in intellect a perfect man: " He went down with
them, and was subject unto them—and increased in wisdom
and stature, and in grace with God and with men."[2]

This history is the only one which has come down to us
concerning the youth of Jesus.   That He passed His youth
at Nazareth, may be safely inferred from the appellation
" Nazaræan " or " Nazarene " which was given Him, and which
even descended to His Church, and from the name " own
city " (πατρίς) of Jesus, by which Nazareth is frequently
designated.[3]   Significant for forming a conception of the youth
and family relations of Christ is the exclamation of the
inhabitants of Nazareth, in Mark vi. 3 : " Is not this the carpenter, the son of Mary, the brother of James and Joses, and
of Judas and Simon ? and are not his sisters here with us ? "
In Matt. xiii. 55, this exclamation is given thus : " Is not this
the carpenter's son ? are there not with us his brethren,
James, and Joses, and Simon, and Judas, and all his sisters ? "
From this we must infer that not only Joseph but also Jesus
Himself was a carpenter (τέκτων); that He had brothers and
sisters according to the flesh; that Joseph was no longer
alive, because in Mark Jesus and His brethren are called the
sons of Mary; and that Jesus had not, before beginning His
ministry, attended some rabbinical school.—" Whence then
hath this man all these things ? "[4]

Sec. 56.   That which is narrated to us by two Evangelists
concerning the childhood of Jesus, and by one Evangelist
concerning His youth, forms a preparatory history, which it did

[1] Luke ii. 49.   [2] Luke ii. 51, 52.
[3] Cf. e.g. Matt. xiii. 54–57 ; Mark vi. 1, etc.   [4] Matt. xiii. 56.

not seem necessary to the other two Evangelists, Mark and John, to relate. The history proper with all begins at the baptism of the Lord.[1] The beginning of His ministry, and a considerable proportion of the after events, have the shore of the Sea of Gennesareth as their theatre. More fully to describe this important point of our earth, the birthplace of Christianity, is the object of the following division.

[1] Matt. iii. 13 ; Mark i. 9 ; Luke iii. 21 ; John i. 33.

DIVISION III.

THE SEA OF GENNESARETH AND ITS ENVIRONS.

SEC. 57. The Land of Promise, strictly speaking, which stretches along the coast of the Mediterranean Sea, is separated from the trans-Jordan domain, the former inheritance of the two and a half tribes, by a level valley (carse), of an average width of 12 miles, which extends north to south from the sources of the Jordan to the Dead Sea, over three and a half degrees of latitude. The upper, northern half of this valley contains the bed of the Jordan (*Jardén*) [1] This stream forms in its course three lakes. The upper, northernmost of these is called Bahr el-Hûleh, and bears this name as early as the time of the Talmudic writings. [2] Erroneously, and in contradiction alike with the Biblical text and with the references of Josephus and Jerome, this lake is on most maps called the *Sea of Merom.* [3] The Jordan, issuing forth from the Hûleh, forms, after a brief course, the second lake, the Sea of Tiberias or Lake of Gennesareth ; then, after a course of about 70 miles, it forms the third lake, called the Dead Sea, which has no outflow. From the *Dead Sea* to the *Aïlatic Gulf* the Ghôr

---

[1] [In the present day it is called the Jordan only *above* the Sea of Tiberias ; below, it is called *Sheriat el-Khebîr.*]

[2] יַמָּא חוּלְתָא ; *Jerus. Ketuboth,* in Ugolini *Thes.* xxx. p. 1001 ; *Jerus. Kilaim,* fol. 31. 1 ; *Bab. Baba-Bathra,* fol. 74 ; cf. Josephus, *Antiq.* xv. 10, sec. 3.

[3] [On the *Hûleh-lake* (Heb. *Chûl,* a circle or district), called by Josephus *Semechonitis-lake,* and described by him in *de Bello,* iv. 1, sec. 1, see Thomson, *Land and Book,* p. 259 ; Tristram, *Land of Israel,* 594, 595 ; cf. Ritter, ii. 209, 210. Since the time of Canon Tristram's visit the lake has been fully explored by Mr. Macgregor in his canoe, the "Rob Roy." The *Phiala-lake* is well described by Robinson, iii. 399, 400 ; Thomson, p. 241 ; Tristram, 589. On this lake, erroneously supposed by Josephus to be the source of the Jordan, compare Ritter, ii. 177 ff. "The river which gushes out at Bânias would exhaust this lake in forty-eight hours" (Thomson).]

is prolonged to a length of 150 miles; nay, the basin of the Dead Sea itself is a continuation of the cleft forming this valley. The whole valley from the Lake of Gennesareth to the Dead Sea is called in the Old Testament the 'Araba;[1] in the present day, however, the name is applied only to the southern part of it, stretching from the Dead Sea; the northern part, on the other hand, which contains the bed of the Jordan, is now called El-Ghôr. The chain of mountains skirting the hollow on either side are as rocky walls, which form the more or less abrupt declivity from the upland plain on either side Jordan. The uppermost source of the Jordan, the Wady Hasbani, lies at Hasbeïa, 568 mètres [1862 feet] above the level of the sea; the Bânias fountain, which the ancients took for the true source of the Jordan, has an absolute height of 383 mètres [1255 feet]. The source of the Little Jordan at Tell el-Kâdi, the ancient Dan, lies 185 mètres [604 feet] above the level of the sea. At the Lake of Gennesareth we are already 189 mètres [617 feet] below the level .of the sea; the depression of the Dead Sea attains 392 mètres [1285 feet]. To the south of the Dead Sea the valley of the 'Araba gradually rises again, until it attains an absolute height of 240 mètres [768 feet], and then falls until, having sunk below the ocean level, it is covered by the waters of the Red Sea.[2]

Sec. 58. **The Lake of Gennesareth** or Sea of Tiberias, now Bahr Tabarîeh, in the Old Testament, Sea of Chinnereth, is formed and fed by the Jordan, which flows through it. Its dimensions are very differently given by different travellers. Its length from north to south seems to be about 14 miles, its breadth 6–8 miles. It is to be reckoned among the shallow lakes; since its medium depth amounts only to 10 fathoms, its greatest depth to not more than 26 fathoms. Its waters are sweet, clear, and very abundant in fish. On the western and the eastern side of the lake run the mountain ranges which form the break in the opposite upland plains. The Galilean range rises about 450 feet above the level of the lake; the opposite, eastern or Gaulonitic range, about 900 feet. In the

---

[1] הערבה, *the wilderness*, Deut. i. 1, ii. 8, iv. 49; Josh. iii. 16, etc.

[2] The altitudes here given are those ascertained by the Duc de Luynes during his travels in 1864.

latter the Haurân basalt, in the former the Jura limestone, is
the prevailing feature.

Sec. 59. **Tiberias,** now Tabarîeh or Tabarîyeh, is at present
the single place of any importance on that sea whose coast
was at the time of Jesus so densely populated. This place
lies on the western shore, about 6 miles from the outflow of
the Jordan, and nearly 9 miles below the entrance of this
stream. The town itself is not mentioned in the New Testament, although John speaks once of the " Sea of Tiberias." [1]
It was built by the tetrarch Herod Antipas, and named after
the Emperor Tiberius. The population, consisting of Gentiles
and Jews, was brought together in part by coercion. The
place on which Tiberias was built was formerly a graveyard,[2]
and on that account unclean for the Jews. According to the
Chronicon of Eusebius, this town was founded in the 14th
year of the reign of Tiberius ; it was therefore still in the
course of erection in the days of Jesus.

Sec. 60. The narrow strip of coast on which Tiberias is
built extends in the same proportions towards the south, as
far as the lower end of the lake. A mile and a half south of
Tiberias are to be found the *Thermal Springs of Tiberias,* now
Hammâm, called by the Talmudists Hamatha, חמת, חמתא
דטיבריא, or " the warm springs of Tiberias," מוי דמוקד דטבריה.[3]
This place affords us an important archæological support ;
since it is one and the same with the Hamath mentioned
with Rekath and Chinnereth, in Josh. xix. 35, as belonging
to Naphtali. This name signifies " warm springs " (*thermæ*),
and *must* be identical with Hammâm, the more so since this
place has from the earliest times been celebrated as a medicinal
spring, and since the ancient Hamath is to be sought for
only on the shore of that lake, to which the sister city of
Chinnereth gives the name. There are still present manifest
traces which go to show that Tiberias at one time extended
as far as Hammâm.

South from the warm springs lie two ruins, a good mile
and a half from each other ; the northern is called *Kades*, the
southern *Kerak*. This latter place is unquestionably the

---

[1] John xxi. 1.   [2] Josephus, *Antiq.* xviii. 2, sec. 3.
[3] *Jerus. Erubin*, fol. 23. 4 ; *Midrash Koheleth*, fol. 116. 2.

ancient *Tarichæa*, according to Josephus 30 stadia distant from Tiberias,[1] on the margin of the lake,[2] with which it communicated by means of a canal.[3] In the neighbourhood of this town lay another, known as Sennabris, which is likewise given as distant 30 stadia from Tiberias.[4] Since Josephus always gives the stadia in round numbers of tens, —so that something may be added to the distance of Tarichæa from Tiberias, something deducted from that of Sennabris,— it becomes highly probable that Sennabris is identical with Kades. In a passage of the Talmud, of which more hereafter, mention is made of two Gennesaroth or Abtinoth, which are called Bethjerach, or better, Beth-Therach[5] and Zennabri;[6] these are thus Tarichæa and Sennabris.

Sec. 61. **Magdala.**—As one journeys northward from Tiberias, the mountain range soon approaches so near to the sea, that there is no longer any room for the road on the beach, but it must pass over the ridge of the hill. Where the road descends again on the north side of the hill, a good three miles from Tiberias, lies a wretched Arab village, *El-Mejdel*, in which is preserved the old name of Magdala. Of this place was, in all probability, Mary Magdalene a native.[7] The name Magdala itself occurs in the New Testament only in Matt. xv. 39, where it is critically doubtful, and must give place to Magadán or Magedán.[8]

Sec. 62. **The Land of Gennesareth.**[9]—Josephus, *de Bello*, iii. 10, sec. 8, describes the land as a fair plain, fruitful and well watered, of 30 stadia long by 20 broad, lying on the western coast of the lake. With this description corresponds the unique, plain El-Ghuweir, situated on the western side of the lake. It stretches northward from Mejdel to a length of about three miles, and is a mile and a half wide from west to east. It is still abundantly watered and fertile. The land

---

[1] Josephus, *Vita*, 32.   [2] *Vita*, 18 ; *de Bello*, ii. 21, sec. 8, iii. 10, sec. 5.

[3] *Vita*, 31 : διώρυγα ποιήσας ἀπ' αὐτῆς (Ταριχαίων) ἐπὶ τὴν λίμνην ἄγουσαν.

[4] Σινναβρίς, *de Bello*, iii. 9, sec. 7.

[5] בֵּית־תִּירַח=בֵּי־תִּירַח=בֵּית־תִּירַה·   [6] צִינַבְרִי·

[7] ἡ Μαγδαληνή, Matt. xv. 40, xvi. 1 ; Luke viii. 1 ; John xx. 1, etc.

[8] See below, sec. 73.

[9] γῆ Γιννησαρίτ, or, according to some MSS., γῆ Γιννησάρ, Matt. xiv. 34 ; בִּקְעַת גִּינֵיסַר with the Talmudists ; Γιννησαρίτις with Josephus.

of Gennesar is often mentioned in the books of Jewish
tradition, and praised especially on account of the excellence
of its fruits. In *Bab. Pesachim,* fol. 8. 2, it is said : " Why
were not the fruits of Gennesar sold at Jerusalem ? Lest
those who came up to the feast should say, We have come
only to taste fruits of Gennesar." In the prophetic benediction
upon Naphtali[1] mention is made of the fulness of blessing
promised to this tribe. The rabbis explain this " fulness " by
saying the plain of Gennesar is meant by it.[2] From this
follows, first, the great value that was attached to this small
strip of land ; but then also—what must here already be
emphatically brought out—that the land of Naphtali, to
which it belonged, extended along the western shore of the
lake.

Sec. 63. **Capernaum.**[3]—In the description of the land of
Gennesar by Josephus, *de Bello,* iii. 10, sec. 8, it is said :
" This land is watered by a very abundant fountain, which the
people of the country call Καφαρναουμ—ἣ πηγὴ διάρδει αι
γονιμωτάτῃ, Καφαρναούμ αὐτὴν οἱ ἐπιχώριοι καλοῦσι. Some
have taken it to be a vein of the Nile, because it brings forth
a sort of fish very similar to the kind called *coracinus* (catfish) in the lake of Alexandria." This name Caphar-Naûm
was given to the fountain of a caphar or village situated there.
There was thus, according to Josephus, a place in the territory of Gennesar known as Kapharnaum. In the El-Ghuweir
there is to be found to the present day a remarkable fountain
corresponding to this description, *Ain El-Mudawarah* (round
fountain), which forms an oval reservoir or basin of about 100
feet diameter, and is walled round. The depth of water may
be two feet. It is beautifully clear and sweet, springs up
with great force, and flows rapidly in a full stream to water
the plain below. Numerous small fishes disport themselves
in its basin.[4] This fountain is on the west side of the El-

---

[1] Deut. xxxiii. 23.   [2] Siphri, in Ugolini *Thes.* xv. p. 979.

[3] Καπερναούμ, or, according to the better MSS., Καφαρναούμ ; in the Talmud
כפר נחום, Nahums-thorp, where, according to the Jewish *Itinerary* of Isaac
Chelo, belonging to the 14th century, cited in Carmoly's *Itinéraire*, p. 259, the
grave of *Nahum, the old* (? *prophet*) was to be found.

[4] Robinson, ii. p. 400. [Canon Tristram, p. 446 ff., comes to the same conclusion as Caspari concerning the identity of *Ain Mudawarah* with Capernaum.

Ghuweir, a mile and a half from the lake. If Capernaum was in its neighbourhood, this town is not to be sought immediately on the shore of the lake, but at some distance from it. It will be easily understood that this town, though situated a mile and a half from the shore, might yet bear the name of παραθαλασσία ;[1] and the more so since this appellation was intended only to distinguish it from another Capernaum, at a distance from the lake, namely, on the Kishon, 18 miles from Cæsarea.[2] Ruins of a town in the vicinity of this fountain have not hitherto been discovered ; this, however, proves nothing against its former existence, in a locality so frequently visited by earthquakes. Thus Schubert[3] found the town of Tiberias utterly destroyed by an earthquake, which had happened on (Sunday) the 1st January 1837. This explains to us how Capernaum might disappear without a trace, even as it was predicted, Matt. xi. 23, that it should disappear. But if this town was in reality early destroyed, it is probable that the place Tell-Hûm, at the northern end of the lake, was already early mistaken for Capernaum. For to Tell-Hûm, and not to the Ghuweir, does the following description of Adamnanus[4] seem to relate : " Quæ (Capernaum), ut Arculfus refert, qui eam de monte vicino prospexit, murum non habens, angusto inter montem et stagnum coarctata spatio, per illam mariti-mam oram longo tramite protenditur, montem ab aquilonari plaga, lacum vero ab australi habens, ab occasu in ortum

He says : " When we come to the Round Fountain of Ain Mudawarah, we find a spot in perfect harmony with the accounts of the evangelists and of Josephus, and, in fact, the only possible locality which will harmonize all the accounts. Here is a fountain in the centre of the western boundary of the plain, sending forth to this day a copious stream which exactly bisects the Ghuweir on its way to the lake, and is the most important source of fertility in the plain. The stream from Wady Hamâm waters the southern end, the Wady of Armûd the northern, while this supplies the central plain, and is not less copious nor less permanent than the others. . . . But the most decisive argument in its favour is to my mind the statement of Josephus, that Capharnaum produced the κορακῖνος, a fish like that of the lake near Alexandria. The fact is, that the remarkable siluroid the catfish, or coracine (κορακῖνος)—*Clarias macracanthus,* Gunthr.—identical with the catfish of Lower Egypt, does abound to a remarkable degree in the Round Fountain to this day." See the argument cited more at length in the appendix to the English translation of Ritter, ii. 410–414.]

[1] Matt. iv. 13.   [2] Guil. Tyr. *de Bello sacro,* x. 26.
[3] *Reisen,* iii. p. 233.   [4] ii. 25.

extensa dirigitur." Even to the present day many Biblical
geographers regard Tell-Hûm as Capernaum, although this
supposition is in glaring opposition to the statement of
Josephus. The cause of it lies in an erroneous conception
as to the boundaries of Naphtali, which shall come under
examination in the succeeding paragraphs. For the position
of Capernaum in the land of Gennesar, we have the testimony
of Jerome and of the Jewish itineraries. Jerome says:[1]
"Lacum Gennesareth, in cujus litore Capharnaum et Tiberias
et Bethsaida et Chorazeim sitæ sunt." In this order of succession could the towns be mentioned only when the pilgrim
visiting the Sea of Galilee is supposed to come down by the
route from Nazareth and Tabor. This ancient highway led
down from the Galilean table-land into the El-Ghuweir, in
the vicinity of the Mudawarah fountain, and thence in a
south-easterly direction by Mejdel and Tiberias, and from
Mejdel northerly, along the lake side to Bethsaida and
Chorazin. If Jerome had conceived of Capernaum as occupying the place of Tell-Hûm, he could not possibly have
enumerated these places in this order. The Jewish itineraries,
too, place Caphar-Nahum in the territory of Gennesar; according to the Isaac Chelo above cited, the place lay between
Arbela and Caphar-Anan. Between these two places, still
known under their old names, Irbil and Kefr Anan, lies El-
Ghuweir, but not Tell-Hûm. Samuel ben Simon, belonging
to the 13th century,[2] travelled from Tiberias through Caphar-
Hanuim to Arbela ; that is to say, he ascended the high
ground by the main route just mentioned, which passes
through El-Ghuweir. There accordingly lay Caphar-Hanuim,
כפר חנוים, which is evidently the name Caphar-Nahum, written
with letters transposed—חנום for נחום. Against this position
of Capernaum, Von Raumer and many others declare themselves. Capernaum, say they, lay on the confines of Zebulon
and Naphtali ; now the western shore belonged to Zebulon,
and Naphtali could touch the lake only at the northern end,
where Tell-Hûm lies ; there, then, Capernaum is to be sought.
It is thus incumbent on us to ascertain the boundaries of these
two tribes.

[1] In Esaiam, ix. 1.   [2] Carmoly, Itin. p. 130.

Sec. 64. **The Boundaries of Zabulon and Nephthaleim.**
—Josephus says:[1] " The Zebulonites obtained as an inheritance the land about Carmel and the sea, extending as far as
Gennesaritis "—Σαβουλωνίται δὲ τὴν μέχρι Γεννησαρίτιδος
καθήκουσαν δὲ περὶ Κάρμηλον καὶ θάλασσαν ἔλαχον. That
γῆν must be supplied to τὴν καθήκουσαν is self-evident; and
that the word Γεννησαρίτιδος be supplemented by γῆς, and
not λίμνης, is demanded by the grammatical structure. The
proposition is thus: the Zebulonites obtained the land about
Carmel and the sea, which stretches on the east as far as the
land Gennesaritis. Gennesar is evidently the name of the
land, for it is formed from גני סר, " the gardens of the (lake-)
basin," and can be transferred to the lake itself only by the
addition of the word λίμνης; where this addition is wanting,
the name can only refer to the land. But when Josephus
represents the territory of Zebulon as extending only *as far
as* the land of Gennesaritis, this land itself, and consequently
also the shore of the lake, remains excluded, and must be
assigned to the tribe of Naphtali. Wholly in harmony
with this, Jerome says:[2] "Naphtali in Galilæa usque ad
Jordanem, ubi Tiberias, quæ olim Chennereth." It is here a
matter of indifference whether or not Tiberias is rightly
identified with Chinnereth; the Church Father, so well versed
in Biblical geography, at any rate says that Tiberias belonged
to Naphtali, that consequently also the shore of the lake was
in the territory of this tribe. That Jewish tradition shares
this view, we have already seen, sec. 62, inasmuch as it
explains the fulness of the blessing of Naphtali by the land
of Gennesar. This tradition is also unanimously of opinion
that the towns of this tribe, Hamath, Rekath, and Chinnereth,
enumerated in Josh. xix. 35, belong to the western shore of
the lake.[3] And, in truth, where should one place Chinnereth,
the town which gave the name to the lake, except on the
lake itself? Where Hamath, except at Hammâm, the place
of warm springs? But if these places were on the shore of
the lake, then its western shore belonged to Naphtali, and
not to Zebulon. Furthermore, it is said in *Bab. Baba-Kamma,*

---

[1] *Antiq.* v. 1, sec. 22. [2] *In Ezech.* 48.
[3] *Jerus. Megilla,* i. 1, in Ugolini *Thes.* xviii. p. 845, and elsewhere.

fol. 81. 2 : " The Sea of Tiberias lies in the portion of the tribe of Naphtali ; " and further : " This tribe possessed, too, a tract of land south of the lake." [1]   When, moreover, we test the description of Zebulon given in Josh. xix. 10–16, we find not the slightest hint which might lead us to suppose that this tribe extended on the east as far as the Jordan or the lake.   Very different is the case with Naphtali, of which the territory is described Josh. xix. 32–39.   Ver. 33 it is said : " Their frontier went from Heleph, from Elon to Zaananim, and Adami ha-Nekeb, and Jabneel ; and the outgoings thereof were at Jordan."   After this it says in the 34th verse : " And the frontier turneth westward to Asnoth-Tabor." This last place was necessarily in the vicinity of Mount Tabor.   Since it lay westward of the point of contact of the frontier of Naphtali with the Jordan, the reference is evidently to the Jordan lying to the east of Tabor, *i.e.* to the Jordan not above the lake, but below it.   Thus much is accordingly certain—that the domain of Naphtali below the lake touched on the Jordan opposite Tabor ; and from this it necessarily follows that the western coast of the lake belonged to this tribe.   But let us still further trace out the boundaries of this tribe.   It began with Heleph.   This place we may pass over as unknown ; it suffices to know that it serves to mark the northern point at which their domain began.   With Zaananim we are acquainted ; according to Judg. iv. 11, it was near to Kedes in Naphtali.[2]   Adami is to be recognised in Damûn, about nine miles E.S.E. from Acco, west from Cabul.   That Adami in reality became transformed in the lapse of ages into Damûn, is vouched for by *Jerus. Megilla,* i. 1,[3] where it is expressly stated that אדמי is דמין.   Naphtali thus formed from Heleph, *i.e.* from the northern side, a narrow strip of land on the western bank of the Upper Jordan to Kedes, where the frontier declined to the west, and extended to the neighbourhood of Acco.   Thence the frontier proceeded to Jabneel.   There were two places of this name in the land

---

[1] So also *Baba-Bathra*, v. 1.   [Cf. " the sea (*yôm*) and the south " of Deut. xxxiii. 23.]

[2] [Kedesh-Naphtali is described by Tristram, p. 583.   The general features of Naphtali are, moreover, vividly portrayed by Thomson, pp. 213, 214.]

[3] Ugolini, *Thes.* xviii. p. 847.

of Israel; first, Jabneel in Judah,[1] later called by the rabbis *Jabne*, by the Greeks *Jamnia ;* and then Jabneel in Galilee, in like manner called by Josephus *Jamnia*, as with the Semitic races in general the sounds of B and M often pass over the one into the other. According to Josephus, *Vita* 37, and *de Bello*, ii. 20, sec. 6, Jamnia was a town of Upper Galilee, which formed one group with Meroth and Achabara. Achabara is still to be recognised in Tell-Achbarah, south of Safed, and Meroth in Mêron, west of Safed. Jabneel (or Jamnia) was, consequently, if not Safed itself,—which is highly probable,—at least in the vicinity of it. Naphtali accordingly possessed a strip of land between Kedes and Safed, which extended on the west as far as Acco. From Jabneel (Safed) the boundary struck southwards as far as the Lower Jordan, opposite Tabor, after it had touched at Lakum.[2] This name we might be content to pass over as unknown, because the direction of the frontier is clear without this. It seems to us, however, that this name has left a trace to the present day. Burckhardt[3] speaks of a plain, Ard-el-Hamma, which lies upon the mountain ridge westward of Tiberias. May not this be the word Ard-el-Lhamma ? if so, Lakum or Lachum is to be recognised in it.—From the Lower Jordan the frontier proceeded westward to Asnoth Tabor, and thence (ver. 34) to Hukkok, now Jakuk or Yakuk, six miles south of Safed. By this line drawn from Tabor to Jakuk is the narrow strip of territory on the sea-side, belonging to Naphtali, separated from Zebulon, which lies to the west of it. With perfect justice, then, it is said, ver. 34 : "Naphtali abuts on Zebulon on the south, on Asher on the west, and on Judah of Jordan on the east." For a line drawn from Damûn to Safed in reality forms the southern boundary of Naphtali, and the northern boundary of Zebulon; the narrow wedge, which penetrates by the coast of the lake into the south, is not here taken into consideration. Of Judah of the Jordan we shall have occasion to treat hereafter in sec. 68.

Sec. 65. It now becomes possible for us to explain the much-discussed passage of Matt. iv. 13–16. It is there said : " Leaving Nazareth, He came and dwelt in Capernaum, which

---

[1] Josh. xv. 11.   [2] Josh. xix. 33.   [3] *Reisen*, p. 577.

is upon the sea-coast, on the confines of Zebulon and Nephthaleim, that it might be fulfilled which was spoken by Esaias
the prophet, saying,[1] ' Land of Zabulon and land of Nephthaleim,
way of the sea, beyond Jordan, Galilee of the nations.' "
Here it is evidently implied that Capernaum lay upon the
confines of the two tribes mentioned, and at the same time
upon the sea route which leads out of Galilee beyond Jordan.
Since the prophet is speaking of two cis-Jordan tribes, and of
Galilee, the words דרך הים עבר הירדן must be translated, " Sea-
way which leads over the Jordan." Now, the main route
from Jerusalem to Damascus, passing by Tabor, descended
into the territory of Gennesar, then from Mejdel passed
along the shore to Khân Minyeh, where it left the shore to
reach the table-land lying to the north of El-Ghuweir ; it
thence advanced in a straight line to the Jacob's Bridge, where
it crossed the Jordan. It is one of the merits of Van de
Velde to have traced out and marked on his map this route,
which during some part of its course is seen to be a *Via
Romana*. This road, which from Tabor northwards indicates
the before-mentioned boundaries of the two tribes, passed
near to the Mudawarah fountain, thus to the true Capernaum ;
Tell-Hûm, on the other hand, was left at a considerable
distance to the east of this route. What is more, Robinson [2]
has shown that no coast route whatever could pass through
Tell-Hûm, the supposed Capernaum.

Sec. 66. **Bethsaida.**[3]—Of the place of this name, called also
Julias, which lay on the east side of the lake, we shall hereafter have to speak, sec. 71. Here we have only to do with
the Bethsaida on this side. That a place of this name lay
upon the western shore, is evident from John xii. 21, where
it is said that Philip was of Bethsaida of Galilee, for Galilee
nowhere extended to the east side of Jordan or of the lake.
But the same Philip was, according to John i. 45, of Bethsaïda,
the city of Andrew and Peter. The place was situated, as
the name itself, which signifies *house of fish*, would lead us to
conjecture, near to the lake,[4] and not far from Capernaum.[5]

[1] Isa. viii. 23–ix. 1 [ix. 1, A. V.].   [2] *Palestine*, iii. 346 ff.

[3] [Written in Matthew and Mark, Βηθσαϊδάν.]

[4] Matt. iv. 18.   [5] Matt. viii. 14 ; cf. vers. 5, 18.

The Lord pronounced the woes upon Bethsaïda no less than upon Capernaum and Chorazin.[1] The geographical hints of the Evangelists with regard to it are too indefinite for determining its position from them, and the name is not found in any other writings, either sacred or profane. The attempt to determine the position of this place can be ventured on only if a trace of the name has been preserved to the present day. Seetzen,[2] in crossing from the district of Jolan, which lies to the east of the lake and the Upper Jordan, to the western shore, at a ford of the Jordan above the lake, came upon the ruins of a Khân Bâtszaida, in the vicinity of a rocky limestone mountain. On the shore was a path or bridle road cut in the rock. The Khân lies six miles from Tabarîye, at the northern opening of the plain of Tabarîye (El-Ghuweir), near to a brook. And he in fact marks upon his map *Bâtszaida* at the north-east corner of the El-Ghuweir, where Robinson places the Khân Minyeh. After Seetzen, no other traveller has heard this name ; but we are not on that account justified in charging this trustworthy investigator with an error. It is well known that since the time of Jesus the population of the western shore of the lake has become entirely changed ; we cannot, therefore, feel surprise that the present inhabitants have lost many of the names, and have no longer any knowledge of Capernaum, Gennesareth, Bethsaïda, etc. It is very different with the wild, independent mountain tribes of the Jolan, who, unchanged, have braved the centuries. Traditions must there have been preserved which on the western side have disappeared. The more recent travellers have all derived their accounts of the Galilean lake district from people about Tiberias or El-Ghuweir ; Seetzen alone had a Bedouin of Jolan as a guide, and from him he learnt the name of Khân Bâtszaida, which therefore appears to us perfectly well attested.

Sec. 67. **Chorazin.**—The place is mentioned only Matt. xi. 21 and Luke x. 13, where the Lord pronounces the woe upon Chorazin, Bethsaïda, and Capernaum, because these towns, notwithstanding the miraculous works (δυνάμεις) wrought in

---

[1] Matt. xi. 21-24 ; Luke x. 13-15.

[2] *Reisen*, i. 344 ; Zach, *Correspond.* xviii. 348 ; Ritter, ii. p. 270.

them, had not repented. The connection with Bethsaïda and
Capernaum gives no nearer direction as to the position of the
place than the hint that it is to be sought in the neighbourhood of the Sea of Gennesareth. The books of Jewish
tradition several times speak of it. In *Bab. Menachoth*[1] it is
said that the place produced wheat of the second quality ; it
is there called Chorazaim, כרויים. In *Jerus. Baba-Bathra*, fol.
15. 1, it is stated that the flocks were driven from Judah
even as far as *Chorasin in Naphtali.* Here the name is
written חורשׁין. Northwards from Tell-Hûm there is found,
according to Van de Velde, upon the rising ground, the ruins
of a town, Bîr Kerâzeh, in which name Chorazin is to be
recognised. According to Eusebius, in the *Onomasticon,*
Χωραζεῖν was a little town of Galilee, ιβ′, *i.e.* 12 miles,
distant from Capernaum. When Jerome has, in his translation of the *Onomasticon,* instead of ιβ′, only II. *Millia*, there
is manifestly an error of the copyist in the question, owing
to which the sign X has been left out in the number xii.
The distance of 12 miles (11 miles English) corresponds
exactly to that from the Ain Mudawarah, the true Capernaum,
to Bîr Kerâzeh.

Sec. 67*b.* It has already been observed that at Khân
Minyeh, or Khân Bâtszaida, the road leaves the lake side and
passes northward upon the mountains, because at this point
the mountain approaches so near to the lake that there is no
longer any room left for it on the shore. Farther north,
where the coast of the lake bends round from west to east,
there opens up again a narrow strip of coast, on the margin
of which lie the oft-mentioned ruins of *Tell-Hûm.* Reland,
Von Raumer, and others, have thought it was to be identified
with the ancient Capernaum. We have above given the
reasons which lead us to reject this opinion. De Saulcy, on
the other hand, thinks Tell-Hûm is Bethsaïda-Julias. The
untenable character of this hypothesis will be made manifest
hereafter, sec. 71. To what ancient town, then, do these
ruins correspond ? Everything seems to us to plead in favour
of the ancient *Thella,* Θελλᾶ, of which Josephus says[2] that

---

[1] Ugolini, *Thes.* xv. p. 392.
[2] Josephus, *de Bello*, iii. 3, sec. 1.

it is near to the Jordan, and marks on one (the eastern) side the length of Upper Galilee, which extends from north to south, beginning in the north at Meroth, to end in the south at Thella. Evidently Tell-Hûm fulfils the condition not merely as regards position, but also as regards the form of the name. As a preliminary remark, we observe that the name is not always written Tell-Hûm; several travellers write it Tell Hunn, or Tel-hhewn.[1] As is well known, *Tell* denotes a hill; now the ruins in question occupy no hill at all, but lie on the shore of the lake. We conclude therefrom that the syllable *Tel* belongs to the root of the name, which is to be written Tellum, Tellun, or Telhewn, from which the Greek form Θελλᾶ then arose. It is, indeed, quite possible, as we have already remarked, that even in the Byzantine period this place was mistaken for the lost Capernaum, and that the ruins of the churches built in pseudo-Capernaum still exist.

Sec. 68. **Judah of the Jordan.**—In Matt. xix. 1 we read : " Jesus departed from Galilee, and came into the confines of Judea beyond Jordan"—ἦλθεν εἰς τὰ ὅρια τῆς ᾿Ιουδαίας πέραν τοῦ ᾿Ιορδάνου. Beyond the Jordan there could be no confines of Judea, because the land to which this name properly belonged was cis-Jordanic. We have here, consequently, to do with a particular district, which bore the name " Judea beyond Jordan." This name we have already met with in sec. 64. According to Josh. xix. 3, Naphtali abutted on Zebulon towards the south, on Asher towards the west, and towards the east on Judah of the Jordan, יהודה הירדן. Since, then, the boundaries of Naphtali in Upper Galilee are known to us, the position of Judah of the Jordan can be open to no doubt. Naphtali had as its eastern boundary the Upper Jordan, the Lake of Gennesareth, and the Lower Jordan at its egress from the lake. Judah of the Jordan is consequently the Jolan, the ancient Gaulonitis ; and the New Testament Judea beyond Jordan is the same district.

But how came the name Judah of the Jordan to be applied to the district of Gaulonitis ? Reland says of this question : " Maximus et insolubilis fere nodus, qui plurimos interpretes

[1] De Saulcy, *Voy.* ii. 199 ff. ; Ritter, *Erdk.* xv. 337.

torsit." This difficult question Von Raumer[1] has most satisfactorily solved. We present here that which is essential in
his argument. According to Deut. iii. 13, 14, Moses gave to
the half tribe of Manasseh all Bashan and the whole tract of
Argob ; but Jair the son of Manasseh took the whole tract
of Argob, to the confines of Geshuri and Maachathi, and called
it after his own name, the " Bashan Havoth Jair " (Bashan of
the villages of Jair) unto this day.[2] What, then, was the
position of Argob and the villages of Jair ?   Jerome answers
in the *Onomasticon:* "Argob, Regis Og, regis Basan *super
Jordanem,*" and, " Avoth-Jair, qui locus nunc vocatur Golan."
The villages of Jair are consequently Gaulonitis, the present
Jolan.   Thus also Josephus[3] translates the expressions. Gilead
and Argob, used of the districts in 1 Kings iv. 13, by
" Galaaditis and Gaulanitis, as far as Lebanon."   The tract
of Argob was counted to Manasseh ; because, according to the
above-cited texts, its possessor was a " son of Manasseh."
But in what sense was he Manasseh's son ?   According to
1 Chron. ii. 3, 4, 21, 24, Judah was the father of Perez,
Perez of Hezron ; to Hezron, Segub was born (out of wedlock)
of the daughter of Machir, the father of Gilead.   Jair was
consequently, on his father's side, of the tribe of Judah ; on his
mother's side, of the tribe of Manasseh.   But since, according
to Num. xxxvi. 7, " every one shall keep himself to the
heritage of the tribe of his fathers," Clericus says justly :
Jair Manassita.   Hic *contra morem* in tribu materna mansit.
The ground of this exception to the rule was the illegitimate
birth of his father, Segub.   This latter was at first cut off
from the tribe of his fathers, but his descendants were afterwards legitimated and received into it again.   A similar
instance is afforded by Jephthah, Judg. xi. 1, 2, 7, 8.   So
long, then, as Jair was excluded from Judah on account
of his illegitimate descent, his land was reckoned part of
Manasseh ; after the legitimation of his family, he and his
land, the tract of Argob, *i.e.* Gaulonitis, were reckoned to
Judah, and this land obtained the name of Judah of the
Jordan.   And thus, too, the state of affairs continued to the

[1] *Palest.* p. 233 ff.   [2] Cf. Num. xxxii. 41 ; Josh. xiii. 29, 30.
[3] *Antiq.* viii. 2, sec. 3.

time of Jesus : for Josephus, *de Bello*, iii. 3, gives a description of the whole Holy Land, as consisting of Galilee,[1] Peræa,[2] Samaria,[3] and Judea, which last again was divided into eleven toparchies ;[4] but, besides these (κἀπὶ ταύταις), there belonged to Judea, Gaulonitis, Gamalitis, Batanæa, and Trachonitis, provinces which belonged too, at the same time, to Agrippa's kingdom. Here, then, Gaulonitis is expressly reckoned as belonging to Judea. Thus it is explained why the eastern boundary of Naphtali was called Judah of the Jordan, and afterwards Judea beyond Jordan. The southern boundary of this district is the Wady Fîk, separating it from Decapolis.

Sec. 69. **El-Batiheh.**—Wilson[5] makes the remark that he was much struck with the similarity of the three little plains on the shore of the Lake of Gennesareth : in the west, El-Ghuweir; in the south, Ard es-Semakh; in the north, El-Batîheh ; which entirely correspond to each other in point of form, soil, extent, and productions. El-Batîheh is a hollow, resembling that of the Ghuweir, but situated on the east side of the Jordan, at its point of influx into the lake. Robinson[6] says that this plain is skirted on the east by the mountains which enclose the lake, and on the north by similar mountains of considerable height, which, farther up, reach down to the Jordan. It is a perfect level, and a more fruitful strip of soil can hardly be conceived of. A striking similarity has often been observed between it and El-Ghuweir in point of form, climate, soil, and productions ; but the Batîheh seems rather to deserve the preference. This extraordinary fertility is to be ascribed not only to the rich black, loamy soil, but also to the abundance of water. No fewer than three perennial streams, besides the Jordan—the streams on the eastern side are almost all of them perennial—contribute to its irrigation. They are, taken in the order from south to north, Wady es - Sanâm, Wady ed - Dâlieh ["vine - valley"], and Wady es-Sufa. In this plain—the name of which Burckhardt writes Battykha—are to be found several of the localities mentioned

---

[1] iii. 3, secs. 1, 2.   [2] iii. 3, sec. 3.   [3] iii. 3, sec. 4.   [4] iii. 3, sec. 5.
[5] *Lands of the Bible*, ii. p. 150. [On the fertility of this plain, see Thomson, p. 361. Compare, on the beauty of the district, Tristram, p. 586.]
[6] *Palestine*, ii. 409–412 ; Ritter, ii. 231, 232.

in the Gospel narratives, among which Bethania beyond Jordan and Bethsaida-Julias are particularly distinguished.

Sec. 70. **Bethania beyond Jordan.**—In John i. 28, the place where John baptized, and where Jesus was pointed out by him as the Messiah, is called Bethany beyond Jordan, $B\eta\theta\alpha\nu\ell\alpha$ $\pi\epsilon\rho\alpha\nu$ $\tau\sigma\hat{\nu}$ 'Ιορδάνου. For that this is the original reading, is now pretty generally acknowledged.[1] Origen instituted inquiries as to the place and position, and came to the conclusion that there was no Bethania on the eastern bank of the Jordan, but there was a Bethabara ; through him the reading $B\eta\theta\alpha\beta\alpha\rho\acute{\alpha}$ was introduced into the MSS. Origen failed to discover it, because, misled by tradition, he sought the scene of John's baptism on the left bank of the *Lower* Jordan. When Seetzen[2] was returning from Fìk, before passing the ford of the Jordan in order to reach the western bank, he came to the village Tellanîje.[3] This place, at which aloes were growing, had a beautiful situation ; the lovely region through which his line of march lay was marked by a dark loamy soil, and intersected between Tellanihje and the Jordan by several brooks. From the Jacob's Bridge, he says,[4] to a point westward from Tellanihje, the Jordan flows through a gorge between basalt mountains. This description corresponds so perfectly with that which Robinson[5] tells us as to the site of Et-Tell, that no doubt can exist as to the identity of Et-Tell and Tellanihje ; the more so, since the maps of both travellers fully correspond on this point. Et-Tell is, says Robinson, the greatest of all the ruins of this plain El-Batîheh. The Tell stretches from the foot of the northern

---

[1] [$B\eta\theta\alpha\nu\ell\alpha$ may also be regarded with a very high degree of probability as the true reading of Mark viii. 22, as pointed out by Ewald (*Götting. gelehrte Anzeigen*, 3d March 1869). It has the support of Codex D and the Italic and Gothic versions, and can hardly have originated in an oversight. In ver. 23, Mark calls $B\eta\theta\alpha\nu\ell\alpha$ a κώμη.]

[2] *Reisen*, i. p. 343.

[3] Written also Tellanihje ; cf. Zach, *Correspond.* xviii. p. 348.

[4] *Reisen*, i. p. 342. [On the *Jacob's Bridge* itself, compare Ritter, ii. 174, 228 ; Thomson, p. 260. The latter says : " Thence it (the Jordan) commences its headlong race over basaltic rocks down to the Lake of Tiberias, a distance of about six miles, and the distance (? plunge), according to my aneroid, is 1050 feet." The Jordan is easily forded at the Tell. Robinson, ii. p. 413. Thomson extends the name *Tellaiya* to the whole valley, p. 366.]

[5] ii. p. 414.

mountain southwards, near to the point at which the Jordan emerges from the mountain. The ruins cover a great part of the same, and are of wide extent ; but consist, so far as could be observed, entirely of unhewn volcanic stones, without any distinct trace of architecture. Robinson and his companions, who recognised the identity of this place with the Tellanihje of Seetzen, could not learn that it had any other name than Et-Tell. This, however, proves nothing against the correctness of Seetzen's information, since Pococke also[1] calls the place Telouy, where we have to read *Telony*. Seetzen had, as has already been observed, sec. 66, a Gaulonitic Bedouin as a guide, whilst Robinson's companions conversed only with the Gwàrineh, who had not long before immigrated from Egypt. Among the primitive occupants of the Jolan alone is a genuine tradition regarding the environs of the Sea of Gennesareth to be looked for. Seetzen drew from the right source. The information he gives us is the more valuable, because he had no theory to support by means of the name he had discovered, and thus was not likely by incautious questioning to call forth an erroneous answer. He, like Robinson, mistook the place for Bethsaida-Julias. The Arabs often substitute the name Tell, hill, for the ancient Beth ; Tell Anihje is Beth Anihje, or Bethania, the place beyond the Jordan where John was baptizing; it lies near the ford of the Jordan, thus complying with the conditions of our text; it is, moreover, the only possible place on the farther shore whence Jesus could reach Cana of Galilee in one day.[2]   In Matt. xix. 1 it is said, Jesus departed from Galilee, and entered the confines of Judea beyond Jordan. In the parallel passage, John x. 40, it is said : " And Jesus went away again beyond Jordan, into the place where John at first was baptizing." Now John was first baptizing at Bethania beyond Jordan—the place lay, consequently, on the farther side of Jordan, *i.e.* in the Jolan, where in reality Tellanihje lies. With regard to the accuracy of our conclusion respecting the site, there can therefore be no doubt.

Sec. 71. **Bethsaida-Julias.**—Josephus[3] relates that the tetrarch Philip had, not long after A.D. 6, built Paneas at the

---

[1] Pococke, ii. p. 106.   [2] John i. 44, ii. 1.   [3] *Antiq.* xviii. 2, sec. 1.

sources of the Jordan, and called it *Cæsarea ;* that he had,
moreover, at the same time raised Bethsaïda, on the Sea of
Gennesareth, formerly a village, to the rank of a city, provided it with many inhabitants and much grandeur, and
conferred upon it the name of the daughter of Cæsar, *Julia.*
According to *de Bello,* ii. 9, sec. 1, the town of Julias was in
Lower Gaulonitis.   On passing Julias—μετὰ πόλιν 'Ιουλιάδα[1]
—the Jordan divides in its course the Sea of Gennesareth
into two equal parts.   Julias marked the western boundary
of the kingdom of Agrippa, as Arpha did its eastern.[2]   That
this town was situated on the shore of the Sea of Gennesareth
is testified also by Pliny :[3] Jordanis amnis . . . in lacum se
fundit, quem plures Genesaram vocant, xvi. m. passuum longi-
tudinis, vi. m. latitudinis, amœnis circumseptum oppidis : ab
oriente Juliade et Hippo, a meridie Tarichæa, ab occidente
Tiberiade.   That no doubt may yet remain as to the trans-
Jordanic locality of this place, we adduce also the testimony
of Jerome, who says :[4] Philippus . . . ex nomine filiæ ejus
(Cæsaris) *Juliadem trans Jordanem* exstruxit.   If, then, Ptolemy[5]
enumerates Julias among the cities of Galilee, this representation must be regarded as erroneous.   Yet upon this evidence
alone H. de Saulcy proceeds to deny the existence of a town
Julias on the east side of the Jordan, and consequently also
to identify a trans-Jordanic Bethsaïda-Julias with Tell-Hûm.[6]
This hypothesis is contrary to all the texts.   The trans-
Jordanic, Gaulonitic Bethsaïda is often mentioned in the New
Testament, especially in the account of the feeding of the five
thousand.   What, then, was the position of this place ?   The
great majority of the geographers, Pococke, Von Raumer,
Robinson, and others, place Julias at Et-Tell.   We have
already seen that these ruins rather mark the site of Bethania
beyond Jordan.   This position, moreover, is in contradiction
with the above-mentioned authorities ; for Et-Tell does not
lie, as Pliny says of Julias, at the *eastern side of the lake,*
neither does it lie, as Josephus tells us of Bethsaïda, imme-

---

[1] *De Bello,* iii. 10, sec. 7.   [2] *De Bello,* iii. 3, sec. 5.   [3] *H. N.* v. 15.
[4] *Ad Matth.* xvi.   [5] Tab. iv. Asiæ.

[6] [For an ingenious but inconclusive argument in favour of the identity of
Bethsaïda-Julias with Bethsaïda of Galilee, cf. Thomson, *The Land and the
Book,* pp. 373, 374.]

diately at the point of the influx of the Jordan into the lake.
Seetzen places on his map a castle of Szeida, " *Schloss Szeida*,"
to the south-east of the mouth of the Jordan, at about the
point where other maps have Aradsh or Mesadijeh. We have
above indicated why we give the preference to the discoveries
of Seetzen, on account of the better knowledge of his Gaulonitic
guide. We regard " Schloss Szeida " as authentic, the more
so because Seetzen makes no use of his discovery, but connects
Bethsaïda-Julias with Tellanihje. Unfortunately, Seetzen's
text affords us no help here. Robinson had pitched his tent [1]
ten minutes' walk to the north of the mouth of the Jordan.
Below the tent, near to the lake, his companions crossed the
river—he himself being confined to his tent by sickness—
and reached in five minutes, in a direction S. 40° E., the
ruins of a village of moderate dimensions, called El-A'raj,
which consisted entirely of unhewn volcanic stones. The
only thing here observable belonging to antiquity was a small
sarcophagus of the same material. Proceeding in the same
direction along the coast, they came, in twenty minutes after
crossing the Jordan, upon Mes'adîyeh, a village in ruins.
These details show, and de Bertou's map confirms the fact,
that Robinson has placed Mes'adîyeh (which is in reality
about fifteen minutes' distance from the mouth of the Jordan)
much too far to the south. El-A'raj lies a little above the
mouth of the river, and Mesadiyeh — or, as it is written
by de Bertou, Maschadieh—opposite to the point at which
the Jordan enters the lake. This latter name, Mesadîyeh,
Mashadieh, is related to *Szaida*, and seems to be only a
corruption of this last. This place we take to be *Bethsaida-
Julias*. On the lake, the northern part of which abounds
with fish, and not on the Jordan, must the " House of Fish "
be looked for. Mesadiyeh, or Seetzen's *Szaida*, lies on the
east side of the lake ; [2] in accordance with the expression of
Josephus, " the Jordan, after (passing) Julias, cleaves the lake
of Gennesareth in the midst." [3]   A camp pitched in the

[1] [On the western bank of the Jordan.] *Palestine*, ii. 410.

[2] [Where Thomson, too, knows of a *Khirbet Saida* (" Ruins of Saida "), but
not of a *Beit Saida ; Land and Book*, p. 366.]

[3] *De Bello*, iii. 10, sec. 7 ; μετὰ πόλιν Ἰουλιάδα διικτέμνει (ὁ Ἰορδάνης) τὴν Γιννησὰρ
μίσην.

vicinity of the Jordan might very well be only a stadium distant from this Julias.[1] It may, indeed, seem surprising that of such a city only insignificant ruins should have remained. Yet we must observe that Robinson's companions are the only travellers who have explored these ruins ; how superficially these explorations were conducted, is evident from the fact that they traversed El-Batîheh in all directions within the space of three hours without anywhere making a stay. It is reserved to future travellers more thoroughly to examine this region, of so great importance in connection with the study of New Testament history.

Sec. 72. **Decapolis.**—This region is mentioned Matt. iv. 25 ; Mark v. 20, vii. 31. Decapolis was a confederacy of Gentile cities existing on Israelitish soil. On the nature of their mutual connection, which in any case was a loose one, we are left in uncertainty ; and just as little is it possible to determine with certainty what towns belonged to this league, since the various ancient geographers differ to some extent in regard to their names. Their number was probably not always the same, and at any rate not always confined to ten. Pliny says[2] that the names of the single towns of the Decapolis were differently given, but that according to the general view the following towns belonged to it : Damascus, Philadelphia, Raphana, Scythopolis, Gadara on the Hieromax, Hippos, Dion, Pella, abounding in water, Gelasa, Canatha. Ptolemy enumerates as the cities of the Syrian Decapolis[3] the following : Abila Lysanion, Saana, Ina, *Damascus*, Samulis, Abida, *Hippos*, Capitolias, *Gadara*, Adra, *Scythopolis*, *Gerasa*, *Pella*, *Dion*, Gadora, *Philadelphia*, *Kanatha*. Josephus nowhere gives an enumeration of the towns belonging to the Decapolis ; he mentions, however, single ones as belonging to this league— Scythopolis,[4] Philadelphia,[5] Gadara, and Hippos.[6] Some of the towns mentioned lie scattered about, or forming little separate groups, such as Abila, Damascus, Canatha ; others are still undiscovered, as Saana, Ina, Samulis. The rest form

---

[1] Josephus, *Vita*, 72.   *H. N.* v. 16.

[3] Κοίλης Συρίας Δεκαπόλεως πόλεις, v. 15 ; Tab. iv. Asiæ ; cf. Reland, *Palæst.* p. 456.

[4] *De Bello*, iii. 9, sec. 7.   [5] *Ibid.* iii. 18, sec. 1.   [6] *Vita*, 65. 74.

a large connected group, spread on both banks of the Hieromax, and forming the region of the Decapolis proper. These are Scythopolis, Hippos, Gadara, Adra, Raphana, Capitolias, Pella, Dion, Gerasa, and Philadelphia, which will now further occupy us.

(*a*) *Scythopolis*, the only one of the Decapolitan towns which lies to the west of the Jordan. In the Old Testament it is called Bethshan,[1] now Beisan or Bîsan, and lies about 12 miles south from Tiberias, and 6 miles west of the Jordan, in the Ghôr. Its domain abutted on that of Gadara and of Hippos.[2]

(*b*) *Hippos*, called by the Talmudists Susitha. It was situated beyond Jordan,[3] 30 stadia from Tiberias,[4] near to Apheka, the Fîk of the present day.[5] This Fîk lies opposite Tiberias, upon the high ground, at the upper end of the Wady Fîk. About a couple of miles to the west of this place is El-Hoesnn,[6] which word signifies " Horse." Hippos and Susitha have the same meaning, from which *we* infer the identity of place. Between El-Hoesnn and the southern extremity of the lake, Burckhardt indicates a ruin, Tell-Hûn.[7] In Ritter, the place is called Kalaat El-Husn.[8] This coincidence between Susitha and El-Husn or Hun is too striking for us to be able to overlook it. In Gen. xiv. 5 it is said : " There came Cadorlaomer and the kings that were with him, and smote the Rephaïm at Ashteroth-Karnaim, and the *Susim* at *Ham*." Ashteroth lay to the north of the Hieromax, and in the same tract of ground wo must look for Susim. In it we really find Susitha, which reminds of Susim, and Hun, which reminds of Ham—the more so since in the Targum Ham, הם, is always represented by Hun, הון. The fact that Susim is written זוזים, while Susitha is written סוסיתא, proves nothing against the identity, since the orthography of the rabbis is arbitrary and without fixed rules. Thus in *Jerus. Demai*, fol. 22. 4, in the description of the tithe-boundaries there stands סוסיתה, and in the repetition of this description in

---

[1] Judg. i. 27 (LXX.) ; Judith iii. 11 ; Josephus, *Antiq.* xii. 8, sec. 5.
[2] Josephus, *Vita*, 9. [3] *Vita*, 31. [4] *Vita*, 65.
[5] *Onomasticon*, art. " Apheca." [6] Burckhardt, p. 437.
[7] Burckhardt, p. 437. [8] Ritter, ii. 281.

Tosaphtha Shibiith[1] there stands ציצ׳תה. According to *Jerus. Shibiith*, fol. 36. 3, Susitha was the land of Tob, Judg. xi. 3.

(c) *Gadara*, the chief town of the land of the Gadarenes—Γαδαρηνῶν, of whom mention is made in Matt. viii. 28. This town was situated, according to Pliny, on the Hieromax.[2] It belonged to Decapolis, and was the metropolis of Peræa.[3] Its distance was 60 stades from Tiberias,[4] and 16 miles from Scythopolis.[5] Answering pretty nearly to these points in the description, and therefore generally taken for Gadara, are the important ruins of Mkès,[6] or Om-keis,[7] [or Um-Keis].[8] The place lies on a mountain, on the southern side of the Mandhûr, the Hieromax of the Greeks, the Jarmuk of the Talmudists. The valley of this river is, at Um-Keis, an immense ravine, in which are to be found the celebrated thermal springs of Gadara. According to Seetzen, Um-Keis is separated by the Wady El-Arab from an adjacent ridge, on which lies the great inhabited cave of Jedur. This name is the modern form of Godor, or Gadara.

(d) *Adraa*, the ancient Edrei, the capital of the kingdom of Bashan,[9] now called Draa or Derâ, on the Upper Mandhûr.[10] According to the *Tab. Peuting.*, Adraa is distant from Bostra 24 miles ; from Capitolias, 16 miles ; from Gadara, 32 miles. In the *Onomasticon* the distance from Bostra is given as 25 miles. These distances show that the position of this place on Robinson's and Van de Velde's maps is incorrectly given.

(e) *Raphana.*—This town, reckoned by Pliny as belonging to the Decapolis, is certainly the Raphon mentioned 1 Macc. v. Timotheus, it is there said, ver. 37, encamped against Raphon,

---

[1] Ugolini, *Thes.* xx. p. 223.   [2] Gadara, Hieromace præfluente, v. 16.

[3] Josephus, *de Bello*, iv. 7, sec. 3. [It was situated "above [the Lower] Jordan, opposite Scythopolis and Tiberias, and to the east of them " (Eusebius, *Onomasticon*). Gadara was, as is indicated by the etymology of the name (נדרה), a fortified place. Cf. Josephus, *Antiq.* xiii. 13, sec. 3. It was rendered yet stronger by its position, 13, sec. 5. This town would seem, from Matt. viii. 28, to have given its name to all the inhabitants of the district as far north as the Wady Semakh.—The name *Jedur* is still given to a large part of the Haurân territory east of Um Keis, and upon the north bank of the Mandhûr. Ritter, *Palestine*, ii. 302.]

[4] *Vita*, 65. According to *Tab. Peuting.* 16 miles [*i.e.* by land].

[5] *Itiner. hieros.*   [6] Seetzen, i. p. 368.   [7] Burckhardt, p. 426.

[8] Thomson, *The Land and the Book*, pp. 376-378.

[9] Num. xxi. 33 ; Deut. i. 4, iii. 10 ; Josh. xii. 4.   [10] Burckhardt, p. 385.

beyond the brook, *i.e.* the Mandhûr, because the writer had
before (ver. 36) been speaking of Bosor, *i.e.* Bostra. Judas
passed over the brook and defeated the Gentiles, who were
commanded by Timotheus. These fled to the temple of
Karnaïm. The Jews burned the temple, with all that were
in it (vers. 42–44). Raphon, or Raphana, was thus in the
vicinity of Karnaïm. Now, Eusebius says in the *Onomasticon*:
" Astaroth, an ancient town of Og, king in Basan, in which
the giants (Rephaim) dwelt. It lies 6 miles from Adar
(Edrei), which again is 25 miles from Bostra ; farther up lies
Astaroth Karnaïm." Of Ashtaroth Karnaïm he says : " The
land of the giants, whom Kador-Laomer defeated. To this
day there are two villages of this name in Batanæa and
Batulua (?), distant 9 miles from each other, between Adra and
Abila." Now, 6 miles from Adra is the present *Mezarib*, and
distant 9 miles from this is *Tel-Ashtereh*. These two places
are consequently the two Ashteroth—towns of the giants, *i.e.*
of the Rephaim—of which one acquired the name of Raphon,
after all only a later form of Rephaim.[1] This name is, however, seen to be preserved in Mezarib, when written Mezar-
Rib or Rif, a name signifying " the sepulchre of the Rephaim."

(*f*) *Capitolias.*—This town was situated, according to the
Tab. Peuting., midway between Adraa and Gadara, and distant
from each of these towns 16 miles. This distance of 16
miles from Capitolias to Adraa and Gadara is twice repeated
in the *Itiner. Antonini*. Now, at the distance indicated
between these two towns lie the ruins of Bêt er-Râs ; thus it
is shown on Seetzen's map and in his text.[2] This place must
be Capitolias, the more so since its present name signifies
Domus Capitis. Von Raumer,[3] misled by the erroneous supposition that the ancient road from Damascus to Gadara
crosses the Mandhûr near to its egress from the mountain,
where it forms an impassable ravine, places Capitolias at
Tseil, near to Nava ; because, according to the *Itin. Antonini*,
the road from Damascus had the following course : From
Damascus to Ære, 32 miles ; thence to Neve, 30 miles ;
Neve to Capitolias, 36 miles ; thence to Gadara, 16 miles.
But he is obliged—and this in itself is fatal to his hypothesis

[1] רפאים, Gen. xiv. 5.   [2] Seetzen, i. 371.   [3] *Palest.* 2

—to change the distance of 36 miles there given, between Neve and Capitolias, into 6 miles. The road from Damascus to Gadara, on the contrary, crossed the Mandhûr near Adraa, and then struck off in a westerly direction to Gadara, along the southern bank of the Mandhûr. On this southern side, consequently, lay Capitolias also.[1]

(g) *Philadelphia.*—This is the Greek name of Rabbath-Ammon, Deut. iii. 11 ; 2 Sam. xi. 14, xii. 31. It is now called Amman, and possesses magnificent ruins.[2] It is situated on the Nahr 'Ammân, *i.e.* the Upper Jabbok.

(h) *Gerasa.*—In the Old Testament this name does not occur. In the present day the place is still called Jerash. It lies 40 miles north of Ammon, and contains ruins of considerable extent. Some MSS. of Matt. viii. 28, Mark v. 1, Luke viii. 26, have Γερασηνῶν—Gerasenes, for Gadarenes or Gergesenes, as other MSS. have it. If this is the correct reading [as it is, so far as Luke's Gospel is concerned, the best supported one], then the term Gerasenes must be taken in the general sense of " inhabitants of the Decapolis." It is possible that, at the time of Christ, Gerasa was the metropolis of Decapolis [situated about 12 miles north of the Lower Jabbok]. Gerasa itself is upwards of 50 miles distant from the lake whose shore is the scene of the events narrated in the passages cited from the Gospels.[3] [The reading *Gergesenes* is adopted by Alford in the text of Mark. According to Josephus, *Antiq.* i. 6, sec. 2, the *name* only of the ancient Γεργεσαῖοι of Scripture (Gen. xv. 21 ; Deut. vii. 1 ; Josh. xxiv. 11, LXX.) existed in his day.[4] Origen, however, asserts

---

[1] The *Tabula Peutingeriana* knows no direct route from Damascus to Gadara, but traces that from Damascus to Capitolias. The *Itinerarium Antonini* has : Damascus, 32 m. ; Aere, 30 m. ; Neve, 36 m. ; Capitoliade, 16 m.—Gadara. The Roman route thus passed to the east. The descent from Fîk into the gorge of the Hieromax was never a *via Romana*.

[2] [For a plan of these ruins, cf. Bædecker, p. 319 ; for those of Jerash, p. 408. For a description of the ruins of 'Ammân, see Tristram, pp. 550–554 ; for a description of those of Jerash, pp. 565, 566.]

[3] [Since the above was written, the author has come to identify the Kersa visited by Dr. Thomson with the Gerasa or Gergesa of the Gospels. It is opposite the plain of Gennesareth, and near the point at which the Wady es-Samakh enters the lake. Cf. *The Land and the Book*, pp. 377, 378.]

[4] Cf. Meyer on Matt. viii. 28.

there was an ancient town of that name still existing near the lake. This might be the Gerasa of Luke.]

(*i*) *Dion.*—Josephus relates that this city was captured by Alexander Jannæus,[1] and that the towns of Hippos, Scythopolis, Pella, and Dion were restored by Pompey to their original Gentile inhabitants.[2] Dion was proverbial for its unwholesome water.[3] In an epigram it reads :

> Νάμα τὸ Διηνὸν γλυκερὸν πότον, ἂν τὸ δὲ πίῃς
> Παύσῃ μὲν δίψης, εὐθὺ δὲ καὶ βιοτοῦ.

Dion's fountain yields a sweet draught ; but, when you drink it,
Quenches for ever the thirst, and soon the life with it.

Now Burckhardt, p. 399, copied at Suf, near Jerash (Gerasa), a fragment of an inscription found by him on a broken stone in the water at the fountain *Ain Keikebe*, which was as follows : *ΔΙΩΝΤΟΙΔΡ. ΑΝΕΤΤΕΡΙΑCΧ . . . ΓΕΤΕΙ ΥΜΟΥ.* These barbaric-Greek words are intended to say, *ΔΙΩΝ ΤΟ ΥΔΡον . . . ΑΝΕΤΤΕΡΙΑC ΓΕΤΕΙ ΩΜΟΥ.*— " The water (of) Dion delivers from old age, and gives you to drink at once (refreshment and death)."

Dion is thus to be recognised in Suf, a village lying four or five miles N.N.W. of Jerash ; and Ain Keikebe is Dion's poisonous spring.

(*k*) *Pella.*—This town is of importance for the Christian investigator ; not only because its position more nearly defined the territory of the Ten Tribes, but also because it was the place of refuge for the early Christian Church of Jerusalem, during the siege and after the destruction of the mother city. In the *Onomasticon* we read : Æmath, urbs quæ cecidit in sortem Ruben. Sed nunc Amathus villa dicitur trans Jordanem in XXImo lapide Pellæ ad meridiem. Amathus lay 21 miles south of Pella. Beyond Jordan there were two places which bore the name of Amath ; that is to say, the warm springs of Gadara, in the ravine of the Mandhûr; and a town of this name, which Josephus speaks of as the principal fortress beyond Jordan.[4] To this last correspond the ruins of Amata, two to

---

[1] Josephus, *Antiq.* xiii. 15, sec. 3. [2] *Ibid.* xiv. 4, sec. 4.
[3] ἧς ὕδωρ νοσερόν, Steph. Byz.
[4] *De Bello,* i. 4, sec. 2 ; *Antiq.* xiii. 1?, sec. 3 ; cf. xiv. 5, sec. 4 ; xvii. 10, sec. 6; *de Bello,* i. 8, sec. 5.

three miles north of the entrance of the Zerka or Jabbok into
the Ghôr. This place is the one intended in the passage
cited from the *Onomasticon;* for Pella, according to *de Bello,*
iii. 3, sec. 3, marked the northern boundary of Peræa. Now,
this province lay to the south of the Mandhûr. Pella could
not, consequently, be 21 miles north of the Amath in the
ravine of the Mandhûr. Ptolemy thus determines the position
of Pella : latitude $67\frac{2}{3}$, longitude $31\frac{2}{3}$. Scythopolis has,
according to the same geographer, a longitude of $67\frac{1}{3}$, and a
latitude of $31\frac{1}{2}$, $\frac{1}{3}$, $\frac{1}{12}$. The diagonal gives a distance of 30
miles from Scythopolis to Pella. If now we take a radius of
30 miles from Bîsan, and another of 21 miles from Amatha,
at the point at which they intersect each other, there will be
found on any good map—that of Raumer, for example—a
place *Erbad* or *Irbid.* Erbad, or a place near to it, is consequently Pella. It is further said in the *Onomasticon,* art.
" Asiroth :" " Jabis trans Jordanem . . . a civitate Pella 6
mill. distans." And, art. "Jabis": "Jabis Galaad . . . nunc
autem est vicus trans Jordanem in sexto milliario civitatis
Pella, *super montem,* euntibus Gerasam." Jabesh itself has
not yet been discovered ; but a Wady Jabes, 14 miles north
of Amata, still recalls to our mind the name of this town in
which Saul and Jonathan were buried. Since it was situated
" upon the mountain," it must necessarily be sought on the
upper eastern opening of the valley of this name. The objection that Jabesh was in that case too far distant from
Bethshan for all that is related, 1 Sam. xxxi. 3–13, to have
been accomplished in a night, is without foundation ; since,
according to the text, only the departure took place on that
night, and Josephus[1] characterizes this deed as the perilous
feat of specially strong and daring men. According to
Seetzen's map, Erbad is in reality situated about 6 miles
north of the upper eastern opening of the Jabesh valley, in
which we look for the town of this name. This lay upon the
route which united Pella with Gerasa. Robinson, Von Raumer,
Van de Velde, and others, believe they have discovered Pella
in Tabakat-Fuhil, five hours' distance northward from Amata.
But Tabakat-Fuhil is distant from Amata, not 21, but 14

[1] *Antiq.* vi. 14, sec. 8.

miles, and from Bethshan not 30, but 10 miles. Further, this place could never have formed the northern boundary of Peræa, if—as Josephus expressly asserts—Gadara, situated a few miles to the north of it, was the metropolis of Peræa. The said geographers have also forgotten to explain how a route passing from Fuhil to Gerasa would be continued over the ravines of the intervening wadys. Stephen of Byzantium says that Pella was formerly called Butis, Πέλλα . . . ἡ Βοῦτις λεγομένη. Now in the *Jerus. Aboda Zara*, mention is made of three celebrated market towns: Gaza, Acco, and Butneh, בוטנה. That this last place, however, is Butis-Pella, is placed beyond doubt by the following considerations:— Seetzen says[1] that the tract between the Mandhûr and the Wady Jabes is called El-Bothin, a name which agrees with Butneh and Butis, and one in which Irbid[2] or Erbad is to be recognised. He further says that the wady, on the edge of which lies Draa (Adraa), is called the Wady Middan. Now Middan signifies "market," or "fair." William of Tyre[3] describes an expedition of the Crusaders from Tiberias against Damascus. The army advanced through the Cavea Rob, and came upon the plain of Medan, a wide level tract, with an open prospect. This plain is intersected by the River Dan, which enters the Jordan between Tiberias and Scythopolis. This River Dan is evidently the Mandhûr; the name owes its origin to a false etymology adopted on the part of the Crusaders, inasmuch as they derived the name of the Wâdy Middan from Mé-Dan, "waters of Dan." We find, moreover, that the Wâdy Middan of Seetzen is represented by Van de Velde as Wâdy Dan. The plain of Medan corresponds to Seetzen's Bothin. The same William of Tyre afterwards describes a second expedition,[4] which set out from Tiberias, and penetrated through Cavea Rob, over the plain of Medan, as far as *Adratum* (Adraa, Edrei). There can thus no longer exist any doubt as to the position, because it lies between Tiberias and Edrei, on the river which flows into the Jordan between Tiberias and Scythopolis. Now, Sanutus says,[5] that in the

---

[1] Seetzen, i. 394.
[2] [Irbid is placed by Robinson at 32° 40′ N. and 36° E.]
[3] *Gesta Dei*, i. 843.   [4] *Ibid.* i. 895.   [5] *Gesta Dei*, ii. 247.

plain of Medan the Saracens yearly held a fair of particular magnificence. This perfectly answers to the requirements of the passage from the Talmud above adduced, and to the true etymology of the word Middan. But since he, too, like his predecessor William of Tyre, derived the word from Mé-Dan, and knew that the ancient Dan lay to the north of the Hûleh lake, he erroneously placed the scene of this fair of the Saracens upon the eastern shore of the Hûleh, where to the present day many maps, *e.g.* that of Raumer, indicate a plain of Midan, when William of Tyre ought surely to have taught them better. The market was held in El-Bothin, the Batueh of the Talmud, the Boutis-Pella of Steph. Byzantinus. If it is then a question of more nearly defining the position of Pella, it must, first of all, be observed that this name no longer exists. It is a known fact that most of the appellations bestowed by the Greeks and Romans upon towns in the East disappeared again, and gave place to the earlier names. Pella is a Macedonian name, of which we cannot expect to find a trace in the present day. If, however, we inquire in those regions for the name Butis, we are embarrassed by the too great plenty. Seetzen found in the neighbourhood of Irbid, in El-Bothin, a brook—Ain Beda—which flows in a deep valley, and forms many foaming waterfalls : also a village of Beda.[1] Now the name Irbid or Erbad seems to us to come from עִיר, city, and בַד or בַט ; so that the original name was עִיר־בַט, Ir-Bat = Boutis-Pella. Since Pliny speaks of *Pellam, aquis divitem,* an abundance of water must be shown to exist at Irbid. But it has been proved in the present day that the great aqueduct, Kanâtir-Fir'aun, was carried past Irbid ; it is possible also that the waters of Ain Beda, which now flow unused into the valley, at one time supplied this town. Buckingham found there a reservoir comparable to the pools of Solomon at Etam.[2]

---

[1] i. p. 383 ff.

[2] Ritter, *Erdk.* xv. 1064. [Bædecker's *Handbuch,* pp. 421, 423, places this reservoir on the route from Mezârib to Bozrah. "In the depression of the valley lies a great reservoir, of 160 paces in length, 65 in width, and about 6 metres [19½ feet] in depth. It is supplied by an aqueduct coming from the north, which is called *Kanâtir Fir'aun* (Pharaoh's arches). The *Kanâtir Fir'aun* are a gigantic work. This channel has a length of 60 miles ; all inequalities in the

(*l*) The region of Decapolis, mentioned in the New Testament, thus lay on both sides of the Mandhûr.   It abutted on the Lake of Gennesareth, from the Wady-Semakh—which formed the southern boundary of Gaulonitis, or Judah of the Jordan—to the southern end of the lake.

Sec. 73. **Magadan.**—The miraculous feeding of the four thousand took place beyond the Sea of Galilee.[1]   After working this miracle, Jesus entered the ship and departed into the confines of Magadan.[2]   The Received Text has, instead of this name, that of Magdala.   The reading Magadan, however, is proved to be the true one; because it is found in the *Codex Sinaiticus*, B *Vaticanus*, D *Cantabrigiensis*, and in the ancient translations, namely, the *Peshito*, *Syriaca Hieros.*, *Persica*, etc.   It is easily explicable how, in place of the unknown name Magadan, the well-known name Magdala was introduced into the manuscripts by conjecture; but it would be inexplicable how this well-known name should be replaced by an unknown one.   Magadan is consequently the correct reading.   Van de Velde indicates upon his map a Wady Madshîdeh, to the west of Bîsan,—the ancient Scythopolis,—which runs down from the south side of Mount Gilboa, the present Jebel Fakûa, into the Ghôr.   On the lower part of this wady, Schultz[3] found considerable ruins of black basalt rock, bearing the name of Mudshiddaah, or, as Van de Velde writes it, Khân Madshîdeh.   This name is clearly one with Magadan, or *Magado*, as it is given in the Peshito.   The region of Magadan, τὰ ὅρια Μαγαδάν, is thus the western domain of Scythopolis, or the "region of the Ten Cities," on this side Jordan.   Christ had withdrawn from the Pharisees—first into the Phœnician territory, then into the trans-Jordanic land near Julias, where the second miraculous feeding of the multitude had taken place.   Thence He

---

ground being spanned over by arches." On the abundance of water in the neighbourhood, cf. Ritter, ii. p. 300.]

[1] Matt. xv. 29.   [2] εἰς τὰ ὅρια Μαγαδάν, Matt. xv. 39.

[3] Ritter, ii. 337. [Robinson says, iii. 314 : "About two hours south of Beisân, at the foot of the same mountains (*sc.* Gilboa), is also a fountain and the ruin of *Mujedda'.*" Robinson supposes the *Wady Mujedda'* of Schultz to be probably another name for the *Wady Kûbôsh.* Otherwise it would be only a small wady. Thomson places on his map a Wady Mujeidah immediately to the south of Beisân.]

returned, not almost into the midst of His enemies, to Magdala, but into the Scythopolitan domain, to Magadan.[1]

Sec. 74. **Dalmanutha.**—Where Matthew says that Jesus went into the confines of Magadan, Mark viii. 10 has: He went into the region of Dalmanutha — ἦλθεν εἰς τὰ μέρη Δαλμανουθά. Some 12 miles to the south of the Sea of Gennesareth, on the eastern bank of the Jordan, lies a village, the name of which Lynch writes Delhemiyeh,[2] as it is also given on Robinson's and Van de Velde's maps. If we strike off from the root of the name Dalmanutha the Aramæan termination—ordinarily תא, but also often נה, or lengthened: נתא-, ניתא-, נותא-—there remains as the name itself, Dalma, which is one with Delamiyeh. This place, too, like Magadan, lies in the Decapolitan Ghôr. Since, then, Matthew does not say that Jesus repaired to the town Magadan, but into the district belonging to it; and Mark, in like manner, does not speak of the township, but of the *region* of Dalmanutha, as the place of retreat of Jesus,—these Evangelists are not in contradiction with each other; the less so, since Jesus there too, as was His wont elsewhere, did not remain domiciled in one place, but journeyed throughout the region. They tell us He repaired to the Decapolitan Ghôr; where He remained, now on this side of the Jordan, now on that, near Mudshîdeh and near Delamîyeh.

[1] Matt. xv. 21, 29, 39.

[2] Ritter, ii. 296. [Robinson, ii. 387, who did not visit it, places Delhemîyeh about half a mile above the mouth of the Mandhûr. So Baedecker, 353, who calls it Delhabîye. At this point it would be only four or five miles from the lake.]

DIVISION IV.

THE FIRST YEAR OF THE PUBLIC MINISTRY OF CHRIST: FROM THE
BEGINNING OF HIS MINISTRY TO THE DEATH OF JOHN THE
BAPTIST, A.U.C. 781, A.D. 28.

SEC. 75. **Synopsis of the Four Gospels.**—Before we enter on
the attempt to present chronologically and geographically the
life and labours of Jesus Christ in time and space, we must
give some explanation as to the mutual relationship of the
sources whence we have to draw the historical material.

The Gospel of Mark appears to us by no means to be, as
has long been asserted, a meagre epitome drawn from the first
and third Gospels; but an original work, composed by Mark
under the personal oversight of the Apostle Peter, and describing the labours of Christ during the last year of His
life, so far as Peter was personally an eye-witness thereof.
It is an error fatal to the right understanding of the Gospel
history, to take one's start from the presupposition that all
the Apostles were wont, during the whole period of the public
ministry of Christ, from beginning to end, constantly and
everywhere to accompany the Lord.   This is true, with important exceptions, only of the last year, but by no means
of the earlier period.   Each of the Apostles returned, after an
often brief intercourse with Jesus, again to his town and to
his social calling.   Peter, in particular, followed the Lord
when He was in Galilee, and remained in Bethsaida when
Jesus repaired to Judea; for to Jerusalem he accompanied
Him only at the last Passover.   Since, then, he related to his
companion and assistant, Mark, only that which he had seen
and heard, the scene of the events narrated by this Evangelist
must necessarily be confined to Galilee.   So soon as we
regard the Gospel of Mark as an original work, we can explain

its relation to the Gospel of Matthew only on the supposition
that the author of this latter took Mark's Gospel as the basis
and framework within which to group his own collection of
the discourses of Jesus.   This might well be the case, since
Matthew was in the same position with Peter, and like him,
followed Jesus only in Galilee.   Luke, who wrote later, would
take these two previous works, which rested on apostolic
authority, as the basis of his own history ; but at the same
time would enlarge, where it was necessary, the framework too
narrow for the material he had collected.   The Apostle John,
on the other hand, was of Jerusalem, where he was known,
and had his own house ;[1] he first became acquainted with the
Saviour at the Sea of Gennesareth, then accompanied Him to
Jerusalem, and there remained and dwelt, accompanying Jesus
only when He was in Judea.   Thus is the fact perfectly explained, that the narratives of this Evangelist—who relates
only what he has himself seen and heard—have almost exclusively Judea as their scene.   *The life of Christ is nothing
better than one-sided and fragmentary, so long as we confine
ourselves either to the Synoptics or to John.   We obtain a har-
monious whole, only when we allow these sources to blend the one
with the other.*   The great thing is to find the certain points
of connection between them.   The Four Evangelists agree in
making the public ministry of Christ begin from the baptism
of John.   Then each one goes his way, until all meet together
again in the account—common to them all—of the miraculous
feeding of the five thousand.   From this point they deviate
from each other again, until they all meet once more in the
history of the Lord's passion, which all record in common.
These points at which the Four Evangelists meet, designate at
the same time important chronological epochs in the life of
Jesus.   From John[2] we learn that the Lord's entry on His public ministry took place shortly before a Passover; and, from the
same Evangelist,[3] that the feeding of the five thousand likewise
took place at the time of Passover.   From this it follows that
the events occurring between the baptism and the feeding of the
five thousand occupy a year ; and that another year separates
this miraculous feeding from the crucifixion of the Lord.

[1] John xviii. 15, xix. 27.   [2] John ii. 13.   [3] John vi. 4.

The present chapter is devoted to the first year of the public ministry of Christ. As regards the material to be arranged within this year, the history of John the Baptist affords us some valuable data from which to form a synoptical view. All that the two first Gospels relate of Jesus after the Temptation — all, consequently, that follows Matt. iv. 12, Mark i. 14—took place after the imprisonment of the Baptist ; and from Matt. xiv. 1, Mark vi. 16 onwards, events are referred to which took place after the execution of the Baptist. John, again, begins his account earlier. In John iii. 22–iv. 1, the Baptist was still at liberty ; in John v. 35, 36, on the other hand, the Lord speaks of him as one who " was," whose labour was brought to a close, either by his imprisonment or by his untimely death. From this it follows that all that is related in John previous to the events of John v. 1, must be inserted before Matt. xiv. 1 and Mark vi. 16. In the Gospel of Luke, the whole history of the Baptist is completed in chap. iii. 1–22. No mention, therefore, is made in the later context of the imprisonment of John, although it is presupposed in chap. vii. 18–35. How much of that related, Luke iv. 14–vii. 17, precedes the imprisonment of the Baptist, will be matter for subsequent inquiry. In Luke ix. 7 the execution is presupposed ; consequently what follows belongs to the time after John's death.

The first year of the public ministry of Christ comprehends thus the following synoptical rubrics :—

	MATT.	MARK.	LUKE.	JOHN.
From the arising of John the Baptist to the baptism of Christ, . . .	iii. 1–17.	i. 1–11.	iii. 1–22.	i. 1–33.
From the baptism of Christ to the beginning of His public ministry, . .	iv. 1–11.	i. 12, 13.	iv. 1–13.	i. 19–28.
From the beginning of Christ's ministry to the imprisonment of the Baptist, .	...	...	iv. 14–vii. 17.	i. 29–iv. 54.
From the imprisonment of John to his death, . . .	iv. 12–xiii. 58.	i. 14–vi. 14.	vii. 17–ix. 6.	v. 1–47.
From the death of the Baptist to the feeding of the Five Thousand, . .	xiv. 1–13.	vi. 14–31.	ix. 7–11.	vi. 1–4.

I.— *The Baptism of our Lord.*

Sec. 76. That John the Baptist was born at the beginning of the year A.C. 2, year of Rome 752, and that Khirbet el-Jehud in the Wady Bettîr was his birthplace, has already (secs. 40-42) been shown to be probable. With regard to his childhood and youth, it is related : " The child grew, and waxed strong in spirit, and was in the deserts till the day of his showing unto Israel." [1] These deserts are not more nearly indicated. It is known that the tradition of the monks speaks of a definite place of the land of Judea as " the desert of John," and points it out as the solitude in which the Baptist spent his youth. This so-called wilderness lies near to 'Ain-Kârim [Fountain of the Vineyard], some six miles west of Jerusalem, and is one of the fairest and most fertile regions of culture in all Judea. [2] Thereby this tradition is, of course, judged. It is, nevertheless, one deserving of attention, inasmuch as it assigns to this same district the birthplace of the Baptist and the dwelling of Zacharias; for this region consecrated to John lies near to his actual birthplace, Khirbet-el-Jehud, in the Wady Bettîr.

Sec. 77. The beginning of John's ministry, as of that of the Lord, fell in the 15th year of the reign of Tiberius, [3] *i.e.* in the beginning of the year 28. [4] The manner of this arising, as well as the scene of it, is thus described by Luke, chap. iii. 2, 3 : " The word of God came unto John, the son of Zacharias, in the wilderness. And he came into all the country about Jordan, preaching the baptism of repentance, for the remission

---

[1] Luke i. 80.   [2] Ritter, iv. 215 ; Bædecker, p. 289.   [3] Luke iii. 1.
[4] Cf. sec. 32. [For like reasons, since we learn from Acts xiii. 25 that the events of Luke iii. 15–18 (cf. iii. 21) belong to a comparatively late period in the ministry of John, we may infer that the date of the 15th year of Tiberius has reference not so much to the time when John arose, as to the time when Christ was baptized by him (sec. 33). With the autumn of the preceding year, U.C. 780, a Sabbatic year began (sec. 53). If John's ministry began with the Sabbatic year, the presence of such great multitudes is easily explained. This would place the arising of the Baptist nearly six months before the call of Andrew, Peter, and John (John i. 35–42). The brief ministry of the Baptist would appear to have been confined to this Sabbatic year ; as he was in all probability imprisoned in the early summer of A.D. 28, soon after the events of John iv. 1. See sec. 104.]

THE BAPTISM OF OUR LORD.

of sins." Since it is said, "He came into all the country
about Jordan," it follows that Luke intended to designate not
the place of his first arising, but the whole theatre of all the
public labours of the Baptist. John in reality, up to the time
of his imprisonment, never forsook the Jordan district, but
continued to baptize in it; if not always in the Jordan itself,
yet sometimes at one spot, sometimes at another, in the Ghôr.
But where did he first arise? According to the Gospel of
John, this took place at Bethania beyond Jordan, in the
province of Gaulonitis, called " Judea beyond Jordan."[1] The
place is thus given by Matthew, chap. iii. 1 : " In those days
came John the Baptist, preaching in the wilderness of Judea—
ἐν τῷ ἐρήμῳ τῆς Ἰουδαίας—and saying, Repent ye . . ." This
wilderness of Judea cannot possibly be the region called in
the Old Testament the "wilderness of Judah,"[2] alike because
this latter district is without water, as because it stands in
close connection with the Dead Sea, but nowhere with the
Jordan, in which John baptized, chap. iii. 6. The wilderness of
Judea is nothing else but Judea beyond Jordan, or Gaulonitis;
in a word, Bethania. The name *wilderness* was very appro-
priately given to this land, since the Jolan is not arable, but
pasture land. Even the glorious fertile plain El-Batîheh is
called a "wilderness!"[3] John and Matthew are thus in this
respect in perfect harmony ; and the more general expressions
of Mark[4] and Luke[5] do not at any rate exclude Bethania.
In Bethania John thus began his labours. For the performance of the baptismal rite this was unquestionably the
best spot that could be chosen. The Upper Jordan before it
enters the lake has a quiet course, is moderately shallow, and,
on account of its sloping banks, is easily accessible. The
Lower Jordan, on the contrary, flows with a strong current
in a deep valley, clothed with timber and brushwood (which
extends through the whole length of the Ghôr), in which the
stream has channelled out its steep-banked bed. This Lower
Jordan is rendered thereby generally inaccessible. Only at

[1] John i. 28, x. 40. Cf. Matt. xix. 1 ; and see sec. 70.
[2] Josh. xv. 61, 62 ; Judg. i. 16. Cf. Robinson, *Palestine*, i. p. 466 sqq.
[3] Matt. xiv. 15.   [4] "John did baptize in the wilderness," Mark i. 4.
[5] In the whole country about the Jordan, iii. 3.

the three fords can it be approached. The first of these is to be found below the point at which the Mandhûr enters the Jordan ; the second, above [1] the mouth of the Jabbok, is called Damieh-ford ; the third is in the neighbourhood of Jericho. The first of these is impossible as the scene of John's baptism, because it was situated on purely Gentile territory ; the last is in winter so perilous, on account of the current, that every year pilgrims bathing there meet with their death ; and at other seasons is, on account of the tropical heat, inaccessible to the inhabitants of the Jewish table-land. The middle ford, Ed-Damieh, by which the route passes from Nablous to Es-Szalt (Ramoth), is probably the Bethabara which Origen introduced into the text of the Gospel of John in place of Bethania. It offers the same perilous depth of stream and rapidity of current, and is exposed to the same tropical climate.[2] That under such circumstances John baptized somewhere on the Lower Jordan, is in the highest degree improbable. What is more, Jewish tradition roundly declares the Lower Jordan to be unclean for the purposes of lustration.[3] In the passage cited it is true the Jordan in general, and not the Lower Jordan, is mentioned ; but, according to *Tosaphtha Berachoth*, vii. 2, it is expressly said that the name Jordan applies only to the lower part of the stream. This is an error, no doubt, but nevertheless it serves to explain that tradition. Had, then, John baptized in this less pure division of the river, he would have incurred the censure of the Pharisees and Sanhedrists : of this, however, there is no trace in John i. 19 ff. ; and according to Matthew, chap. iii. 7, many even of the Pharisees underwent baptism at his hand. Bethania beyond Jordan, on the contrary, was in every respect suitable as a place of baptism ; and was situated, more than any other ford, on peculiarly Israelitish territory, between Naphtali and Judah of the Jordan.

Sec. 78. The work of John was the preaching of repentance, baptism for the remission of sins, the proclamation of the coming of Messiah, and the pointing out of His person. This

---

[1] Not below, as Van de Velde supposes ; *vid.* Ritter, *Erdk.* xv. 718, 1035 ; Stanley, p. 296.

[2] Ritter, iii. 28.   [3] *Mishna Para*, viii. 10.

last was even his chief mission.[1] It is not conceivable that the fulfilment of this, his chief mission, had long to be waited for. The baptism of Jesus, by which He was manifested as the One who should come, must be preceded only by so much time as was necessary, in order that John and his labours might become known in the land, and the people flock to him. The Sanhedrim of Jerusalem, which watched with such jealous care over every spiritual movement in the land, would certainly have waited several months before instituting an inquiry as to John's work and aims. If now, as is evident from John i. 19, 26, the deputation from Jerusalem came to John only after the baptism of Jesus, this baptism must fall in the earliest period of the labours of the Baptist.[2]

Sec. 79. The baptism of Jesus and the accompanying circumstances are related in perfect accord by all Four Evangelists.[3] When Jesus first came forth in public, John, according to the Fourth Evangelist, instructed his disciples concerning Christ's baptism and the circumstances attending it. From this it follows that, of the persons then surrounding the Baptist, no one had been present at the baptism of the Lord, that a considerable time had thus elapsed between the baptism and the coming forth of Jesus in Bethania ; but as to what this time was, and where Jesus had meanwhile remained, John is silent. The Synoptists, however, supply us with information on both these points.[4] They tell us that Jesus remained forty days in the wilderness ; where He fasted, and was tempted of the Devil. Why did the Evangelist John pass over this history in silence ? Modern criticism thinks John could not relate the history of the Temptation, because it is in conflict with his idea of the Christ. Much more simply, more naturally, and more honestly is this silence explained by the recognition of the principle, manifestly prevailing with

---

[1] Matt. iii. 2, 3 ; Mark i. 2, 3–7 ; Luke iii. 4, 16.

[2] [But the first fresh impulse to a national reformation must have by this time given place to a spirit of critical questioning. The watchword of the Baptist, John iii. 30, was already receiving its exemplification.]

[3] Matt. iii. 13–17 ; Mark i. 9–12 ; Luke iii. 21, 22 [ὡσεί, ver. 23, as in i. 56, ix. 28 : *towards, approaching*]. John i. 32–34, *ipsissima verba* of the Baptist.

[4] Matt. iv. 1–11 ; Mark i. 12, 13 ; Luke iv. 1–13.

H

John, of relating only that which he has seen with his own
eyes, and heard with his own ears.

Sec. 80. The Synoptists do not tell us in what wilderness
the temptation took place : all hypotheses with regard to it
would therefore be rash conjecture. If, however, we must
express an opinion, we should say—since Bethania on the
Jordan was the point from which the Lord was impelled by
the Spirit into the wilderness,[1] and at which He first appeared
again among men — the wilderness may have been the
Gaulonitic one, a region which, as we have before seen, was
called simply " the wilderness." The Christian tradition, with
which Arculfus is already acquainted,[2] assigns as the scene
of the forty days' fasting in the wilderness the *Quarantania*
mountain, in the neighbourhood of Jericho. This opinion is a
natural result of the other, which represents Jesus as being
baptized near Jericho, and of course falls with it.

We have no thought of following certain exegetes, who seek
to identify the mountain from whose summit the Tempter
showed to the Lord all the kingdoms of the world.[3] We
observe only, that in the other act of temptation it is not said,
either in Matt. iv. 5 or in Luke iv. 9 : The devil set Him
on a pinnacle of the temple ; but what *is* said is : He set Him
on the pinnacle, or summit, of the sanctuary, ἐπὶ τὸ πτερύγιον
τοῦ ἱεροῦ. The roof of the *royal portico* is meant, which
formed the limit of the outer court on the southern side, and
towered in dazzling height above the valley of the Kedron.[4]

II.—*The Beginning of the Public Ministry of Christ.*

Sec. 81. The description of the first days in the public life
of our Lord, as given in John i. 28 ff., certainly leaves upon
every unprejudiced reader the impression that he has here
before him the account of an eye-witness, upon whose memory
and heart that scene of so great importance for his whole life
had indelibly impressed itself. This pregnancy of representation, this mode of narration, in speaking of the different
persons by their own names, not forgetting the hour of the

---

[1] Mark i. 12.   [2] l. ii. c. 11 ; *circa* A.D. 670.
[3] Matt. iv. 8 ; Luke iv. 5.   [5] Josephus, *Antiq.* xv. 11, sec. 5.

day, and other details in themselves insignificant,—all compels
us to believe that the narrator had seen and heard these things
for himself. On the day after that on which the deputation
from Jerusalem had interrogated the Baptist as to his acts,
he beheld Jesus coming, and testified: This is the Lamb of
God.[1] The " next day," thus the first day after the coming
forth of Jesus, the second after the inquiry of the Sanhedrists,
" about the tenth hour," *i.e.* four o'clock in the afternoon, there
joined Him His first disciples, namely, Andrew, and that
disciple never mentioned by name, consequently John himself,
and through them also Simon Peter.[2] The next day, the
second after the coming forth of Jesus, when the Lord was
preparing to go into Galilee, He called Philip to follow Him,
and Philip brought Nathanael to the Lord.[3] On the third
day Jesus went to Cana of Galilee.[4] Since Jesus was the
day before on the point of departing for Galilee, it is to be
supposed He fulfilled this intention, and did not pass the night
in Bethania.   He thus probably went with His disciples to
Bethsaïda, the city of Andrew, Peter, and Philip.[5] There also
does the interview of Nathanael with Christ seem to have
taken place; for had it been at Bethania, Nathanael would
have heard from the mouth of the Baptist the testimony that
Jesus was the Christ, and Nathanael and Philip could not
have spoken as, according to i. 45, 46, they did speak.   " On
the third day there was a marriage in Cana of Galilee."   The
terminus a quo is the day when John became acquainted with
the Lord, and not the day when the deputation arrived from
Jerusalem ; for the former, and not the latter event, was that
which marked an epoch in the life of the apostle.

Sec. 82. **Cana of Galilee.**—Upon the plateau to the west
of the Sea of Gennesareth there extends between Hattîn and
Sepphoris the considerable plain of El-Buttauf.[6] At the foot
of the range of hills forming its northern boundary, at
about 15 miles from the lake, and 6 or 8 miles to the
north of Nazareth, lie the ruins called Kânet el-Jelîl.   On the
southern side of the same plain, a good hour's distance from
Nazareth, lies Kefr Kenna.   The tradition of the present

---

[1] John i. 29–34.   [2] i. 35–43.   [3] i. 45 ff.   [4] ii. 1.
[5] i. 44.   [6] " The plain of 'Ασωχίς " of Josephus (*Vita*, 41).

day points to this last place as the Cana of the New
Testament; its claim, however, must yield to that of the
ancient name still existing. As early as the time of the
Arabic translation of the New Testament, Κανὰ τῆς
Γαλιλαίας is rendered by Kânet el-Jelîl. Tradition seems
always to have wavered between these two places. Saewulf[1]
clearly favours Kânet el-Jelîl. He says: "From Nazareth
Chana of Galilæa, where the Lord at the wedding turned
water into wine, is distant six _milliaria_,[2] situated to the
north, on a mountain : there is nothing there now but a
monastery, called _Architriclini_. Midway between Nazareth
and Galilæa—so he abbreviates Cana of Galilee—lies a
Castellum Roma." [3] Adrichomius, in the sixteenth century,
says that Cana has a mountain on the north, and a broad, fair,
fruitful plain in the south. This description, like the preceding, applies to Kânet el-Jelîl.[4] Cana of Galilee was the
city of Nathanael.[5] This may well have occasioned the first
visit of our Lord to it, of which we have the record in John
ii. 1–11. A second visit is narrated in John iv. 46–54.[6]

Sec. 83. If the Lord came, as is ordinarily supposed, direct
from Bethania beyond Jordan to Cana in a single day, He
would have a journey of 21 miles ; if He came from Bethsaïda,
on the western side of the lake, He would have a journey of
15 miles. It must thus become evident how important for the
right understanding of the Gospel narrative is this outwork,
Biblical geography; for by the true determination of the
position of Bethania and Cana important objections to the
authenticity of John's Gospel are thoroughly invalidated.
Schenkel, _e.g._, in his _Charakterbild Jesu_, bases his conclusion,
that this Gospel could not have proceeded from an eye-witness,
partly upon the statement made in it that Jesus journeyed in
one day from the place where John was baptizing to Cana.
A long distance truly, if it is supposed that this place of

---

[1] A.D. 1103.

[2] His _milliaria_ are longer than the Roman ; for he gives the distance from
Tabor to the lake as 6 miles, whereas it is 13 Roman miles.

[3] _i.e._ Tell Rûme.

[4] On this place, comp. Robinson, _Palestine_, ii. 346 ff., and Schulz, in the
Zeitschrift der deutsch. morgenl. Gesellsch. iii. 50.

[5] John xxi. 2.   [6] See also Sepp, _Architecton. Stud._ p. 202.

baptism was in the neighbourhood of Jericho; for the Lord would then have to go over something like 90 miles in order to reach Cana—more than three days' journey.

The miracle which Jesus wrought at Cana in changing water into wine, and the circumstances accompanying this miracle, call forth questions of an archæological, but neither of a topographical nor chronological nature.

Sec. 84. " After this Jesus went down to Capernaum, He, and His mother, and His brethren, and His disciples ; and continued there not many days. And the Passover of the Jews was at hand; and Jesus went up to Jerusalem." [1] This passage affords us a firm chronological point of rest in determining the history of Jesus Christ. The year of the commencement of His public ministry was the year 28 of the Dionysian era.[2] In this year the 15th Nisan fell on the 30th March.[3] It would have fallen on the 29th April if this had been an intercalary year; but since it was a Sabbatic year, the intercalation could not take place. The time required for the Lord to be present at Jerusalem, from Capernaum, on the 14th Nisan, the few days which He spent in Capernaum —οὐ πολλὰς ἡμέρας—and the journey from Bethania to Cana, occupy together about 14 days. We can thus assert with a tolerable degree of certainty, that—

> Our Lord was baptized by John about the 1st of February ; [4]
> He returned to Bethania, 40 days later, about the 12th of March ;
> He came to Cana on the 15th March ;
> He came to Capernaum on the 17th March ;
> He came to Jerusalem on the 29th March (14th Nisan).

The beginning of the ministry of the Baptist is to be placed about a month before the baptism of Christ—thus about the 1st January U.C. 781.

The way in which the evangelist narrates the journey of our Lord to Capernaum as taking place, namely, in the society of His whole family, justifies us in the conjecture that the true and proper migration to Capernaum is here intended. That event, it is true, is placed by Matthew, chap. iv. 12–17,

---

[1] John ii. 12, 13.   [2] Cf. sec. 34.   [3] Cf. sec. 37.

[4] [The date of Christ's baptism cannot be fixed much earlier, since the fig-tree was already in leaf at the time of Nathanael's call ; nor any later, as the whole time from the early part of March is required for the succession of events before Passover.]

in the time after the imprisonment of John. But this evangelist, who begins his general account of the labours of Jesus
only with the epoch of this imprisonment, might well leave
out of the account the few days during which, according to
John ii. 12, He dwelt at Capernaum, and begin the removal
with the first lengthened sojourn of the Lord in that town.

III.—*The First Passover. Tuesday, 30th March,*
A.U.C. 781, A.D. 28.

Sec. 85. The opening act of the ministry of Christ in
Jerusalem was **the cleansing of the Sanctuary.**[1] " He found
in the sanctuary those that sold oxen and sheep and doves, and
the changers of money sitting. And He made a scourge of
cords, and drove them all out of the sanctuary, with the sheep
and oxen ; and poured out the change of the money-changers,
and overthrew the tables ; and said to them that were selling
the doves, ' Carry these things hence : make not my Father's
house a house of merchandise.' "   At the time of Christ the
Jews had in use Roman and Herodian money, which could not
be employed for sacred purposes ; there were therefore money-
changers, who changed the current money into the money of
the temple.   Every adult Israelite was required to contribute a
half-shekel annually to the temple, and the time appointed for
its payment was the month of Adar.   Now, in *Mishna Shekalim*,
i. 3, we read : " On the 15th Adar the money-changers seated
themselves at their tables in the city, but on the 25th they
seated themselves in the sanctuary."   Since, then, at the
paschal festival, the money tribute was at the same time paid

---

[1] John xi. 14–17. [The court of the Gentiles in this sanctuary was separated
from the inner court by a stone wall, bearing an inscription which forbade any
Gentile to pass it, under pain of death ; *Antiq.* xv. 11, sec. 5. The pillar on
which this inscription was graven was discovered not long ago by M. Clermont-
Ganneau, who communicated at the time an account of the discovery to the
columns of the *Athenæum*. It appeared likewise in the *Revue d'Archéologie*,
1872, vol. xxiii. p. 214 sqq. Subjoined is a copy of the inscription, furnished
by M. Caspari :—

(1) ΜΗΘΕΝΑ ΑΛΛΟΓΕΝΗ ΕΙΣΠΟ·   (2) ΡΕΤΕΣΘΑΙ ΕΝΤΟΣ ΤΟΥ ΠΕ·
(3) ΡΙΤΟΙΕΡΟΝΤΡΤΦΑΚΤΟΤΚΑΙ   (4) ΠΕΡΙΒΟΛΟΤΟΣΔΑΝΛΗ·
(5) ΦΘΗ ΕΑΤΤΩΙΑΙΤΙΟΣΕΣ·   (6) ΤΑΙΔΙΑΤΟΕΞΑΚΟΛΟΤ·
(7) ΘΕΙΝΘΑΝΑΤΟΝ, *i.e.* Μηθένα ἀλλογενῆ εἰσπορεύεσθαι ἔντος τοῦ περὶ τὸ ἱερὸν
τρυφάκτου καὶ περιβόλου· ὃς δ' ἂν ληφθῇ ἑαυτῷ αἴτιος ἔσται διὰ τὸ ἰξακολουθεῖν θάνατον.]

and deposited in the thirteen chests of the temple, this custom or abuse may have thus crept in. At the great festivals a temple-market was held, the Court of the Gentiles serving for holding it. The merchants, as well as the money-changers, crowded into the Court of Israel ;[1] from this place, which no less than the temple itself was called the " house of God," [2] did Jesus expel the merchants and money-changers. The same or a similar fact is narrated by the Synoptists on the occasion of the last Passover.[3] Here, then, there are three cases possible : either the Lord performed the cleansing of the sanctuary twice, or He did so only once, at the beginning of His ministry ; or, finally, only once, but at the end of His ministry. No slight grounds may be adduced in favour of the repetition. The cleansing of the sanctuary was a symbolical act, by which the Lord visibly represented that which He desired and at which He aimed ; it was thus entirely in place at the very outset of His public ministry, and equally so at the close too of His labours. By this repetition He implied, " What I desired two years ago, that I desire still." Matthew and Mark relate nothing concerning a dialogue between the Lord and the Jews ; but Luke [4] records one, and according to him the Lord answered something very different from that which He answered in John ii. 19. It is certainly remarkable that John tells us nothing of a cleansing of the sanctuary before the last Passover, of which he must nevertheless have been an eye-witness. For that that which is related, John ii. 14–20, belongs necessarily to the first Passover, and not to the last, follows from the chronological reference of John ii. 20 ; so that it cannot be admitted that John had merely transposed this account. It is rather possible that the Synoptists, who, strictly speaking, relate the history only of the last year of the Saviour's life, have, for the sake of the completeness of the account, introduced into their only narrative of the appearing of Christ publicly in the temple much which took

---

[1] *Vid. τὸ ἱερὸν τοῦ Θεοῦ*, Matt. xxi. 12. [Cf. the בכנעני of Zech. xiv. 21.]

[2] *τὸν οἶκον τοῦ πατρός*, John ii. 16. [According to Mark's account, the Lord cited Isa. lvi. 7 in such wise as to vindicate *for the Gentiles too* the same right of worship. Cf. Ellicott, p. 295, note 3.]

[3] Matt. xxi. 12–16 ; Mark xi. 15–18 ; Luke xix. 45–48.   [4] Luke xx. 3–8.

place in Jerusalem in earlier years.[1] In favour of this view
it may be advanced also, that, according to Matt. xxi. 15 ff.,
the Jews took offence only at the solemn entry, but not at
the act of temple-cleansing. Be this as it may, it must be
maintained that this act took place at the first Passover, as
related by John.

Sec. 86. On that first paschal festival took place the discourse narrated John iii. 1–21. It belongs not to our task to
explain the purport of this conversation. Wholly without
ground have certain expositors assumed that Christ was on
this occasion absolutely alone with Nicodemus, and then
naïvely raised the question, Whence could John have learnt
all this ? We cannot indeed see why John, in whose house
it is highly probable the conversation was held, may not have
been present at it. We must hold firmly to the principle
that John relates only what he saw and heard. Because he
did not personally witness the Ascension, for instance, at which
only " Galilean men " were present,[2] he does not relate this.
In the whole Gospel of John there is to be found only a
single account, which does not seem to have been derived
from personal observation, namely, the conversation of the
Lord with Pilate ;[3] and even in this case it is not absolutely
impossible that John may have heard it. Into the Prætorium
the Jews also were permitted to enter, but they would not,
lest they should be defiled ; but a John, who was much more
concerned about the fate of his Master than about a question
of Levitical purity, may well have entered.

Sec. 87. " After these things came Jesus and His disciples
[from Jerusalem] into the land of Judea, and there He tarried
with them and baptized. [During the month of April, and
part of May.] And John also was baptizing in Ænon, near
to Saleim . . . for John was not yet cast into prison."[4] Who
were these disciples ? The supposition that it was even then
the company of the apostles is a baseless one. Disciples of
Jesus were all those called who attached themselves to Him,

---

[1] [The traces of several earlier visits have been rightly observed in Matt.
xxiii. 37 ; Luke xiii. 34. *Vid.* Kienlen, in his recension of this work, *Revue
Chrétienne*, 1869, p. 747.]

[2] Acts i. 11. [3] John xviii. 33 ff. [4] John iii. 22–24.

although many of them afterwards fell away from their allegiance.[1] That Peter, who is to be regarded as the principal authority for the Gospel of Mark, was not then present, although he was already a disciple before his actual vocation to the apostolic office, which took place on the shore of the Sea of Galilee a year later, but was quietly plying his avocation as a fisherman somewhere about Bethsaïda, we are justified in concluding, from the silence of the Synoptists concerning the labours of Jesus at this time, as also from the silence of John concerning the names of the disciples; since the same Evangelist afterwards, for the most part, mentions by name Peter and the other disciples, not only where they were taking part in the history, but also where they were only present. During the first sojourn of Christ in Judea He was accompanied more or less exclusively by Judean disciples, with John, and perhaps Nathanael.[2] This sojourn of Jesus in Judea was not limited merely to the paschal visit, and the journeying to and fro consequent upon it; but " He tarried there," διέτριβε. The duration of this sojourn may, it seems to us, be inferred from John iv. 35. Near to Sychar, in the moment at which He had left Judea, our Lord spoke the words : " Behold, the fields are white already to harvest." In the neighbourhood of Sychar the harvest falls towards the end of May ; Christ had consequently remained in Judea during the month of April and a part of the month of May. It is true, indeed, that these words of Jesus were employed in a figurative sense ; but His figures were, as a rule, taken from the existing aspect of things. The words, " Do ye not say (at sowing-time), ' Yet four months, and it is harvest' ? " might have been spoken either at seed-time or harvest. We conclude it was the latter, from the Lord's words, " Behold, the fields are white already to harvest." The cause of the Lord's withdrawing from Judea is given in John iv. 1–3 : " When the Lord knew how the Pharisees had heard that Jesus made and baptized more disciples than John ... He left Judea." At that time John was still at liberty ; but his

---

[1] John vi. 60, 66.

[2] This is rendered probable by the fact of our Lord's at once repairing, on His return to Galilee, to Cana, the city of Nathanael.

imprisonment must have taken place shortly afterwards, for as early as John v. 35 [latter summer] Jesus speaks of him as one who " *was.*"

Sec. 88. **Ænon, near to Saleim.**—" John was baptizing in Ænon, near to Saleim, because there was much water there ; and they came and were baptized. For John was not yet cast into prison."[1] Where was it situated, this place—as would appear, the last scene of John's ministry ? In the *Onomasticon* it is said, art. " Salem," that 8 miles from Scythopolis in the plain—that is to say, in opposition to the mountain-land, in the great plain of the Jordan, the Ghôr—there lies a village which is called *Salumias,* and corresponds to the New Testament Saleim. Jerome says :[2] Oppidum est juxta Scythopolin, quod usque hodie appellatur Salem. Of Ænon it is said in the *Onomasticon :* " To the present day this place is shown 8 miles south of Scythopolis, near Salem and the Jordan." In the direction indicated, and at that distance from Bisan, at the opening of the Wâdy Khusneh into the Ghôr, Van de Velde marks a spring, Shech *Sâlim,* by which our place would seem to be designated ; for in the vicinity are to be found Bir (well), Ain Bêda, and other waters, of which one was Ænon.

Sec. 89. " Jesus left Judea, and departed again into Galilee. And He must needs go through Samaria. He comes then to a town of Samaria, called Sychar, near to the ground which Jacob gave to his son Joseph ; and Jacob's well was there."[3]

Samaria, the town, in Hebrew *Shomron,* was, from the time of Omri, metropolis of the kingdom of Israel, and bore its ancient name until the time of Herod the Great, who renewed it, and called it, in honour of Augustus, *Sebaste.*[4] The small village on its ruins is to the present day called Sebustîeh.[5] The name Samaria, Σαμάρεια, passed over to the province mainly occupied by that people who were attached to the sect of the Samaritans.[6] This sect dwelt principally at

---

[1] John iii. 23, 24. [2] *Epistola* lxxiii.
[3] John iv. 3–6. [4] The Greek equivalent to *Augusta.*
[5] Robinson, ii. 304 ff. Stanley, *Sinai and Palestine,* pp. 244–246.
[6] Josephus, *Antiq.* xiii. 2, sec. 3. Luke xvii. 11 ; Acts i. 8, viii. 1, ix. 31, xv. 3.

Sichem, the Nablûs of the present day, at the foot of Gerizim, on which the Samaritan temple once stood, and which has continued, notwithstanding the destruction of the temple by John Hyrcanus,[1] to be the sacred mountain of this people to the present day. The name Samaria is used in John, alike in iv. 7 as iv. 5, to denote not the *town*, but the *province*. This province consisted principally of the valley of Sichem, extending from west to east, and lying between Mount Gerizim on the south and Mount Ebal on the north. In this well-watered and fruitful valley[2] the town of Sichem existed so early as Jacob's time.[3] This city was for a time the residence of King Jeroboam.[4] John Hyrcanus destroyed it, together with the temple on Gerizim. At the time of Christ it appears in history under the name of *Neapolis*, which it has retained under the shortened form of Nablûs to the present day. Since the destruction of the temple, its former site, a levelled surface of the rock, has continued to be the place of worship of the Samaritan sect, in the present day as in the age of our Lord.[5]

Below Nablûs the valley widens through the receding of Mounts Ebal and Gerizim, and opens up at the eastern end of these mountains into the valley running from south to north, called *Wâdy el-Mochna*.

Sec. 90. **Jacob's Well.**[6]—When Jacob, in returning from Mesopotamia, came to Shalem, the city of Shechem, he pitched his tent before the city, and purchased of the sons of Hamor, father of Shechem, the piece of land on which he had encamped.[7] In the piece of ground which Jacob had bought of the sons of Hamor was Joseph's body buried after the return from Egypt. From these passages it has been inferred that Shechem, or Sichem, where Joseph was buried, and

---

[1] *Antiq.* xiii. 9, sec. 1.   [2] Cf. Ritter, iv. 301 ff.
[3] Gen. xxxiii. 18, xxxiv. 24, xxxvii. 12 ff.   [4] 1 Kings xii. 25.

[5] On this place of prayer, see Robinson, *Pal.* ii. 275–280 ; Stanley, 234, 248 ; Tristram, 152 ; and especially de Saulcy, *Voyage autour de la mer morte*, ii. p. 407, and plan.

[6] [For an admirable description of the locality, see Tristram, pp. 145–147.]

[7] Gen. xxxiii. 19. [Knobel and others would translate שלם as an adjective = *unscathed ;* but Robinson's discovery (ii. 279) presents a solution better corresponding to the requirements of the text ; cf. Ellicott, p. 128, note 1.]

Shalem, or Salem, where the field lay, are names belonging to one and the same town.   Rather is the field of the sons of Hamor conceived of sometimes as in the neighbourhood of Salem, sometimes of Sichem, because it was situated midway between the two.   Jacob's field lies at the opening of the Sichem valley into the Mochna valley, a mile from Nablûs. The mountain chain rising to the east of the Mochna valley bears upon its ridge, at a distance of about three-quarters of an hour from Nablûs, half an hour from Jacob's well, the place now called *Sâlim,* corresponding to the ancient Salem.   In this Jacob's field, where the Sichem valley widens out, there lies on the north side of the valley, nearer to Ebal than to Gerizim, the grave of Joseph, of which there is no sufficient ground for doubting the authenticity.   In the same field, three to four hundred feet to the south, lies Ain-el-Belad, the Jacob's well, 20 minutes' distance to the east of Nablûs. According to Quaresmius[1] it is 105 feet deep; according to Wilson,[2] 75 foot, and 9 foot in diameter, with 15 feet of water.   It is covered at the top with rough stones.   Above the well itself are traces of a former Christian chapel and of an altar.   "Jesus then, being wearied with the journey, sat thus at the fountain : and it was about the sixth hour."[3]

Sec. 91. **Sychar.**—Herr Rosen (Prussian Consul at Jerusalem) has given[4] a description and plan of Nablûs and its immediate environs, which we may with confidence accept as our guide.   According to this, there is, 8 minutes' walk north from Joseph's grave—10 minutes, thus, from Jacob's well—a village called *El-Askar,* a name in which that of Sychar is preserved.   Some 150 paces farther north is a fountain, Ain el-Askar, which issues from a remarkable structure,—a vaulted passage leading to the foot of Ebal, 6 feet high, built of large well-smoothed stones,—and presently flows into a tank enclosed with square stones.   The existence of this place and name has, moreover, been sufficiently vouched for

[1] ii. 801.

[2] *Lands of the Bible,* ii. 53. [Now for the most part without water : Robinson, ii. 283, 284; iii. 132.   Eli Smith, cited by Barnes on John iv. Stanley, p. 241.   Tristram, p. 147.]

[3] [ἐπὶ τῇ πηγῇ, John iv. 6.   Called from its depth also φρίαρ, vers. 11, 12.]

[4] *Zeitschrift der deutschen morgenl. Gesellsch.* 1860, ii. 334 ff.

by other travellers. Walcott says:[1] "Askar and Belad, two little villages, lie at the opening of the valley of Nablûs towards the east; Askar on the north side of the valley, Belad on the south." Many Biblical geographers have maintained that Sychar, in the text in question from John's Gospel, is to be taken as identical with *Sichem*. It is true that in one or two MSS. the name $\Sigma\upsilon\chi\acute{\epsilon}\mu$ stands for $\Sigma\upsilon\chi\acute{\alpha}\rho$ or $\Sigma\iota\chi\acute{\alpha}\rho$; it is, however, pretty generally acknowledged that the first of these readings (Sychem) is an exegetical conjecture. The doubt as to the separate existence of Sychar is based partly on a want of acquaintance with the geography of the country, partly on a misapprehension of some passages in the Church Fathers. Jerome, in *Epitaph. Paulæ*, says of this pilgrim : " transivit *Sichem* (non ut plerique errantes legunt, *Sichar*), quæ nunc Neapolis appellatur." This passage has been explained as though Jerome denied the separate existence of Sychar. This, however, is incorrect : he means only that, according to his own (individual) opinion, Sichem is the true reading in John iv. 5 ff. Eusebius, in the *Onomasticon*, says : "*Sychar, in front of Neapolis,* near the field which Jacob gave to his son Joseph, where our Lord and Redeemer, according to the Gospel of John, spoke with the Samaritan woman at the well, and where now a church is erected." In the *Itiner. Antonini* it is said, that a mile from Scythopolis there is a place called Sechar. The name occurs also in Jewish tradition. In *Machoth* x. 2 it is related that, in an especial and exceptional case of necessity, the two loaves of Pentecost were brought from Ain-Sychar (בקעת עין סוכר). At the time of our Lord, Palestine was probably ten times as populous as at present, and there are therefore good grounds for the supposition that Sychar, which now is a little hamlet or clachan, but was then a town,[2] extended considerably farther to the south, and that consequently a considerable portion of it lay nearer to the Jacob's well than to the fountain Ain el-Askar, and that thus the inhabitants of this southern part of the town drew their supply of water from the Jacob's well; the more so since a special value was attached to this water.[3] On the other hand, it is inexplicable that a woman should

[1] *Biblioth. Sacra*, 1843, i. 74. [2] John iv. 5. [3] John iv. 12.

have come half an hour's journey in the noontide heat,[1] from Sichem or Nablûs, abounding in fountains and water, to this well to fetch water. *Sychar* is consequently not Sichem, but *El-Askar.*

Sec. 92. In the conversation of Christ with the Samaritan woman—of the dogmatic significance of which we have not here to speak—there occur several topographical and chronological allusions, of which we must take note in order to bring them into relief. In John iv. 11 it is said that the well was deep; in iv. 20, that its position was within sight of Gerizim, where the Samaritans had their place of worship. In the conversation with the disciples the Lord says:[2] "Do ye not say (proverbially): Yet four months, and harvest is there? Behold, I say unto you, lift up your eyes, look on the country round, it is already white to the harvest." These words seem to us to have the following sense: "At seed-time the husbandman consoles himself with the thought, 'Four months of patience, and the harvest comes!' Behold now his hope fulfilled, the corn is ripe. At the spiritual seed-time, however, one has ordinarily no such certainty of hope that the seed will quickly ripen into fruit; and yet, behold, only a few moments ago I sowed, in speaking to that woman words of life, and already is the harvest-field whitening." The Lord pointed beyond the fields ripe for the harvest to the multitude of people streaming to Him from Sychar[3]—which was His harvest. If this explanation is the true one, Jesus must have been at the Jacob's well towards the end of May, which is the harvest-time in that district. It would indeed be possible to assume as our starting-point, that Jesus was in Sychar at seed-time. But in this case a chronological difficulty would arise, fatal to the acceptance of this hypothesis. Jesus travelled from Sychar into Galilee, and returned to Jerusalem at the festival of Atonement.[4] Since this festival was observed before seed-time, the one which Jesus visited could not have been Atonement A.D. 28, but that of A.D. 29; the public ministry of our Lord would thus have continued not two, but three years; the chronology of John would no longer harmonize with that of Luke; and, most surprising of

---

[1] John iv. 6.   [2] John iv. 35.   [3] John iv. 40.   [4] Cf. secs. 95, 96.

all, we should have an entire year of our Lord's labours about which nothing is recorded by the Evangelists. We must therefore assume that the Lord came to Sychar at harvest-time.

Sec. 93. After a sojourn of two days in Sychar, "Jesus went into Galilee: for He Himself (Jesus) testified that a prophet is not honoured in his own city—ἐν τῇ ἰδίᾳ πατρίδι. When, then, He came into Galilee, the Galileans received Him, having seen all the things that He did at Jerusalem at the feast: for they also went to the feast. He went then again to Cana of Galilee."[1]

Here John ceases to be our only authority. For, if we compare Luke iv. 14–30 with John iv. 43–45, a striking similarity between the two narratives appears. Jesus returned to Galilee, whither His fame had preceded Him;[2] He testified that a prophet is lightly esteemed in his own city:[3] only in Luke this utterance is called forth by the reception which the people of Nazareth accorded their countryman.[4] It is true indeed that the account of Luke follows immediately upon the history of the Temptation;[5] but it is said, chap. iv. 16, "He went, *as was His wont,* into the synagogue on the Sabbath-day, and stood up to read;" further, chap. iv. 23, "Ye will surely say unto me . . . *Whatsoever we have heard was done in Capernaum,* do also here in thine own city."[6] This manifestly presupposes a public activity of Jesus already begun, so that a gap must be supposed to exist in the third Gospel between this history and that of the Temptation— a gap which the fourth in part fills up by that which has hitherto been narrated.

IV.—*Our Lord's Second Sojourn in Galilee.*
Summer, A.U.C. 781, A.D. 28.

Sec. 94. John, as we have seen, relates that Jesus, on His coming to Galilee from Sychar, did not settle in the town of His youth, but repaired to Cana. There He healed the son

---

[1] John iv. 43–46.
[2] Luke iv. 14, 15 ; John iv. 43, 45.
[3] Luke iv. 24 ; John iv. 44.
[4] Luke iv. 16–30.
[5] Luke iv. 1–13.
[6] [Cf. John ii. 12.]

of the nobleman, who had come to Him from Capernaum.[1] Here the narrative of John breaks off, as concerns the further labours of Christ at that time in Galilee; for in that which follows we find the Lord again in Jerusalem.[2] He had, with other disciples,[3] accompanied the Lord into Galilee, and had enjoyed beyond others the privilege of being constantly in the company of Jesus. For we must certainly suppose that while those disciples were gone to buy food, he had remained at the Jacob's well, and had listened to the conversation between Jesus and the Samaritan woman. The Galilean disciples, Andrew, Simon, and others, had not accompanied Jesus to Jerusalem at the first Passover, but had remained at home following their avocation. John now returned to Jerusalem with the same object in view.

Sec. 95. At the point at which John ceases, Luke now resumes the narrative, and relates—Luke iv. 31 ff.—that Jesus repaired to Capernaum, where on the Sabbath He taught in the synagogue,[4] and there healed a possessed one.[5] On the same day " He arose out of the synagogue " and came into Simon's house, where He healed Simon's mother-in-law of a fever.[6] The house of Simon was accordingly at Capernaum ; [7] whereas John, i. 45, speaks of Bethsaïda as " the city of Peter." Are the two Evangelists here in conflict ? We think not. For it seems that Bethsaïda did not constitute a township in itself, but was part of Capernaum, a suburb lying on the coast of the lake, the fisher haven of this town. Of such majumas or havens of the seaside towns, there were several in Palestine, e.g. that of Gaza [or of Jamnia]. This explains the fact that neither in Josephus, nor in Jewish tradition, nor elsewhere, is mention made of this Bethsaïda ; it is counted as part of Capernaum. We can say with certainty only of the Evangelist John that he mentions this place. The Synoptists often, indeed, speak of a town of this

---

[1] [βασιλικός, an officer of the court of Herod Antipas, John iv. 46–54.]

[2] John v. 1 ff.   [3] John iv. 27.   [4] Luke iv. 31, 32.

[5] Luke iv. 33–37.   [6] Luke iv. 38, 39.

[7] Country fever is to this day very prevalent in this seething plain and its borders, and such a position as Ain Mudawarah would be peculiarly subject to it. The dry, elevated, rocky ground of Tell Hûm cannot be considered as a probable fever locality.—(Tristram, p. 448, note.)

name, but the trans-Jordanic Julias is always meant. The only passage which might possibly have reference to this place is that of Matt. xi. 21, Luke x. 13, where the Lord pronounces the woe upon Bethsaïda. But since this woe finds its explanation in the fact that the Lord had wrought "mighty works" in this place, and the Synoptists relate no single miracle which was wrought there, it is probable that even in this case the woe relates to Bethsaïda Julias, in the neighbourhood of which they record the healing of the blind man and the feeding of the five thousand as taking place.[1] For the Synoptists, the western Bethsaïda was an integral part of Capernaum, the "fish-house" of this town ; for them Simon the fisherman was a dweller at Capernaum; while John, more nearly defining, places his house at Bethsaïda.

Sec. 96. After the healing of Peter's mother-in-law, Jesus was, *with the close of the Sabbath*,[2] so greatly besieged with suppliants, that He retired to a desert place; but even there the people discovered Him, and they held Him that He should not depart from them.[3] "And He said unto them, I must preach the kingdom of God to the other cities also, for therefore am I sent. *And He preached in the synagogues of Judea*."[4]   In all editions of the New Testament the reading here is ἦν κηρύσσων ἐν ταῖς συναγωγαῖς τῆς Γαλιλαίας. This reading has the great majority of MSS. in its favour. But the two oldest (uncial) manuscripts give a different reading. Codex C Regius has ἐν ταῖς συναγωγαῖς τῆς Ἰουδαίας ; Codex א Sinaiticus, B Vaticanus, and L Parisiensis, εἰς τὰς συναγωγὰς τῆς Ἰουδαίας ; so also the Coptic version and the Peshito. If then we are called to decide on internal grounds as to which is the true reading, it must be admitted that in the place of Ἰουδαίας, the form Γαλιλαίας might easily be substituted ; for Christ was in Galilee when He spoke these words, and immediately after—Luke v. 1—we find Him still, or again, in Galilee ; a mention of Judea in the interval must appear so strange, that the word was set down to an error of the copyist, and was replaced by "*Galilee*." On the other

---

[1] Luke ix. 10, 11 and parall. places.
[2] Luke iv. 40 and parall. places.   [3] Luke iv. 40–42.
[4] Luke iv. 43, 44. [As before in those of Galilee, chap. iv. 15.]

I

hand, one cannot at all explain how in a history in which Jesus appears, immediately before and after this reference, at the Sea of Galilee, the name Galilee could have been pushed aside by that of Judea. On the testimony, therefore, of the most ancient codices and translations, and on important internal grounds, we regard the reading τῆς Ἰουδαίας as the true one. Since, then, Luke here mentions a journey to Judea, John v. 1 —where we find Jesus again in Jerusalem—attaches itself immediately to Luke iv. 44. The sojourn of Jesus by the lake, Luke iv. 31–43, was in any case of short duration; perhaps two or three days. The preaching of our Lord throughout Judea, on the other hand, must have occupied a considerable period of time. Luke relates only that He preached in the synagogues of Judea; there were consequently no Galilean disciples with the Lord on this journey, and John met Him only at Jerusalem at the festival of Atonement. What towns our Lord visited on this journey must remain to us for ever unknown.[1] [After this festival, we have no further record of the ministry of Christ until we meet with Him again on the shores of the lake of Galilee, in the spring of the year 782 (A.D. 29), when the four apostles were called.]

V.—*Our Lord's Visit to Jerusalem, at the Day of Atonement.*
10th *Tisri*, 18–19th *September*, A.U.C. 781, A.D. 28.

Sec. 97. "After that was the festival of the Jews, and Jesus went up to Jerusalem." [2] What festival is here intended ? Many exegetes have sought a nearer definition of it in the form of expression " festival *of the Jews*," and regarded it as a festival instituted after the Captivity, which was not a Mosaic and Israelitish, but specially Jewish institution, like the feast of Dedication or of Purim. But the argument is baseless; since John calls also the Passover and the feast of Tabernacles ἡ ἑορτὴ τῶν Ἰουδαίων.[3] We hope to be able to

---

[1] [If Judea is the genuine reading in Luke iv. 44, the events to which this verse refers must immediately follow those of Mark i. 39, which, like the present verse, forms the point of transition to a new period in our Lord's life. The healing of the leper, Mark i. 40–45, is placed by Matthew and Luke in another connection, namely, immediately after the call of the four apostles.]

[2] John v. 1.   [3] John vi. 4, vii. 2.

prove that, alike in this passage and in chap. vii. 8, the Day of Atonement is that which is meant. The Greek word stands for היומא, the rabbinical name for the Day of Atonement. We arrive, too, necessarily at the Day of Atonement by a process of elimination, whereby all other festivals are excluded. The majority of exegetes conjecture the feast of Purim, which was observed on the 14th or 15th of Adar, a month before Passover. [The 14th Veadar, 19th March 782 (A.D. 29), would have satisfied the condition of falling on a Saturday;[1] but, on the other hand, allows an interval of nearly twelve months to elapse between our Lord's first and second visits to Judea. The character of this festival is, moreover, such that our Lord could not possibly observe it.] It is a festival commemorating the deliverance of the Jews from the persecution of Haman, and the bloody revenge taken by the Jews on their enemies. Its observance consisted in the reading of the required Megillah, *i.e.* the Book of Esther. After this it was incumbent on every one to abandon himself to mirth. He was to cry, " Cursed be Haman, blessed be Mordechai ;" to drink and shout, until he no longer knew what he was crying, and stammered, " Blessed be Haman, cursed be Mordechai."[2] Since the poor also were to be mirthful, the giving of alms on this day was greatly commended. Of all the Jewish festivals, Purim was the only one which was not observed in the temple, but at home. To such a festival of revenge, cursing, and drunkenness, to which no festive guests were invited, would Jesus have journeyed up to Jerusalem? Or would He at once have left the Holy City to sojourn during the Passover by the Lake of Gennesareth?[3]—Others have supposed that the festival in question was a Passover. [This, however, is impossible ; since the only festivals, the eve of which fell on a Saturday during the public ministry of our Lord were, the *Day of Atonement*, A.D. 28, and the *feast of Purim*, A.D. 29.] It is, moreover, impossible, because in the next chapter a Passover is spoken of as being nigh.[4] Had then a whole year of the Lord's life passed away in such inactivity that John is not able to say a word concerning it ?—Pentecost is in like manner impossible,

[1] John v. 9.

[2] *Jerus. Taanith*, fol. 63. 3.

[3] John vi. 4.

[4] John vi. 4.

whether that of A.D. 28 or A.D. 29. The latter, because then nearly a whole year of inactivity would intervene between John v. and John vi. ; the former, because Jesus was, according to chap. iv., at Sychar about the time of Pentecost (May 19th). Except the festal month of Tisri, there was only one other festival in addition to those above mentioned, namely, the feast of Dedication, on the 25th Kisleu,[1] which was observed seven days. Had John meant this feast, it is incomprehensible why he should not here, as in chap. x. 22, have mentioned it by name. This festival took place in winter, which in Jerusalem is sufficiently cold. How is the presence of a throng of sick persons desirous of bathing, as seen in John v. 7, to be explained ?—There remains thus only the festive month of Tisri. Had John meant the feast of Tabernacles, he would have indicated it by name, as in chap. vii. 2. He had therefore before his mind the Day of Atonement. He does not mention it by name ; for the reason that the Jews were not wont so to speak of it, but designated it by the name of " the Day," יומא.

Sec. 98. During this visit, on the Sabbath, took place at the Pool of Bethesda the healing of the man who had been 38 years diseased.[2] This called forth the first passionate outburst of hostility on the part of the Jews towards Jesus. On this occasion our Lord appealed to the testimony of the Baptist, " He was a burning and a shining lamp." [3] Jesus here speaks of John as one who was, ἦν. He had accordingly quitted the scene of his labours, for captivity or death. " John, in shining for others, consumed himself," i.e. he was a brilliant meteor, quickly burning itself out ; which, rising but a few months before, had already vanished. His labours had continued only for a period of about eight months.

Sec. 99. **The Pool of Bethesda.**—" At Jerusalem there is, by the sheep-gate, a pool, called in Hebrew Bethesda, which has five porches (or porticos)." [4] This name Bethesda [= בֵּית חִסְדָּא, cf. Syriac], which signifies " House of Mercy," occurs nowhere

---

[1] This fell in the year 28, on the 1st December.

[2] John v. 2–9. [With the following sunset the Day of Atonement began.]

[3] 'Εκεῖνος ἦν ὁ λύχνος ὁ καιόμενος καὶ φαίνων. [" He was the torch which burned and shone,"—the wedding torch, in whose light the Jews were willing for a time to exult. LUCENDO CONSUMEBATUR.]

[4] John v. 2.

else. The position of this pool, however, is to be determined by the remark that it was situated near the *sheep-gate*; for that after ἐπὶ τῇ προβατικῇ, not κολυμβήθρᾳ, but πύλῃ is to be supplied, is generally acknowledged. In Neh. xii. 39, 40, it is said that the second choir, at the dedication of the walls of Jerusalem, went " past the gate of Ephraim, and past the fish-gate, the tower of Hananeel, and the tower of Meah, even unto the sheep-gate; and they stood still at the gate ha-Matara: and so the two choirs stood by the house of God." The towers Hananeel and Meah belonged to the fortification of the Birah, later replaced by the Antonia; the sheep-gate consequently lay eastward of Antonia, in the northern wall of enclosure of the holy mountain. In that locality lies in the present day the pool called *Birket Israïn*, which later tradition regards as Bethesda. It may be right in so doing, yet, according to a still earlier tradition,[1] the pool near the church of St. Anne, north of the Birket Israïn, although now entirely choked up, is rather to be regarded as the Pool of Bethesda. This latter, however, is less probable, because the sheep-gate cannot be sought there. These two pools are enclosed within the third wall, built by Agrippa, and consequently at the time of Christ were without the city walls; but at the time when John wrote his Gospel the third wall already existed, and thus he could say, Bethesda " is in Jerusalem." [2]

[1] Cf. Robinson, i. 330, note. Ellicott, p. 139, note 2. [Bædecker's editor decides in favour of the *Hummâm esh-Shefa* of Robinson (i. 343); *probably* on account of the natural properties of the water. See Bædecker, p. 191.]

[2] See the Appendix : *Topography of Jerusalem*.

DIVISION V.

THE SECOND YEAR OF OUR LORD'S MINISTRY : A.U.C. 782, A.D. 29.

SEC. 100. After the Lord's sojourn at Jerusalem, during the anonymous festival, which we believe we have shown to be the Day of Atonement, John, vi. 1 ff., presents Him to us again in Galilee, and soon after,—as we know from the Synoptists,—beyond the lake, where (shortly before Passover A.D. 29) He wrought the miracle of feeding the five thousand. This miracle is related in the same manner by all the evangelists : Matt. xiv. 13 ; Mark vi. 30 ; Luke ix. 10 ; John vi. 2.   This fact consequently affords us a trustworthy chronological starting-point, whence to obtain a synoptical view of the Gospel history.   John relates but little of that which happened on the lake side before the miraculous feeding of the multitude ; he only says, " A great multitude followed Him, because they saw the miracles which He did on them that were diseased." [1]   From this it at least follows that the feeding of the five thousand did not at once take place on the coming of Jesus into Galilee, but that miraculous healings were before this wrought by the Lord.   What these deeds and wonders were he does not relate ; probably because he was not present.   This blank is filled up by the Synoptists.

We have shown above [2] that Luke iv. 14–44 runs parallel with John iv. 43–46, and precedes the anonymous festival. What is there related by Luke is also narrated, although partly in different order, it is true, by Matthew and Mark. We may therefore assume that all three evangelists begin the history of Jesus with His sojourn in Galilee before the anonymous festival.   Their accounts are as follow :—

[1] John vi. 2.   [2] Cf. secs. 93, 94.

	JOHN.	LUKE.	MATT.	MARK.
The rejection of Christ at Nazareth, . .	iv. 44.	iv. 14–30.	xiii. 53–58.	{i. 14, 15. {vi. 1–8.
He comes to Capernaum. Healing of the demoniac,	...	iv. 31–37.	[iv. 12–17.]	i. 21–28.
Healing of Peter's wife's mother, . .	...	iv. 38–41.	viii. 14–17.	i. 29–34.
Journeyings of Christ. *Preaches in the synagogues of Galilee. In the synagogues of Judea. Goes up to the festival at Jerusalem,* . .	v. 1.	iv. 42–44.	...	i. 35–39.

Matthew and Mark relate that all which they record of the ministry of our Lord occurred after the imprisonment of the Baptist.[1] We shall hereafter show (sec. 104) that this imprisonment in reality took place during the sojourn of Jesus at Cana, related John iv. 46 ff.

The Lord's ministry in Galilee, after the return from the anonymous festival, Luke v. 1, begins with the miraculous draught of fishes, and the calling of the three (four) first apostles. The first subsequent event of which we can precisely determine the chronology, is the disciples' plucking the ears of corn on the second-first Sabbath, Luke vi. 1; and after that, the feeding of the five thousand. After this last event, the Gospel of John speaks of four different occasions on which the Lord was absent in Judea; namely, at the feast of Tabernacles, chap. vii. 1 ff.; at the feast of Dedication, x. 22; on His visit to Bethany, where He raised Lazarus, xi. 17; and, finally, at the last Passover, xii. 12. Entirely in harmony with this is Luke, who mentions a journey to Jerusalem, ix. 51; speaks of His presence at Bethany, x. 38; indicates anew a journey to Jerusalem, xiii. 22; and, finally, marks the last journey through Jericho to the feast of Passover, xviii. 31. We thus obtain as the synoptical points: John vii. 1 = Luke ix. 51; John x. 22 = Luke x. 38; John xi. 17 = Luke xiii. 22; John xii. 12 = Luke xviii. 31. Of these journeys the last two belong to the year A.D. 30.

[1] Matt. iv. 12; Mark i. 14.

The first two, on the other hand, belong to the year A.D. 29 ; consequently, to the present division.

Below is given a general outline of the history of Christ, as recorded by Luke and John, to the time of the last Passover, together with a synoptical view of the history to the feeding of the five thousand.

(I.) SUCCESSION OF EVENTS TO THE LAST PASSOVER.

ORDER OF TIME.	PLACE.	ARRANGEMENT OF JOHN.	ARRANGEMENT OF LUKE.
YEAR I.			
Beginning of the ministry, .	Galilee.	i. 1–ii. 13.	iii. 21–iv. 13.
First Passover, . . .	Judea.	ii. 14–iv. 1.	...
Departure. Sojourn in .	Galilee.	iv. 2–54.	iv. 14–43.
Journey to the anonymous			
festival. Sojourn in .	Judea.	v. 1–47.	iv. 44.
YEAR II.			
From the approach of the			
second Passover. Sojourn			
in	Galilee.	vi. 1–vii. 9.	vi. 1–ix. 50.
Departure, ...	...	vii. 10.	ix. 51.
Journey in	Judea.	...	ix. 52–x. 37.
Sojourn at feast of Taber-			
nacles, ...	...	vii. 11–x. 21.	...
Bethany, ...	...	...	x. 38–42.
Feast of Dedication, . .	...	x. 22–39.	...
Sojourn beyond Jordan, .	...	x. 40–42.	xi. 1–xiii. 21.
YEAR III.			
Departure to Bethany, .	...	xi. 1–53.	xiii. 22–xvii. 10.
Ephraim. Journey between			
Galilee and Samaria, .	...	xi. 54–57.	xvii. 11–xix. 28.
Jericho, Bethany, . .	...	xii. 1.	xix. 29.

Sec. 101. Division of the historical material to Passover A.D. 29 :—

(II.) SYNOPTICAL VIEW OF THE HISTORY FROM THE BEGINNING OF A.D. 29 TO THE FEEDING OF THE FIVE THOUSAND.

ORDER OF EVENTS.	MARK.	LUKE.	MATTHEW.
Calling of the first apostles, . . .	i. 16–20.	v. 1–11.	iv. 18–22.
Capernaum.—Healing of one possessed, . .	i. 21–28.	cf. sec. 100.	...

ORDER OF EVENTS.	MARK.	LUKE.	MATTHEW.
Healing of Peter's mother-in-law, . . .	i. 29–34.	...	viii. 14–17.
Jesus retires into a desert place, ...	i. 35–37.	...	...
Healing of the leper. Jesus withdraws again to the wilderness, .	i. 40–45.	v. 12–14.	viii. 1–4.
After some days returns to Capernaum. Healing of the paralytic, . .	ii. 1–12.	v. 15–26.	ix. 1–8.
Repairs to the seaside. Calling of Levi, . .	ii. 13–17.	v. 27–32.	ix. 9–13.
Christ discourses concerning the fasting of John's disciples, . . .	ii. 18–22.	v. 33–39.	ix. 14–17.
The disciples pluck the ears of corn on the Sabbath day, . . .	ii. 23–28.	vi. 1–5.	xii. 1–8.
Healing of the withered hand. The Pharisees and Herodians consult to put Him to death, .	iii. 1–6.	vi. 6–11.	xii. 9–14.
Jesus retires to the sea. Several acts of healing,	iii. 7–12, 20–30.	...	xii. 15–45.
His mother and His brethren, . . .	iii. 31–35.	viii. 19–21.	xii. 46–50.
Jesus preaches by the sea,	iv. 1–34.	viii. 4–18.	xiii. 1–35.
Returns to the house. There instructs the disciples. The pearl of great price, . . .	...	...	xiii. 36–52.
The Lord preaches throughout Galilee, .	...	...	iv. 23–25.
Ordaining of the twelve apostles, . . .	iii. 13–19.	vi. 12–16.	...
The Sermon on the Mount,	...	vi. 17–49.	v. 1–vii. 29.
Capernaum.—Healing of the centurion's servant,	...	vii. 1–11.	viii. 5–13.
Nain. — Raising of the widow's son, . .	...	vii. 12–17.	xi. 1 [?].
Message of the Baptist, .	...	vii. 18–35.	xi. 2–19.
The three woes,[1] . .	...	...	xi. 20–24.
The Saviour's hour of joy,	...	...	xi. 25–30.
The woman that was a sinner, . . .	...	vii. 36–50.	...
The ministering women,	...	viii. 1–3.	...
Crossing of the sea: storm,	iv. 35–41.	viii. 22–25.	viii. 18–27.
Jesus in the land of the Gadarenes, . . .	v. 1–20.	viii. 26–39.	viii. 28–34.

[1] [Unless the historical connection of these words is that of Luke x. 13–15 ; towards the close of the Lord's ministry, cf. sec. 137.]

ORDER OF EVENTS.	MARK.	LUKE.	MATTHEW.
Capernaum.—Healing of the woman. Raising of Jairus' daughter,	v. 21–43.	viii. 40–56.	ix. 18–26.
Healing of two blind men, and of one who was dumb.	...	...	ix. 27–35.
First sending forth of the apostles,[1]	vi. 7–13.	ix. 1–6.	ix. 36–x. 42.
Death of the Baptist,	vi. 14–29.	ix. 7–9.	xiv. 1–12.
Return of the Twelve.	vi. 30.	ix. 10.	...
Feeding of the five thousand. Bethsaida-Julias. Jesus walks upon the sea, JOHN. vi. 1–21.	vi. 31–56.	ix. 11–17.	xiv. 13–36.

Sec. 102. Mark and Luke arrange the historical material in the same order; it is otherwise with Matthew. This evangelist places *before* the history of the disciples plucking the ears of corn a succession of events which the other two evangelists place *after* that history — namely, the message of the Baptist,[2] the storm on the sea, the healing of the demoniac, and the sending forth of the twelve. Luke, on the other hand, relates two histories not contained in the other Gospels, which are narrated by him after the plucking of the corn-ears—that, namely, of the raising of the young man at Nain, and that of the anointing of Jesus' feet. We find Mark more explicit in point of time and place than the other evangelists, who often employ indefinite expressions to designate the change of locality and succession of days. We therefore regard Mark's arrangement as that preserving the more strictly chronological order.

I.—*From the Return of our Lord to Galilee to the Second-First Sabbath.* (*From Beginning of the Year till 4th April* A.D. 29.)

Sec. 103. **The Second-First Sabbath.**—Thus Luke designates the Sabbath on which the plucking of the ears of corn

---

[1] [Cf. Luke xxii. 35.]   [2] Not recorded by Mark.

took place. The date of this occurrence was at any rate somewhere about the beginning of the month Nisan, A.D. 29. The
subsequent feeding of the five thousand falls shortly before
the 15th Nisan; much more must the Sabbath in question
precede the Passover. Ripe ears of barley may be found in the
Ghuweir as early as the beginning of April, but not earlier.
The given day can, however, be more nearly defined. Luke
tells us [1] that the disciples plucked the ears (of corn) on the
second-first Sabbath, ἐν σαββάτῳ δευτεροπρώτῳ. There are
few expressions in the New Testament to which such diverse
explanations have been given as to this. Without entering
into the merits of these, we simply give our own interpretation — one resting upon no mere hypothesis. We have
already [2] cited a passage from *The Preaching of Peter*, in
which it is stated that the Jews, when the moon does not
shine, do not observe the " so-called first Sabbath," σάββατον
τὸ λεγόμενον πρῶτον, which preceded, and was connected
with the Neomenia, *i.e.* the first day of the new month. Now
we have above remarked [3] that the Jews at a distance from
Jerusalem were always in uncertainty whether the month
just closed consisted of 29 or 30 days, and whether,
consequently, the first day of the new month would correspond to the 30th or the 31st day of the old. They
therefore observed both as festivals or Sabbaths; the first
of these days was called, as we learn from *The Preaching of
Peter*, σάββατον πρῶτον; the second *must* accordingly be
called σάββατον δευτερόπρωτον. Since, then, in the year A.D.
29, the Adar [Veadar] consisted of 29 days (cf. p. 13), the
1st Nisan was consequently the " first Sabbath," and the 2d
Nisan the " second-first Sabbath;" the "first Sabbath" thus
began on the evening of Sunday, 3d April, and the "second-
first " on the evening of Monday, 4th April.

Sec. 104. **The Imprisonment of John the Baptist.—**
Herod the tetrarch cast John into prison, because he had said
it was not lawful for Herod to have Herodias, his brother
Philip's wife.[4] Josephus says : " Herod slew John, called the
Baptist, who was a good man, and who exhorted those Jews

---

[1] Luke vi. 1.   [2] Cf. sec. 11.   [3] Cf. sec. 14.
[4] Matt. xiv. 3, 4 ; Mark vi. 17, 18 ; Luke iii. 19, 20.

that were intent upon virtue, were righteous towards each
other and pious towards God, to come to baptism. . . . Now
when people crowded to him on all sides, and were carried
away by his words, Herod feared he might abuse his influence over the people to stir up a rebellion, since they
seemed inclined in all things to be obedient to his suggestions.
He thought it therefore advisable to put him out of the way
before he should attempt any commotion. . . . In consequence of this suspicion on the part of Herod, he was bound,
sent to Machærus, and there put to death." [1]   Machærus was
a fortress beyond Jordan, or rather beyond the Dead Sea; in
the present day the place is called Mkaur, and lies upon a
high mountain, Attarûs by name, on the southern bank of the
Wady Zerka Maîn. [2]—The time at which John was imprisoned
can no longer be determined with precision.   Thus much is
certain, that after the Passover of the year A.D. 28 he was still
at liberty, and at the Fast of the Atonement of the same year
was already a prisoner ; if, namely   of which there can be no
room for doubt—the anonymous festival in which the Lord
spoke of John as one *who was*, [3] is to be regarded as the Day
of Atonement.   At some time, then, between these two dates,
John was cast into prison.   If, as we conclude, [4] that event
took place while Jesus was at Cana of Galilee, [5] where He
arrived during the month of May, at harvest time, Matthew
and Mark are justified in dating the beginning of their narrative from the imprisonment of the Baptist.   To the time preceding the anonymous festival belongs, as we have seen, [6]
Luke iv. 14–44, and consequently also Matt. iv. 12–17 and
Mark i. 14 ff.   We can hardly escape the inference that our
Lord, during His sojourn at Cana, was led, by the intelligence
that John had been cast into prison, to come forth by the Sea
of Gennesareth, *i.e.* to enter on a wider circuit of labour, and
take up His abode at Capernaum.

[1] *Antiq.* xviii. 5, sec. 2.

[2] [According to Bædecker (p. 317), 3860 feet above the Dead Sea, and 2546
above the Mediterranean.   On the fortress itself, see Ritter, iii. 70.   Cf. Ellicott,
p. 129, note 2.]

[3] John v. 35.

[4] [From Matt. iv. 12 ff. as compared with John iv. 43, 44.]

[5] John iv. 46.   [6] Cf. sec. 93.

Sec. 105. **Herod the Tetrarch.**—The author of John's death was a son of Herod the Great and of Malthace. After the death of his father he became tetrarch of Galilee and Peræa.[1] His first wife was the daughter of Aretas, king of Petra. He subsequently took to himself Herodias, wife of his brother Herod.[2] The daughter of Aretas fled to her father, who later made war with Herod on account of this injury. John the Baptist had said to Herod, " It is not lawful for thee to have thy brother's wife." This was the cause of his imprisonment. The same Herod Antipas was the founder of the city of Tiberias, which, at the time of our Lord's ministry, was still building. Herod, however, seems already to have had his residence in this town ; a consideration by which the fact is explained that our Lord, who avoided this prince, never entered Tiberias. The relation of the Lord to Herod is touched upon in Luke ix. 7 ff., xiii. 31 ff. ; Mark viii. 15.

Sec. 106. Nothing would prevent our placing the beginning of our Lord's ministry at the lake in the latter part of the year 28, since the Baptist had then at any rate been already long in captivity, if the Synoptists had related to us somewhat more than they have done of the Lord's work at that time. But that which takes place before the second-first Sabbath is in too great numerical disproportion with that which is related of the next fourteen days, for us to be able to conceive of the first event, **the miraculous draught of fishes,** as happening earlier than the beginning of the year 29. The place which was the scene of this miracle is not mentioned by name : it admits of no doubt, however, that it was Bethsaïda, the town of Peter, the fisher-haven of Capernaum, the present Khân Betszeida, or Minyeh. This miraculous draught was immediately followed by the calling of Peter, James, and John, according to Luke ; of Andrew also, according to the other Synoptists. This calling to the apostolate is not to be identified with the calling to the discipleship, described in John i. 37 ff., which took place a year earlier. The manner

---

[1] Josephus, *Antiq.* xvii. 8, sec. 1 ; 11, sec. 4.

[2] So he is called by Josephus, *Antiq.* xviii. 5, sec. 1 ; in Matt. xiv. 3 he is called Philip. He was probably called Herod Philip ; as the tetrarch of Galilee and Peræa was called Herod Antipas.

in which the sons of Zebedee, James and John, are introduced by the Synoptists might call forth surprise.   Zebedee and his sons were citizens of Jerusalem, where they had their home and associations; and here it would appear as though they, like Andrew and Peter, were inhabitants of Bethsaïda.   On this matter the books of Jewish tradition afford us light. In *Bab. Baba Kama*, fol. 80. 2, it is expressly said that every Israelite, wherever might be his abode, had a right to engage in the fishery on the Sea of Tiberias.   Of this right many denizens of Jerusalem would naturally avail themselves; especially at the time of the Passover, when it was a question of providing the Holy City with provisions for a million and a half of pilgrims.   If we think of Zebedee as such a citizen of Jerusalem, who with Simon and Andrew plied the fishing, every difficulty and objection disappears.   This labour seems to have been pursued with special zeal in February and March ; for at this season in the year 28 we found John in company with Simon and Andrew on the shore of the lake, and now it is the same again in 29.   It is probable that Nathanael, the man of Cana, was present on a like errand at Bethsaïda, when he became the Lord's disciple.[1]

When, in consequence of this vocation, it is said: " They left all, and followed Him," it results that such following in the narrower sense had not previously existed; although these men had already been a year the disciples of Jesus,—a connection and acquaintance which the Synoptists too presuppose, since they, and especially the two first evangelists, assign no reason for the following of the disciples immediately upon the call.   If the association of these men with Jesus was not as yet a constant one, we cannot feel surprise that they were not with Him in Jerusalem, and that John, the Jerusalemite, alone could give an account of that which took place there. Even for the subsequent period the following of the disciples was no constant one in the stricter sense ; we shall still have often to indicate the absence of one or other of the apostles.

Mark i. 21 brings into immediate connection with the calling of those four *the healing of a demoniac* in the synagogue

[1] Cf. sec. 81.

at Capernaum. He says, they came away after Him: and
they enter into Capernaum, and straightway[1] on the Sabbath
day He entered into the synagogue, where He wrought the
miracle of healing. Luke places this miracle at an earlier
period.[2] We cannot decide which of them observes the true
order. The same is the case also with *the healing of Peter's
mother-in-law.* This took place on the same day as the
healing of the demoniac;[3] so that the same chronological uncertainty attaches to it. Here Mark mentions, chap. i. 38, 39,
a *tour of Jesus through Galilee,* which is one with that to
Judea, related in Luke iv. 42. The unquestioned reading of
" Galilee " in Mark was on harmonistic grounds substituted in
place of the " Judea " in Luke.

According to Luke, the first miracle wrought by Jesus on
His return from Judea, after the anonymous festival, was *the
healing of the leper.* Where the scene of this miracle was,
cannot be learnt from the narrative in the evangelists.
According to Matthew, chap. viii. 1, it took place after the
Sermon on the Mount, before the Lord entered Capernaum.
That it did not take place at Capernaum, we learn also from
Mark i. 40, 45, ii. 1. According to Luke v. 12, it took place
" in one of the towns," ἐν μιᾷ τῶν πόλεων.

The healing of the paralytic was, according to Mark ii. 1,
wrought at Capernaum, some days after the healing of the
leper.[4] The place was without doubt Capernaum, although
this is nowhere expressly stated. On the same day,[5] while
Jesus was going from Capernaum to the sea,[6] was the *call of
Levi.* The customs house lay consequently on the sea-side, *i.e.*
at Bethsaïda ; placed there probably on account of the fishery,
which was not likely to be toll free. On the same day Jesus
gave judgment on the fasting of John's disciples.[7] After this,
but without definite connection in point of time with what
precedes, is related the history of the plucking of the ears.

---

[1] καὶ εὐθέως ; Mark i. 21.   [2] Luke iv. 31 ff.; cf. sec. 95.
[3] Mark i. 29 ; Luke iv. 38.
[4] εἰς τὴν ἰδίαν πόλιν, Matt. ix. 1 ; cf. Luke v. 16, 17.
[5] Luke v. 27.   [6] Mark ii. 13.
[7] Matt. ix. 14–17 ; Mark ii. 18–22 ; Luke v. 33–38. [From Mark's account,
an actual fast-day ; therefore probably a Monday or Thursday. Cf. Luke
xviii. 12.]

II.—*From the Second-First Sabbath to the Storm upon the Sea.*

Sec. 107. The second-first Sabbath we have already shown to be the 1st Nisan, *i.e.* the 4th April, A.D. 29. Mark and Luke make mention, immediately after the history of the plucking of the corn-ears, which belonged to the events of that Sabbath, of the healing of the man with the withered hand, upon a Sabbath day, in the synagogue of Capernaum. In Matthew the facts are placed in another connection. In Mark, chap. iii. 1, the transition from the plucking of the ears to the said healing is brought about by the words, "And He entered again into the synagogue; and there was a man there which had a hand withered. And they watched Him, whether He would heal him on the Sabbath." According to this evangelist, the healing of the withered hand thus took place on the same day on which the disciples had plucked the corn. On this day the Pharisees, already embittered, wished to test by an actual case the question how the Lord stood with regard to the Pharisaic Sabbath tradition. He had permitted an act to His disciples which seemed to them a Sabbath-desecrating labour: they would now see—for by them had the presence of the sick man been contrived—whether Jesus would feel Himself justified in performing an act which, according to their tradition, was a toil. Now, that the healing of a sick man was really regarded as a Sabbath-breaking labour, is evident from the *Jerus. Berachoth*, iii. 1, where it is related that Rabbi Meïr, the teacher of Rabbi Jehuda the holy, proposed tempering this too severe precept, to the extent of permitting in future oil and wine to be applied as remedial agents. The healing wrought by the Lord now completed the rupture with the Pharisaic party.[1]

Luke, chap. vi., connects the healing of this man with the plucking of the corn, by the words: ἐγένετο δὲ καὶ ἐν ἑτέρῳ σαββάτῳ εἰσελθεῖν αὐτὸν, κ.τ.λ. If we understand by these words " on another Sabbath," there is a contradiction between Mark and Luke; if, however, we render them by, " on the remaining part of the Sabbath," *i.e.* on the morrow, the con-

[1] Mark iii. 6.

tradiction disappears.[1] The plucking of the ears had taken place on the evening of the 4th April, after the second-first Sabbath had begun ; on the same Sabbath, but on the following day, 5th April, Jesus went again into the synagogue and healed the withered hand. As the Pharisees now took a decisive step, so also our Lord. He left Capernaum, repaired to the sea, and presently after to a mountain, where He ordained the Twelve.[2]

Sec. 108. **The Sermon on the Mount.**—According to Luke, chap. vi. 13, the Lord ordained the Twelve upon the mountain, calling them to Himself as soon as it was day. He then went down with them, and took His stand upon a level place,[3] where He addressed to the great assembled multitude the discourse recorded vers. 20-49. The Sermon on the Mount is placed by the Evangelist Matthew, the collector of the discourses, at the head of his Gospel, as the programme of the kingdom of God. It cannot, however, by any means be regarded as the first public act of Jesus, for a series of acts must at any rate have preceded it, in order that the multitude spoken of in Matt. iv. 25 might be gathered out of all the lands there mentioned — Galilee, Decapolis, Jerusalem, Judea, Peræa. That which is said Matt. iv. 18-23 does not suffice to explain it. We hold, therefore, that Luke gives this discourse in its true chronological order.

A very old tradition, already favoured by Jerome,[4] against which no reasonable objection can be raised, places the mountain, called from the blessings contained in the discourse there pronounced the " Mount of Beatitudes," *Mons Beatitudinum,* upon the Karûn Hattîn. This mountain, on which there are two knolls or horns, lies upon the high plateau which stretches westward from the lake. It is situated at about four miles S.W. from Ain-Mudawara, or Capernaum. At its foot extends the plain of Hattîn. There were the people assembled, to

---

[1] [That is to say, Luke speaks of the next day, which was also Sabbath, as another Sabbath. Cf. sec. 126 on Luke ix. 37.]

[2] Mark iii. 7-10 ; Luke ix. 6-12.

[3] ἐπὶ τόπου πεδινοῦ, Luke vi. 17.

[4] *Ep.* 44 *ad Marcell.* t. iv. p. 522, ed. Mart.

whom Jesus came down ; and the discourse which He held to them was none the less delivered on the mountain, in approaching which from the land of Gennesar one must make a considerable rise. That which leads many geographers, *e.g.* Von Raumer,[1] to reject this tradition, is the unsuitable misplacing of Capernaum at Tell-Hûm, and the incongruous story of the monks, who point out the same mountain as the scene of the feeding of the five thousand ; whereas this last must certainly be sought on the other side of the Sea of Galilee. That a very ancient tradition of the Christians attaches to Karûn Hattîn, is shown by the fact that among the Arabs certain blocks of rock upon this mountain bear the name of Hejâr Nasâra, *i.e.* stones of the Christians (or, of Christ the Nazarene ?). Robinson,[2] who in coming up from the south climbed the eastern horn of the Tell-Hattîn, says : " As seen on this side, the tell or mountain is merely a low ridge, some 30 or 40 feet in height, and not 10 minutes in length from east to west. At its eastern end is an elevated point or horn, perhaps 60 feet above the plain, and at the western end another not so high. These give to the ridge at a distance the appearance of a saddle, and are called Kurûn Hattîn, the ' Horns of Hattîn.' But the singularity of this ridge is, that on reaching the top you find that it lies along the very border of the great southern plain [of el-Lûbieh], where this latter sinks off at once, by a precipitous offset, to the lower plain of Hattîn, from which the northern side of the tell rises very steeply, not much less than 400 feet. Below, on the north, lies the village of Hattîn, and further towards the north and north-east a second similar offset forms the descent to the level of the lake.

" The summit of the eastern horn is a little circular plain, and the top of the lower ridge between the two horns is also flattened to a plain. The whole mountain is of limestone. On the eastern horn are the remains of a small building, probably once a Wely, with a few rough ruins of no import; yet the natives now dignify the spot with the name of el-Medîneh. This point commands a near view of the great plain [to the south] north of Tabor, and also of the basin Ard el-Hamma ;

[1] *Pal.* p. 37.   [2] *Pal.* ii. 370 ff.

the latter lying spread out before us with fields of varied hues, like a carpet. On the other side the eye takes in, even here, only the northern part of the Lake of Tiberias, and on its western shore the little plain of Gennesareth; while in the north and north-west Safed and a few other villages are seen upon the hills. The prospect is in itself pleasing, but bears no comparison with that which we had just enjoyed from Mount Tabor. This tell is nearly on a line between Tabor and Hermon, the latter being about N.N.E. $\frac{1}{2}$ E., and the former nearly S.S.W. $\frac{1}{2}$ W."

Sec. 109. "When He had ended all His sayings in the audience of the people, He entered into Capernaum," it is said in Luke vii. 1. There He healed the centurion's servant.[1] This miracle, which Mark does not relate, is narrated by Matthew as occurring after the Lord's return to Capernaum from the Mount of Beatitudes. One proof the more that the Sermon on the Mount, as related by Matthew, and the discourse of our Lord in Luke vi. 20 ff., are one and the same. Here Luke, chap. vii. 11–17, inserts the history of the *raising of the young man at Nain ;* which history may find its point of attachment in the journeyings of our Lord, when " He went thence to teach and preach in their cities." [2]   Matthew has immediately before, chap. x. 1–42, described the constituting of the apostolate of the Twelve ; the same as Luke, with the omission of the Sermon on the Mount, which had already been communicated chap. v.–vii. " The following day," says Luke, ἐν τῇ ἑξῆς, consequently, on the day after the Sermon on the Mount and the healing of the centurion's servant, " Jesus went into a city called Nain : " at the gates of this city He raised the young man.[3]

Sec. 110. **Nain.**—This place, which in the present day still bears the ancient name, lies in the plain of Esdraelon, at the northern foot of the Jebel ed-Duhi (Lesser Hermon), southward from Mount Tabor, about 24 miles from Capernaum. Since the Esdraelon plain passes over, without any considerable plunge, into the Ghôr, at Bîsan, it is to be

---

[1] Luke vii. 2–10 ; Matt. viii. 5–13.   [2] Matt. xi. 1.
[3] Luke vii. 11–17.

supposed that our Lord proceeded from the Ghôr to Nain, coming by ship to the southern end of the lake.[1] This journey, thus understood, would not occupy more than two days.

Sec. 111. **The Message of the Baptist.**—John sent two of his disciples to Jesus and asked, "Art thou He that should come, or do we look for another?" This fact is related by Matthew and Luke.[2] When and where did this happen? Luke leaves us in doubt whether these messengers came to Him in the vicinity of Nain or at Capernaum, where the events of chap. vii. 36–50 must have taken place. Matthew leads us to suppose that it was at Capernaum. Luke places this history after the second-first Sabbath; Matthew, on the other hand, before it. From the second-first Sabbath to the feeding of the five thousand is an interval of twelve or thirteen days, of which that which is related until now takes up seven or eight. Now John's death falls [according to the order observed in the narrative of Matthew and Mark][3] two or three days before the feeding of the five thousand; but that would be about the day when John's disciples were with Jesus, and they consequently would not have found their master alive on their return. The place assigned by Matthew to the sending of these messengers seems therefore to us to be the true one. Luke perhaps placed this narrative after that of the raising of the young man at Nain, in order that the words of the Lord (ver. 22), "Dead ones are raised," might rest upon an accomplished fact. [Nothing, however, prevents our believing these two events to have happened in the order recorded by Luke, and at the time indicated by Matthew, *i.e.* before the second-first Sabbath. From

---

[1] Stanley says of this ruined hamlet : "One entrance alone could it have had, that which opens on the rough hill-side in its downward slope to the plain."— *Sinai and Pal.* p. 357, ed. 5. Van de Velde says in his *Memoir*, that the rock on the west side of Nain is full of sepulchral caves, whence he infers that the Lord approached it on that side. See Ellicott, p. 181, note 2. Tristram refers to the traces still remaining of the ancient walls, as showing that it was once a *walled* town, and so with *gates*, as in the Gospel narrative.—*Land of Israel*, p. 129. Thomson saw a large number of tombs on the *east* side of the village.— *Land and Book*, p. 445.

[2] Matt. xi. 2-19 ; Luke vii. 18-35.   [3] Matt. xiv. 6-12 ; Mark vi. 21-29.

Luke ix. 7–9 the Baptist must have been put to death *early* in that year,—some considerable time before Passover A.D. 29.] [1]

Sec. 112. After the history of the messengers of John, probably on the evening of the same day, Luke relates [2] that Jesus went to be a guest with a Pharisee, Simon by name. There a woman that was a sinner anointed His feet, and the Lord related the parable of the two pardoned debtors. This history is not given in Matthew and Mark. In place of it we read, Matt. xii. 22 ff., the history of one healed by the Lord, a demoniac who was blind and dumb. The Pharisees exclaimed, " He casteth out the devils by the Prince of the devils." This drew forth from the Lord the warning regarding the sin against the Holy Ghost. Since the scribes and Pharisees required a sign, the Lord promised them the sign of the prophet Jonah. " While He yet talked to the people, behold His mother and His brethren stood without, desiring to speak with Him. . . . And stretching forth His hand towards His disciples, He said, ' Behold my mother and my brethren.' " [3] In Mark iii. 20 ff. the same reproach also is found, though introduced in another connection, the reproach of casting out devils by Beelzebub, as well as the saying about Jonah, and the coming of his mother and his brethren. This account, so far as concerns the mother and the brethren, is found also in Luke viii. 19 ff.; but after the parable of the sower, and immediately before the crossing over the sea. The two first evangelists, after they have reported the discourse in which the Lord says who are His mother and His brethren, add : " On the same day Jesus went out of the house and sat by the sea ; [4] and . . . He entered into a ship, and the whole multitude stood on the shore, and He spoke to them in parables." The parables which are given in Mark iv. 1–33 are those of the seed on different ground, of the growth of the seed without the intervention of man, and of the grain of mustard seed. Matthew, chap. xiii. 1–35, has the same, with the

---

[1] Cf. sec. 115.

[2] Luke vii. 36–50. On this history, compare the remarks of Ellicott, p. 182 note 2.

[3] Matt. xii. 46–50.   [4] Matt. xiii. 1.

exception of that of the growth of the seed; instead of which we have the parable of the tares in the field, of the hidden treasure, of the pearl of great price, and of the net with which are taken fish of every kind. Matthew next relates the Lord's journey to Capernaum and to Nazareth.[1] In Mark, on the other hand, the parables are immediately succeeded by that crossing of the sea which led to the feeding of the five thousand; while in Luke the passage to the land of the Gadarenes follows the words touching His mother and His brethren.

Sec. 113. **The first crossing of the Lake.**—This event is related alike by all the Synoptists.[2] Jesus proceeded from the western shore (Bethsaïda) across the lake. During the passage a tempest arose, and filled the disciples with dismay,—a tempest which was presently stilled by the Lord.[3] On the other side of the lake, in the district of the Gadarenes, Gergesenes, to Gerasenes, He healed a demoniac.[4] When did this first crossing of the sea take place? According to Matthew's order of narrating, it belongs to a period considerably earlier, at any rate before the second-first Sabbath, perhaps before the anonymous festival, because it is related shortly after the healing of Peter's wife's mother. According to Mark and Luke, it preceded by only a few days the feeding of the five thousand. Since these two last evangelists are wont in general to observe the chronological succession of events more strictly than Matthew, we accept their order as the correct one in this case too. As concerns the place, it may be difficult to determine which of the three readings merits the preference, whether χώρα Γεργεσηνῶν, or Γαδαρηνῶν, or Γερασηνῶν. The name *Gergesa* is absolutely unknown in geography. *Gerasa* may, at the time of Jesus, as being the

---

[1] Matt. xiii. 36, 53–58. [πατρίς, as distinguished from ἰδία πόλις, always means Nazareth.]

[2] Matt. viii. 18–31; Mark iv. 35–v. 20; Luke viii. 22–39.

[3] [On the peculiar features of this miracle, cf. Ellicott, 167, n. 3. It is touchingly commemorated in the beautiful lines of M'Cheyne, beginning: "Behind the hills of Naphtali."]

[4] According to Matthew, viii. 28 ff., there were *two* demoniacs healed. [With reference to the silence of the other evangelists as to the presence of a second demoniac, cf. Ellicott, *Lectures on the Life of our Lord*, p. 188, note 2.]

metropolis of the Decapolis in the general sense of *Regio Decapolitana*, have also comprehended under its name the eastern shore of the Sea of Galilee.[1] The same remark applies to Gadara, of which the township, moreover, extended directly to the sea.[2] But if the name of the region is doubtful, the region itself is not. That it belonged to the Decapolis is evident from Mark v. 20, as compared with Luke viii. 39. Now to this domain belonged that part of the eastern coast which extended from the Wady Semakh to the southern end of the lake.[3] We are accordingly told, Luke viii. 26, that the said region lies over against Galilee— ἀντιπέρα. Jesus, in healing the demoniac, permitted the demons to enter into a herd of swine, who rushed down the precipitous side of the hill—κατὰ τοῦ κρημνοῦ—into the sea.[4] This took place then on a part of the coast where the eastern mountain range slopes down with a steep declivity to the very edge of the lake ; which seems to be especially the case in the region of Adveriban. On account, however, of the striking resemblance between *Chersa* and Gerasa, or Gergesa, the scene of the miracle is probably to be placed by the Wady Semakh.

Sec. 114. The sojourn of Jesus on the Decapolitan domain was of but brief duration.[5] When He landed on the western coast at Bethsaïda a great crowd of people awaited Him, among them Jairus, whose daughter He raised from the dead. The scene of this miracle was evidently Capernaum. On the way thither, the woman who had the issue of blood was healed by the touch of His garment's hem. This is followed, according to Mark vi. 1, by a journey of Jesus to Nazareth. Matthew also, chap. xiii. 54, places this journey shortly before the feeding of the five thousand. Luke does not mention it, unless it is identical with the one recorded by him, chap. iv. 16. This evangelist relates immediately after the raising of the daughter of Jairus a first mission of the apostles.[6] " And," it is said, chap. ix. 6, " going forth [from Capernaum], they journeyed through the villages, τὰς

---

[1] Cf. sec. 72, *h*.   [2] Cf. sec. 72, *c*.
[3] Cf. sec. 72, *l*.   [4] Luke viii. 33.
[5] Matt. viii. 34 ; Mark v. 17 ; Luke viii. 37.   [6] Luke ix. 1–6.

κώμας, everywhere evangelizing and healing." There is thus
here no reference to any considerable journey and prolonged
absence ; but to a journeying through the villages of the
western seaboard, which does not call for more than a single
day for its accomplishment.

Sec. 115. The fact next following is now the feeding of
the five thousand. If we then from this point review the
historical material which the Synoptists have piled up between
the history of the plucking of the ears and that of the feeding
of the five thousand, we must regard it as impossible to range
all this within the brief period of something like a fortnight,
from 1st to 14th Nisan : we must therefore conclude that the
evangelists did not design to follow any strictly chronological
order. The attempt to determine the exact date of each
single event must thus be abandoned as an impracticable
undertaking. We must be content with fixing in general the
limits of time ; and these we may look upon as already
satisfactorily established.

III.—The Feeding of the Five Thousand.

Sec. 116. The immediate occasion of the second crossing of
the lake by Jesus was **the death of John the Baptist.** For
Herod, who had beheaded John, thought, when he heard of
the deeds of Jesus, that this was the Baptist risen from the
dead.[1] The Lord, to avoid this tyrant, repaired therefore to
the eastern side of the lake.[2] In connection with this, the
Synoptists relate the manner and cause of the execution of
the forerunner of Christ. The place of the execution was,
according to Josephus, the fortress of Machærus, on the east
side of the Dead Sea.[3] The evangelists do not mention the
place ; nothing thus hinders our accepting the statement of
the Jewish historian as true.[4] The *time* of the execution of
the Baptist cannot be very nearly determined from the Gospel
accounts. According to Luke vii. 18, John was still alive

---

[1] Matt. xiv. 1, 2 ; Mark vi. 14 ; Luke ix. 7.
[2] Matt. xiv. 13.   [3] Cf. sec. 104.
[4] [Wieseler places the scene of his death at *Livias* ; but cf. Ellicott, p. 129,
note 2.]

eight days after the second-first Sabbath ; he was dead when
Jesus went to Bethsaïda-Julias, about the 12th Nisan : the
execution is thus perhaps to be placed between the 12th and
16th April A.D. 29. Some chronologists, among others
Wieseler,[1] have sought more nearly to define this day from
the statement, Matt. xiv. 6, Mark vi. 21, that the beheading
was ordered at the time when Herod was celebrating his
γενέσια. This term may indicate either the birthday or the
day of accession to the throne. If it signifies the birthday,
this statement avails us nothing, since it is unknown on what
day Herod Antipas was born ; if it signifies the day of his
accession to the throne, it is still a question whether Herod
dated this from the time of his appointment by the Emperor
Augustus, or from that of the death of his father, Herod the
Great. Wieseler supposes this latter. We cannot, however,
by any means accept this view, since Herod was not tetrarch
by inheritance or by his father's will ; on the contrary, Herod
had by his will formally disinherited Antipas and the other
sons, and bequeathed his whole kingdom to Archelaus. This
will was overthrown, and Augustus appointed Antipas tetrarch.[2]
The date of the appointment by the Emperor is unknown ; at
any rate, not in the month of April. The only chronological
result to be gained from these γενέσια is the determination of
the month of Herod's birth,—a date to which no interest
attaches. In order to arrive by another method at the year
of the Baptist's death, appeal has been made to Josephus,
Antiq. xviii. 5, sec. 2. It is there said that the Jews
attributed the defeat inflicted on Herod by Aretas, king of
Petra, to the judgment of God on account of the death of
John the Baptist. Herod suffered this defeat shortly before
the death of the Emperor Tiberius, A.D. 36. From this, however, it does not at all follow that the Baptist was put to
death A.D. 36 rather than A.D. 29. A calamity overtaking
Herod seven years after the crime might still be regarded as
a punishment for that crime.

---

[1] Wieseler, *Synopsis*, p. 266 ff. of Engl. trans.

[2] Josephus, *Antiq.* xvii. 8, sec. 1 ; 11, sec. 4. [The general purport of
Herod's will appears, however, to have been carried out by Augustus ; cf. *de
Bello,* i. 23, sec. 7 ; ii. 6, sec. 3.]

Sec. 117. Jesus withdrew again beyond the Sea of Galilee[1] to a city which is called Bethsaïda;[2] and a great multitude of people followed Him. Now the Passover, the festival of the Jews, was nigh.[3] There, in a solitary place,[4] where there was much grass,[5] He fed five thousand men with five loaves and two fishes.[6] As concerns the time at which this miracle was wrought, we shall be guilty of no rashness in concluding that the day in question was the 12th or 13th Nisan [15th or 16th April]. That Bethsaïda beyond Jordan, called also Julias, and identical with the castle of Szeida, is here meant, has been shown above, sec. 71.

When Jesus perceived that they would come and carry Him off to make Him king, He retired to a mountain alone to pray. The disciples, when it was already evening, began to cross the sea. In the midst of the sea, however, they had to contend with contrary winds.[7] About the fourth watch of the night,[8] when they had proceeded some five and twenty furlongs,[9] they saw Jesus walking on the sea, coming to them. They received Him into the ship; and immediately the ship was at the land, whither they went.[10] The land to which they were going was Capernaum;[11] there, consequently, in the haven of Capernaum, at Bethsaïda, they landed. Now, Matthew, as well as Mark, says that they landed in the country of Gennesareth.[12] The position of Capernaum must thus, as we have already determined it, have been in the land of Gennesar, the El-Ghuweir. The accepting of Tell-Hûm as the site of the Lord's city (ἰδία πόλις) would involve John in contradiction with the Synoptists. One proof the more for

[1] John vi. 1.   [2] Luke ix. 10.   [3] John vi. 2-4.
[4] Mark vi. 35. [The scene of this miracle is well described by Thomson, p. 372.]
[5] John vi. 10.
[6] Matt. xiv. 19; Mark vi. 39; Luke ix. 14; John vi. 10.
[7] Matt. xiv. 24; Mark vi. 47; cf. John vi. 14.
[8] Matt. xiv. 25.   [9] John vi. 19.
[10] John vi. 21. [For a vivid description of a similar tempest witnessed on the lake, see Dr. Thomson, *The Land and the Book*, p. 375; and especially Tristram, *Land of Israel*, pp. 433, 434; for some excellent remarks on this whole history, Ellicott, pp. 208, 209.]
[11] John vi. 17.
[12] εἰς τὴν γῆν Γιννησαρίτ, Matt. xiv. 34; Mark vi. 53.

the correctness of the position we have assigned to Capernaum, sec. 63. John's account appears to differ from that of the Synoptists to the extent that, according to these latter, the meeting of the disciples with Jesus took place in the midst of the sea; whilst John states that so soon as they had received Jesus on board the ship, they were immediately at the shore. The contradiction, however, is only apparent. When they were in the midst of the sea, or yet more definitely, with John, when they had made 25 out of the 40 stades of the sea's width,[1] they saw one walking on the sea, whom they did not at once recognise as the Lord; when at length they recognised Him, and received Him into the ship, they came immediately to the shore.[2] Here again we have a fresh proof that Capernaum is not Tell-Hûm. From Bethsaïda to Tell-Hûm is scarcely the half of the total breadth of the lake, about 20 stades therefore; thus, after having already traversed 25 stades in this direction, they could no longer be on the high sea.

Sec. 118. On the day after the feeding of the five thousand, the Lord, according to John vi. 22–59, held in the synagogue at Capernaum, the discourse concerning the eating of His flesh and the drinking of His blood. It became a critical turning-point for the disciples of Jesus, of whom many from that time drew back from following Him.[3] It seems to us to be the place here to enter upon the question why the Evangelist John, in the description of the last paschal meal, does not mention the institution of the Lord's Supper. That the discourse now before us has the design of, in some measure, making amends for this silence, has often been asserted, and certainly with perfect justice; but those who assert this have, it seems to us, stopped short at half-way. A meal of this nature—of which the Supper on the eve of the Lord's death was only a somewhat modified continuation—seems to have

---

[1] Cf. Josephus, de Bello, iii. 10, sec. 7.

[2] John says: "They *were willing* then to receive Him" (vi. 21). The contrast he institutes is with the terror they had before displayed. That Christ was willing to enter the ship it was not necessary to say. Upon His coming on board the wind ceased, and immediately they were at the shore. The narrative is in undesigned agreement with that of the Synoptists.]

[3] John vi. 60 ff.

been already ordained at the paschal season of the year 29,
which Jesus spent on the shore of the Lake of Gennesareth.
If one considers the expression so frequently recurring in the
Gospels, " He was made known to them in the breaking of
the bread," [1] as well as the oft-repeated formula, " He took
the bread, gave thanks, brake it, and gave to the disciples,"
which occurs alike at the institution of the Supper, at the
feeding of the five thousand, and at that of the four thousand,
—the thought suggests itself that all these were sacramental
repasts, to which the words of John vi. 22 ff. form the commentary.   As early as the Passover A.D. 29 had the Lord, if
not already substituted His Passover for the Mosaic one, yet
instituted it side by side with the other, and drawn His
disciples closer to Himself, and confirmed them in personal
communion with Himself, by that meal which He distributed
to them.   Such a step, from the previous mere proclamation
of the coming kingdom of God to the actual summoning of
followers, must frighten away the undecided ; but, on the other
hand, must call forth and stimulate true believers.   This very
effect it is described as having in John vi. 60–71.   The mere
words could not produce this ; it must have now come to a
decisive act.   The so-called institution of the Lord's Supper
was thus only to such an extent an instituting, as something
already existing was enriched with new thoughts, and destined
to continuance after the Lord's death.   But since this new
element was for the Apostle John already virtually communicated in every meal till then blessed and distributed by the
Lord from the time of the Passover by the lake, the last meal
also was for him nothing else than each previously partaken
of—namely, a sacrament of communion of life with the Lord.
This discourse of Jesus is communicated only in the Gospel
of John ; but the effect it produced, namely, the falling away
of some, the joyful confession of others,—in a word, the crisis,
—is simultaneously indicated by Matthew and Luke.[2]

[1] Luke xxiv. 30, 31, 35 ; John xxi. 13 ; cf. Luke xxii. 19 ; Mark vi. 41, viii
6, and parallel places.
[2] Luke ix. 19–27 ; Matt. xiv. 33.

IV.—*Synopsis of the Events following the Feeding of the Five Thousand, during the Year* A.D. 29. (Matt. xv. 1–xix. 1; Mark vii. 1–x. 1; Luke ix. 18–xiii. 30; John vii. 1–x. 40.)

Sec. 119. Up to the time of the feeding of the five thousand, the Gospel of Luke, by virtue of its more numerous points of contact with the Johannine accounts on the one hand, and with the accounts of the two first Synoptists on the other, formed a sure element from which to obtain a synopsis of the four Gospels. This, however, is, so far as concerns the events of the year 29, henceforth unfortunately in much less degree the case; since the three Synoptists are very sparing with regard to chronological and topographical data. Nevertheless we may attain, with some degree of certainty, an historical groundwork, by means of the tables of contents of the four Gospels, given below.

(III.) SUCCESSION OF EVENTS, ACCORDING TO THE FIRST TWO EVANGELISTS.

CONTENTS OF THE NARRATIVE.	REF. IN MATT.	REF. IN MARK.
Immediately after the return from the feeding of the five thousand, Jesus converses, with the scribes and Pharisees from Jerusalem, on the washing of hands, . .	xv. 1–20.	vii. 1–23.
Journey of Jesus in the district of Tyre and Sidon, . . .	xv. 21–28.	vii. 24–30.
Return to the Galilean Sea, region of Decapolis, ...	xv. 29–31.	vii. 31–37.
Feeding of the four thousand, .	xv. 32–38.	viii. 1–9.
Passage to Magadan (Dalmanutha),	xv. 39–xvi. 4.	viii. 10–12.
Passage to Bethsaïda (Julias), .	xvi. 5–12.	viii. 13–22.
Healing of the blind man, . .	...	viii. 22–26.
Journey to Cæsarea Philippi, .	xvi. 13–28.	viii. 27–ix. 1.
Transfiguration of Jesus, . .	xvii. 1–21.	ix. 2–29.
Journey through Galilee, . .	xvii. 22, 23.	ix. 30–32.
Jesus at Capernaum. Temple tribute, ...	xvii. 24–xviii. 35.	ix. 33–50.
Jesus in Judea beyond Jordan, .	xix. 1.	x. 1.

(IV.) Succession of Events, according to Luke.

Contents.	Reference.
Jesus asks the disciples, Whom do the people say that I am? (cf. Matt. xvi. 13 ; Mark viii. 27),	ix. 18–27.
Transfiguration of Christ,	ix. 28–50.
Journey to Jerusalem, through the land of the Samaritans,	ix. 51–62.
Second mission of the disciples. Woe upon Chorazin, etc. (cf. Matt. x. 20–28),	x. 1–37.
Jesus at Bethany. Mary and Martha,	x. 38–42.
Doctrine of prayer. Healing of the dumb man,	xi. 1–36.
Jesus at table with a Pharisee,	xi. 37–54.
Words and works,	xii. 1–xiii. 30.
Jesus warned against Herod. " It cannot be that a prophet perish out of Jerusalem,"	xiii. 31–35.
Jesus is guest at the house of an archon of the Pharisees. Heals one suffering from dropsy. Parables,	xiv. 1–xvii. 10.
Journey to Jerusalem, through the confines of Samaria and Galilee. The ten lepers,	xvii. 11–xviii. 30.
Last journey to Jerusalem, by Jericho,	xviii. 31.

(V.) Succession of Events, according to John.

Contents.	Reference.
Jesus remains in Galilee after the feeding of the five thousand until the feast of Tabernacles, 14th Nisan–10th Tisri (17th April–7th Oct.) A.D. 29,	vii. 1–9.
Jesus at Jerusalem at the feast of Tabernacles. Healing of the man born blind (Tisri, until?),	vii. 10–x. 21.
Jesus at Jerusalem during the feast of Dedication, 25th Kisleu (20th Dec.) A.D. 29,	x. 22–39.
Jesus withdraws beyond Jordan, where John at first baptized, and remains there,	x. 40–42.
Resurrection of Lazarus. (This belongs to the events of the year 30,)	xi. 1.

Between the feast of Dedication and the resurrection of Lazarus—thus from the end of A.D 29 to the beginning of A.D. 30—Jesus tarried, according to John, in the place where John at first baptized, *i.e.* at or near Bethania in Judea beyond Jordan. Thither also we find the Lord repairing, according to Matt. xix. 1 and Mark x. 1. We have thus here a synchronistic datum, according to which all that precedes Matt. xix. 1 belongs to the year 29. Luke does not give this journey to Judah of the Jordan; his synopsis with John must therefore be arrived at in another way. After the feeding of the five thousand, John knows of three journeys of Jesus to Judea; the going up to the feast of Tabernacles, the coming to Bethany for the raising of Lazarus, and the journey from Ephraim to the eventful Passover. It is doubtful whether or not a fourth journey is to be presupposed. Did Jesus remain at Jerusalem from the feast of Tabernacles to the feast of Dedication? On this question we find nothing to guide us in John x. 21, 22. In Luke ix. 51, we find mention of a journey to Jerusalem; x. 38, of a sojourn in Bethany; xvii. 11, of a journey to Jerusalem, "through the middle ground of Samaria and Galilee," *i.e.* necessarily *through the marches between these two provinces;* otherwise it must have been said, through the midst of Galilee and Samaria. Now this was the route of Jesus from Ephraim, through the Ghôr, to Jericho, in order finally, after passing through Bethany, to celebrate His last public entrance into Jerusalem. Before this journey between Samaria and Galilee, mention is made, chap. xiv. 1, of a meal of which Jesus partook in the house of an archon of the Pharisees. Such archons, members of the Sanhedrim, are to be sought in the neighbourhood of Jerusalem, perhaps at Bethany. We have thus here to do with the short sojourn of Jesus at Bethany, on the occasion of the raising of Lazarus. Previously, chap. xiii. 31, we read of a warning addressed to Jesus, with regard to the danger threatening Him on the part of Herod. These conditions perfectly correspond to those we are led to presuppose by the flight of Jesus to the place where John at first was baptizing.[1] Whence it follows: Luke ix. 18–xiii. 30 = John vii. 1–x. 40 = Matt. xv. 1–xix. 1 = Mark vii. 1–x. 1. The journey to Jerusalem and sojourn in Bethlehem, Luke ix. 51–x. 42, synchronizes with the sojourn of Jesus at Jerusalem, at the feasts of Tabernacles and Dedication, John vii. 1–x. 39, during which Jesus spent the nights on Olivet, John viii. 1, therefore beyond doubt at Bethany.

From this we gain the following general arrangement of the historical material:—

[1] John x. 40; Matt. xix. 1.

(VI.) SYNOPTICAL VIEW OF THE HISTORY TO THE FEAST OF DEDICATION, A.D. 29.

CONTENTS OF THE NARRATIVE.	REFERENCE IN			
	MATTHEW.	MARK.	LUKE.	JOHN.
I. Sojourn in Galilee.				
Jesus in Galilee from the feeding of the five thousand to the feast of Tabernacles,	...	...	...	vii. 1, 2. [vi. 22-71.]
a. Jesus at Capernaum, Matt. xiv. 34-36; Mark vi. 53-56,	xv. 1-20.	vii. 1-23.	...	...
b. Journey in the district of Tyre and Sidon,	xv. 21-28.	vii. 24-30.	...	...
c. Return by the seaside into the region of Decapolis,	xv. 29-31.	vii. 31-37.		...
d. Feeding of the four thousand. Passage to Dalmanutha (Magdala),	xv. 32-xvi. 4.	viii. 1-12.		
e. Passage to Bethsaida-Julias,	xvi. 5-12.	viii. 13-26.	...	...
f. Journey to Cæsarea-Philippi,	xvi. 13-28.	viii. 27-ix. 1	[ix. 18-27.]	...
g. The Transfiguration, and journey through Galilee,	xvii. 1-23.	ix. 2-32	ix. 23-50.	...
II. Journey to the feast of Tabernacles.				
a. Jesus leaves Galilee later than His brethren,				vii. 3-10.
b. He takes His way through Samaria,			ix. 51-62.	
c. Second mission of the disciples. Woes on the three cities,			x. 1-37.	
III. Jesus at the feast of Tabernacles. Jerusalem.				
a. In the midst of the festival, He arose in the sanctuary and taught,				vii. 14-36.
b. On the last day of the festival Jesus again teaches there,				vii. 37-53.
c. He retires to the Mount of Olives, to Bethany,				viii. 1.
d. The pardon in the sanctuary of the woman who was taken in adultery,[1]			x. 38-42.	viii. 2-11.
e. Discourses of Jesus (in the so-called Court of the Women),				viii. 12-59.
f. Healing of the man born blind. Pool of Siloam,				ix. 1-x. 21.
IV. Jesus at the feast of Dedication.				
a. (Does a journey of Jesus intervene between this festival and the last?) [Cf. sec. 133.]				
b. Jesus teaches in Solomon's porch,				x. 22-42.
c. Journey of Jesus to Judea beyond Jordan,[2]	xix. 1.	x. 1.	(xi. 1 ?)	x. 40.

[1] [An unquestionably apostolic tradition; although, chiefly for doctrinal reasons, not appearing in the four earliest existing MSS. It first appears (or re-appears) in the important MSS., codex D. On the whole question of its genuineness, cf. Lange *in loc.* Ellicott, p. 253, considers the proper place of this narrative to be at the end of Luke xxi.]

[2] [On the place of Matt. xvii. 24-xviii. 35 = Mark ix. 33-50, cf. sec. 137.]

V.—Journey of Jesus within the confines of Tyre and Sidon.

Sec. 120. After the feeding of the five thousand, Jesus held a conversation with scribes and Pharisees, who had come down from Jerusalem to Capernaum (after the festival), and complained to Him that His disciples eat with unwashen hands. The manner of the Lord's answer offended them ;[1] therefore "Jesus went thence, and withdrew to the confines of Tyre and Sidon." Here He healed the diseased daughter of the Canaanitish mother. At the time of Christ the domain of Tyre and Sidon extended in the north of Galilee from the Mediterranean to the Jordan.[2] It cannot be determined in what part of the Phœnician domain Jesus tarried, probably in the vicinity of the Jordan. [According to the best MSS. of Mark, however, Jesus sojourned within the confines of Tyre (ver. 24), and returned *through Sidon* (διὰ Σιδῶνος, ver. 31) to the Sea of Galilee. The spiritual significance of this fact has not escaped the attention of Ellicott. Cf. *Lectures,* p. 218, note 3.]

VI.—The Feeding of the Four Thousand.

Sec. 121. From the Phœnician domain Jesus came, on the [eastern] side of the Sea of Galilee,[3] to the confines of the Decapolis.[4] There they brought to Him one deaf, and with difficulty speaking.[5] In those days when great multitudes were with Him,[6] upon a mountain[7] He fed four thousand men with seven loaves and a few fishes (ἰχθύδια). The place where Jesus wrought this miracle is not more nearly defined; at any rate, it was more southerly situated than the place of the feeding of the five thousand, since it "was in the midst of the confines of Decapolis," thus to the south of the Wady Semakh, the northern boundary of the Decapolis.[8] After the feeding of the four thousand, Jesus, we are told by Matthew, entered the ship, and came into the district of Magadan. In Mark it is said that, "embarking on the ship with His disciples, He

---

[1] Matt. xv. 12.   [2] Josephus, *de Bello,* iii. 3, sec. 1.   [3] Matt. xv. 29.
[4] Through the midst of the confines, Mark vii. 31.   [5] Mark vii. 32 ff.
[6] Mark viii. 1.   [7] Matt. xv. 29 ff.   [8] Cf. sec. 72, *l.*

came to the parts (about) Dalmanutha." [1] We have shown, in sec. 73, that Magadan, not Magdala, is the true reading in Matthew. The place is to be recognised in Mudshiddah, westwards of Beisan. This place must at one time have formed a sort of frontier town at the boundary line between the Scythopolitan domain belonging to Decapolis, and the provinces of Galilee and Samaria. The place was consequently exceedingly favourably situated for Jesus, who would retire before the machinations of His enemies. Dalmanutha is identical with Delhemîyeh,[2] on the left bank of the Jordan, about four hours' distance below the lake. This place, too, belonged to the Decapolitan territory. Probably Jesus repaired first to Dalmanutha, and then to Magadan.

VII.—*Passage of Jesus to Cæsarea Philippi.*

Sec. 122. According to Mark viii. 11, Jesus, while at Dalmanutha, met with Pharisees, who required a sign from Him. On this account He went on board again, and crossed the sea.[3] During the passage Jesus warned the disciples of the leaven of the Pharisees, and of Herod. The supposition is possible that this passage brought Jesus to the western shore, whence He reached Magadan. Yet the manner in which Jesus speaks of the feeding of the four thousand, Mark viii. 19, 20, gives the impression of a reminiscence of something which had taken place a while ago, rather than of that which had happened on the same day.[4] After some length of sojourn in the Decapolitan Ghôr, Jesus, disturbed by the Pharisees, went on board the ship, and sailed for Bethsaïda.[5] Bethsaïda-Julias, to the east of the lake, appears to be here intended. First, because the Synoptists never mention the western Bethsaïda,[6] but treat it as an integral part of Capernaum ; and

---

[1] Matt. xv. 39 ; Mark viii. 10.   [2] Cf. sec. 74.

[3] πάλιν ἐμβάς, Mark viii. 13–29.

[4] [The parallel in Matthew also favours the supposition of an eastward voyage, namely, from the district about Magadan. From a comparison of Matt. xvi. 1–4 with Mark viii. 10–13, the scene of the conversation with the Pharisees would seem to be in each case identical, *sc.* in the Ghôr, between Magadan and Dalmanutha.]

[5] Mark viii. 22. Some codices have Βηθανίαν.   [6] [On Mark vi. 45, see Lange.]

then, because Jesus was at this time evidently avoiding
the western shore on account of His enemies, the Pharisees
and Herod. At Bethsaïda He healed a blind man,[1] and
then repaired to the region of Cæsarea Philippi. In Matthew,
the passage to Bethsaïda, and the healing of the blind man,
is not mentioned; but immediately after the sojourn at
Magadan we have the account of the journey to Cæsarea
Philippi.[2]

Sec. 123. **Cæsarea Philippi.**[3]—The sources of the Jordan
rise at the south-west foot of Hermon, in a cave which in
antiquity was consecrated to Pan, and called Paneion. On
this spot Herod the Great built a temple in honour of the
Emperor Augustus.[4] His son Philip, to whose tetrarchy the
place belonged,[5] adorned and enlarged the town built near to
the Paneion, and formerly known as Paneas—called by the
Rabbis *Pamias*, פמייס, now known as *Bánias*. To this place he
gave the name of Cæsarea. In order to distinguish it from
the Cæsarea Palæstina situated on the coast of the Mediterranean south from Carmel, the name of the founder was
usually added to it. The population was mostly heathen;
but there were also Jews dwelling there.[6] This town lies 25
to 30 miles north of the Sea of Gennesareth, in the most
charming region of Palestine.[7] Owing to its being situated
on Gentile territory, and under the dominion of the peaceful

---

[1] Mark viii. 23.

[2] [Matthew xvi. 13, as compared with xvi. 5, indicates that they would probably land at Bethsaïda. Their route would thus lie through Bethania, in
journeying to Cæsarea Philippi.]

[3] [Tristram says of this place (p. 586) : "Dean Stanley calls it a Syrian
Tivoli, and certainly there is much in the rocks, caverns, cascades, and the
natural beauty of the scenery to recall the Roman Tibur. Behind the village,
in front of a great natural cavern, a river bursts forth from the earth, the 'upper
source' of the Jordan. Inscriptions and niches in the face of the cliff tell of the
old idol-worship of Baal and of Pan." The description is continued on the next
two pages. Beside the admirable remarks of Tristram should be read the no
less brilliant historic sketch of Stanley, pp. 397–400. Compare also the excellent description of Robinson, iii. 409–413.]

[4] Josephus, *Antiq.* xv. 10, sec. 3.   [5] Luke iii. 1.   [6] Josephus, *Vita*, 13.

[7] The peculiar beauty of this Hûleh district is described in glowing terms by
Thomson, *Land and Book*, p. 225. Its solitude is illustrated by the fact that
it is the only district in Palestine where he found the pelican, pp. 260, 261.
Compare also Ritter, ii. 163–167.

Philip, it offered a secure asylum to Jesus and His disciples. A very ancient Christian legend[1] relates that the woman who was healed by the touch of the hem of Christ's mantle was a Gentile woman of Cæsarea Philippi; and that out of gratitude to Jesus, she had a statue of Him made and set up in front of her house. The godless Julian cast it down, and substituted for it his own image; but a flash of lightning smote and destroyed this latter. The statue of Jesus was brought into a church, and by this statue sprung up an herb which healed all diseases. This tradition at any rate proves that very early a Christian church flourished in this place.

Sec. 124. In this region of Cæsarea—according to Mark viii. 27, on the way thither—the Lord asked the disciples who the people said, and who they themselves said, He was. Upon which Peter confessed, " Thou art the Christ, the Son of the living God."[2] Six days afterwards the Transfiguration took place, as related by Matt. xvii. 1 ff., Mark ix. 2 ff., and Luke ix. 28 ff. This last evangelist tells us that it took place " about an eight days" after the confession of Peter. He relates nothing of the visit of Jesus to the Tyro-Sidonian territory, of the feeding of the four thousand, and of the journey to Cæsarea. It seems thus as though the confession of Peter took place immediately after the feeding of the five thousand, in the vicinity of the lake ; and eight days after the said feeding, the Transfiguration. This view has in its favour the fact that Peter's confession of Luke ix. 20 thus synchronizes with that of John vi. 68, 69. Yet that which is related by the two first Synoptists, between the feeding of the five thousand and the Transfiguration, bears so clearly the stamp of chronological succession, that we cannot hesitate to regard it as given in its due order. Luke ix. 18 offers a place for the insertion of that which has been omitted, by the indefinite formula, καὶ ἐγένετο ἐν τῷ εἶναι αὐτὸν προσευχόμενον—" it came to pass (once), when He was praying . . ."

---

[1] Glycas, *Ann.* iv. ; cf. Reland, *Palœst.* 922.

[2] Matt. xvi. 13-20 ; Mark viii. 27-30 ; Luke ix. 18-21. [In *Mark* the same confession appears in a shorter form, " Thou art the Christ ; " while *Luke* has simply, " The Christ of God." Peter's confession at Capernaum, " Thou art the Holy One of God " (John vi. 69), thus strikes the first note of this later Confession of Faith.]

This praying may be conceived of as immediately following the feeding of the five thousand; but also equally well as taking place a considerable period after that event.[1]

VIII.—*The Transfiguration.*

Sec. 125. "Jesus taketh Peter, James, and John his brother, and bringeth them up into an high mountain apart, and was transfigured before them . . ."[2] Among the chosen disciples who witnessed this scene John also is mentioned. Whence is it that this apostle does not mention in his Gospel the event of the Transfiguration? John, it is true, relates only what he has himself seen; he does not, however, relate *all* that he has seen, but only that which might confirm the readers' faith in Jesus as the Christ, the Son of God,[3] and that by which His glory was manifested. The Transfiguration could not, however, be adduced as proving this; partly because it was witnessed only by three persons, but especially because the seeing of the disciples was no objective and physical one, but an inner vision. This is shown by the form of expression ὤφθησαν αὐτοῖς, "there appeared unto them Moses and Elias;" and especially by the statement of Mark ix. 6, that Peter knew not what he should say; as also that of Luke ix. 32, that they—the three disciples—"were heavy with sleep." Such inner visions and revelations, in a condition of sleep or of dream, occur frequently in the New Testament.[4] It would be a great mistake to wish to take from these events the subjective character which Scripture evidently attaches to them; on the contrary, it is of great importance to distinguish between such subjective experiences and those miracles to which Holy Scripture distinctly and definitely ascribes an objective character. If the apologetes mingle subjective with objective, the right is conceded to subversive criticism to do the same, and to rarefy the whole gospel history into that which is subjective, inner, and spiritual. Inner spiritual experiences, like the vision

---

[1] [Manifestly a distinct occasion from that of Matt. xiv. 33; Mark vi. 46; John vi. 15. Cf. Ellicott, p. 212, note 1.]

[2] Matt. xvii. 1–13; Mark ix. 2–13; Luke ix. 28–36.   [3] John xx. 30, 31.

[4] Matt. ii. 12, 13, 19; Acts x. 10, 11; 2 Cor. xii. 2, 3, and elsewhere.

the apostles had of the glorification, exerted a refreshing, consoling power upon the disciples themselves; but as arguments for others, they are not to be employed and are not employed. John could and would thus omit the history of the Transfiguration, as not bearing upon the object he had in view.

Sec. 126. Which was the high mountain on which the Transfiguration took place? From the accounts of Matthew and Mark, we should be inclined to look for it in the district about Cæsarea Philippi. According to Luke—who entirely passes over the three journeys on Gentile territory—one would rather think of it as situated in the neighbourhood of Capernaum. Hints, too, are not wanting in the first two Synoptists which would favour the supposition of a mountain in Galilee.[1] A multitude, such as here appears,[2] did not surely follow Jesus as far as Cæsarea? Since the Gospels neither mention the mountain by name, nor more clearly define it, it is a thankless task to attempt to discover it. A very ancient tradition, already advocated by Jerome and Cyril of Jerusalem, points out Tabor as the Mount of the Transfiguration.[3] Jerome, in *Epitaphio Paulæ*, says, " Scandebat (Paula) montem Tabor, in quo transfiguratus est Dominus." At any rate the Transfiguration *cannot* have taken place, as tradition represents, upon the *summit* of Tabor; since at the time of Christ a town—the *Atabyrion* of Polybius, the *Itabyrion* of Josephus—existed there, which is contrary to the conditions of the text, privacy and solitude. And if *this* mountain had been the scene of the Transfiguration, the evangelists would assuredly not have omitted to mention it by name.[4] When Jesus had come

---

[1] [Whither there would be no difficulty in journeying during the six or eight days which preceded the scene of the Transfiguration.]

[2] Matt. xvii. 14 ; Mark ix. 14 (καὶ γραμματεῖς) ; Luke ix. 37.

[3] [The summit of Tabor is, according to Tristram, only 1300 feet from its own base, and 1865 feet above the sea ; according to Von Schubert, 2283 feet above Lake Tiberias. Its position in relation to the surrounding country gives it the appearance of an altitude it does not possess. It is well described by Stanley, pp. 550, 551. The beauty of the prospect from Tabor is celebrated by all travellers ; cf. especially Tristram, p. 503, and Ritter, ii. 314 ff. A small church on the plateau of Tabor, belonging to the former Convent of Elias, dates, according to Fogüé, from the fourth to the fifth century. Its width is 13 feet, its length 17 to 20 feet. The floor is inlaid with black and white mosaic. Cf. Bædecker, p. 380.]

[4] [Ellicott, p. 226, favours the view which places the scene of this miracle on

down with the three apostles from the mountain,[1] on the following night-day in the Jewish sense, thus on the same day
after sunset, He healed the youth who was possessed.   Immediately after He entered on a journey through Galilee,
which, by reason of the words of Jesus then spoken concerning His approaching death, attaches itself to Luke ix. 51,
where a journey to Jerusalem is recorded.   Between the
Passover, at which Jesus fed the five thousand, and the feast
of Tabernacles, was an interval of fully six months.   On this
whole period we should know next to nothing, if we were
confined to the narratives of Luke and John.   Here, however, the two first Synoptists satisfactorily fill up the gap.
During this period Jesus abode partly in Galilee,[2] but principally in Gentile lands, because the Pharisees and Herod
" held counsel against Him how they might destroy Him."

IX.—*Journey of Jesus to the Feast of Tabernacles at Jerusalem.*
15th to 22d Tisri, 12th to 20th Oct., A.D. 29.

Sec. 127. The brethren of Jesus, who believed not in Him,
called upon Him, since the feast of Tabernacles was at hand,
to manifest Himself to the world. Jesus answered them,
My time is not yet come. . . . Go ye up to the feast ; I do
not go up to this feast, because my time is not yet fulfilled.
—He remained in Galilee. When His brethren were gone up,
He also went up to the feast, but, as it were, in private.[3]
The manner in which Jesus answered His brethren has been
characterized as an infraction of the law of truth. We must
certainly assent to this judgment, if Jesus had attended the
festival of which He had said : " I go not up to this feast."
This, however, was by no means the case. The Jews who
came up from a distance to Jerusalem naturally arranged to

Gentile territory—" on one of the lofty spurs of the snow-capt Hermon." (So
Ellicott, with an allusion to Shakespeare.) It is remarkable that the scene of
the baptism, the transfiguration, and the manifestation to the five hundred, is, in
any case, to be sought in the country north of Judea proper.]

[1] Matt. xvii. 14 ff. ; Mark ix. 14 ff. ; Luke ix. 37, ἐν τῇ ἑξῆς ἡμέρᾳ.

[2] [Only *passing through* Galilee in privacy and seclusion, παριπορεύοντο, Mark
ix. 30.]

[3] John vii. 2–10. [As a prophet coming up out of seclusion.—Lange.]

be in Jerusalem on the Day of Atonement, which was held
on the 10th Tisri, five days before the feast of Tabernacles;
partly for the sake of this festival itself, partly because the
thrice sacred Sabbath of Atonement, on which the severest
fasting was enjoined, under penalty of being cut off from
among the people, must have been in the highest degree in-
convenient for the festive journey.   At this festival, εἰς τὴν
ἑορτὴν ταύτην, Jesus did not purpose being at Jerusalem;
nor did He go.   Unquestionably He said this to His brethren
iu such a way that they understood that precisely the first
part of the festal season—the Day of Atonement—was intended.   Our Lord journeyed from Galilee in such wise as to
be able to arise in the sanctuary in the midst of the festival,
i.e. on the third or fourth day of the feast of Tabernacles.[1]
The route which He took is made known to us by Luke,
who says:[2] "It came to pass, when the days were being
accomplished that He should be received up, He steadfastly
set His face to go to Jerusalem. . . . And they went and
entered into a village of the Samaritans, to make ready for
Him.   And they (the Samaritans) did not receive Him. . . ."
The starting-point was unquestionably Capernaum; for there
dwelt His brethren, with whom He had previously spoken
about the festival.   From the shore of the lake three routes
led to Jerusalem.   The one went from Capernaum over the
western uplands, past Tabor, by Nazareth, through the plain of
Esdraelon, and through Samaria to the Jewish uplands.   This
is still the ordinary route.   A second route went from Capernaum along the coast of the lake into the Ghôr, then through
the plain of Esdraelon, past Nain, into the land of the Samaritans, where it united with the former one.   The third continued in the Ghôr as far as Jericho, and then ascended the
mountains by the sharp ascent of Adumim to Bethany, and
then down the Mount of Olives.   Those Biblical geographers
who are not acquainted with these two last pilgrim routes
usually say that two routes led from Capernaum to Jerusalem:
the one (our first) through Samaria; the other, through the
Ghôr on the eastern side of the Jordan to Jericho.   Of this
route there is no trace in history.   It is asserted that Jesus

[1] John vii. 14.   [2] Luke ix. 51, 52.

took this route on His last journey to Jerusalem ; but this, as we shall see, is an error. The shortest and most frequented route was the first, which, moreover, was pursued by Jesus when He went up to the feast of Tabernacles. It was often rendered insecure by the hostility of the Samaritans, through which scenes of blood were sometimes enacted.[1] Jesus, too, was on this occasion inhospitably received by the Samaritans. On this account James and John thought it was a case for calling down fire from heaven upon them ; to such an extent that the Lord must correct them, by reminding them that they knew not of what spirit they were the children.[2]

Sec. 128. **The Feast of Tabernacles** was, according to the law,[3] one of the three festivals which called for the personal appearing of the Israelite before the face of Jehovah in the sanctuary. It was observed in the seventh month, Tisri, five days after the Day of Atonement: it began on the 15th of the month, and lasted eight days. During these eight days the Israelites were to dwell in tabernacles made of green boughs, in commemoration of their fathers' dwelling in tents in the wilderness. The first day and the eighth were observed as Sabbaths.[4] After the Captivity this festival was the favourite one, and the greatest of all.[5] In the sanctuary the altar of burnt-offering was hung round with green boughs ; the festive pilgrims carried in their hand the *Lulab* (? palm-leaf), and a bough with citrons on it. On the occasion of the morning sacrifice took place that water libation peculiar to the feast of Tabernacles. A priest filled a golden vessel from the fountain of Siloa, entered through the water-gate into the sanctuary, and poured it out at the foot of the altar.[6] This practice, however, peculiar to the Jews after the Captivity, was not universally regarded as obligatory. The Sadducees disapproved of it.[7] It happened once that a Sadducean high priest—it was Alexander Jannæus—instead of pouring the libation water upon the altar, poured it out at his own feet. By this act a tumult was stirred up, and the pilgrims pelted him with

---

[1] Josephus, *Antiq.* xx. 6, sec. 1. [2] Luke ix. 53–56.
[3] Lev. xxiii. 33–44. [4] Lev. xxiii. 39.
[5] ἑορτῶν μεγίστη, Philo, *Opp.* ii. 286. Josephus, *Antiq.* viii. 4, sec. 1 ; xv. 3, sec. 3.
[6] *Mishna Succa*, iv. [7] *Jerus. Shbiith*, fol. 33. 2.

the citrons which they carried in their hands. In that storm
the altar lost one of its horns.[1] On the evening of these
feast days the sanctuary was, by means of torches in the
Court of the Women, burning upon candelabra of fifty cubits
high, so brilliantly illuminated, that all Jerusalem was flooded
with light; [2] the Levites stood upon the fifteen steps of the
gate leading from the Court of the Women to the Court of
Israel, and sang with musical accompaniment the so-called
Psalms of degrees (Ps. cxx.–cxxxiv.) ; at the same time the
sages and leading men of Jerusalem joined in a torch dance
in the Court of the Women ; while the women, apart from the
men, were spectators of it from a separate platform.[3] Rabban
Simeon ben Gamaliel distinguished himself in this dance by
the dexterity with which he cast into the air eight torches,
and caught them again, without ever letting one of them fall
to the ground.[4] In short, " He who has not seen the joy of
the drawing-house (בית השואבה, for so this festive solemnity
was called) knows not what joy is."[5] Whether, as is thought
by many exegetes, Jesus alluded to the water libation in the
words of John vii. 37, we leave an. open question. We only
remind of the fact that the libation-water was not drunk, but
poured forth ; and Jesus says, " If any man thirsteth, let him
come unto me and *drink*." These words spoke Jesus " on the
last, the most glorious day of the feast." [6] It has already been
said that the eighth day was observed as a Sabbath.[7] It
formed a separate festival in itself, called especially for the
personal appearing in the presence of Jehovah, and bore the
name of " Assembly." [8]

Sec. 129. This sojourn of our Lord made manifest the decided hostility of the hierarchs and Pharisees, till then more or
less veiled. It is well known that the Sanhedrim accused
Jesus of a threefold crime ; hostility towards the holy place, the
misleading of the nation, and declaring Himself to be God, or
the Son of God.[9] The first charge rested upon a perversion of

---

[1] *Mishna Succa*, vi. 9. *Bab. Joma*, fol. 39. 1. *Bab. Rosh hashanna*, fol.
16. 1, fol. 48. 1.

[2] *Succa*, v. 2. 9. *Jerus. Succa*, fol. 55. 2. *Bab. Succa*, fol. 52. 2.

[3] *Succa*, v. 2–4.

[4] *Tosaphtha Succa*, iv. 2.　　[5] *Ibid.*　　[6] John vii. 37.　　[7] *Succa*, v. 6.

[8] עצרת, Lev. xxiii. 36.　　[9] Mark xiv. 58, 61 ; John xix. 7, 12.

the words He had spoken at the first Passover ;[1] where He was accused of having said : " I will break down the temple, and in three days raise it up." From that time dates the hostility of the hierarchs. The hostility of the Pharisees was not so quickly developed; nevertheless it was already beginning to show itself at the anonymous festival, when Jesus healed a sick man at the Pool of Bethesda on the Sabbath day,[2] and He was declared to be a contemner of the Sabbath.[3] Through the eating of the disciples with unwashen hands His disregard of the traditionary ordinances of the fathers was made manifest.[4] But to an open hostility, which demanded the death of the Lord, matters came only at the feast of Tabernacles, where He was declared to be a seducer of the people.[5] Later than this the charge was added of proclaiming Himself to be God.[6] The nation was divided, they knew not what to think of Jesus ; yet the multitude was more for Him than against Him, and eagerly awaited His arrival at the festival.[7] The journey of Jesus to Jerusalem, which is mentioned Luke ix. 51, and seems to us to indicate this visit to the feast of Tabernacles, is announced in the words, " It came to pass, when the days were being fulfilled that He should be received up "—ἐγένετο ἐν τῷ συμπληροῦσθαι τὰς ἡμέρας τῆς ἀναλήψεως αὐτοῦ. We have already, in the introduction, explained how they are to be understood. Here we may further add, that this journey was in reality one fraught with the most important results, and paving the way for the final decision ; since the hostility of the Jews was brought to a climax by the sojourn of Jesus in Jerusalem at the feast of Tabernacles.

Sec. 130. At the end of the eighth day Jesus went to the Mount of Olives :[8] in connection with this we have probably to think of Bethany. To this period might belong Luke x. 38–42 ; but it is, as we shall hereafter show, more probable that this sojourn at Bethany belongs to the period of the feast of Dedication. When, on the next day, Jesus entered again into the temple, the incident of the woman taken in

[1] John ii. 19.
[2] John v. 16.
[3] John vii. 20–25.
[4] Mark vii. 1 ff.
[5] John vii. 12, 32, 44, 52.
[6] John x. 33.
[7] John vii. 11–13. [Cf. Ellicott, p. 250, note 2.]
[8] John viii. 1.

adultery occurs.[1] Whether or not this history was really incorporated by John himself into his Gospel, is a question of criticism which we are not called to solve; if, however, it is authentic, it is our province to determine the place in the sanctuary where the scene occurred. In *Mishna Sota*, i. 5, we read that the women accused of adultery were judged at the Nicanor Gate, and especially had to undergo the judicial test which consisted in the drinking of the bitter waters prepared from the ashes of a red heifer which had been burnt. There indeed Jesus was called to give judgment in the case of the accused woman. The Nicanor Gate, known also as the Eastern Gate, the Corinthian Gate, and the Beautiful Gate, led from the Court of the Gentiles to the Court of the Women on the east, and lay facing the Great Gate which by means of the fifteen steps connected the Court of the Women with the Court of Israel; so that from the Nicanor Gate one had, through the Great Gate, a view of the altar and the temple. That the Nicanor Gate belonged to the Court of the Women is already apparent from the judgment there held upon the adulteress; for the women were not permitted to enter into the Court of Israel. That it lay towards the east, is twice said in *Mishna Middoth* (i. 4, ii. 6). That it was identical with the Corinthian Gate described by Josephus,[2] follows from *Middoth*, ii. 2, where it is said that the Nicanor Gate was of brass, whereas all the other gates of the sanctuary were gilded. That, moreover, Jesus was then in the Court of the Women is to be inferred, not only from the fact that at the feast of Tabernacles all the festivities were held there, but also from John viii. 20, where it is said that Jesus was then teaching by the temple-coffer in the sanctuary.[3] According to *Mishna Shekalim*, vi. 1 and 6, the temple-coffer, with its thirteen boxes for offerings, stood in the Court of the Women;[4] and Josephus[5] says, in describing the Court of the Women, that the porticos which surrounded it on three

---

[1] John viii. 3 ff.   [2] Josephus, *de Bello*, v. 5, sec. 2.

[3] [In the portico which contained the temple-coffer, ἐν τῷ γαζοφυλακίῳ.]

[4] [So called because the women were not allowed to pass *beyond* it. In this court was always to be found the greatest concourse of those going and coming. Cf. Mark xii. 41.]

[5] Josephus, *ut supra*.

sides lay over against the Treasury—γαζοφυλάκια. This was found consequently on the fourth (western) side, which separated the Court of the Women from the Court of Israel. The history of the woman taken in adultery falls on the first day after the day of the Assembly.

Sec. 131. After this festival, on a Sabbath [? 23d October], Jesus healed the man born blind, anointing his eyes with a clay made with spittle, and bidding him wash in the Pool of Siloam.[1] The Pool of Siloam, Siloah, or Siloa, is situated in the lower Tyropœon valley, which separates the temple mountain from the so-called Mount Zion, a few minutes' distance from the city of Jerusalem. It is a small, deep, oblong reservoir of 18 feet wide, which receives its water from a yet smaller basin, of 5 or 6 feet in width, hewn out in the rock, and lying a few feet higher. Into this last basin the fountain of Siloa discharges itself. The fountain is now called Ain Silwân, and by means of a subterranean channel carried through the rocks, and running from N.E. to S.W., serves as an outflow to the Fountain of the Virgin.[2] At the time of Christ the city wall extended as far as the fountain of Siloa.[3] To the fortifications in the vicinity of the fountain belonged no doubt the tower in Siloam, spoken of Luke xiii. 4.

X.—*Jesus in Jerusalem at the Feast of Dedication.* (*Evening of* 20*th to* 28*th December,* A.D. 29.)

Sec. 132. The festival of Dedication, τὰ ἐγκαίνια, was celebrated eight days, from the 25th Kisleu, in commemoration of the restoring of the temple service by Judas Maccabæus.[4] The ceremony consisted—in addition to the special sacrifices—in a brilliant illumination of the sanctuary, and all the houses in Jerusalem.[5] Hence the Greek name of the festival is ἐγκαινίων ἑορτή, or φῶτα; whilst the Hebrew name, יום הנוכה, signifies day of consecration. The occasion of this illumination is not known. Jewish tradition invents with regard to it the fable, that when the Jews entered into

---

[1] John ix. 1 ff. [In going out ; cf. Acts iii. 2.]   [2] Robinson, *Pal.* i. 338 ff.
[3] Josephus, *de Bello,* v. 4, sec. 1.   [4] 1 Macc. iv. 45 ff.
[5] *Bab. Shabbath,* fol. 21. 2 ; *Antiq.* xii. 7, sec. 7.

the sanctuary desecrated by the heathen, in order to cleanse it
and restore the worship, they could find no pure oil for the
sacred light, save a single bottle, which bore the seal of the
high priest.   In the ordinary course this oil would only have
met the requirement of a single day, but by a miracle it was
caused to suffice for seven days.   Hence the feast of lights.[1]
According to the school of Shammai, there were kindled for
the illumination on the first day eight lamps, on the second
seven, and so on; every day one less.   According to the
school of Hillel, there was conversely, one lamp lit on the
first day, on the second two, and so increasing to the eighth
day, when eight lamps were enkindled.[2]

Sec. 133. Immediately after the actions to which the healing
on a Sabbath day, shortly after the feast of Tabernacles, of one
born blind, had given rise, the Evangelist John, chap. x. 22 ff.,
relates the words and work of Christ at the feast of Dedication.   Where did Jesus remain during the two months which
intervened between these festivals?   The Gospel of John
affords us no information on this point.   That Jesus spent
this whole time at Jerusalem is not probable; first, because so
long a sojourn in one place was not in accordance with the
Lord's practice, and then especially because the hostility of
the Jewish rulers had now attained so high a degree as to
render impossible a quiet sojourn of two months in their
vicinity.   We have already remarked that the journey to
Jerusalem through Samaria, of Luke ix. 51, coincides with
that to the feast of Tabernacles; and that the account of the
appearing of Jesus at Bethany mentioned soon after, chap.
x. 38–42, harmonizes best with the sojourn of Jesus at
Jerusalem during the feast of Dedication.   Then, too, Luke
relates, chap. x. 1–37, a second mission of seventy disciples,
with a discourse of the Lord, in which the woe upon Chorazin,
Bethsaïda, and Capernaum is pronounced.   It must indeed be
acknowledged that it is more probable Jesus pronounced these
woes upon the three cities, as related by Luke, towards the
end of His ministry, rather than at the beginning of it, as we
should be led to suppose from Matt. xi. 20–24, were we to
take for granted that Matthew gives this discourse of Jesus in

---

[1] *Megillath Taanith*, ix., 25th Kisleu.   [2] *Ibid.*

a purely chronological order. If, however, Jesus pronounced the woe upon those cities on the occasion of His afresh sending forth His disciples, we must certainly believe that the words were pronounced, not somewhere in the neighbourhood of Jerusalem, but within sight of the cities addressed. From this it follows that between the feast of Tabernacles and that of Dedication, Jesus was on the shore of the lake, and there appointed to the Seventy their mission.

Sec. 134. "Now it was the feast of Dedication at Jerusalem. It was winter. And Jesus walked . . . in the portico of Solomon."[1] As concerns the stoa [portico or colonnade] of Solomon, we refer the reader to the Appendix, on the topography of Jerusalem, 20, where it is shown that this is the subterranean portico still existing under the mosque of El-Aksa.

[1] John x. 22, 23.

DIVISION VI.

THIRD AND LAST YEAR OF OUR LORD'S LABOURS, A.U.C. 731, A.D. 30.

I.—*Synopsis of the Historical Material.*

Sec. 135. Synoptical view of the history, from end of A.D. 29 to the Resurrection, 9th April A.D. 30.—See pp. 178, 179.

Sec. 136. The journey of Jesus, mentioned by the fourth evangelist, to the place where John at first was baptizing— thus to Bethania beyond the Jordan — is introduced by Matthew with the words, " He came into the confines of Judea beyond the Jordan ; " for in the land of this name had John his first place of baptism. In Mark it is said : " He cometh into the confines of Judea, *and* beyond the Jordan." This evangelist thus indicates that there were two journeys of Jesus ; the former expression implying the visit to Judea at the feast of Dedication, and the second that from thence beyond Jordan. The two first evangelists thus complement each other, and thus complemented their account perfectly tallies with that of John. In Matthew and Mark the two journeys apparently blend in one — namely, the visit to Bethany, and then the last journey by way of Jericho. But here again Luke steps in to remove the discrepancy. The journey to Jerusalem of Luke xiii. 22 is the journey to Bethany for the raising of Lazarus ; the sojourn in Ephraim testified by John is with Luke [1] a sojourn on the frontier line between Samaria and Galilee. On this frontier line did Jesus descend into the Ghôr, through which He came down on the west side of the Jordan to Jericho. The three Synoptists now agree in mentioning the journey from Jericho to Bethphage-Bethany, where, according to John xii. 1, was held the supper

[¹ Luke xvii. 11.]

at which Jesus was anointed. After this took place the public entry of Jesus into Jerusalem.[1] The Synoptists place the anointing after this entry. From this point it becomes easy to harmonize the narratives of the four evangelists.

II.—*Jesus remains in Judea beyond Jordan.*

Sec. 137. From Jerusalem, whither He had gone to the feast of Dedication, our Lord retired to the place where John was at first baptizing, and abode there.[2] This place was Bethania, the present Tell-Anihje,[3] in the El-Batîheh. But this belonged to Judea beyond Jordan, by which is meant the ancient Gaulonitis, the Jolan of the present.[4] Yet Jesus seems to have paid a brief visit to Capernaum, where the events connected with the temple-tribute occurred.[5] According to Ex. xxx. 13, every Israelite was required to contribute yearly half a silver shekel to the sanctuary.[6] This obligation was still in full force after the Captivity.[7] The time fixed for paying over the tax into the temple treasury was, according to *Mishna Shekalim,* ii. 4, from the 15th to the 25th Adar. But since the sums collected were paid over in the order of the different townships and provinces, the collection of the didrachma—for this is the value of the half shekel—must be made at the latest by the beginning of the month Adar. That which is related, Matt. xvii. 24 ff., thus took place at the beginning of the month Adar, or even during the month of Shebet [middle of February]. According to John, Jesus in reality tarried in that region from the end of Kisleu, during the months of Thebet and Shebet, until the beginning of Adar. That, however, the tax referred to in this history is not, as Wieseler supposes, the poll-tax to be contributed to the civil authority, but the temple-tribute, follows first from the fact that Peter was asked whether his Master was wont to pay the didrachma or not; for the poll-tax was not a voluntary one, whilst at the time of Christ the temple-tax was to such extent optional that no compulsory measures could be taken against

---

[1] John xii. 12 ff.   [2] John x. 40–42.   [3] Cf. sec. 70.
[4] Cf. sec. 68.   [5] Matt. xvii. 24 ff.
[6] Cf. 2 Chron. xxiv. 6.   [7] Josephus, *de Bello,* vii. 6, sec. 6.

M

(VII.) SYNOPTICAL VIEW OF THE HISTORY, FROM END OF A.D. 29 TO THE RESURRECTION, 9TH APRIL A.D. 30.

CONTENTS OF THE NARRATIVE.	REFERENCE IN			
	MATTHEW.	MARK.	LUKE.	JOHN.
Jesus at Capernaum. The tribute money,	xvii. 24–xviii. 35.	[ix. 33–50.]	...	...
After the sojourn at Bethany (at feast of Dedication) Jesus goes away again beyond Jordan, and abides there. In a certain place teaches His disciples to pray,	xix. 1–xx. 16.	x. 1–31.	xi. 1–13.	x. 40–42.
Healing of a demoniac who was dumb. Other deeds and discourses,	...	...	xi. 14–xiii. 21.	...
Journey to Bethany for the raising of Lazarus,	...	...	xiii. 22–30.	xi. 1–45.
He is warned against Herod. "It cannot be that a prophet perish out of Jerusalem,"	...	...	xiii. 31–35.	...
Deeds and discourses,	...	...	xiv. 1–xvii. 10.	...
The Sanhedrim decides on the death of Jesus,	...	...	...	xi. 46–53.
Sojourn at Ephraim,	...	...	...	xi. 54–57.
Last journey of Jesus to Jerusalem, through the confines of Samaria and Galilee. The ten lepers,	xx. 17–28.	x. 32–45.	xvii. 11–xviii. 34.	...

Jesus passes through *Jericho*,	xx. 29-34.	x. 46-52.	xviii. 35-xix. 27.	...
Six days before the Passover comes to *Bethany*. Anointing of Jesus,	[xxvi. 6-13.]	[xiv. 3-9.]	...	xii. 1-8.
Triumphal entry into Jerusalem on the following day,	xxi. 1-11.	xi. 1-10.	xix. 28-44.	xii. 9-50.
Jesus returns to Bethany in the evening,	xxi. 17.	xi. 11.	...	...
On the morrow cleanses the sanctuary,	xxi. 12-16.	xi. 15-18.	xix. 45, 46.	...
The barren fig-tree,	xxi. 18-22.	{ xi. 12-14. / xi. 19-26. }	...	...
Jesus teaches during the day-time in the sanctuary, and passes the nights upon Olivet,	...	...	{ xix. 47, 48. / xxi. 37, 38. }	...
Returns to the sanctuary,	xxi. 23-xxiv. 1.	xi. 27-xiii. 1.	xx. 1-xxi. 4.	...
Discourses upon the Mount of Olives,	xxiv. 1-xxv. 46.	xiii. 1-37.	xxi. 5-36.	...
Two days before the Passover. Decision of chief priests and elders. Treachery of Judas,	xxvi. 1-16.	xiv. 1-11.	xxii. 1-6.	...
The paschal supper on first day of unleavened bread,	xxvi. 17-30.	xiv. 12-26.	xxii. 7-38.	xiii. 1-xiv. 31.
Gethsemane. The apprehension,	xxvi. 31-57.	xiv. 27-53.	xxii. 39-54.	xv. 1-xviii. 13.
Jesus before the high priest,	xxvi. 57-75.	xiv. 53-72.	xxii. 54-71.	xviii. 13-27.
In the morning taken before Pilate [and Herod],	xxvii. 1-30.	xv. 1-19.	xxiii. 1-25.	xviii. 28-xix. 15.
The Crucifixion,	xxvii. 31-56.	xv. 20-41.	xxiii. 26-49.	xix. 16-30.
The Burial,	xxvii. 57-66.	xv. 42-47.	xxiii. 50-56.	xix. 31-42.
The Resurrection,	xxviii. 1-20.	xvi. 1-18.	xxiv. 1-49.	xx., xxi.
The Ascension,	...	xvi. 19, 20.	xxiv. 50-53.	...

those refusing to pay it, as indeed the Sadducees did refuse to pay it. That the temple-tribute is meant, follows also from the reason adduced by Jesus to show that it cannot be claimed as due from Him, because He is a Son,[1] *i.e.* a Son of God, and not, *e.g.*, of Herod or of Cæsar. A sure chronological point of support is not afforded us by this history, partly because the time of the collection of the temple-tribute is uncertain, and partly because the place occupied by this account, in strictly chronological order, is also doubtful. Immediately after the account of this incident we read in Matthew of the controversy among the disciples on the question who of them should be the greatest—a controversy which, according to Mark [?] and Luke, belongs to an earlier period.[2]

III.—*The Raising of Lazarus (about 27th February,* A.D. 30).

Sec. 138. While Jesus was with His disciples in Judea beyond Jordan, the sisters of Lazarus sent to tell Him that their brother was sick. After two days of further sojourn in that place, Jesus revealed to His disciples the fact that Lazarus was dead, and made known His resolution of going to Bethany. Which of the apostles accompanied Him on this journey? That John, and also Thomas,[3] belonged to the company is certain; but equally certain, too, that Peter did *not* belong to it, because his reporter, Mark, does not relate anything of this raising of Lazarus. As a whole, the journey has the appearance of being made with but a small company of disciples, without imposing circumstances, and in haste. We have already said that Luke xiii. 22, where it says, " He went through towns and villages, teaching and journeying towards Jerusalem," is to be explained of this journey.[4] It is true, indeed, that on this occasion He did not proceed so far

---

[1] υἱός, Matt. xvii. 25.

[2] Mark ix. 33 ; Luke ix. 46. [Luke, who also places the scene in Galilee, but records it immediately after the Transfiguration, does not appear to have observed the chronological order.]

[3] John xi. 16.

[4] [A journey of three days, before that event which should constitute the crowning and closing act of His personal *ministry ;* Luke xiii. 32. Henceforth He presents Himself as *King*—for acceptance or rejection.]

as Jerusalem itself; but a journey to Bethany, which was distant only 15 stades from this city,[1] might well be called a journey to Jerusalem. The warning given to the Lord to flee, since Herod was seeking His life,[2] called forth from the Lord the answer, that to Jerusalem belonged the high prerogative of slaying the prophets, and a lament over Jerusalem specially in harmony with the then state of affairs.[3] The raising of Lazarus is related, John xi. 17–44, with great fulness of detail, and in a manner which must draw from every unprejudiced reader the confession that we have here before us the narrative of an eye-witness. That Jesus had been already previously acquainted with Lazarus and his sisters, is to be gathered with certainty from the account, and especially from the words of the message : Lord, behold, *he whom Thou lovest* is sick.[4] With John, however, there is no mention of this relation of friendship ; Luke, on the other hand,[5] speaks of it in a narrative which appears to coincide in point of time with the sojourn of Jesus at Jerusalem during the feast of Dedication.

Sec. 139. The intelligence of the miracle wrought at Bethany was for the enemies of Jesus the occasion of a decisive step. The Sanhedrim was called together, and the sentence of death pronounced against Him.[6] And since Jesus withdrew Himself out of their hands, the injunction was issued that whosoever knew His place of abode should reveal it, that He might be taken.[7] It has been urged as an argument against the authenticity of the Gospel of John, that the author of the fourth Gospel has been guilty of an oversight which could not have happened in the case of an eye-witness — the omission, namely, of the judgment of the Sanhedrim passed upon Jesus. And, indeed, no trial is reported in John xviii. 12–27. But the fact has been overlooked that the sentence had long been pronounced, and that the whole significance of the then sitting of the Sanhedrim was merely to receive Jesus as one already condemned, and captured by their authority. What is here said finds its full confirmation in the following remarks :—

[1] John xi. 18.
[2] Luke xiii. 31.
[3] John x. 39, xi. 8, 16.
[4] John xi. 3.
[5] Luke x. 38–42.
[6] John xi. 47–54.
[7] John xi. 57.

The books of Jewish tradition contain so many odious and infamous fables about Jesus, that the whole has been rejected in the lump; and any historic value whatever has been denied to the Talmudic accounts concerning the Lord.   There is, however, found in these writings a passage to which a real historic character must be acknowledged.   In *Mishna San-hedrin*, vi. 1, it is said that when any one was condemned to death by the Sanhedrim a public crier proclaimed the sentence, in order that witnesses in favour of the condemned might have time and opportunity for presenting themselves. Now, as an instance of this proceeding, there is cited in *Bab. Sanhedrin*, fol. 43. 1, a passage taken from the *Baraitho*, a supplement to the *Mishna* codex, which reads thus : " Jesus was crucified (literally, *hanged*) on the eve of the Passover. A public crier went forth with regard to him during forty days (proclaiming) : ' One who is to be stoned, because he has bewitched and seduced Israel, and led it into schism. Whoever can bring forward anything in his justification, let him come and testify for him.'   But no justification was found for him ; so they crucified him on the eve of the Pass-over "   (ליסקל יוצא יום 'מ לפניו יוצא והכרון לישו תלאוהו פסח בערב והתניא על שביישף והיסית והידית את ישראל כל מי שיודע לו זכות יבא וילמד עליו ולא מצאו לו זכות ותלאוהו בערב פסח).

For the right understanding of this passage we must observe that, according to *Jerus. Sanhedrin*, vi. 7, the bodies of those stoned were to be hanged until the evening ; the hanging was consequently a Jewish custom.[1]   The Rabbis, however, employ the word denoting this act, תלא, also simply for crucifixion.   M. Renan, in his *Life of Jesus*, infers from the passage above cited that Jewish tradition declares Jesus to have been stoned.   But the text does not say this.   It asserts, on the contrary, that Jesus was indeed sentenced to be stoned ; but the execution was not by stoning, but by hanging, *i.e.* by crucifixion, as it is twice stated in the text. But if the Sanhedrim condemned Jesus to stoning, how comes it to pass that, contrary to the sentence, He was crucified ? On this point again, Jewish tradition itself gives us explicit information.   In *Jerus. Sanhedrin*, i. 1, it is said that the

[1] [Cf. Deut. xxi. 22, 23.]

Sanhedrim, forty years before the destruction of the temple, was deprived of the right to carry out the death punishment. The words ascribed to the Jews in the Gospel of John :[1] " We may not put any one to death," are thus testified to by the Talmud itself. Jesus was crucified forty years before the destruction of Jerusalem. At that time the Sanhedrim was already—for *forty* is with the Rabbis a favourite round number—deprived of the power of executing the capital sentence, but was obliged to seek its execution at the hands of the Roman Procurator, who changed the sentence of stoning pronounced by the Sanhedrim into that of crucifixion.[2] Between the condemnation and the execution of the sentence there thus intervened, according to our text, a period of forty days. During this period the crier published the sentence with regard to Jesus (לפניו), and summoned the people who had anything to bring forward in favour of the condemned to put in an appearance. But with this agrees the Gospel of John, which states that the Sanhedrim pronounced the sentence of death upon Jesus immediately after the raising of Lazarus ; so that the sojourn of Jesus at Ephraim falls between the condemnation and the execution. That the evangelists, and especially John, mention nothing of the function of the crier, proves nothing against the matter, for John relates only what he himself saw and heard ; and since at the time in question he was not at Jerusalem, but in the wilderness with Jesus, he was not acquainted with this fact from personal observation. But that the sentence of the Supreme Council was in reality published, is clearly implied in the saying of John xi. 54, that Jesus could no longer walk openly among the Jews ; and in that of xi. 57, that the chief priests had issued injunctions (ἐντολάς)—probably by means of the public crier—that any one who knew should give information where Jesus was, in order that they might apprehend Him. From this it follows that the assembly of the Supreme Council on the night before the Lord's crucifixion was not really a session for passing

---

[1] John xviii. 31.

[2] [The cry of σταύρου, σταύρου αὐτόν, Luke xxiii. 21, and parall., only shows that the Jews knew how to accommodate themselves to the altered circumstances. The execution of Stephen was, on the other hand, a violation of Roman law.]

judgment, but for the final examination of witnesses. We shall presently see that the statement of the Talmudic text, that Jesus was crucified—not on the day of Passover itself, but—on the preparation day, *i.e.* the 14th Nisan, is perfectly true. We have thus, in the passage cited, a highly important and thoroughly genuine historic document. The forty days mentioned in this text are not to be greatly pressed, for it is well known that with the Semitic races the number "forty" was, and still is, a round number, signifying "many." Yet it is by no means impossible to take it here in the literal sense. The sentence was executed on the 14th Nisan, and must therefore have been passed on the 5th Adar. Jesus would thus have left Bethania beyond Jordan on the 2d Adar (24th February), and might still be in the neighbourhood of the Sea of Galilee when the half-shekel was collected there. We may suppose with certainty that Jesus spent about a month in the wilderness near Ephrem.

IV.—*Our Lord's Sojourn at Ephraim.*

Sec. 140. "Jesus therefore walked no more openly among the Jews, but went away from thence to the country near the wilderness, to a town called Ephraim (Ἐφραίμ), and abode there with the disciples."[1] The words immediately following these : "And the Passover of the Jews was nigh," belong not to this, but to the following sentence, and refer to the end of the "abiding" at Ephraim,—which, as we have just re-marked, may certainly be estimated at a month, if not at fully forty days. The meaning of this journey is clearly indicated. Jesus was withdrawing from the plots of the hierarchs and Sanhedrim, which had condemned Him to death, and now sought to obtain possession of Him. As regards the name of the place whither Jesus withdrew, in the Received Text it is written Ἐφραίμ, in some MSS. it is called Ἐφρέμ,[2] in others Ἐφράμ and Ἐφραθά. Eusebius, in the *Onomasticon*, regards this place as identical with Ephron, which was situated 8 miles (northward ?) of Ælia [Jerusalem]. Jerome, on the other hand, says, by way of correction, that Ephron, and consequently

---

[1] John xi. 54.   [2] [ℵ L, Coptic version.]

Ephraim, was 20 miles north of Jerusalem. But we have serious doubts as to the identity of Ephrem at all with Ephron. Ephron, and the Bethel mentioned with it,[1] belonged to Judah, and was too near Jerusalem, and too much under the immediate influence of the authorities in that city, to be able to afford Jesus a secure hiding-place. Only a district bordering on Samaritan territory could accomplish this purpose. In the Samaritan domain, about 35 miles north of Jerusalem, 6 miles N.E. from Nablûs, on the road to Beisan, lies a place visited by Schultz called El-Faria or El-Farah, at the beginning of a wady which runs down into the Ghôr, known as the Wady El-Faria or El-Farah. With the Hebrew article this name would be Ha-pharah. It is possible, moreover, that the original name, Ephram, has been metamorphosed by the Arabs into El-Pharah. Nevertheless, our Ephrem might be the Ἀἰφρααΐμ of the *Onomasticon*, which was situated 6 miles north of Legio. The place is now called Afûleh, and is situated between Ledjûn and Nazareth,[2] where, immediately to the east, begins the wilderness of the Jebel ed-Dûhy. At this point fits in remarkably well the account of the Evangelist Luke,[3] where it says : " It came to pass, as He was journeying to Jerusalem, that He also passed through the confines of Samaria and Galilee :" διὰ μέσου Σαμαρείας καὶ Γαλιλαίας.[4] Ginæa, the present Jenîn [En-gannim],[5] was the northern frontier town of Samaria,[6] and thus the southern frontier of Galilee. Thither Jesus repaired, in order to travel along the confines into the Ghôr, and thence to Jericho. On this route, on the frontiers between Samaria and Galilee, the Lord healed the ten lepers.[7] The discourses and deeds of the Lord, recorded Luke xvii. 20–xviii. 34, took place on the way.

[1] 2 Chron. xiii. 19. Josephus, *de Bello*, iv. 9, sec. 9.

[2] [On the northern confines of the plain of Jezreel, about 8 miles north of Jenîn (*Ginæa*).]

[3] Luke xvii. 11 ff.

[4] Not, as ordinarily rendered, " through the midst of Samaria and Galilee ; " for the way which goes first through Samaria and then through Galilee leads not *to* Jerusalem, but farther and farther *from* that city. It must have been written, " through the midst of Galilee and Samaria."

[5] [Formerly belonging to the tribe of Issachar, Josh. xix. 21.]

[6] Josephus, *de Bello*, iii. 3, sec. 4.

[7] Luke xvii. 12–19.

Among these is specially to be emphasized the proclamation of His approaching death and resurrection.[1]

V.—*The Last Journey of Jesus to Jerusalem.*

Sec. 141. According to the three Synoptists, Jesus came to Jerusalem, on His last journey, through Jericho.[2] In what way did He reach this town ? It is pretty generally assumed that Jesus came down on the eastern bank of the Jordan from the district of the Sea of Galilee, until opposite Jericho, and then crossed the Jordan, and so entered Jericho. All this, however, is pure hypothesis ; not the slightest indication of it is found in the texts. More than this, the absolute silence of the narrative regarding a passing across the Jordan renders such a supposition in the highest degree improbable. Jesus, after quitting Ephrem, passed along the frontiers between Samaria and Galilee into the Ghôr, and then pursued down the Ghôr the route described in the *Tabula Peutingeriana* from Scythopolis to Jericho, on the western side of the Jordan. The way on the eastern side of this river would have gone through the territory of Herod, the tetrarch of Galilee and Peræa, whom Jesus had every reason for avoiding ;[3] whereas He proceeded by the much shorter cis-Jordan route, with a protecting caravan of festive pilgrims.

Sec. 142. **Jericho.** — In the region where the Jordan empties itself into the Dead Sea, the Ghôr forms, on the western side of the river, the well - watered and naturally fruitful oasis of Jericho. In this oasis there exists at the present day a miserable village named Rîha, or er-Rîha. This name — formerly written Erîha — resembles that of Jericho.[4] The village, however, does not indicate the site of the ancient city : this latter was situated at the Elisha-Fountain [Ain es-Sultan], a mile to the north of Rîha. The town of Jericho at the time of Christ seems, moreover, not to have occupied exactly the place of the former city destroyed by Joshua. Important in this connection is the remark of Eusebius in the *Onomasticon*, that the town of Jericho visited

---

[1] Luke xviii. 31–34.   [2] Matt. xx. 26 ; Mark x. 46 ; Luke xviii. 35.

[3] Luke xiii. 31.   [4] [Cf. יְרִיחוֹ.]

by the Lord was destroyed by the Romans at the time of the
siege of Jerusalem, on account of the faithlessness of its
inhabitants; that to replace this the third city was built,
which existed in Eusebius' time; " the traces also," he adds,
" of the two former cities are shown to this day." The oasis
of Jericho was at the time of Jesus world-famed for the
culture of the balsam and date-palm; it has—owing to the
protection of the surrounding mountains, and its depression
below the level of the sea, which amounts to more than a
thousand feet—a really tropical climate, and brings forth
tropical productions.

At Jericho—before His entrance into the city, according
to Luke xviii. 35; after He had passed through it, according
to Matt. xx. 29; Mark x. 46—Jesus healed the blind man,
and turned aside to sojourn (καταλῦσαι) in the house of the
publican Zacchæus.[1]

Sec. 143. In order to reach Jerusalem from Jericho, the
traveller must climb the mountain-wall which supports the
Judean uplands, and forms the western boundary of the Ghôr.
The height to which he must rise attains to something like
3500 feet; since Jerusalem lies 3700 feet above the level of
the Dead Sea, and Jericho only 200 feet above that level.
The route lies through a gloomy desert of cretaceous and
calcareous hills. The distance amounts to about 18 miles.
This road is still and was always rendered unsafe by robbers
and highwaymen, and especially was the ascent of Adumim
(*Khân Hadrûr*) notorious on this account.[2] From the uplands
to which this road leads Jerusalem is divided by the valley
of Jehoshaphat—the upper part of the Kidron—running from
north to south. The western declivity of these uplands, lying
opposite Jerusalem, is called **the Mount of Olives**.[3] This rises
above the valley of Jehoshaphat like a far-stretching wall of
rock, spreading from north to south. At its summit it assumes
a less rugged form than at its base. It rises terrace-wise, in
perpendicularly shelving layers and strata of limestone, to its

---

[1] Luke xix. 1–10. [If the healing took place *on the way to the house of*
Zacchæus, there is no discrepancy between the different narratives.]

[2] Luke x. 30 ff. Cf. Stanley, *Sin. and Pal.* chap. xiii. p. 424.

[3] [Called *Olivet* in Luke xix. 29, xxi. 37; Acts i. 12.]

three principal plateau-like summits,—somewhat higher than the rest of the mountain, yet flattened at the top,—which tower only by about 200 feet above the highest parts of the city. The absolute height of the Mount of Olives is 2500 feet ; opposite to St. Stephen's Gate it rises 600 feet above the Kidron. A moderate number of the olive trees, from which it takes its name, still adorn the mountain ; and at its western foot the oldest group of its veterans in the Garden of Gethsemane is world-famed as a spot sacred to the Christian pilgrim. A great part of the mountain is occupied with level fields ; and even the highest peak is ploughed up, and sown with barley. The southernmost of these three summits is known under the name of " Mountain of Offence," with reference to the idolatry of Solomon recorded 1 Kings xi. 7. The northernmost is called " Viri Galilæi." [1]   The centre one, and at the same time the highest, bears on it the Chapel of the Ascension. On the eastern side of this last summit lies the Arab village *El-Azirieh*, or, what is better, El-Lazirieh, *i.e.* Lazarus. It has already been remarked that the Arabs have attached to many ancient localities the name of some renowned man belonging to them. Thus they call Hebron El-Khalil, the friend (*sc.* of God), *i.e.* Abraham ; Rama of Samuel, Neby Samwîl. So also *Bethany*, after Lazarus, *El-Lazirieh*. The place in reality corresponds to all the requirements of the sacred text. It lies 2 miles from Jerusalem,— the distance thus agreeing with the 15 stadia of John xi. 18. From El-Azirieh Jerusalem is not visible, owing to the intervening Hill of the Ascension. The traveller gains a view of the city only when he has left behind him half the way, has gone round the Hill of the Ascension, and has reached the slope of Olivet.[2]   Thus also, according to Luke xix. 37, 41,

---

[1] [Cf. Acts i. 11.]

[2] [In connection with the history of the Lord's descent from Olivet on the occasion of His last triumphal entry, the student should ponder the memorable description of Stanley, *Sin. and Pal.* chap. iii. pp. 192, 193. With this let him compare the account of Tristram : " There is but one true approach to Jerusalem, and, if possible, even at the cost of some hours' *détour*, let the pilgrim endeavour to enter from the east, the favourite approach of our Lord, the path of His last and triumphant entry. It is a glorious burst as the traveller rounds the shoulder of Mount Olivet, and the Haram wall starts up before him

Jesus first gained a view of the city a considerable time after He had left Bethany.

Sec. 144. **Bethphage.**—In the account given by Matthew Bethany is not mentioned, but it is said [1] that when Jesus had gone up from Jericho, and had drawn near to Jerusalem, He came to Bethphage, and from that point sent out two of His disciples. . . . In Mark xi. 1 and Luke xix. 29, on the other hand, it is said : " And when they were come unto Bethany and Bethphage, εἰς Βηθφαγῆ καὶ Βηθανίαν, He sendeth forth two of His disciples. . . ." Had Bethphage been a village, its site must have been eastwards of Bethany, since it is mentioned before this latter village. Jesus makes a halt, to wait for the bringing up of the ass on which He is to ride into the city ; this point of halting and of rest was Bethphage *and* Bethany. How could Jesus be waiting in two villages at one time ? In connection with this question it must at once strike one, that while ancient and modern Biblical geographers agree with tradition in pointing out with certainty the site of Bethany, they are, with regard to Bethphage, uncertain and mutually contradictory. All difficulties vanish, however, so soon as we understand by Bethphage not a village, but a whole district—namely, the Mount of Olives from the eastern wall of Jerusalem as far as Bethany ; and that this is really meant by the term Bethphage, may be proved with certainty from the books of Jewish tradition. If at the feast of Passover millions of pilgrims came up to Jerusalem, it is evident that only a comparatively small proportion of them could find

from the deep gorge of the Kedron, with its domes and crescents sparkling in the sunlight—a royal city. On that very spot He once paused and gazed on the same bold cliffs supporting a far more glorious pile, and when He beheld the city He wept over it. . . . We gazed for a few moments, grouped in silence. ' That is the mosque,' ' There is the Mount of Olives,' ' That is the Church of the Holy Sepulchre,' were remarks enough. The one thought, ' This is Jerusalem,' absorbs all others. ' Thy servants take pleasure in her stones.' It is like revisiting a father's grave or the home of one's youth, and no one is disposed to expatiate on the outline or details of the landscape which rivets itself upon the soul with magnetic power, for over it hover the memories of redemption achieved, and the victory over the grave " (*Land of Israel*, p. 174). The devout and judicious remarks of Andrew Bonar, *Narrative*, before cited, p. 157, are also worthy of careful attention.]

[1] Matt. xxi. 1.

quarters in the city ; the great majority encamped outside the city, where also they must prepare their Paschal meals. But since this must, according to the law, be performed in " the camp," *i.e.* according to later conceptions, at Jerusalem, the district lying eastward of Jerusalem, and comprising the Kidron and the Mount of Olives, was " sanctified," *i.e.* declared an integral part of " the camp," in which every sacred act which should be performed by the Israelite at Jerusalem was permitted and valid. This supplement of the Holy City was called by the Rabbis Bethphage, בית פגי. In this sense is to be understood the oft-reiterated assertion : " Bethphage is without the city ; but since it rests immediately upon the holy mountain, the bread prepared there is sacred." [1] Since Bethphage is the whole Mount of Olives, sanctified as part of the " camp," the evangelists could say with justice that Jesus came to Bethany *and* Bethphage ; for it then means that He came into the district known as Bethphage, and into the particular spot of this district which is called Bethany.

Sec. 145. That which Jewish tradition tells us about Bethphage and Bethany, affords us important information on points connected with the history of the Sanhedrim in the age of Jesus. The Pharisaic Talmudists often reproach the Sadducees with being bloodthirsty and ferocious in the application of capital punishment. Thus it is said in *Bab. Sanhedrin*, fol. 14. 2, and in *Bab. Sota*, fol. 45. 1, that the Sanhedrim of Bethphage condemned to death those elders—*i.e.* members of the Great Council—who opposed the decrees of the majority. What is to be understood by this Sadducean Sanhedrim at Bethphage ? According to *Bab. Rosh hashanna*, fol. 31. 1, and *Bab. Sanhedrin*, [2] the Synedrium had originally its seat in Leshkath ha-Gasith, on the south side of the Court of Israel; but forty years before the destruction of the temple this supreme court of judicature migrated, and removed to Hanioth; and later, from thence to Jerusalem—into the city, but not into the sanctuary ; then to Jabne (at the time of the destruction of Jerusalem), etc., until at last it came to Tiberias.

[1] *Bab. Pesachim*, fol. 63. 2 ; *Menachoth*, vii. 6, ii. 2 ; *Tosaphtha Menachoth*, ii. 2 ; Siphri in Ugolini, *Thes.* xv. p. 399.

[2] Ugolini, *Thes.* xxv. 589.

Further, we read in *Bab. Baba Mezia*, fol. 88. 1, " Hanioth, חניות, the place of the sons of Hanan, בני חנן, was destroyed before the overthrow of the temple ; and why was Hanioth at Héno, חניות של הינו, destroyed ?   Because they (*i.e.* the Bené Hanan) at Hanioth founded their decrees on the law alone, without regard to the traditions of the fathers." The San-hedrim at Hanioth, whose members were called, on account of the place of session, Bené Hanan, was thus—like that of Bethphage on the Mount of Olives—*Sadducean*.   But Hanioth too was situated on the Mount of Olives.[1] From this it fol-lows that the Sanhedrim of Hanioth and that of Bethphage is one and the same, and Hanioth or Hanio is nothing else than *Beth-hania* or Bethany. We observe that the orthography of this name with the Talmudists is in the highest degree unsettled.   As corresponding with the above-cited חניות של הינו, we read in *Bab. Pesachim*, fol. 53. 1, היני ; in *Bab. Erubin*, fol. 28. 1, בית יוני ; in *Tosaphtha Trumoth*, vii. 6, בית אוני. The most natural etymology seems to us to be a contracted בית חני, *i.e.* בית חניות.   The word חניות signifies booths or tents, set up by the merchants in the fairs or markets.   That tents of this kind were to be found at the encampment of the pilgrims who came up to the festival, will be self-evident. The locality in which they were mainly to be found was Bethany.

Sec. 146. We have already[2] cited a passage from the Tal-mud, to the effect that forty years before the destruction of the temple, the Sanhedrim was deprived of the right of inflict-ing capital punishment.   In the citation just made, it is said that, forty years before the destruction of the temple, the Sanhedrim removed from Leshkath Hagasith to Bethany; this migration, and that loss of a privilege which, according to the Talmudists, stood and fell with the possession of Leshkath Hagasith as a place of sitting, belong thus to one and the same occasion.   Later, probably after only a brief sojourn at Bethany of Bethphage, the Great Council withdrew to Jeru-salem ; where, in reality, it held its sessions during the period of the life of Christ now under consideration.[3] The number

---

[1] *Jerus. Taanith*, iv. 8, fol. 69, 2.   [2] Sec. 139.
[3] John xviii. 13 ; Matt. xxvi. 57, 58 ; Mark xiv. 53 ; Luke xxii. 54.

forty is not, as we have already said, to be taken literally. The Sanhedrim was in the year 783, thus forty years before the destruction of Jerusalem, already in this city; the time of their assembling at Bethany falls thus somewhat earlier. It would seem that at Bethany-Bethphage the Great Council was exclusively Sadducean; at Jerusalem it was composed of Pharisees and Sadducees combined;[1] and shortly before the destruction of Jerusalem it became exclusively Pharisaic, under the influence of the Rabban Johanan Ben Zacchai.[2] Remarkable, in connection with this name, is the following passage of the Talmud:[3] "Forty years before the destruction of the temple"—thus in the year of the death of Christ—"the doors of the temple opened of themselves. Johanan Ben Zacchai began to chide them, and said, 'Temple, why openest thou of thyself? From this I see that thine end is near, for it is written (Zech. xi. 1), Open thy doors, O Lebanon, that the fire may devour thy cedars.'" Does not this spontaneous opening of the doors of the temple, in the year of the death of Christ, remind of Matt. xxvii. 51, "The veil of the temple was rent in twain, from the top to the bottom"?

VI.—*The Mode of observing Passover at the Time of Christ.*

Sec. 147. The right understanding of the history of the passion, even as respects its chronology, depends in a high degree upon a true insight into the order of observance for the Jewish Passover. In the law, Ex. xii. 1–18, it is commanded: "The month Abib (Nisan) shall be unto you the first month. On the tenth day of this month shall every man take a lamb for a house ... without blemish, a male, of a year old. On the fourteenth day of this month shall they kill it, the whole assembled congregation of Israel, between the two evenings (בֵּין הָעַרְבַּיִם), and shall eat the flesh in that night, roasted with fire; and mazoth (unleavened bread) shall they eat to bitter herbs ... Seven days shall ye eat mazoth; even on the first day shall ye put away leaven out of your houses.

---

[1] Acts iv. 1 ff., v. 17, 21, 34, 40.
[2] *Megillath Taanith*, 27th Marchesvan.
[3] *Bab. Toma*, fol. 39. 2.

... On the first day and on the seventh day shall be holy convocation: no labour shall be done, save the preparation for the eating. In the first month, on the fourteenth day of the month, at even (בערב), shall ye eat mazoth, until the twenty-first at even." This order for the observance of the Passover is repeated, with some variations, in Lev. xxiii. 5–14 ; Num. xxviii. 16–25 ; Deut. xvi. 1–8. Taken as a whole, the directions are distinct. The single difficulties connected with exegesis and harmonistics we may disregard, since our object is only to see how the Jews, at the time of Christ, understood them and carried them out.

Sec. 148. The 14th Nisan is invariably designated in the Talmudic writings by the expression ערב הפסח, eve of the Passover ; in the same sense in which ערב השבת denotes the Jewish sixth day, preceding the Sabbath. In the N. T. the 14th Nisan is called παρασκευὴ τοῦ πάσχα, very properly translated by Luther, " Rüsttag." On the evening of this 14th, *i.e. at its beginning,*—since the Jewish day begins with the evening, and " evening and morning "[1] make up the day,—the Jews began to eat the mazoth.[2] This could not but be the case, since on the evening of the 14th Nisan all leaven must be put away by daylight.[3] This preparation day, the 14th Nisan, was—equally as the Passover day, the 15th, or as the " Day of Convocation," the 21st—a festival,[4] although the practice with regard to it was somewhat different in the different provinces. In Judea, work was permitted on the preparation day until the dawn of the morning ; in Galilee, the *whole* day, evening, night, and morning, was kept sacred.[5] Besides the putting away of the leaven, and the beginning of the eating of the mazoth, the principal event of the 14th Nisan was the offering of the paschal lamb in the sanctuary. This offering of the lamb consisted not, however, as is maintained by many exegetes, in the eating of it, but in the killing of it in the sanctuary. This was to take place בין העברים, " between the two evenings." We have not to investigate

---

[1] Gen. i. 5.   [2] Ex. xii. 18.   [3] *Mishna Pesachim,* i.–iii.
[4] *Jerus. Chagiga,* iii. 7 : ערב הפסח כפסח יום טבה בעצרת.
[5] ביהודה חיו עושין מלאכה בערבי פסחים עד חצות ובגליל לא היו עושין כל עיקר.—*Pesachim,* iv. 5.

what significance this expression had in the Mosaic writings, but merely how it was understood in the age of Christ.   The *thamid*, or evening sacrifice, was, according to Ex. xxix. 38, 39, xii. 6, Num. xxviii. 3, 4, to be presented " between the two evenings."   Now we read in *Mishna Pesachim*, v. 1: " Thamid was killed at the eighth hour and a half, and offered at the ninth hour and a half.   On the preparation for the Passover it was killed at the seventh hour and a half, and offered at the eighth hour and a half.   But if the preparation for Passover fell on a Friday, thamid was killed at the sixth hour and a half, and offered at the seventh hour and a half; and after this followed Passover."   By this is explained the signification of the expression " between the two evenings: " it is the time at which both the thamid and the paschal lamb were offered, thus between the sixth hour and a half and the twelfth hour; or from half an hour after mid-day to six o'clock in the evening, or rather to sunset.   On the 14th Nisan, when the following day did not coincide with a Sabbath, the evening sacrifice was killed at half-past one, offered at half-past two, and then, at about half-past three, the Israelites began to slay the paschal lamb.   The offering of the Passover consisted in the burning of the fat, and in the pouring out of the blood of the lamb at the foot of the altar of burnt-offering.   Josephus [1] says that the paschal lamb was offered, or slain, between the ninth hour and the eleventh,— thus between three and five in the afternoon.   The lamb was then skinned, prepared, and roasted.

Sec. 149.   The 15th Nisan was a " Day of Convocation," like the 21st, and bore the name of Sabbath, which might also be that of the week-day on which it fell.[2]   In the night with which this day began the paschal lamb was eaten.   That this was, and must be, an eating by night, follows from Ex. xii. 8, 10.   It did not thus take place on the 14th Nisan, which ended with sunset.   This would have been, in the nature of things, impossible ; since the roasting of a whole lamb, which was killed only at five o'clock in the evening, could not possibly have been accomplished before the close of the night-

---

[1] Josephus, *de Bello*, vi. 9, sec. 3.
[2] Lev. xxiii. 6, 7, 11.

day. It is consequently an error, when it is asserted that the paschal lamb was consumed at the end of the 14th Nisan. The 15th Nisan was observed strictly as a Sabbath: the following days, from the 16th to the 20th Nisan, were work days, only the use of leavened bread was interdicted on them. Yet on the 16th took place the special celebration of the harvest, and the presentation of the paschal sheaf.[1] The barley sheaf was gathered in, by those deputed by the Sanhedrim, immediately upon the setting of the sun, thus at the beginning of the 16th Nisan. For this purpose, a field in the neighbourhood of Jerusalem, in the valley of the Kidron, was ordinarily chosen; because in this valley, which sank down abruptly to the tropical Ghôr, the corn was ripe considerably earlier than in the rest of Palestine.[2] The presentation took place at the time of the morning sacrifice, and proclaimed the beginning of the harvest. From this 16th Nisan was determined the feast of Pentecost, which fell seven weeks later. It thus took place fifty days later than the 15th Nisan, on the next day of the week. If, for instance, the 15th was a Sabbath, — as was the case in the year A.D. 30,—then the day of Pentecost was Feria I.[3] The 21st Nisan was again a "Day of Convocation," which was observed as a Sabbath, and brought to a close the feast of the Mazoth.

Sec. 150. In the modern Jewish calendar, the new moon, and consequently the 1st Nisan, is no longer determined by the phase, but by astronomical calculation. It can, moreover, be arbitrarily postponed. The 1st of Nisan is therefore in such wise ordered in the modern calendar that the 15th never falls on the second, fourth, and sixth days of the week, i.e. on Monday, Wednesday, and Friday, in the Jewish sense. That, however, this limitation did not exist in the ancient Jewish period, but that at that time—consequently also in the age of Christ—the Passover might fall on any day of the week, may be proved with certainty from the Talmud. In *Mishna Pesachim*, vii. 10, it is said that the remains,

---

[1] Lev. xxiii. 10 ff. Josephus, *Antiq*. iii. 10, sec. 5.
[2] *Tosaphtha Menachoth*, x. 10. [Cf. Tristram, p. 596.]
[3] Cf. Lev. xxiii. 15 ff. Josephus, *Antiq*. iii. 10, sec. 6.

bones, etc., of the Easter lamb were burnt on the 16th Nisan; but that, if this fell on a Sabbath, the burning took place on the 17th. From this it follows that the 16th might fall on a seventh day, and consequently the 15th might be a sixth day, or Friday. So also in *Mishna Chagiga*, ii. 4, the case of the day of Pentecost falling on a Sabbath is discussed. We might have passed over this fact without notice, had not some interpreters sought additional support for their position that the 15th Nisan in the year of the death of Jesus was not a Friday, as is generally supposed, but a Saturday, by an appeal to the law that the 15th Nisan could never fall on a Friday. We maintain the same position, that in the year of the death of Christ the day of Passover fell on a Sabbath. It was incumbent on us, therefore, to say why we did not avail ourselves of this argument. It is because this rule does not apply to the age of Christ.

VII.—*The Time of Christ's Suffering, according to the single Evangelists.*

Sec. 151. **The time of the Passion according to the Gospel of John.**—The question dominating and conditionating every other is this: On what Jewish day of the week and month was Jesus crucified? Now, in John xix. 14 it is said that the day on which the Lord was crucified was the preparation day of the Passover, ἦν δὲ παρασκευὴ τοῦ πάσχα. That by this is meant the Rabbinical ערב הפסח, cannot be explained away by any exegetical artifice. If the evangelist is not to be charged with employing expressions necessarily misleading to the reader, it must be admitted that he places the day of the crucifixion of Christ on the 14th Nisan. To the same conclusion does John xviii. 28 necessarily lead, where it is said: " They (the Jews) led Jesus from Caiaphas unto the prætorium; but they themselves went not into the prætorium, that they might not be defiled, but might be able to eat the Passover," ἵνα μὴ μιανθῶσιν, ἀλλ᾽ ἵνα φάγωσι τὸ πάσχα. That the " eating of the Passover " is not *of necessity* to be understood of the partaking of the paschal lamb, we admit, and even postulate; but that it *may* imply the eating of the paschal lamb must equally be admitted. The observance of the feast of Unleavened Bread was an eating of the Passover in the proper sense of the term ; but to this observance was not attached the condition of Levitical purity ; for even those who were unclean might, yea must, partake of unleavened bread in these days, for other bread was interdicted to every one, under pain of being cut off. The Jews, however, in the passage cited, have before their mind an eating of the Passover which is permitted only to those ceremonially clean: this could only be the eating of the paschal lamb. Some exegetes have asserted that the festive thank-offering, Chagiga, and the sacrificial meal which follows it, is what is meant. It is said, Deut. xvi. 16, 17, " Three times in a year shall all thy males appear before the face of Jehovah thy God, in the place which He shall choose, namely, at the feast of the Mazoth, at the feast of Pentecost, and at the feast of Tabernacles. And there shall not any one appear empty before Jehovah, according as his hand can give, and according to the blessing which Jehovah hath given to each one." This " not appearing empty " the Jews understood in the sense of a thank-offering, and the meal which follows this, which they called Chagiga. That was generally presented on the 15th Nisan, but could also be offered on the 14th, simultaneously with the paschal lamb ; [1] but the sacrificial flesh thereof could be preserved two days and a night.[2] Since, then, the entering into a Gentile house defiled only until evening,[3] there would still have been time enough for the Jews to partake of the sacrificial meal a day later, if they had entered into the prætorium. But the main reason why we cannot regard the eating for which they should preserve themselves clean as Chagiga is, that to this sacrifice there is wanting any special paschal character, since it could be presented on all festivals, and must be presented at Pentecost and Tabernacles ; the expression, " to eat the Passover," does not therefore rightly apply to it. The Jews avoided entering the prætorium in order that they might be able to eat the

[1] *Mishna Pesachim*, vi. 3, 4.
[2] *Ibid*. vi. 4.
[3] Judith xii. 7-9.

paschal lamb on the night which was before them,—the night
with which the 15th Nisan began; the day on which they
had used such precaution was thus the 14th Nisan. On this
day, consequently, was Jesus crucified.

Sec. 152. According to John, Jesus was judged,[1] crucified,[2]
and buried,[3] on the 14th Nisan. Further, as concerns the day
of the week, it must have been on the sixth day, a Friday;
since, according to xx. 1, Jesus rose on a Sunday,—τῇ μιᾷ
τῶν σαββάτων,—after being buried at the end of the day of
preparation,[4] and lying in the grave over the Sabbath, the
great one,[5] which was thus both a week Sabbath and the high
day of Passover. In the year U.C. 783, A.D. 30, the 15th
Nisan was in fact a Sabbath; and consequently the 14th,
Feria VI., a Friday. The statement of the Gospel of John thus
perfectly tallies with that of Jewish tradition, which is to the
effect that Jesus was crucified on the preparation day of the
Passover, בערב הפסח.[6]

Sco. 163. It will be self-evident that, if Jesus was crucified
on the 14th Nisan, the last supper which He held with His
disciples will also be on the 14th Nisan. Yet this fact may
be immediately proved. In John xiii. 1, 2 it is said, " Before
the feast of the Passover . . . supper being come . . . Jesus
riseth from supper," πρὸ δὲ τῆς ἑορτῆς τοῦ πάσχα . . . καὶ
δείπνου γενομένου.[7] The paschal festival was observed on the
15th; before the feast of the Passover was, consequently, the
14th. That this meal took place at night is seen from chap.
xiii. 30. This night then, in which, after the supper, Jesus
was in Gethsemane, belonged to the 14th Nisan. This 14th
Nisan had begun with sunset, and consequently with the
evening of our Thursday.

The relation of the Jewish night-days of that paschal
season to our days, which begin with midnight, will be
apparent from the following scheme :—

[1] John xviii. 28.   [2] John xix. 14.
[3] John xix. 31, 42.   [4] John xix. 42.
[5] John xix. 31.   [6] Cf. sec. 139.
[7] [Tischendorf, with the Sinaitic and Vatican MSS., reads γινομίνου. The
meaning would then rather be, "supper beginning," or "coming on :" γινομίνου
(retained by Alford) is "being come."]

JULIAN DAY.		JEWISH NIGHT-DAY.

Thursday, 6th April.
- Midnight till morning.
- Forenoon.   . . .
- Afternoon.   . . . — 13th Nisan, Feria V.

- Evening till midnight.

Friday, 7th April.
- Midnight till morning.
- Forenoon.   . . .
- Afternoon.   . . .
- Evening till midnight. — 14th Nisan, Feria VI.

The Last Supper ; beginning of the Mazoth ; Gethsemane ; putting away of the leaven ; judgment.

Crucifixion and burial. — Offering of the paschal lamb.

15th Nisan, Sabbath. — Eating of the paschal lamb. Jesus in the grave. } Passover.

Saturday, 8th April.
- Midnight till morning.
- Forenoon.   . . .
- Afternoon.   . . .
- Evening till midnight.

Sunday, 9th April.
- Midnight till morning.
- Forenoon.   . . .
- Afternoon.   . . .
- Evening till midnight. — 16th Nisan, Feria I.

Jesus in the grave ; ingathering of first-fruits. Resurrection of Jesus.

Sec. 154. Every unprejudiced reader is surely convinced by what has been already said, that John places the crucifixion of Jesus on the preparation day of the Passover, *i.e.* the 14th Nisan, and not on the great day of Passover. Further proof is not necessary. Yet, by way of supererogation, we may adduce still further the passage John xiii. 29. After the meal, while it was night,[1] Jesus had said to Judas, "That thou doest, do quickly." "Some of them thought, because Judas had the purse, that Jesus had said to him, Buy what we have need of against the feast." That feast is the 15th Nisan. Now if Jesus was crucified on the 15th, the supper would have taken place on the same night-day; but on the 15th Nisan, the great Sabbath, no "buying" was possible ; this must have been looked after on the 14th. Jesus then spoke the words we have cited, on the 14th Nisan, at the beginning of that night-day in the second half of which the crucifixion took place.

If, then, many interpreters have nevertheless attempted to show that John admits of the supposition that Christ was

[1] John xiii. 30.

crucified on the 15th Nisan, this takes place on harmonistic grounds. They seek to bring John's account into harmony with that of the Synoptists, who, as is supposed, fix as the day of the Lord's death the great day of Passover itself, the 15th Nisan. Of this we shall now speak in the following section.

Sec. 155. **The time of the Passion according to Luke.—** In Luke xxii. 7, 8 we read : " Then came the day of unleavened bread, on which the Passover must be killed. And Jesus sent Peter and John, saying, Go and prepare us the Passover, that we may eat." For the moment we leave undecided the question as to what this paschal meal was, contenting ourselves with saying that it does not follow with absolute necessity that this was the eating of the paschal lamb, for the very reason that no mention is made of any lamb. The day of unleavened bread, when the Passover should be offered, *i.e.* the lamb should be slain, its blood poured forth on the altar, and its fat be consumed, was the 14th of Nisan—and only on tho 15th followed the eating. The command to prepare the Passover was given to the disciples on the afternoon of Thursday, 6th April; the eating took place on the same date, after sunset of the Thursday, on what was consequently already the 14th Nisan, the Jewish Feria VI. If, as is ordinarily supposed, Jesus had given the command at the end of the 14th Nisan, in such wise that the meal took place at the beginning of the 15th, then Luke could not have said that the day *came*, on which the Passover must be killed. He must, on the contrary, have said that the day on which the Passover must be killed was drawing to its close ; for at that hour of the afternoon the offering of the paschal lamb was, if not already accomplished, in the full course of accomplishment.

Sec. 156. If the meal which Jesus held with His disciples had been the eating of the paschal lamb, the Lord must have partaken of it proleptically, and against the rule, at the beginning of the 14th Nisan ; for at this time, according to Luke no less than John, did the eating take place. It must in that case be explained how the disciples came to be authorized by the priests, proleptically and against the law, to slay their lamb in the sanctuary a day earlier than others. But if it had really been the case that Jesus had already partaken of

the paschal lamb on the 14th Nisan, it would follow therefrom that He was also crucified on the 14th; for, after the
eating of the supper, Jesus addressed to Peter the words, " I
say unto thee, Peter, the cock will not crow *this day*, σήμερον,
until thou shalt thrice have denied that thou knowest me." [1]
From this follows that Peter's denial took place on the same
night-day on which the meal was partaken of.—Another
passage, Luke xxiii. 26, proves that the day of the Lord's
death could not possibly fall on the 15th Nisan. It is there
said that Simon the Cyrenian was coming up from the field,
ἀπ' ἀγροῦ, when they compelled him to bear the cross of
Jesus. Of a man who is returning from a Sabbath walk it
cannot be said that he is coming up from the field; [2] this
expression, on the contrary, implies that he was returning from
field labour. Now field labour was not permitted to any one
on the great day of the Passover; although it was so, where
necessity required it, on the preparation day.

Sec. 157. When Jesus had expired upon the cross, Joseph
of Arimathea buried the body ; and " it was the preparation,
and the Sabbath drew on." [3] The name " preparation,"
παρασκευή, *may* denote either the day before the Passover or
the day before the week Sabbath. In this last sense—as
preparation day for the week Sabbath—is it taken by those
interpreters who suppose that Jesus was crucified on the 15th
Nisan, a Friday. But for whom must not a difficulty lie in
the supposition that the greatest and most sacred festive
Sabbath of the whole year should here be called simply the
preparation of the Sabbath, as any other Friday of the year ?
The 15th Nisan was, on the other hand, so exceptionally
sacred, that the week Sabbath might serve as preparation day
for this. When the 15th Nisan fell on the Jewish Feria I.,
and consequently the 14th Nisan was a Sabbath, it was permitted to break this last to such extent as was required by
the preparations for the festival. [4] From this it follows that
the Passover was more sacred than the week Sabbath, and
consequently could not serve as preparation day to it. The

---

[1] Luke xxii. 34.
[2] Compare, for the use of ἀγρός, Luke xiv. 18 ; Matt. xxii. 5.
[3] Luke xxiii. 54. [4] *Mishna Pesachim*, iii. 6, vi. 1; *Jerus. Pesachim*, fol. 33. 1.

Paraskeue in Luke thus signifies, as we have already found to be the case in John, the preparation day for Passover, the 14th Nisan. From this it follows that, according to Luke, Jesus observed the supper at the beginning of the 14th Nisan, Thursday after sunset; and that on the same Jewish night-day, the 14th Nisan—though, according to our mode of reckoning, on the Friday—He was condemned, crucified, and buried. In the meantime the Sabbath drew on, with the sunset of Friday; and this night-day was at once the week Sabbath, Feria VII., and the great paschal Sabbath. This Sabbath they passed in quiet, according to the commandment.[1] On the Sunday following, τῇ δὲ μιᾷ τῶν σαββάτων, Jesus rose from the grave.[2] The chronology of Luke thus perfectly harmonizes with that of John.

Sec. 158. **The Paschal Meal.**—That the "eating of the Passover" *may* signify the eating of the paschal lamb is beyond doubt, and is, moreover, proved from John xviii. 28. But that it has not exclusively this signification, we have now to show. That the last supper, as John relates it, was not the eating of the paschal lamb, is perfectly clear. If, then, that described by Luke had been the paschal lamb of the 15th Nisan, we must assume a manifest contradiction between these two evangelists. The opinion, however, that Luke designates the 15th Nisan as the day of the supper and of the crucifixion, is based simply and alone upon the fact that the evangelist calls this meal "the Passover;" for the other chronological hints point, as we have already seen, rather to the 14th Nisan. If Luke had anywhere expressly said that at this meal the lamb was eaten, we should be confined to the paschal supper of the 15th; but the word "lamb" does not at all occur in his narrative. In chap. xxii. 14–23 he has described this supper carefully and in detail : Jesus gave to the disciples the cup to drink;[3] then the bread to eat, which is His body,[4] and the cup of the New Testament to drink, which is His blood;[5] but of a lamb not a trace. If anywhere surely here, the *argumentum e silentio* is valid. Luke does not speak of the paschal lamb; therefore it was not the

---

[1] Luke xxiii. 56.   [2] Luke xxiv. 1.   [3] Luke xxii. 17, 18.
[4] Luke xxii. 19.   [5] Luke xxii. 20.

eating of the paschal lamb. But what was this paschal meal ?
Here Jewish tradition alone can afford us any light. The
paschal meal of the Jews is described with fulness of detail in
the *Mishna Pesachim,* x. This tractate teaches us in what the
eating of the Passover consisted, and when it took place. It
began with the head of the family passing round the first cup
of wine,[1] and then followed the eating.[2] After this followed
a second cup ;[3] the son asked the father concerning the meaning of the festival, and the father instructed him concerning
it.[4] After this they began to intone the great Hallel, Ps.
cxiii.–cxviii.; then was handed forth the third cup, called by
the Rabbis "the cup of blessing."[5] The singing of the Hallel
was continued, and at the close of it the fourth cup was
administered ;[6] by which the meal was brought to an end.
That which was eaten on this occasion is enumerated x. 3,
where it says : "They set before him (the head of the family)
lettuce for dipping, until the dessert comes. There is set
before him unleavened bread, lettuce, and sweet paste,[7]
and the two dressed dishes. . . . Rabbi Eliezer bar Zadok
says, *Mazoth !* and they set before him the body of the Passover in the sanctuary." (הביאו לפניו טבל בחזרת עד שמגיע לפרפרת
דפת הביאו לפניו מצה וחזרת וחרוסת ושני תבשילין אף על פי שאין חרוסת
מצוה · רבי אליעזר בר צדוק אומר מצות ובמקדש היו טביאים לפניו גופו של
פסח.) The body of the Passover is the paschal lamb. In
the whole carefully detailed account of the paschal meal in
the Mishna, this is the only reference to the paschal lamb.
The remark of R. Eliezer is evidently designed to say that in
the eating of the Passover, the Mazoth is that which is obligatory ; in addition to this, the eating of the lamb is also
obligatory, but only for those who observe the festival in the
sanctuary. The Mishna consequently describes the paschal
meal as it was observed by all Israelites without distinction.
Not only at Jerusalem was Passover eaten, but also in every
Israelitish family, wherever they might dwell; and this meal

---

[1] *Pesachim*, x. 2.   [2] *Ibid.* x. 3.   [3] *Ibid.* x. 4.
[4] *Ibid.* x. 5, 6.   [5] כסא דברכה, cf. 1 Cor. x. 26.   [6] *Pesachim*, x. 7.
[7] [The *Charoset*, a sort of sweet paste composed of dates, figs, etc., and
made of the colour of a brick, in order to remind of the Egyptian bondage. Cf.
Meyer on Matt. xxvi. 23. Into this the unleavened bread and bitter herbs
were dipped. Winer, art. "Pascha."]

had as the essential element the mazoth. This meal does not presuppose personal presence in the sanctuary ; yea, what is more, it does not even require the existence of the sanctuary for its observance. It was held, and is still held, in banishment, and at a time when neither temple, nor altar, nor sacrifice existed. But at the time when the sanctuary existed, it was equally so held by all Israelites who could not, might not, or would not appear in the sanctuary. It is thus an error when it is asserted that φαγεῖν τὸ πάσχα denotes necessarily the eating of the paschal lamb ; the earliest Jewish tradition teaches definitely the contrary : the mazoth meal, observed with solemnity in every Israelitish house, was a φαγεῖν τὸ πάσχα. Now it is further asked, *When* was this meal held ? *Pesachim*, x. 1, says, " On the evenings of the Passover we eat first about the time of the *Mincha* prayer, when darkness is come on : then they eat in Israel the bread of affliction." What is to be understood by " the evenings of the Passover, ערבי פסחים ? If the expression is equivalent to ערב הפסח, it signifies the 14th Nisan, the day of the Paraskeue ; but it *may* signify the evening with which the 15th Nisan begins. In the first case it would mean that the Jews observed the paschal meal, which they held at home, on the beginning of the preparation day ; in the second case it would fall on the 15th Nisan. We do not intend to enter on this philological examination, because it has no importance with regard to the object we have in view. If the paschal meal was held as a rule on the 14th Nisan, then the last supper of the Lord coincides with it ; if, on the other hand, it was as a rule held on the 15th, then the Lord's Supper, which was held on the 14th, was an anticipation, not permitted indeed with regard to the paschal lamb, but which, so far as eating of the mazoth was concerned, might without difficulty take place, where sufficient grounds were present. Such ground, however, the Lord supplies, Luke xxii. 15, " With desire have I desired to eat this Passover with you, *before I suffer.*" The anticipation of the mazoth meal presented no difficulty, because this was not dependent, as was the case with the lamb, upon a priestly act in the sanctuary, but upon the will of the father of the family alone. The 14th Nisan was in any case the day of the mazoth. It seems to us, however, that this anticipation has not necessarily to be presupposed. The ערבי פסחים in question stands, we think, in the very common signification of ערב הפסח, preparation day. In that night which began with the 14th Nisan, the leavened bread was destroyed and all leaven put away; at the supper at the beginning of this night-day they therefore necessarily partook of mazoth. Now, it is only to be expected that to the first partaking of this festive bread was attached a certain solemnity, which is precisely that described in the Mishna. Luke does not say, any more than John, that the supper consisted in the partaking of the paschal lamb; and so soon as the erroneous supposition, that only the eating of the lamb could be understood by it, is set aside, there is not the slightest ground for this hypothesis in his account. More than this, if that meal had been the paschal lamb, we could not but feel surprise that the evangelist—who enters into so many details in describing it—does not devote a single word to the mention of that which was the main point, neither to the buying, nor to the killing, nor to the offering, nor to the eating of the lamb.

Sec. 159. **The time of the Passion according to Mark.** —"After two days was the Passover, the feast of unleavened bread, and the chief priests and the scribes sought how they might take Him by craft and put Him to death. But they said, *Not at the feast*, lest there be an uproar of the people."[1] If this wish of the chief priests, "not on the feast day," was not carried into effect, but Jesus was taken on the 15th Nisan, we cannot in any way see a reason why Mark should make mention of such a futile resolution; he would either have passed over it in silence, or have made mention of its non-fulfilment. But if, as is manifestly implied by the evangelist, this resolution was carried out, and Jesus was not taken captive on the great day of the Passover, the 15th Nisan, then neither was He crucified on this day; for, according to Mark, no less than the other evangelists, Jesus was crucified on the same night-day on which He was apprehended. Hence this passage of Mark definitely excludes the

[1] Mark xiv. 1, 2.

supposition of the 15th Nisan as the day of the crucifixion. At that time, two days before the Passover, thus on the 13th Nisan, Jesus was in Bethany, where, according to the order of relating on the part of this evangelist, He was anointed. After this, thus on the same night-day, Judas Iscariot went to the chief priests to betray Jesus, " and he sought how he might have opportunity to betray Him." By a " timely" betrayal (εὐκαίρως) he evidently meant, at the time designed by the Great Council : " not on the feast day." [1]

" On the first day of the unleavened bread, when they killed the Passover, His disciples say to Him, Where wilt Thou that we go and prepare, that Thou mayest eat the Passover ? " [2] That the reference here cannot be to the partaking of the paschal lamb on the 15th Nisan, is shown by these words, " not on the feast day." That Jesus did not eat the paschal lamb, proleptically, before the time, on the 14th Nisan, is evident from the fact that the proposition with regard to the paschal meal proceeded, not from the Lord, as foreseeing His speedy death, but from the disciples ; for these asked the Lord, not *whether* (*this* was understood without their asking), but *where* they should prepare for Him. That here, too, as in Luke, only the above-described [3] first eating of the mazoth, on the evening or beginning of the 14th Nisan, is in case, will need no extended demonstration. Mark, too, represents the last meal as an eating by night ; [4] he, too, describes it without making any mention of the lamb ; [5] he, too, says that Simon the Cyrenian was " coming from the field ; " [6] he, too, calls the day of crucifixion " the preparation or fore-Sabbath," [7] and affords not the slightest indication that the day on which the Lord was crucified was a sacred feast-day of the Jews ; and he, too, places the resurrection of the

---

[1] [The reference is evidently not to the *place*, but to the *time* of the feast The plan of the Sanhedrim, however, may have been to take the Lord *after the festival was over*. This plan, if such it was, was set aside by the premature action of Judas. Only in the event of His apprehension taking place on the 15th Nisan would any explanation be necessary on the part of the evangelist. Since no such explanation is made, St. Mark's statement favours the supposition of His being taken during the first part of the 14th Nisan.]

[2] Mark xiv. 12.   [3] Sec. 158.   [4] Mark xiv. 17.
[5] Mark xiv. 18 ff.   [6] Mark xv. 21.   [7] Mark xv. 42.

Lord on a Sunday. This evangelist also thus agrees with John and Luke in assigning the 14th Nisan as the date of the supper and the crucifixion.

Sec. 160. **The time of the Passion according to Matthew.** —The narrative of that which took place during the Passion-week comes forth with less distinctness from Matthew than in the other two Synoptists; but his statements perfectly agree with theirs. Matthew makes known to us, like Mark, the resolution of the Great Council to take Jesus captive. This resolution, which was taken two days before Passover, makes provision that His capture should take place "not on the feast day."[1] Judas engages "at the fit time" to reveal the Lord's place of abode,[2] by which covenant the 15th Nisan, as the day of His apprehension, is excluded. The account of the supper,[3] and the prediction of the Lord that "in this night" Peter will deny Him,[4] is in harmony with Mark's narrative, and shows that the night-day of the supper and of the crucifixion is the same. That the day of the crucifixion was the preparation day, is said in chap. xxvii. 62; and that the day of the resurrection was a Sunday, is taught us in chap. xxviii. 1. That the παρασκευή signifies the pre-paration for Passover, and not simply the preparation for the week-Sabbath, is especially clear from chap. xxvii. 62, where it is said, "On the next day that followed the day of the preparation, the chief priests and Pharisees came together unto Pilate." If this morrow had been an ordinary Sabbath, Matthew would certainly not have designated it by this strange expression: the Paraskeue, from which he designates the following day, must have a character distinguishing it from each weekly recurring Friday; that is to say, it must have been the Paraskeue of the Passover, yea, a festival day in itself. According to Matthew, the day of resurrection was a Sunday; the day on which Jesus remained in the grave a Sabbath; the day of the crucifixion the preparation for Passover. Thus the 15th Nisan was no other than the Sabbath of the rest in the grave.

Sec. 161. As soon as the difficulty connected with the

[1] Matt. xxvi. 2–4.	[2] Matt. xxvi. 15.
[3] Matt. xxvi. 17.	[4] Matt. xxvi. 34.

eating of the Passover is removed, and it is acknowledged that this was not the eating of the paschal lamb, but the solemn mazoth-meal, which was eaten in every Jewish house in the evening, *i.e.* in the beginning of the 14th Nisan ; so soon is the apparent discrepancy between the Synoptists and John, and the contradiction in which each of the Synoptists stands with himself, entirely removed. We say the contradiction of each one of the Synoptists with himself; for had they regarded the Last Supper as the eating of the paschal lamb, which could be partaken of only at the beginning of the 15th Nisan, the apprehension of the Lord would have taken place " on the feast day." This would have been in contradiction with the saying, " not on the feast day ;" with the intimation that Judas betrayed the Lord " at the fit time," *i.e.* the time intended; and with the statement that Simon the Cyrenian was " coming from the field." According to all the four Gospels, the day of the Lord's death was the preparation day, the 14th Nisan,—a Friday. With this perfectly tallies the result obtained by a calculation of the paschal month, according to which, in the year A.D. 30, the 15th Nisan fell on a Sabbath ; and the datum of Jewish tradition, which fixes the preparation day of the Passover as the day of the crucifixion. We must not overlook the fact that the books of ancient Jewish tradition have rendered us on these points a threefold and very important service ; inasmuch as they tell us, in the first place, that the day of the crucifixion was on the preparation day of the Passover ; in that they further tell us the condemnation of Jesus had been pronounced forty days before the crucifixion ; and, finally, in that they have made us acquainted with the character of the paschal meal. It is evident that the study of the Talmud, conducted in the spirit of rational criticism, might yield results of great value for the interpretation of the New Testament. It is true, as we have shown above, if one blindfolds his own eyes, and perverts and falsifies the meaning by parenthetical interpretations, they will not be able to afford any light.

One reason why the exegetes cling with such tenacity to the 15th Nisan as the day of the Lord's death, is to be found in the tradition of the Christian church of the West; but in opposition to this stands that of the church of Asia Minor, which teaches that the 14th Nisan was the day of the crucifixion. These traditions shall be discussed in the following chapter.

VIII.—*The Time of the Suffering of Christ, according to Christian Tradition.*

Sec. 162. Eusebius [1] reports from Irenæus : " Anicetus [2] was not able to induce Polycarp [3] no longer to observe the Passover on the 14th of the month; an observance which Polycarp based on the fact that with John, the disciple of the Lord, and the other apostles, he had always held it then : " Οὔτε γὰρ 'Ανίκητος τὸν Πολύκαρπον πεῖσαι ἐδύνατο μὴ τηρεῖν (σελήνης τὴν τεσσαρεσκαιδεκάτην), ἅτε μετὰ 'Ιωάννου τοῦ μαθητοῦ τοῦ κυρίου ἡμῶν καὶ τῶν λοιπῶν ἀποστόλων, οἷς συνδιέτριψεν, ἀεὶ τετηρηκότα. In giving this fact he gives the first beginning of the afterwards so complicated and tedious Easter controversy. The Christians of the West in such wise observed Eastertide that the day of the Lord's death always fell on a Friday, and the resurrection on a Sunday; because, according to the Gospels, the events then celebrated occurred on the said days of the week. The churches of Asia Minor, on the other hand, laid the stress not upon the day of the week, but upon the date of the moon, which with the Jews determined the time of Passover. The peculiarity of the observance on the part of the churches of Asia Minor consisted in the paschal meal, which they observed on the 14th Nisan. The passage cited teaches us to see in Polycarp the representative of the Eastern rite, and at the same time supplies the foundation on which he rested it— namely, that of a genuine apostolic tradition, immediately transmitted.

Sec. 163. Baur and his school judge after this fashion from the above text : " John taught Polycarp that Jesus held the paschal supper on the 14th Nisan; from this it follows that, according to John, Jesus was crucified on the 15th Nisan; John's oral teaching is thus in contradiction with that

---

[1] *H. E.* v. 24.   [2] Bishop of Rome, A.D. 165–175.   [3] Bishop of Smyrna.

of the fourth Gospel attributed to the same John. But, since
Polycarp vouches for the genuine Johannine tradition, the
fourth Gospel—which contradicts this tradition—cannot proceed from the same John, the disciple of the Lord." How
such sheer nonsense could be asserted and maintained on the
part of discreet and learned persons, and could become for
hundreds a reason for standing in doubt of the Gospel of
John, is for us a real enigma. The critical school has left
unnoticed the fact that those of Asia Minor reckoned, and
could only reckon, alike the months and the days after the
Jewish fashion, so soon as they determined the paschal season
according to the Jewish fashion and with the Jews. If, then,
John taught orally that Jesus observed the paschal meal on
the 14th Nisan, he *must* consequently at the same time have
taught that Jesus was crucified on that same 14th Nisan, for
the supper, held after sunset, necessarily took place on the
same night-day as the crucifixion ; alike the supper, as the
crucifixion, occurred on the same Jewish feria (6), although
on two different dates when the day is begun with midnight.
John had thus by word of mouth taught Polycarp, what the
fourth Gospel teaches in writing, that on the Paraskeue, the
14th Nisan, Jesus held the supper, and that towards the end
of the same night-day He was crucified. Nothing, consequently, prevents our regarding the same John as the source
of the oral tradition in question, and as the author of the
fourth Gospel.

Sec. 164. At the head of the *Chronicon Paschale* there is
found, instead of an introduction, a series of excerpts from the
writings of the Church Fathers of the first centuries on the
Passover. Foremost stands an excerpt from Peter, Bishop
of Alexandria, and martyr, in proof that beyond controversy
the Hebrews, until the destruction of Jerusalem, preserved
the order of beginning the Passover with the 14th of the first
lunar month : Πέτρου, 'Επισκόπου 'Αλεξανδρείας καὶ Μάρ-
τυρος, ὅτι ἀπλανῶς ἔταξαν οἱ ῾Εβραῖοι τὴν ιδ῀ τοῦ α΄ μηνὸς τῆς
σελήνης, ἕως τῆς ἁλώσεως τῶν ῾Ιεροσολύμων. This Peter, who
died a martyr's death in the year 311, and thus belongs to
the second half of the third century, says :[1] " Therefore did

[1] Page 2, edit. du Frêne.

the law (among the Hebrews) rightly prescribe that Passover
should be held after the spring equinox, on the 14th of the
first lunar month, on what week-day soever it might fall : "
῎Οθεν καλῶς νενομοθέτηται ἀπὸ τῆς ἐαρινῆς ἰσημερίας, εἰς
ὁποίαν δ᾽ ἂν ἐβδομάτα ἐμπέσῃ ἡ τεσσερακαιδεκαταία τοῦ
πρώτου μηνός, ἐν αὐτῇ ἐπιτελεῖν τὸ Πάσχα. This passage
confirms the order above[1] ascribed to the Jewish calendar.
After this, page 4, Peter of Alexandria says : " The Lord,
before His preaching and during His preaching, observed with
the people the legal and typical Passover, in eating the typical
lamb. . . . After the preaching (*i.e.* when His time of labour
was expired at the last Passover), He eat not the lamb, but
Himself suffered as the true lamb at the paschal feast, as the
theologian and Evangelist John teaches us in his Gospel. . . .
On that day, on which Jesus would eat the Passover at even-
tide, was our Lord crucified. For ' even Christ was offered
for us as our Paschal Lamb (Passover),' and not—as some
suppose through ignorance—after eating the paschal lamb
was He delivered up (to be crucified). At the time, then, in
which our Lord suffered for us in His flesh . . . He eat not the
legal Passover, but, as He Himself said, as the true Lamb He
was slain for us in the typical Passover on the preparation
day, the 14th of the first lunar month." Καὶ αὐτὸς σὺν τῷ
λαῷ ἐν τοῖς ἔτεσι τοῖς πρὸ τοῦ κηρύγματος, καὶ τοῖς ἐν τῷ
κηρύγματι, τὸ νομικὸν καὶ σκιῶδες Πάσχα ἐπετέλεσεν, ἐσθίων
τὸν τυπικὸν ἀμνὸν . . . ἐπεὶ δὲ ἐκήρυξεν οὐκ ἔφαγε τὸν ἀμνὸν,
ἀλλ᾽ αὐτὸς ἔπαθεν ὡς ἀληθινὸς ἀμνὸς ἐν τῇ τοῦ Πάσχα ἑορτῇ,
καθὼς διδάσκει ὁ Θεολόγος καὶ Εὐαγγελιστὴς Ἰωάννης . . . Ἐν
αὐτῇ οὖν τῇ ἡμέρᾳ, ἐν ᾗ ἔμελλον οἱ Ἰουδαῖοι πρὸς ἑσπέραν
ἐσθίειν τὸ Πάσχα, ἐσταυρώθη ὁ Κύριος ἡμῶν. Καὶ γὰρ τὸ
Πάσχα ἡμῶν ὑπὲρ ἡμῶν ἐτύθη Χριστός, καὶ οὐχ ὡς τινές
ἀμαθείᾳ φερόμενοι διαβεβαιοῦνται, ὡς φαγὼν τὸ Πάσχα παρε-
δόθη. . . . Ἐν ᾧ οὖν καιρῷ ἔπαθεν ὑπὲρ ἡμῶν κατὰ σάρκα ὁ
Κύριος ἡμῶν . . . τὸ κατὰ νόμον οὐκ ἔφαγε Πάσχα, ἀλλ᾽ ὡς
ἔφην αὐτὸς ὡς ἀληθὴς ἀμνὸς ἐτύθη ὑπὲρ ἡμῶν ἐν τῇ τοῦ
σκιώδους Πάσχα ἑορτῇ, ἐν ἡμέρᾳ Παρασκευῇ, τῇ ιδ᾽ τοῦ
πρώτου μηνὸς τῆς σελήνης. From this passage it follows
incontestably that the Apostolic Fathers of Egypt taught, in

[1] Cf. sec. 10.

harmony with those of Asia Minor, that Jesus was crucified
on the preparation day, the 14th Nisan; and that the supper
was not the eating of the paschal lamb.

As an introduction, the *Chronicon Paschale* further gives
extracts from Hippolytus, martyr for righteousness, called
Bishop of the Portus, a place near to Rome, who in his
writing, *Against all Heresies*, says, word for word : " I see,
then, what is the ground of the controversy. He (the heretic)
says thus : ' Christ held the Passover (eat the paschal lamb)
at that time, on the day on which He suffered ; therefore it
is meet for me also to do as the Lord did.' But he errs, since
he does not know that Christ, at the time in which He
suffered, did not eat the legally-appointed paschal lamb ; for
He Himself was the Paschal Lamb predicted, and on the
appointed day fulfilled." Ἱππόλυτος . . . ἔγραψεν ἐπὶ λέξεως
οὕτως· Ὁρῶ μὲν οὖν ὅ, τι φιλονικίας τὸ ἔργον. Λέγει γὰρ οὕτως·
Ἐποίησε τὸ Πάσχα ὁ Χριστὸς τότε τῇ ἡμέρᾳ καὶ ἔπαθε· διὸ
κἀμὲ δεῖ ὃν τρόπον ὁ Κύριος ἐποίησεν, οὕτω ποιεῖν. Πεπλά-
νηται δέ, μὴ γινώσκων ὅτι ἐν ᾧ καιρῷ ἔπασχεν ὁ Χριστὸς οὐκ
ἔφαγε τὸ κατὰ νόμον Πάσχα· οὗτος γὰρ ἦν τὸ Πάσχα τὸ προ-
κεκηρυγμένον καὶ τελειούμενον τῇ ὡρισμένῃ ἡμέρᾳ.[1]   In this
Hippolytus, who lived at the close of the second century and
at the beginning of the third, we have thus an Italian witness
who teaches, in harmony with those of Asia Minor and of
Egypt, that Christ did *not* eat the paschal lamb at the last
supper ; but that on the day on which the paschal lamb was
offered, thus on the 14th Nisan, He was Himself offered as the
Paschal Lamb.—We read further in the *Chronicon Paschale* :
" The same Hippolytus, moreover, said in his treatise on the
Holy Communion : ' He (Christ) who said, I eat no more the
paschal lamb, manifestly held His supper before the (time
of the) paschal lamb : He eat not the paschal lamb, but
suffered ; for it was no time for such eating :' " Πρόδηλον ὅτι
ὁ πάλαι προειπὼν· Ὅτι οὐκ ἔτι φάγομαι τὸ Πάσχα, εἰκότως
τὸ μὲν δεῖπνον ἐδείπνησε πρὸ τοῦ Πάσχα, τὸ δὲ Πάσχα
οὐκ ἔφαγεν, ἀλλ' ἔπαθεν· οὐ δὲ γὰρ καιρὸς ἦν τῆς βρώσεως
αὐτοῦ.[2]

After this the *Chronicon Paschale* cites,[3] in proof that the

---

[1] *Chronicon Paschale*, p. 5.   [2] *Ibid*.   [3] Page 5.

Lord, when He suffered, did not eat of the typical lamb, Apollinaris, Bishop of Hierapolis, who lived in the second half of the second century. "Apollinarius . . . who stood near to the apostolic times, taught the same in the book concerning Easter, in which he says: Some contend on these things out of ignorance, and say that on the 14th the Lord eat the lamb with His disciples, and that He suffered on the great day of the unleavened bread; and appeal to Matthew, of whom they say that he favours their view. Therefore is their opinion in contradiction with the law, and they appear to have the Gospels against them. Further, the same (Apollinaris) in the same book wrote as follows: The fourteenth of the true Passover of the Lord is the great sacrifice, the Son of God instead of the lamb, the bound One who bound the strong man, the judged One, a judge of the quick and the dead, the One delivered into the hands of sinners for crucifixion, the One exalted upon the horns of the unicorn, who was pierced in His sacred side, who also shed forth the two streams of cleansing virtue, water and blood, word and Spirit, and who was in the grave on the day of Passover, the stone being placed on the grave:" Καὶ Ἀπολιναρίος . . . ὁ ἐγγὺς τῶν Ἀποστολικῶν χρόνων γεγονὼς ἐν τῷ περὶ τοῦ Πάσχα λόγῳ τὰ παραπλήσια ἐδίδαξε, λέγων οὕτως· Εἰσὶ τοίνυν οἵ δι' ἄγνοιαν φιλονεικοῦσι περὶ τούτων, . . . καὶ λέγουσι, ὅτι τῇ ιδʹ τὸ πρόβατον μετὰ τῶν μαθητῶν ἔφαγεν ὁ κύριος, τῇ δὲ μεγάλῃ ἡμέρᾳ τῶν Ἀζύμων αὐτὸς ἔπαθε· καὶ διηγοῦνται Ματθαῖον οὕτω λέγειν ὡς νενοήκασιν· ὅθεν ἀσύμφωνός τε νόμῳ ἡ νόησις αὐτῶν, καὶ στασιάζειν δοκεῖ κατ' αὐτοὺς τὰ Εὐαγγέλια. Καὶ πάλιν ὁ αὐτὸς ἐν τῷ αὐτῷ λόγῳ γέγραφεν οὕτως· Ἡ ιδʹ τοῦ ἀληθινοῦ τοῦ Κυρίου Πάσχα, ἡ θυσία μεγάλη, ὁ ἀντὶ τοῦ ἀμνοῦ Παῖς Θεοῦ, ὁ δεθεὶς, ὁ δήσας τὸν ἰσχυρὸν, καὶ ὁ κριθεὶς κριτὴς ζώντων καὶ νεκρῶν, καὶ ὁ παραδοθεὶς εἰς χεῖρας ἁμαρτωλῶν, ἵνα σταυρωθῇ, ὁ ὑψωθεὶς ἐπὶ κεράτων μονοκέρωτος, καὶ ὁ τὴν ἁγίαν πλευρὰν ἐκκεντηθεὶς, ὁ ἐκχέας ἐκ τῆς πλευρᾶς αὐτοῦ τὰ δύο πάλιν καθάρια, ὕδωρ καὶ αἷμα, λόγον καὶ πνεῦμα, καὶ ὁ ταφεὶς ἐν ἡμέρᾳ τῇ τοῦ Πάσχα, ἐπιτεθέντος τῷ μνήματι τοῦ λίθου. According to Apollinaris, the 14th Nisan was thus the day on which Jesus was crucified. The error with which he charges the opponents is not that of maintaining that the supper took place on the 14th Nisan, for this is the true date; but with asserting that this meal was the eating of the paschal lamb, which he does not admit, and, what he equally contests, that Jesus was crucified on the great day of unleavened bread, that is, on the 15th Nisan; for on this day He was reposing in the grave.

The *Chronicon Paschale*, finally,[1] adduces as a witness Clemens Alexandrinus, who lived in the middle of the second century, citing his testimony in the following words : " But also Klemes, the holy priest of the church of Alexandria, a man of very early antiquity, who was born not far from the apostolic times, teaches like doctrine in the book concerning Easter, writing as follows : In the earlier years the Lord used to eat the slain (lamb) with the Jews, in keeping the feast of the Passover; but when He proclaimed that He Himself was the Passover, the Lamb of God, led as a sheep to the slaughter, immediately He taught His disciples the hidden meaning of the type on the 13th Nisan, on which day they also ask Him, Where wilt Thou that we prepare for Thee to eat the Passover ? On that same day, then, took place both the hallowing of the unleavened bread (Ἄζυμοι) and the preparation for the feast. Therefore also John writes that the apostles were already prepared, in that their feet were washed by the Lord. On the next day our Saviour suffered, Himself being the Paschal (Lamb), offered by Jews an acceptable sacrifice. And after other things he says : So afterwards, on the 14th, the day on which He also suffered, the chief priests and scribes led Him at dawn of day to Pilate; but did not themselves enter into the prætorium, that they might not be defiled, but might unhindered at evening eat the paschal lamb :" Ἀλλὰ καὶ Κλήμης ὁ ὁσιώτατος τῆς Ἀλεξανδρέων ἐκκλησίας γεγονὼς ἱερεύς, ἀνὴρ ἀρχαιότατος, καὶ οὐ μακρὰν τῶν Ἀποστολικῶν γενόμενος χρόνων, ἐν τῷ περὶ τοῦ Πάσχα λόγῳ τὰ παραπλήσια διδάσκει, γράφων οὕτω· Τοῖς μὲν οὖν παρεληλυθόσιν ἔτεσι τὸ θυόμενον πρὸς Ἰουδαίων ἤσθιεν, ἑορτάζων ὁ Κύριος Πάσχα· ἐπεὶ δὲ ἐκήρυξεν αὐτὸς ὢν τὸ Πάσχα ὁ ἀμνὸς τοῦ Θεοῦ, ὡς πρόβατον ἐπὶ σφαγὴν ἀγόμενος, αὐτίκα ἐδίδαξε μὲν τοὺς μαθητὰς τοῦ τύπου τὸ μυστήριον τῇ ιγʹ ἐν ᾗ καὶ πυνθάνονται

---

[1] Page 5.

αὐτοῦ· Ποῦ θέλεις ἑτοιμάσωμεν σοι τὸ Πάσχα φαγεῖν; Ταύτῃ οὖν τῇ ἡμέρᾳ καὶ ὁ ἁγιασμὸς τῶν Ἀζύμων καὶ ἡ προετοιμασία τῆς ἑορτῆς ἐγένετο. Ὅθεν ὁ Ἰωάννης ἐν ταύτῃ τῇ ἡμέρᾳ εἰκότως ὡς ἂν προετοιμαζομένους ἤδη ἀπονίψασθαι τοὺς πόδας πρὸς τοῦ Κυρίου τοὺς μαθητὰς ἀναγράφει. Πέπονθε δὲ τῇ ἐπιούσῃ ὁ Σωτὴρ ἡμῶν, αὐτὸς ὢν τὸ Πάσχα, καλλιερηθεὶς ὑπὸ Ἰουδαίων. Καὶ μετὰ ἕτερα· Ἀκολούθως ἄρα τῇ ιδ', ὅτε καὶ ἔπαθεν, ἕωθεν αὐτὸν οἱ Ἀρχιερεῖς καὶ οἱ Γραμματεῖς τῷ Πιλάτῳ προσάγοντες οὐκ εἰσῆλθον εἰς τὸ πραιτώριον, ἵνα μὴ μιανθῶσιν, ἀλλ' ἀκωλύτως ἑσπέρας τὸ Πάσχα φάγωσι. The succession of time given by Clement is as follows : Before the Passover, on the 13th Nisan, Thursday before sunset, the disciples asked the Lord where they should prepare for Him the Passover, which was to be partaken of on the night immediately following, the 14th Nisan. The disciples were prepared for this, and knew that in that year the Lord would not eat the typical paschal lamb, but would Himself be sacrificed as the Lamb. That they were thus prepared is shown, according to Clement, from the fact that John, chap. xiii. 10, represents them as being prepared for the footwashing as pure. This chronology is perfectly correct. Since the supper was to be partaken of at the very commencement of the 14th Nisan, the preparation for it must have taken place on the preceding day,—i.e. the 13th Nisan, Thursday before sunset,—and consequently also the question of the disciples. Clement rightly terms this 13th Nisan the day before the preparation, the preparation for the preparation day, which last began with the eating of the unleavened bread. The supper, the footwashing, the crucifixion, Clement further places on the 14th, i.e. Thursday evening and Friday.

Whether the succeeding passage, page 6 of the *Chronicon Paschale*, belongs to the citation from Clement's writing or not, we cannot decide. At any rate, it perfectly sums up that which has been already said. It reads thus : " At the time, then, in which the Lord suffered, He did *not* eat the legal, typical lamb ; but He Himself, as the true Lamb, was sacrificed for us on the preparation day, the 14th of the first lunar month :" Ὅτι μὲν οὖν ἐν ᾧ καιρῷ πέπονθεν ὁ Κύριος ἡμῶν καὶ Σωτὴρ, οὐκ ἔφαγε τὸν νομικὸν καὶ σκιώδη ἀμνὸν, ἀλλ' αὐτὸς ὡς

ἀληθὴς ἀμνὸς ἐτύθη ὑπὲρ ἡμῶν ἐν ἡμέρᾳ Παρασκευῇ τῇ ιδ´ τοῦ
πρώτου μηνὸς τῆς σελήνης.

It was necessary to place before the reader these texts *in
extenso*; since they have hitherto been either overlooked, or
for the most part cited in a fragmentary way, and, apart from
their connection, wrongly explained and misapplied. Upon
an examination of them, it must become manifest that, if the
paschal controversy of the first centuries has remained involved in darkness, the modern interpreters alone must bear
the blame of it. That such is the case may be seen to one's
full satisfaction in any church history or in any commentary
on the history of the Passover. The gist of the whole question in the paschal controversy lay in deciding whether or not
the Lord, before He was crucified, eat the paschal lamb; and
whether He was crucified on the 14th or 15th, on the
Paraskeue or on the great day of the Passover. This controversy, in which those were in the right who held to the 14th
as the day of the crucifixion, was set aside by the Council of
Nicæa,[1] in their deciding that the Christian Passover had as
its conclusion and point of culmination the day of the resurrection, the 16th Nisan, the day of the sheaf; and that, since
that day was a Sunday, it should be henceforth held on a
Sunday. Since, then, the Jewish method could not and might
not any longer serve for the determining of this day, the nine
years' Easter cycle was established.[2] With this testimony
also agrees that of Julius Africanus (circ. A.D. 200), who says,
" Before the first day of the Passover the things concerning
the Saviour took place:" πρὸ δὲ τῆς μιᾶς τοῦ Πάσχα τὰ περὶ
τὸν Σωτῆρα συνέβη. On the other hand, the fact must not be
concealed that Origen, Jerome, Chrysostom, and others place
the crucifixion of Christ on the 15th Nisan. On this side
also—wrongly as it seems to us—has Justin Martyr been
cited, who, in the *Dial. cum Tryphone*, says to the Jews: " On
the day of the Passover did you apprehend Him, and on the
Passover did you crucify Him" (καὶ ὅτι ἐν τῇ ἡμέρᾳ τοῦ
Πάσχα συνελάβετε αὐτὸν, καὶ ὁμοίως ἐν τῷ Πάσχα ἐσταυρώ-
σατε, γεγράπται); for here πάσχα is the paschal lamb, the
day thereof the 14th Nisan. The earliest Christian tradition

---

[1] *Chron. Paschale*, p. 6 ff.   [2] *Ibid.* p. 11.

consequently taught that Jesus held the supper on the 14th Nisan, on the night of the Thursday; that on the same Jewish night-day (but, according to Western reckoning, on the Friday), at the time of slaying the paschal lamb, He was crucified; and that on the following day (Saturday) was the great paschal festival. The Christian tradition, rightly understood, teaches thus — as all the Gospels, and as Jewish tradition — that Jesus was crucified on the 14th Nisan, a Friday. If afterwards, in the angry paschal controversy which ensued, another opinion prevailed, this does not concern us.

IX.—*Synopsis of the History of the Passion.*

Sec. 165. By the determination of the day of Christ's death on the 14th Nisan, feria 6, that is, the 6th to the 7th April, U.C. 783, A.D. 30, we have gained a foundation for the chronology of the single facts of the Passion week, which are now to be synoptically arranged. The conception we have already formed as to the character of John's Gospel, as the narrative of an eye-witness, compels us to take the data of this book as the basis of the synopsis. " Six days before the Passover "—thus on the 9th Nisan—" Jesus came to Bethany, where Lazarus was, which had been dead, whom He raised from the dead." [1] From the Synoptists we know that He came thither from Jericho.[2] The account of the Synoptists, taken alone, would lead us to suppose that Jesus remained at Bethany only until the disciples could bring the ass, upon which He entered Jerusalem without delay. John teaches us that the Lord previously passed the night at Bethany. The 9th Nisan was a Sunday; Jesus had consequently remained over the Sabbath in Jericho, in the house of Zaccheus,[3] and had taken the journey to Bethany on the 9th Nisan, *i.e.* on the 2d of April. There a supper was prepared for Him, and during the supper Mary anointed Him.[4] This took place thus on the 10th Nisan, after sunset on the 2d April. On the following day, the 10th Nisan, but the 3d April, a

---

[1] John xii. 1.   [2] Matt. xxi. 1; Mark xi. 1; Luke xix. 29.

[3] [Compare the expressions μεῖναι and καταλῦσαι, in Luke xix. 5, 7.] John xii. 2-8.

Monday, Jesus made His triumphal entrance into Jerusalem.[1] This took place five days before the Passover.
John relates nothing concerning the following days, until the
evening before the Passover, when the last supper was held.
In the interval, it would seem, Jesus lived greatly in retire-
ment with His disciples at Bethany ; for it is said, John xii.
36, " Jesus departed and hid Himself from them." The Synoptists relate the same facts as John, but in the contrary
order—first, the entrance into Jerusalem, then the anointing.
The entering recorded in John xii. 12 ff. is the same as that
described Matt. xxi. 1 ff., Mark xi. 1 ff., Luke xix. 29 ff.
After this Jesus returned to Bethany, where He passed the
night. Then, on the following morning,—i.e. if we follow
the order of time supplied to us by the fourth Gospel,—on
Tuesday, 4th April, He pronounced judgment upon the fig-
tree which bore no fruit ;[2] and on this day, according to
Mark, chap. xi. 15, Jesus cleansed the sanctuary of the buyers
and sellers. According to the order of Matthew, this had
already taken place before the sentence upon the fig-tree. The
events connected with this cleansing are recounted by all
three Synoptists,[3] with this difference, that Matthew and Luke
bring these into immediate connection with the public entry,
while Mark separates the entry and the cleansing of the
temple by the night at Bethany. John does not relate this
cleansing of the sanctuary at all ; perhaps because He had
already, chap. ii. 14, related a similar history of that which
had occurred two years before. It is possible that we have
inserted here on the part of the Synoptists, where they are for
the first time recording the appearing of Jesus in Jerusalem,
that which, in its due order of narration, belongs to a period
two years earlier.[4] For the recurrence of the event, thus
that the cleansing recorded by the Synoptists belongs to the
period before the last Passover, pleads the fact that, according
to Luke xx. 1, 2, Jesus was called to account by the elders
for this act.[5] In the evening Christ returned again to

[1] John xii. 12.   [2] Matt. xxi. 17–19 ; Mark xi. 11–14.
[3] Matt. xxi. 12; Mark xi. 15 ; Luke xix. 45.   [4] Cf. sec. 85.
[5] [As also the evident allusion to the calling of the Gentiles in the case of the
last cleansing, Mark xi. 17.]

Bethany.[1] On the next morning, thus on Wednesday, 5th April, Jesus returned to the sanctuary, and the disciples on the way saw the fig-tree already withered up.[2] When, in the evening, He had again left the temple, and was seated opposite thereto upon the Mount of Olives, and the disciples admired the structure of the sacred buildings, He predicted the destruction of this sanctuary and this city.[3] Two days before the Passover,[4] thus on the 13th Nisan,—which began with the evening of the 5th April,—took place the anointing of Jesus, according to the order of narration observed by the Synoptists.[5] The contradiction with John is solved by our understanding that Mark, by the words, " And after two days was the feast of the Passover," intends to give, not so much the date of the anointing as the date of Judas' betrayal of the Lord to the chief priests.[6] But since the reproof received on the occasion of the anointing [7] seems to have contributed somewhat to the resolution of Judas, the anointing is related out of its chronological order, in connection with the act of the traitor on this day.

Sec. 166. The succession of events seems to have been the following. See table, p. 220.

Sec. 167. **The Supper.**—The time at which this was prepared and partaken of is thus indicated by Matthew.[8] " On the first day of unleavened bread the disciples asked Jesus, Where wilt Thou that we prepare for Thee to eat the Passover ? . . . And when it was become evening, He sat down with the twelve." The first day of unleavened bread is the 14th Nisan : on this day, late in the evening, Jesus sat down to the table. For the object of the evangelist is evidently to make known the date of the eating, and not the date of the asking; since this last was an incident without significance, the other, on the contrary, a fact of great importance. Now, the evening of the 14th Nisan was its commencement. Mark in like manner teaches that the meal was held in the latter part of the evening.[9] The day he indicates in the words,

---

[1] Mark xi. 19.   [2] Mark xi. 20 ff.
[3] Mark xiii. 1 ff. ; cf. Matt. xxiv. 1 ; Luke xxi. 5.   [4] Mark xiv. 1.
[5] Matt. xxvi. 1 ; Mark xiv. 1.   [6] Mark xiv. 10.   [7] John xii. 4–7.
[8] Matt. xxvi. 17, 20.   [9] Mark xiv. 12, 17.

DATE.			EVENTS.
April.	Nisan.	Feria.	
2d.	9th.	1	{Six days before the Passover, on the Sunday, Jesus came to Bethany.
2d.	10th.	2	Anointing of Christ.
3d.	10th.	2	{Entry into Jerusalem. Jesus spends the night at Bethany. *Monday.*
4th.	11th.	3	{Sentence upon the fig-tree. Cleansing of the Sanctuary. *Tuesday.*
4th.	12th.	4	Return to Bethany.
5th.	12th.	4	{Return to Jerusalem. The fig-tree is seen to be withered. *Wednesday.*
5th.	13th.	5	{Return to Olivet. Prophecy of the destruction of Jerusalem. According to Mark's order, anointing of Jesus. *Wednesday.*
6th.	13th.	5	{Judas bargains with the high priests to deliver the Lord up. *Thursday.*
6th.	14th.	6	The Last Supper. *Thursday.* Betrayal.
7th.	14th.	6	{Jesus before the high priests. Denial, crucifixion, and burial. *Friday.*
7th.	15th.	7	{The great paschal Sabbath begins. Jesus in the grave.
8th.	15th.	7	Jesus in the grave. *Saturday.*
8th.	16th.	1	Jesus in the grave.
9th.	16th.	1	Resurrection of Jesus. *Sunday.*

" On the first day of unleavened bread, when they used to offer the Passover, His disciples say to Him, Where wilt Thou that we go and prepare, that Thou mayest eat the Passover ?" They were wont to offer the Passover at the end of the 14th Nisan. If, when the disciples asked, it was the time of the offering of the Passover, the eating was the beginning of the 15th. But against this lies the emphasis which the evangelist himself lays upon the resolution of the Supreme Council, " Not on the feast day ; "[1] the words ὅτε τὸ Πάσχα ἔθυον must consequently be taken in the sense of ἐν ᾗ ἔθυον, " the day on which they offered the Passover." Luke[2] says, " Then came the day of unleavened bread, when the Passover must be killed. And He sent Peter and John, saying, Go and prepare us the Passover, that we may eat." That day is the 14th Nisan, on which the Passover was slain. In the first hours of this night-day the meal was provided. Here, as

[1] Mark xiv. 2.   [2] Luke xxii. 7, 8.

in Matthew and Mark, the preparation and eating are placed, not at the end, but at the beginning of the 14th Nisan. Had they meant the end of that day, they must have said, When the day on which the Passover must be killed was at an end. John, finally,[1] places the supper "before the feast of the Passover," πρὸ τῆς ἑορτῆς τοῦ πάσχα, at the beginning of the preparation day of the Passover, at the end of which Jesus was crucified;[2] consequently on the 14th Nisan. With John, too, the meal is held at night.[3]   It was observed in the city of Jerusalem, in a private house.[4]   That it was not, according to any of the evangelists, the eating of the paschal lamb; that in none of them is found a trace of the eating of the paschal lamb, has been above shown in detail. It was, on the contrary, the first solemn mazoth meal, as described by Jewish tradition: this is vouched for by the elements exclusively present in the supper—wine and bread with bitter herbs, the dipping of the morsel, the great hallel.[5] All the four evangelists tell us that during this supper Judas' treachery was made known to his fellow-apostles.[6]   John does not describe the meal itself, but simply relates what occurred during the meal,[7] especially the washing of the disciples' feet. From this it follows that the single events can be thought of only in the following order: (1) The mazoth meal; (2) the sacrament of the Lord's Supper attached to this; (3) the washing of the disciples' feet; (4) manifestation of the traitor; (5) withdrawing of Judas. The attempt to present these facts in another order arises from the wish to remove the traitor as unworthy, before the sacrament. On the other hand, we must freely or perforce admit that Judas partook of the Lord's Supper.

Sec. 168. It is perfectly right to speak of that new element which the Lord attached to the paschal or mazoth supper, as the institution of the Lord's Supper; yet only in the sense that what was given on this evening was not something absolutely new, but that the sacrament already instituted at the feeding of the five thousand[8] was here constituted a

[1] John xiii. 1, 2.   [2] John xix. 14.   [3] John xiii. 30.
[4] Matt. xxvi. 18, 19 ; Mark xiv. 13-16 ; Luke xxii. 10-13.
[5] Matt. xxvi. 30 ; Mark xiv. 26.
[6] Matt. xxvi. 21 ; Mark xiv. 18 ; Luke xxii. 21 ; John xiii. 21.
[7] δείπνου γενομένου, John xiii. 2.   [8] Cf. sec. 118.

legacy for the future, and brought into more definite connection with the death of the Lord.   The existence of the sacrament, which had been dispensed to the disciples during the
last year every time the Lord broke to them the bread,
explains why John makes no mention of it on this occasion.
It would have been a repetition of that which is said in John
vi. 27 ff. The Synoptists do not record the washing of the
disciples' feet; yet they do record the occasion of this sym-
bolic action.[1]

Sec. 169. After the supper Jesus went with His disciples
out of the city, beyond the brook,[2] into a garden called Gethsemane, and situated on the Mount of Olives,[3] where He
passed the night in conflict of soul.   Whether the traditional
Gethsemane, with its venerable olive trees, lying opposite to
the so-called " Eternal Gate " in the Haram wall, is the place
where Jesus spent His last night on earth, must remain
undetermined; yet it is not to be denied that the tradition
attaching to this place appears to be a very ancient one.[4]
Here Jesus, during the night,[5] but towards morning, was
taken captive.[6]

Sec. 170. When Jesus was taken captive in the Garden of
Gethsemane, " all the disciples forsook Him, and fled." [7]   This
statement admits of some limitation; for John, and in part
Peter, were witnesses of that which afterwards took place.
On this account also the Gospel of John, as the account of
an eye-witness, must in that which follows be our principal

---

[1] Luke xxii. 24–30, especially ver. 27 ; cf. John xiii. 14.

[2] The *Kedron* in any case, even though the reading of John xviii. 1 is
doubtful.

[3] Matt. xxvi. 30, 36 ; Mark xiv. 26, 32 ; cf. Luke xxii. 39.

[4] Robinson, i. 235. [Thomson, *Land and Book*, p. 634, is very unfavourable
to the authenticity of the traditional Gethsemane.   Andrew Bonar, who visited
it with M'Cheyne in 1839, is equally favourable.   An interesting account of his
visit is given in his *Narrative of a Mission to the Jews*, pp. 161, 162 ; where he
well observes, from John xviii. 2, that Gethsemane was often appointed by the
Lord as a meeting-place, "when His disciples, dispersed through the city by
day, were to join His company in the evening, and go with Him over the hill to
Bethany."   The same thing has been since brought out by Lange, on John
xviii. 2.]

[5] Luke xxii. 53.

[6] Matt. xxvi. 47 ff. ; Mark xiv. 13 ; Luke xxii. 47 ; John xviii. 3 ff.

[7] Matt. xxvi. 56 ; Mark xiv. 50.

guide, in connection with whose data the statements of the Synoptists are to be viewed.

According to John, chap. xviii. 12 ff., the band [cohort], the Chiliarch, and the servants of the Jews, took Jesus, bound Him, and led Him away to Annas first, the father-in-law of Caiaphas—" who was that same year high priest "—and afterwards Annas sent Him bound to Caiaphas the high priest.[1] While Jesus was in the power of Annas, the denial on the part of Peter began, and was repeated a second and third time when Jesus was already delivered over to Caiaphas.[2] Since, now, Peter was the whole time, with the " other disciple," i.e. John, in the palace, or rather in the court of the high priest,[3] and was warming himself at the same fire, and saw all that happened to Jesus,[4] certain exegetes have raised an objection in regard to the matter, and asked how Peter in the palace of Caiaphas could see into that of Annas? Of course this difficulty must furnish a new and important testimony against the authenticity of John's Gospel. But what if Annas, the father-in-law of Caiaphas, and, moreover, the former high priest, who now and later continued to bear the title of high priest, should be found to dwell with his daughter's husband in the high priest's palace, perhaps in another wing of the building, but one looking into the same court? Then Peter and " the other disciple " could, without leaving the fire in the court, observe all that took place in the open porticos facing the court, both in the case of Annas and Caiaphas ; for the leading away of Jesus from the one to the other took place across that same courtyard. The leading away of Jesus from Annas to Caiaphas was the delivering up of the condemned to the executive power of the high priest. The Great Council had assembled in all haste in the house of Annas, on the intelligence that Jesus was apprehended. We have already observed earlier, sec. 33, that possibly Annas in his character of Nasi of the Sanhedrim bore the title of high priest : the assembling at the house of this man would thus be sufficiently explained. Perhaps, however, they met here because Annas was an ordinary member of the Great Council. At any rate,

---

[1] John xviii. 24.

[2] John xviii. 17, 25-27.

[3] εἰς τὴν αὐλὴν τοῦ ἀρχιερέως, John xviii. 15.

[4] Luke xxii. 61.

the Sanhedrim must still pronounce a judgment, before Jesus was delivered over to the executive power. Nothing prevents our supposing that Caiaphas, as a member of the Great Council, attended the sitting for judgment, and was the high priest mentioned in John xviii. 19 as interrogating Jesus. But as high priest, he obtained power over Jesus only by the fact that Jesus was delivered over by judgment and condemnation to his executive power.

Sec. 171. The objection has been raised against the Johannine relation, that it, properly speaking, describes no trial at all, and makes mention of no sentence ; and especially that it says nothing of that which took place before Caiaphas. To this it must be rejoined, that at that time no trial in the strict sense of the word was held ; for trial and sentence had been given a month earlier.[1] Of this John reminds us when he says, chap. xviii. 14, " Now Caiaphas was he which gave the counsel to the Jews : It is expedient that one man should die for the nation." When Caiaphas spoke these words,[2] the trial, properly speaking, was held ; from the time of that sitting of the Great Council Jesus was condemned to death. The object of the present sitting of the 14th Nisan was only to hear such new witnesses as might present themselves, and to confirm the sentence previously passed. Before Caiaphas there was now no trial held. It is true Matthew, chap. xxiv. 57, places the scene of the trial not before Annas, but before Caiaphas ; but since both dwelt in the same palace, and both were members of the Sanhedrim, and Caiaphas, as Sanhedrist and as high priest, took an active part in the matter, no importance attaches to the apparent contradiction.

Sec. 172. These events in the palace of the high priest took place before sunrise, about the time of cock-crowing,[3] thus from three to five in the morning. With the first dawn,[4] they led Jesus away to the prætorium to Pilate. Where was this prætorium ? Pilate fixed his residence not at Jerusalem,

---

[1] Cf. sec. 139.   [2] John xi. 47–57.

[3] Matt. xxvi. 74 ; Mark xiv. 72 ; Luke xxii. 60 ; John xviii. 27.

[4] πρωίας δὲ γενομένης, Matt. xxvii. 1 ; ἐπὶ τὸ πρωί, Mark xv. 1 ; ἦν δὲ πρωί, John xviii. 28.

but at *Cæsarea Maritima.* When, as at the time of the Pass-over A.D. 30, he came to Jerusalem, he dwelt in one of the two fortresses occupied by the Romans,—either in the royal palace of Herod in the Upper City, or in the citadel of Antonia, on the north-west side of the Temple Mountain. By a hint occurring in John xix. 13, the site of the prætorium may be determined with probability. For Pilate, when he gave judg-ment, took his seat on the tribunal, called Lithostroton, and in the Hebrew Gabbatha. Now Josephus mentions[1] that the whole surface of the Temple Mountain was paved with varie-gated mosaic work. Pilate accordingly, in order to pronounce the sentence, came forth from the Antonia into the northern court of the sanctuary, to the Lithostroton ; by which in any case a definite place in Jerusalem is to be understood, and not the moveable and portable tesselated pavement which the Roman judges used to carry about with them, in order to fix their tribunal upon it — and for this reason, that it has a special Hebrew name. To the Antonia, as the scene of the trial of Jesus, points also an ancient tradi-tion, of which the Pilgrim of Bordeaux (A.D. 333) already testifies.[2]

Sec. 173. By far the most difficult point to determine in the history of the Passion is the hour of the crucifixion. According to John xix. 14,[3] Pilate took his seat upon the tribunal, in order to pronounce sentence, about the *sixth* hour; and, according to Mark xv. 25, about the *third* hour they crucified Jesus. All kinds of attempts have been made to remove this contradiction ; some would refer the sixth hour mentioned by John to something else than the trial and crucifixion; others suppose that John counts his hours from mid-night, while Mark counts his from sunrise. 1. Can " the sixth hour" be referred to anything else than the condemnation to the death on the cross ? The words read, " It was the preparation day of the Passover, about the sixth hour :" ὥρα ἦν ὡσεὶ ἕκτη,

---

[1] *Antiq.* v. 5, sec. 2.   [2] See Appendix, 19.

[3] [ὥρα ἦν ὡς ἵκτη, *towards* the sixth hour, *i.e.* between nine and twelve A.M. The Lord's examination before Pilate would thus begin before six A.M., and end between nine and twelve. According to Mark, the *third* hour had come *before* the crucifixion, *i.e.* the day was already in its second quarter. The *second*, *fourth*, and *fifth* hours are not mentioned in the New Testament.]

P

or ὡς ἕκτη.[1] Von Gumpach proposes to read, ὥρᾳ δὲ ὡσεὶ
ἕκτη, and to translate, "The time of preparation was at about
the sixth hour." He takes the proposition as a parenthesis,
designed to explain why Pilate hurried the trial through ;
namely, in order that the execution might be accomplished
before the time of the preparation. Thus understood, the
passage says nothing as to the time of the crucifixion, and it
remains possible to accept as the hour of the crucifixion the
hour mentioned by Mark. But against this explanation it
is to be objected, that (a) all MSS. with one accord have ΩΡΑ-
ΕΚΤΗ, and not ΩΡΑΙ-ΕΚΤΗΙ ; the alteration of the text
is consequently an unsupported conjecture. (b) It is presupposed that παρασκευὴ τοῦ Πάσχα—and therefore the synonymous ערב הפסח—signifies "the time of preparation," which is
conceived of as beginning only at mid-day ; whereas the term
denotes the whole 14th of Nisan. And (c) it is taken for
granted that Pilate, in order to please the Jews, did hurry the
trial through a presupposition not at all warranted by the
Johannine text. This conjecture is consequently untenable.
2. Has John an epoch from which to reckon the hours, other
than that of Mark ? It is beyond question that, at the time
of Christ, the Jews, like the Romans, divided the day into
twelve hours, of which the first began with sunrise : this
custom is followed by the Synoptists. Of John, it is asserted
that he counted the hours from midnight to midnight, as with
us. In this case, the sixth hour would correspond pretty
nearly to our six in the morning. If Jesus was condemned
at this hour, the carrying out of the sentence might well take
place at the time indicated by Mark, about the third hour, i.e.
towards nine A.M. But, to render this hypothesis acceptable, it
must be shown that such a division of hours was then current,
side by side with the other ; and this proof is wanting. If,
what is with reason doubted, it were really the case that the
Romans thus reckoned their hours judicially from midnight, it
would still be incomprehensible that Pilate should be able to
pass sentence upon Jesus by six A.M., when Christ had been

---

[1] [The reading of the Receptus is ὥρα δὲ ὡσεὶ ἕκτη, which, like the Latin circa,
expresses less strongly than ὡς the idea of approaching a given number : about,
nearly, not far from, almost.]

brought into the prætorium only at early morning (πρωί), *i.e.* at the soonest about five A.M.   This difficulty is the greater, when we take into account the many intervening circumstances, occupying together a considerable interval, such as the sending away of the accused to Herod, and the determining of the question whether Christ or Barabbas was to be set free.

Sec. 174. John, like the Synoptists, reckoned his hours from the time of sunrise ; and indicates in the passage before us that about the sixth hour, *i.e.* towards noon, Jesus was delivered over to be crucified, and it is clear that the datum thus afforded us is not an erroneous one, but veritable history.   Matthew and Luke do not expressly mention the hour of the crucifixion ; but they tell us [1] that a darkness came over the whole land from the sixth hour to the ninth.   This darkness is evidently represented by the evangelists as a miraculous one, designed to show that creation veiled itself in mourning on account of the act of transgression then wrought by man.   But that miracle possessed demonstrative force, only inasmuch as the darkness occupied precisely the time during which Christ hung on the cross.   If thus any one would come to a judgment from Matthew and Luke as to the hour at which Jesus was crucified, he would without doubt conclude that it was about the sixth hour, at which time also the sun was darkened. Matthew and Luke are consequently in harmony with the statement of John.   But this account of a darkening of the sun from the sixth to the ninth hour is found equally in Mark, chap. xv. 33 ; so that this evangelist also regards the sixth hour as that of the crucifixion of Christ.   Against this conclusion it is objected that the Synoptists do not mention the darkness at the beginning of their account of the crucifixion, but only in the course of the same ; so that what is recorded before the mention of this darkness also took place before it, while that recorded afterwards took place during its prevalence.   Let us then try whether this objection will stand.   In Matt. xxvii. 45, 46, 50, we read: " And from the sixth hour there came a darkness over the whole land until the ninth hour ; and about the ninth hour Jesus cried with a loud voice, Eli, Eli, lama sabachthani. . . . And Jesus again

[1] Matt. xxvii. 45 ; Luke xxiii. 44.

having cried with a loud voice, yielded up the ghost." Matthew consequently does not give an account of the darkness at the time of its beginning; but when, simultaneously with the death of Jesus, it came to an end. For the beginning of the darkness we have thus no other *terminus a quo* than the crucifixion itself, which consequently began about the sixth hour. Entirely the same account is given us in Mark, chap. xv. 33, 34, 37: "And from the sixth hour there came a darkness upon all the land until the ninth hour. And at the ninth hour Jesus cried with a loud voice . . ." Equally do we see that Luke, chap. xxiii. 44–46, mentions the account of the darkness simultaneously with the death of Jesus. We conclude from this that the sixth hour was the hour of the crucifixion, not only according to John, but also according to the Synoptists, Mark included. If now it is said, Mark xv. 25, that Jesus was crucified about the *third* hour, a false number must here have crept into the text: the τρίτη must be spurious, even though all the MSS. were unanimous in giving this reading. This, however, is not the case; in some MSS. is found ἕκτη, and several ancient versions read the same.[1]

Sec. 175. If we are right in regarding the sixth hour as that at which Jesus was given up to crucifixion, the proceedings in the prætorium lasted about six hours. This time is not too long, when it is considered that Pilate sent Jesus to Herod,[2] and that the discussion as to whether Jesus or Barabbas should be set free occupies a considerable time. We understand, therefore, that Jesus was taken prisoner soon after midnight; that the interpellation in the palace of the high priest took place about the time of cock-crowing, *i.e.* three A.M.; that towards six o'clock in the morning Jesus was led away into the prætorium, and about noon was crucified; that simultaneously with the crucifixion there supervened a darkness not explainable on natural and astronomical grounds, but arising from a supernatural cause; that, finally, after hanging upon the cross three hours, Jesus expired at about three in the afternoon.

---

[1] Jerome, on Ps. lxxvii., says that the *three* in Mark arose from the fact that many in place of the Greek ϛ (σταῦ) read a Γ.

[2] Luke xxiii. 6 ff.

Sec. 176. The place where Jesus was crucified was situated outside of the city,[1] but near to it,[2] and was called Golgotha, which is translated, " place of a skull."[3]   If Golgotha signifies " place of a skull," the original name was Golgoltha (גלגלתא), from which גלגתא arose by abbreviation.   That this etymology was generally accepted at the time of Christ, is evident from the consensus of the evangelists.   It is not an impossible one, for contractions of this kind frequently occur in names.   We adduce as an example only Bezetha, which, according to Josephus,[4] signifies καινόπολις, i.e. Newtown : the original form must have accordingly been Bethhadatha, ביתחדתא. Krafft's conjecture, however,[5] that the name is rather to be derived from Golgoatha (גלגועתא), " Hill of Death," i.e. place of execution, is deserving of attention. This topograph connects the name with the place Goath (גועת), mentioned Jer. xxxi. 39, as well as with the gate Gennath of Josephus, Bell. v. 4, sec. 2, which, in important MSS., is written Γυάθ, Guath,[6] and consequently appears to be the gate which led to the place or pile, hill (גל) Goath.   These statements will be found to be examined in the Appendix.

Sec. 177. According to Christian tradition, Golgotha, the place where Jesus was crucified, and the grave in which His body was laid, are both enclosed within the Basilica of the Holy Sepulchre.   The union of the two places, the place of crucifixion and the grave, under one and the same roof, presents no difficulty.   It is justified by the expression of John :[7] " There was at the place (ἐν τῷ τόπῳ) where He was crucified a garden, and in the garden a new sepulchre . . . there laid they Jesus."   The great thing now is to ascertain whether this tradition is worthy of credence or not.   Eusebius relates in his Life of Constantine,[8] that after the Council of Nicæa this emperor caused a magnificent temple to be erected above

---

[1] ἐξῆλθεν, John xix. 17 ; ἐξερχόνται, Matt. xxvii. 32.
[2] ἰγγὺς ἦν ὁ τόπος τῆς πόλεως, John xix. 20.
[3] κρανίου τόπος, Matt. xxvii. 33 ; Mark xv. 22 ; Luke xxiii. 33 ; John xix. 17.
[4] De Bello, v. 4, sec. 2.   [5] Topogr. Jerus. p. 158.
[6] [Γυάθ is not found, however, among the various readings of Cardwell's Oxford edition, 1837.   This reading seems in reality, as asserted by Robinson, to have originated in an error on the part of Krafft.]
[7] John xix. 41.   [8] Vit. Constant. iii. 25-40.

the grave of Jesus. This grave the heathen had in former times stopped up with earth, and built thereon a temple of Venus. That the place on which Constantine built this temple is the site of the present Church of the Holy Sepulchre has been confirmed by such unbroken tradition from the time of Constantine downwards, that it is acknowledged even by the opponents of the authenticity of the sepulchre. The first link in this chain of tradition is formed by the Pilgrim of Bordeaux, who visited Jerusalem in 333. He says that in proceeding from the prætorium of Pontius Pilate (*i.e.* from the Antonia at the north-west corner of the Temple Mountain) to the Neapolitan Gate (Gate of Nablûs, now Damascus Gate, Bâb-el-Amûd), he had on his left hand (*i.e.* to the westward) the hill of Golgotha, where the Lord was crucified. A stone's-throw from thence is the cave where His body was laid, and where He rose on the third day. There, at the command of the Emperor Constantine, a Basilica of surprising beauty was lately erected: a sinistra autem parte est monticulus Golgotha, ubi Dominus crucifixus est. Inde quasi ad lapidis missum, est cripta, ubi corpus ejus positum fuit et tertia die resurrexit. Ibidem modo jussu Constantini imperatoris basilica facta est miræ pulchritudinis. . . . This description points, beyond doubt, to the position of the present Church of the Holy Sepulchre.

Sec. 178. That such a tradition might be perpetuated from apostolic times can be doubted by no one ; for the Christians were never banished from Jerusalem for a whole generation together, not even under Hadrian. That the first Christians knew where the place of the crucifixion was is certain ; that they held this place in reverence, they who held in honoured memory the grave of the least of the martyrs, is equally certain, as it is that it was in accordance with the practice of the heathen to erect a fanum upon every place reputed sacred. Constantine was thus able to learn by a sure tradition the identity of the place which, as the place of the grave of Jesus, he adorned with a temple. If, instead of a genuine tradition, a pious fraud had obtained ; if a deceiver, merely in order to satisfy the emperor, had pointed out any place at random as the sacred spot, he would never, in order to preserve the semblance of probability, and to obtain credence for his fiction, have selected as the desired spot a place within the city of Jerusalem, but outside its walls ; for at that time, equally as now, the Scripture was known, which says that Jesus was crucified and buried without the city. This unsuitable, improbable site in the midst of the city vouches for the genuineness of the tradition ; a pious fraud or a scientific research would have led to a result more in accordance with probability. The temple of Venus, which may have been designed to mislead the Christians with regard to the site, served only the more definitely to mark it out.

Sec. 179. A veritable crusade has been directed against the Church of the Holy Sepulchre, and countless volumes have been written to show that the place assigned by tradition is not the true Golgotha. The principal argument which is urged against this site of Golgotha is this : " Jesus was crucified and buried outside of Jerusalem. But the place which is claimed as the scene of the crucifixion lies within the walls, and must have lain within them at the time of Christ ; this tradition is therefore spurious." The first proposition is well-founded : the scene of the crucifixion was without the city. The second proposition is also true : the Church of the Holy Sepulchre lies nearly in the middle of the present city. But whether this place was already enclosed within the city walls at the time of Christ, is the very point at issue ; and on this unquestionably depends the genuineness or spuriousness of the tradition which makes this site to be Golgotha. From Josephus, de Bello, v. 4, secs. 1–4, we know that the third wall, which surrounded the New City, the northernmost quarter of the city of Jerusalem, was built a short time before the destruction of Jerusalem ; this quarter was consequently at the time of Christ—that is to say, forty years before this destruction, and about twelve years before the building of said wall—not yet incorporated with the city. If, then, the Church of the Holy Sepulchre lies in this quarter of the New City, the place was still without Jerusalem at the time of Christ ; but if the place lies within the second wall, it already belonged to the city at the time of Jesus, and cannot therefore by any possibility be the locality of the grave of

Christ. We content ourselves here with the remark that the more recent researches and excavations prove with ever-increasing certainty that the site of the Church of the Holy Sepulchre was without the second wall, and consequently was first incorporated into the city by the third wall ; and on this account nothing prevents our regarding this as the locality of the true grave, and of Golgotha. The further discussion of this important question we reserve for the Topographical Appendix, No. 24.

Mount Calvary, or Golgotha, lies 110 feet E.S.E. of the Holy Sepulchre ; both sacred places, as we have said, being enclosed within the one structure of the Basilica. It is not here the place to enter into a detailed description of this church—such description is to be found in Ritter's *Erdkunde*,[1] and especially in Von Raumer's *Palestina*, p. 303 ff.

Sec. 180. **The Crucifixion.**—The form of death to which Jesus was condemned was by no means a Jewish punishment. It is true Josephus relates[2] that Alexander Jannæus caused about eight hundred of his Jewish opponents to be crucified ; but it does not follow therefrom that in this mode of revenging himself he conformed to the custom of his ancestors. If the Sanhedrim had possessed the authority to carry out the sentence of death, they would have stoned Jesus ; even as the Jewish tradition testifies He was sentenced to be stoned.[3] But since their sentence must be confirmed and executed by the Roman procurator, the latter condemned Jesus to the death of the cross. The matter seems to us to have had the following course : The Sanhedrists demanded of Pilate that he should ratify the sentence they had pronounced ; had this been done, they would themselves have carried out the sentence, and stoned Jesus. But since the procurator refused to confirm the sentence on their mere recommendation, entering upon a revision of the process, and having the air of being resolved not to sacrifice a single human life to the law of the Jews, they changed their accusation, charged Jesus with rebellion against Cæsar, and delivered up the Lord to

---

[1] [Ritter, *Palestine*, Engl. trans., iv. pp. 135-140.]

[2] *Antiq.* xiii. 14, sec. 2.

[3] [And as Stephen actually was stoned, in violation of the Roman law.]

the Gentiles, who condemned Him as a state criminal against
the Romans, to the crucifixion awarded to those guilty of
revolt. So soon as the Jews accused Jesus before the Roman
tribunal, they were fully aware what punishment the procurator must impose upon Him, if he adjudged Him guilty ;
for this reason they cried, Crucify, crucify !¹ as an answer to
the question, What shall I do to this man ?²

Crucifixion³ was one of the most painful and dishonourable
modes of punishment,⁴ and as such was inflicted upon revolted
slaves, those engaged in sedition, and highwaymen. Those
condemned to crucifixion must, after undergoing scourging,⁵
themselves bear their cross to the place of execution.⁶ They
were then deprived of their garments,⁷ and affixed to the cross
previously erected.⁸ This cross might vary in point of height.
Whether they were affixed by the hands and feet, or by the
hands alone, is difficult to determine. No universal custom
seems to have obtained with regard to it. Lucan. vi. 547
speaks of nails in hands.⁹ The New Testament does not
express itself decisively on the question. The body of the
crucified rested upon a projecting piece of wood ($\pi\hat{\eta}\gamma\mu\alpha$),
fixed at about the middle of the upright beam of the cross,¹⁰
and was, moreover, fast bound with cords.¹¹ Death ensued
under the most horrible sufferings—rarely before the twelfth
hour of the crucifixion, not seldom only after two days.
Origen says, " Miraculum erat, quomodo post tres horas
receptus est (Jesus), qui forte biduum victurus erat in cruce,
secundum consuetudinem eorum, qui suspenduntur quidem
non autem percutiuntur." After the execution the crucified
ones continued to hang upon the cross until they were consumed by the birds. The Jews, however, were wont to take

---

¹ Properly, *Hang,* תלה.
² John xix. 15 ; Matt. xxvii. 23 ; Mark xv. 14.
³ Cf. Winer, *Realw.* i. 677.
⁴ Crudelissimum teterrimumque supplicium, Cic. *Verr.* v. 64.
⁵ Livius, xxxiii. 36.   ⁶ Plutarchus, *de Serâ Vind.* c. 9.
⁷ Artemidorus, ii. 53.
⁸ Cicero, *Verr.* v. 66. Josephus, *de Bello,* vii. 6, sec. 4.
⁹ Insertum *manibus* chalybem. [Meyer, however, has shown from Plautus,
Justin Martyr, and Tertullian, that the nailing of *the feet also* was general.
Comm. on Matt. chap. xxvii. 35.]
¹⁰ Iren. *Adv. Hær.* ii. 42. Justin, *Dial. c. Tryph.*   ¹¹ Lucan. vi. 543 sqq.

them away and bury them.[1] The breaking of the legs (τὰ σκέλη)[2] took place as a *coup de grace* on account of the approaching festival. This was inflicted only upon the two crucified with Jesus, because He was already deceased. (? From a rupture of the heart, or of an artery.) The piercing of the side had as its object to guard against the taking down from the cross one who had possibly merely swooned.

Sec. 181. **The taking down from the cross** took place " when even was come," " when the Sabbath drew on."[3] At about the ninth hour, *i.e.* about three in the afternoon, Jesus had died. The obtaining of permission to take Him down from the cross and bury Him had occupied some time. The burial nevertheless took place before the time of the great paschal Sabbath.[4] Among those engaged in this work is especially mentioned a member of the Sanhedrim, a secret disciple of Jesus, named Joseph of Arimathæa.[5] The question where this Arimathæa was situated is of but slight importance. Arimathæa is evidently the Græcised Aramaic form of Ha-Ramathaim. Among the different places known as Rama, only the one Rama of Samuel has this dual form of the name.[6] That this Ramathaim, and consequently Arimathæa, is to be recognised in Neby Samwîl, N.W. from Jerusalem, has already been shown.[7] How Biblical geographers have been able to see Arimathæa in Ramleh—a name which denotes *sand*—we are at a loss to explain.

Sec. 182. That **the grave,** in which the body of Jesus was laid, was one similar to other Jewish graves, hewn out horizontally in the rocks and closed with a door of stone, is evident from Mark xv. 46, Matt. xxvii. 60, Luke xxiii. 53, John xix. 41. The grave shown in the Basilica is really such an one, although the rock above it has been in part cut away, for the sake of building the tomb over.

Sec. 183. After the burial, which had taken place in haste, and could be only a preliminary one, the women who had followed Jesus out of Galilee, and had seen the grave,

---

[1] Josephus, *de Bello*, iv. 5, sec. 2.   [2] John xix. 31.
[3] ὀψίας γενομένης, Matt. xxvii. 57 ; Mark xv. 42 ; cf. Luke xxiii. 54.
[4] ἡμέρα ἦν παρασκευή, Luke xxiii. 54.
[5] Matt. xxvii. 57 ; Mark xv. 43 ; Luke xxiii. 50 ; John xix. 38.
[6] 1 Sam. i. 1.   [7] Cf. sec. 49.

returned to the city, prepared spices and ointments, and were resting on the Sabbath day according to the commandment.[1] Now this Sabbath is brought into relief, as one of special sacredness and importance. John xix. 31 calls it the Great Sabbath day—ἦν γὰρ μεγάλη ἡ ἡμέρα τοῦ σαββάτου—and all the Evangelists call the day which precedes it "the preparation day."[2] Had then, as is supposed by the majority of exegetes, the day of Christ's death been the 15th Nisan, the great sacred paschal Sabbath, it could not be at all explained how this highest festival of the Jews should be characterized as the preparation day for an ordinary week Sabbath, and by no other distinctive mark whatever. How can we suppose that during this feast day, termed in the law Sabbath, one could buy[3] and go to the field;[4] whilst the week Sabbath, which could be broken for the sake of the paschal Sabbath, must be esteemed so sacred? Why should the Sabbath following Passover be termed "the great Sabbath day," when the 16th Nisan in itself was only a working day, and the week Sabbath falling at this date could be broken by the gathering in of the sheaf. Precisely in the history of the burial of Jesus does it come forth clear as day, that not only according to John, but according to all the Synoptists, the day of the burial was the 14th Nisan, the day before the great paschal festival, which in this year fell on a week Sabbath.

The day of the Lord's repose in the grave, on which the Sanhedrim importuned Pilate to set a watch upon the sepulchre, is the 15th Nisan.

X.—History of the Resurrection of Christ.

Sec. 184. We cannot deny that it is a much more difficult task to present a harmony of the four Gospels as regards the history of the resurrection, than is the synoptical arrangement of the history of the Passion.

[1] Luke xxiii. 55, 56.

[2] ἡ παρασκευή simply, Matt. xxvii. 62 ; παρασκευή, ὅ ἐστι προσάββατον, Mark xv. 42 ; ἡμέρα ἦν παρασκευή, Luke xxiii. 54 ; παρασκευὴ ἦν . . . παρασκευὴ τῶν 'Ιουδαίων, John xix. 31, 42.

[3] John xiii. 29 ; Luke xxiii. 56.   [4] Mark xv. 21.

A first difficulty arises from the suspicion of non-genuine-
ness which attaches to the history of the resurrection in Mark
xvi. 9–20. This section is wanting in the *Sinaiticus, Vaticanus* [and earliest codices of the Armenian version], and is represented as doubtful in several other codices. The Canones of
Eusebius end with xvi. 8. Eusebius himself testifies[1] that,
according to Mark, Jesus did not appear to the disciples. From
the Schol. in Codd. L. and *Syr. Philoxenus*, on the margin, one
sees that there was another ending of this Gospel.[2] On the
other hand, all codices, except א B, and all versions [except
the Armenian], have this pericope xvi. 9–20 in a text agreeing with ours. If Mark had really closed his Gospel with
chap. xvi. 8, we might certainly conceive, and even expect,
that a later hand would have added an appendix concerning
the manifestations of the Risen One; but it is inconceivable
that Mark xvi. 9–20 should be such addition. A history of
the resurrection appended by later Christians could manifestly
have been nothing more than an excerpt from the other
Gospels. But the pericope is no such excerpt; for in ver. 18
it contains additional particulars not related by the others,
and relates the history of the Ascension in a connection not
in harmony with that of Luke, but rather in apparent contradiction with it. It is difficult, moreover, in such case to
comprehend how it could find its way into almost all the MSS.
and versions. On the other hand, it is easy to explain how
this pericope, if it was originally found in Mark's Gospel,
should become suspected; since Mark apparently contradicts
himself, inasmuch as the appearing of the Risen One was in
ver. 7 promised in Galilee, and according to ver. 9 took place
in Jerusalem, and especially because it is difficult to bring it
into harmony with Matthew and Luke. We therefore regard
the pericope as genuine; without, however, wishing to attach
to it all the value of an undisputed account.

Sec. 185. "On the first day of the week cometh Mary
Magdalene early, while it was yet dark, unto the sepulchre,

---

[1] Schol. b. Victor Antioch. ii. p. 208.

[2] Ver. 8 : . . . ἐφοβοῦντο γάρ. Φέρεται ποῦ καὶ ταῦτα· Πάντα δὲ τὰ παραγγελμένα
τοῖς περὶ τὸν Πέτρον συντόμως ἐξήγγειλαν. Μετὰ δὲ ταῦτα καὶ αὐτὸς ὁ Ἰησοῦς ἀπὸ
ἀνατολῆς καὶ ἄχρι δύσεως ἐξαπέστειλι δι᾽ αὐτῶν τὸ ἱερὸν καὶ ἄφθαρτον κήρυγμα τῆς αἰωνίου
σωτηρίας.

and she seeth the stone taken away from the sepulchre. Then she runneth, and cometh to Simon Peter, and to the 'other disciple' whom Jesus loved, and saith unto them, They have taken away the Lord out of the sepulchre, and we know not where they have laid Him." [1] On this occasion of the first visit to the grave, Mary Magdalene alone is mentioned. She did not go there alone, however, but in company with others; for she does not say, I know not—but, We know not (οὐκ οἴδαμεν), where they have laid Him. Who they were who were with her at the grave is recorded by the Synoptists. Of this we shall hereafter have occasion to speak.

" Peter then and the other disciple went out and came to the sepulchre. The two ran together : and the other disciple did run before, more quickly than Peter, and came the first to the sepulchre. And stooping down, he seeth the linen clothes lying there ; yet did he not go in. Peter then cometh following him, and went into the sepulchre, and looks upon the linen clothes lying there, and the napkin, which was about His head, not lying with the linen clothes, but apart, rolled up, in a separate place. Then went in also that other disciple which came first to the sepulchre, and saw, and believed." [2] This vividness of presentation, this bringing into bold relief of the minor details, which for every other person would have been without significance, this feverish alternation of tenses and of verbs, could proceed only from an eye-witness, who, after an interval of many years, realizes to himself the scene as though it were still before his eyes. The two disciples now returned. Mary Magdalene, however, went again to the grave, where she was favoured with the first manifestation of the Risen One.[3] That which follows in the Gospel of John carries us to the evening hours of that Sunday. Before we enter on the treatment of this part of our subject, it is necessary here to compare that which is said by the Synoptists.

Sec. 186. Luke relates, chap. xxiv. 1–12, " On the first day of the week, at early dawn, came they—the women from Galilee, mentioned xxiii. 55, of whom (chap. xxiv. 10) Mary Magdalene and Johanna, and Mary of James are mentioned

---

[1] John xx. 1, 2.   [2] John xx. 3–9.   [3] John xx. 11–18.

by name, with the addition, 'and the others with them'—to
the sepulchre, bearing the spices which they had prepared.
And they found the stone rolled away from the sepulchre;
but when they entered in they found not the body [1] [*of the
Lord Jesus*]. Two men, who stood near them, proclaimed to
them that Jesus was risen. They made all this known to the
apostles." Then Peter ran to the grave, stooped down, and
saw the linen clothes lying alone.[2] The time of the visit to
the grave is with Luke, as with John, the time of the grey
dawn; for ὄρθου βαθέως is equivalent to πρωὶ, σκοτίας ἔτι
οὔσης; the plurality of the women is indicated, as we have
seen, by John too; that the stone was rolled away is equally
recorded by both. That the object of the women was to complete the preparations for the burial, is not in contradiction
with John xix. 40, since it may at any rate be supposed that
that first preparation remained, on account of the haste with
which it was performed, an incomplete one; that Luke does
not speak of John, as well as Peter, as visiting the grave is of
slight importance. The most striking difference between the
two accounts is the mention on the part of Luke of the two
men in shining garments, who confirmed the fact of the resurrection of Jesus, but of whom John says nothing. The narrative of Luke has not the oral accounts of John as its source;
otherwise he would have mentioned John with Peter in
xxiv. 12.[3] But so soon as it is seen that Luke derived his
report from other witnesses, the agreement with the teaching
of the fourth Gospel must be brought into prominence, as a
matter of great importance.

Sec. 187. Mark xvi. 1–8 begins the account yet earlier.
"When the Sabbath was over, Mary Magdalene, and Mary of
James, and Salome, bought spices, that they might come and
anoint Him." This took place thus on the evening of the
Saturday, when the Sabbath, which was at the same time the
Sabbath of the festival and of the week, was at an end.
From Luke xxiii. 56 it would seem as though the buying of

---

[1] [σῶμα, never πτῶμα.]   [2] Cf. Luke xxiv. 22-24.
[3] [This verse, which is wanting in Codex D and some of the early versions, is
omitted by Tischendorf. The visit of Peter and John is in any case alluded to
in the 24th verse.]

the spices had taken place already on the Friday evening, before the beginning of the Sabbath; but this is not expressly said there, and consequently the account given by Mark remains uncontradicted. "And very early on the first day of the week they went to the sepulchre, at the rising of the sun. They saw that the stone was rolled away. When they entered the sepulchre they saw a youth in a white robe, sitting at the right hand side . . . who proclaimed to them that Jesus was risen, and bade them tell the disciples and Peter, 'He goeth before you into Galilee, there shall ye see Him.' And they fled, and said nothing to any one; for they were afraid." This account is in contradiction with that of John and of Luke, as regards the time when the women came to the grave, if we translate ἀνατείλαντος τοῦ ἡλίου by "when the sun was risen;" but it is also in contradiction with itself, since the time when the sun is already risen cannot be called "exceedingly early," λίαν πρωί. It seems to us that, both here and often elsewhere in the N. T., the aorist participle is used in the sense of the participle of the future, and that ἀνατείλαντος must be translated, "when it was about to rise."[1] That Mark speaks only of one man, Luke of two, is without significance. Of greater importance, however, is the directing of the disciples to Galilee, as the place where they should see the Lord,—of this we shall speak hereafter,—and the statement that the women said nothing to any one; whereas, according to Luke, they related it to the apostles. Yet these words can only mean that they said nothing to the people whom they met by the way; for, since they had received an express commission with regard to the disciples and Peter, it is not to be supposed that they neglected to fulfil it.

Sec. 188. Matthew says, chap. xxviii. 1, Ὀψὲ δὲ σαββάτων, τῇ ἐπιφωσκούσῃ εἰς μίαν σαββάτων, ἦλθε Μαρία ἡ Μαγδαληνὴ καὶ ἡ ἄλλη Μαρία, θεωρῆσαι τὸν τάφον. In order to bring this passage into approximate harmony with the accounts of

---

[1] [The aorist does not here denote the actual phenomenon, but is—as remarked by Ellicott—to be regarded only as a general definition of time. Compare the ὑπὸ τὴν ἕω (about the time of the dawn), φωτὸς ἤδη τὴν γῆν ὑπαυγάζοντος. "Notum est solem non uno momento oriri."—Elsner.]

the other evangelists, various translations have been proposed.
De Wette translates, "Now after the Sabbath, on the dawn of
the first day of the week, came Mary Magdalene and another
Mary, to see the sepulchre." Others render it, "When the
week was at an end, and the first day of the new week began
to appear. . . ." By this means, no doubt, we arrive at the
Sunday morning; but the violence done in such translations
is evident, since they are equivalent to, "Late on the Sabbath,
when the light of the first day of the new week began to
appear, came Mary, etc." But *late on the Sabbath* points to
the sunset on Saturday evening, not to the Sunday morning.
If the passage is taken in this way, Matthew will be brought
into absolute contradiction with the other evangelists, who
place the visit to the grave on the Sunday morning. But,
however it is translated, the use of the aorist θεωρῆσαι continues to present a difficulty, since we should rather expect
θεωρεῖν or θεωρῆσειν; unless we suppose that here also the
sense of the future is to be attributed to the aorist.[1] If we
regard the matter from the point of view that Matthew, so far
as the *history* is concerned—for in the collection of discourses
he is original—stands in a relation of dependence on Mark,
the supposition forces itself upon us, that Matt. xxviii. 1 is
formed from the combination in one proposition of the two
propositions of Mark xvi. 1, 2, of which the one tells us
what was done in the evening, the other towards morning.
In Matthew the mention of the purchase made in the evening
has dropped out, and the time at which it was made has
remained standing. The restoration of the text would give
something like the following: "At the close of the Sabbath
[the women of Galilee purchased spices]; when the first day
of the new week began to dawn (thus, early on the Sunday
morning), went Mary Magdalene . . . to see the sepulchre."[2]

[1] [Kühner (*Smaller Grammar*, sec. 257, 1 obs. c.) says, "The aorist infinitive
has the signification of *past time* only after expressions of *saying* or *thinking*, and
in the *accusativus cum infinitivo* with the article. . . . In all other cases it has
the signification of the *present*."]

[2] [These remarks are based on the fact that in the N. T. and the LXX.
ὀψία or ὀψί means towards the close of day (Matt. xx. 8), sunset (Mark iv. 35),
the dusk (Mark xiii. 35), the time at which the lamps were kindled (Ex. xxx.
8); though not necessarily the time after sunset (Matt. xxvii. 57). Cf. sec. 5.]

Equally, in vers. 5–10, are the two visits of Mary to the grave combined in one; so that the women accompanying Mary Magdalene—at least the other Mary—were witnesses with her of the first manifestation. Whether or not the two women were present at the wondrous scene of xxviii. 2–4, is not clear.[1] The manifestation of the Risen One is promised in Galilee; and only this is described, in addition to the manifestation which was vouchsafed to the women at the sepulchre.[2]

Sec. 189. The fact proclaimed alike by all the evangelists is, that Mary Magdalene, with other women from Galilee, found the grave empty, and that to Mary Magdalene the Lord first manifested Himself; from that point, however, the narrative of the two first evangelists differs considerably from that of the two last; inasmuch as the former mention nothing of the other manifestations at Jerusalem, recorded by the latter, but point at once to Galilee. That the command to repair to Galilee was obeyed by the disciples after the completion of the paschal season, must be accepted as a fact. One and another of them, however, would seem to have fled to Galilee immediately after the Lord's crucifixion, among whom was probably Matthew, so that they could speak from their own experience only of that which took place there.

Sec. 190. After Mary Magdalene, Peter was the first who saw the Lord.[3] That John is silent as to this event, arises not from his jealousy of his fellow-apostle, but simply from the fact that John relates only that which he has himself witnessed. To this principle he remained true from the beginning of his Gospel to its end. He departs from it only when he treats of facts which stood in causal connection with that which he had himself experienced, and which were communicated to him by eye-witnesses, as is the case with that which was witnessed by Mary Magdalene, chap. xx. 1, 11–18.

Sec. 191. The third manifestation is that on the way to Emmaus.[4] It took place after Peter had seen the Lord, on the very day of the resurrection. A nearer defining of the

---

[1] [But compare Mark xvi. 3.]   [2] Matt. xxviii. 9–20.
[3] Luke xxiv. 34; 1 Cor. xv. 5.   [4] Luke xxiv. 13–35; Mark xvi. 12, 13.

time is given in the words of the disciples, chap. xxiv. 29,
" Abide with us, for it is towards evening, and the day is
far spent (κέκλικεν)." This urgency is not necessarily to be
explained as a warning addressed to the unknown one
against travelling alone by night, but rather as an act of
hospitality. We know already the wide application of the
word " evening" with the Jews ; it includes the whole afternoon, from half-past twelve, " when the sun inclines towards
evening."

Emmaus.—Of this place Luke says that it is a village,
κώμη, distant 60 stades from Jerusalem.[1] A very ancient
tradition identifies this place with Ammaus, the later Nicopolis, and present Amwâs, S.E. from Lydda. It is favoured
by Eusebius in the *Onomasticon*, and Jerome *in Dan.* viii.,
and *Ezek.* xlviii. This town, however, is distant not 60, but
180 stades from Jerusalem. Besides this Ammaus near to
Lydda, another Ammaus is known to Josephus. This latter
must now claim our attention. *De Bello*, vii. 6, sec. 6, he
mentions that Cæsar (Titus) assigned as a residence to
800 veterans discharged from the army a place (χωρίον)
called Ammaus, 'Αμμαοῦς, distant from Jerusalem 60 stades.
This Ammaus thus became a colony of veterans. Now, there
is to be found in the present day, at a distance of 60 stades
W.N.W. of Jerusalem, a place called Kolonieh—a name confessedly derived from *Colonia*. But Josephus knew only of a
single Roman colony in the neighbourhood of Jerusalem,
namely, this place evidently corresponding with the Emmaus
of Luke. Emmaus is consequently Kolonieh. This conclusion is confirmed, moreover, by the Talmud. In *Mishna
Succa*, iv. 5, it is said that the green willow branches, with
which the altar was decorated at the feast of Tabernacles, were
brought from a place near to Jerusalem called Maûza, מוצא.
In the Babylonian Talmud *Succa* it is observed that Maûza is
Kolonieh. If we give the name of the place with the article
prefixed—as it is also written Josh. xviii. 26—we have המוצא,
Hammaûza, which is evidently identical with Ammaus. There
is therefore no rashness in asserting that in *Kolonieh* the
Emmaus of the Gospel is certainly discovered. Travellers tell

---

[1] Luke xxiv. 13.

us but little about this place.   Tobler[1] visited it, and found
there a considerable spring.[2]

Sec. 192. From Emmaus the two disciples returned to
Jerusalem, after they had seen and recognised the Risen
One. The intelligence they had to bring lent speed to their
feet, so that they did not require two hours to leave behind
them the 60 stades; whilst from Nicopolis they would have
had a six hours' journey, and could not hope to reach Jerusalem the same evening. They found, it is said Luke xxiv.
33, the Eleven gathered together, and others with them.   It
is here the place to observe that before the treachery of Judas
" the Twelve," and after that treachery " the Eleven," means
just the apostles, without regard to the number,[3] and it is
not necessary that the number should be always complete.
On this occasion Matthew was wanting,[4] as also Thomas
and Peter, of whom they speak in Luke xxiv. 34 as an
absent one.   During the account given by the disciples from
Emmaus, the Lord manifested Himself to the assembled
apostles.[5] That Mark xvi. 14, 15 does not belong to this
place is shown in the following section. Whether 1 Cor.
xv. 5b belongs to this, or designates the following manifestation, must be left undecided. But it is certain that in John
xx. 19–23 the same appearing of the Risen One is intended,
from a comparison of John xx. 19, 20 with Luke xxiv.
36, 37.   In John it is said, " When it was now evening "
(not, was becoming evening) " on that Sunday." With the fall of
night the Emmaus-disciples were able to be again in Jerusalem.

Sec. 193. Eight days later,—the 16th April, Sunday,—
another manifestation of the Risen One was, according to
John xx. 24–29, vouchsafed in the presence of the assembled
apostles. Among these was now present Thomas, who had
not witnessed the previous one. This manifestation is the
one referred to in Mark xvi. 14, 15, and probably also in

---

[1] *Denkblätter*, p. 662. [Andrew Bonar, *Narrative*, p. 125. Robinson, iii.
158.]

[2] The author had regarded the site of Emmaus as his own discovery. All this
was recognised and written before Sepp's works, *Jerusalem and the Holy Land*,
and *New Architect. Studies*, had been seen by him. From these it is evident
that the discovery had already been made in the same manner long since.

[3] [Cf. 1 Cor. xv. 5b.]   [4] Sec. 189.   [5] Luke xxiv. 36–43.

1 Cor. xv. 6. What place was the scene of it? John does
not tell us; and this silence would lead to the conjecture
that, as in the case of the former appearing, so of this too,
the scene is at Jerusalem. But when we consider that an
express command was given to the apostles and disciples to
repair to Galilee, where they should see the Lord, there is
every reason for supposing that they obeyed this command
without delay, after the completion of the eight days of the
paschal festival, and that thus this manifestation took place
in Galilee, at Capernaum, or Bethsaïda. Anything by which
the acceptance of this view could be absolutely precluded
does not exist. On the contrary, John, chap. xxi. 1, seems in
the words, "Jesus manifested Himself again to the disciples
at the Sea of Tiberias," to presuppose an earlier, before-
mentioned manifestation on this sea. If the scene of this
manifestation was Galilee, the way is prepared for arriving at
the desired harmony with the two first Synoptists. Mark
xvi. 7 leads to expect a manifestation—the one mentioned
xvi. 14, 15 must thus be intended; but this [probably]
corresponds to that described John xx. 26, and [certainly] to
that related Matt. xxviii. 16, as is seen from the command
recorded alike in both Gospels,—Matt. xxviii. 19; Mark
xvi. 15: "Go ye into all the world, and preach the gospel."
In Matthew, it is true, this manifestation is spoken of as
taking place upon the mountain, consequently in the open
air; in Mark and John, on the other hand, in a house during
the meal, the doors being closed. But it would seem that
here, as often elsewhere, Matthew has combined the two facts
in one in his narrative, namely, the appearing in the presence
of the apostles in a house, with that upon the mountain in
the presence of all the disciples. Such manifestation unquestionably took place, although the evangelists do not make
distinct mention of it; for, 1 Cor. xv. 6, it reads: "After
that He was seen of above five hundred brethren at once; of
whom the greater part remain unto this present, but some are
fallen asleep." Equally silent are the evangelists concerning
a manifestation of the Lord vouchsafed to James, of which
the apostle speaks in ver. 7, which must yet have been a
well-known occurrence.

Sec. 194. The manifestation on the Sea of Gennesareth, John xxi. 1–25, appended by John as a supplement to his Gospel, is called the *third* ;[1] namely, of those witnessed by the apostle himself. He does not reckon among them the appearing of the Lord to Mary Magdalene, because the account of this does not rest on his own ocular contemplation. Because he was not personally present, he does not record the Galilean manifestations.

Sec. 195. We have already several times availed ourselves of the right—now in the case of one evangelist, now of another—to make divisions where the text appeared to proceed without break. The authorization thereto is rendered unquestionable by the following example. In Acts i. 1–11, Luke relates that the Lord manifested Himself from time to time during the forty days, until His Ascension. None the less is it the case with the same evangelist that all these manifestations are in his Gospel blended in a single one— that of chap. xxiv. 36–51. We must necessarily suppose that a new section begins with xxiv. 41, which probably ends with ver. 43, and forms the parallel of John xxi. 1. A second section, xxiv. 44–48, probably corresponds to Matt. xxviii. 18–20, and—as to its contents—to John xx. 21. The last section, finally, Luke xxiv. 49–53, belongs to the end of the forty days. [Corresponding to Mark xvi. 19, 20.] Then the Galilean apostles were again at Jerusalem, and received from the Lord the promise of power from on high, for which they were to wait *henceforth* in Jerusalem.[2] The command, "But tarry ye in Jerusalem," was not given to the disciples as early as the day of the Resurrection,—by which, of course, all that belongs to their sojourn in Galilee would have been rendered impossible,—but forty days later, after they had returned from Galilee. From the Ascension to Pentecost they did in fact remain at Jerusalem.

Sec. 196. The manifestations of the Risen One recorded by the different evangelists may, consequently, be presented in the following order :—

1. Mary Magdalene sees the Risen One on the morning of the Resurrec-

---

[1] John xxi. 14.   [2] Καθίσατε ἐν τῇ πόλει, Luke xxiv. 49.

tion—Sunday. The four evangelists have this account in common. Cf. sec. 189.

2. Peter alone sees the Lord on the afternoon of the same day. Luke and Paul vouch for this fact. Cf. sec. 190.

3. The two disciples on the way to Emmaus see Him on the same afternoon. The witnesses are Mark and Luke. Cf. sec. 191.

4. On the evening of the same day the Lord manifests Himself to the disciples, the doors being shut, after the return of the two disciples from Emmaus. This manifestation is reported by John and Luke. On this occasion there were absent Thomas, Peter the authority for the second Gospel, as well as the author of the first. Cf. sec. 192.

5. Eight days later the Lord manifested Himself to His disciples under similar circumstances,—but probably in Galilee,—Thomas being present. This is given on the authority of John, Mark, and Paul ; those who vouch for the facts of the first and of the third Gospel were absent. Cf. sec. 193.

6. Jesus manifests Himself in Galilee upon the mountain : this is reported by Matthew and Paul. John and Peter were not present. Cf. sec. 193.

7. Jesus the Risen One was seen upon the shore of the lake. John alone records this fact. Cf. sec. 194.

8. Last manifestation at Jerusalem, immediately before the Ascension, Witnessed by the Galilean disciples alone, John being absent. Cf. sec. 195.

Sec. 197. The Ascension is presupposed as a fact by all the evangelists and apostles, inasmuch as they speak of Jesus as the Lord in heaven, in the glory at the right hand of God. But the event itself is recorded only by two evangelists, Mark and Luke. The narrative of the former of these is such as to leave it doubtful whether the Ascension took place before the eyes of the disciples or not. It is there said, " The Lord then, after He had spoken to them, was received into heaven, and sat down at the right hand of God.[1] Luke, however, represents the fact as one taking place before the eyes of the Galilean disciples. According to the Gospel,[2] He led them out (from the city of Jerusalem) as far as Bethany, lifted up His hands and blessed them ; and while He blessed them [He was parted from them and] was carried up into heaven. In the Acts of the Apostles there are to be found further notes of time and place: the time during which the Risen One manifested Himself to His disciples was forty days ;[3] the place of the Ascension was " Olivet, which is nigh to Jerusalem, being distant a Sabbath-day's journy." [4]   A Sabbath-day's journey

[1] Mark xvi. 19.   [2] Luke xxiv. 50.   [3] Acts i. 3.   [4] Acts i. 12.

contains 2000 cubits, or 6 stades. If Luke intends in this place only to indicate in general the distance of Olivet from Jerusalem, his statement tallies with that of Josephus, who fixes it at 5 or 6 stades.[1] If, however, he intends to mark the distance of the place of the Ascension, this datum corresponds pretty nearly to the site of the Chapel of the Ascension, where tradition indicates the point from which the Lord rose to heaven. In this case, however, the Acts would be in contradiction with the Gospel, in which the scene of the Ascension is placed at Bethany, a village 15 stades from Jerusalem.[2]

Sec. 198. The Lord before His exaltation left with His disciples the injunction to tarry in the city of Jerusalem until they were endued with power from on high.[3] This promise had its accomplishment " when the day of Pentecost was being fulfilled,"[4] that is to say, on the second part of the night-day on which the feast of Pentecost fell. Now Pentecost was held fifty days after Passover, and consequently always fell on the same week-day as the 16th Nisan. In the year 30 A.D. Passover was a Sabbath, and thus Pentecost a Sunday. When this night-day was drawing towards its close, i.e. on the day after the eve of Pentecost, the promised outpouring of the Holy Ghost took place—thus on a Sunday, as is maintained by Christian tradition. This could not have been the case if—as is erroneously supposed by the great majority of exegetes—the 15th Nisan in that year had fallen on a Friday. In the year 30 the 15th Nisan was, as we have seen, a Saturday, 7-8th April ; the day of the Resurrection, 9th April ; the day of the Ascension, 18th May ; and the day of the gift of the Holy Ghost, Pentecost, 27-28th May. The events of Acts ii. 1 ff. accordingly took place on the morning of Sunday, 28th May, at about the third hour,[5] i.e. nine A.M. The place where the disciples were assembled was

---

[1] *Antiq.* xx. 8, sec. 6 ; *Bell.* v. 2, sec. 3.

[2] The contradiction, however, disappears if in Luke xxiv. 50 we read, with א B C, ἕως πρὸς Βηθανίαν, or, with D, simply πρὸς Βηθανίαν. For it then says, He led them out *in the direction of Bethany*, thus not into it. The site of the Church of the Ascension may then, according to the better supported reading of Luke, be the true one ; since it lies immediately above Bethany, on the mountain.

[3] Luke xxiv. 49.

[4] Acts ii. 1, ἐν τῷ συμπληροῦσθαι τὴν ἡμέραν ; cf. Luke ix. 51.   [5] Acts ii. 15.

" a house ; " [1] but that it could not be a private house follows
from the statement that they were all together, ἅπαντες
ὁμοθυμαδόν, thus at least 120 in number,[2] in the same; for a
room of such magnitude cannot be supposed to exist in private
dwellings.   It is well known that a very ancient tradition,
vouched for by Cyril of Jerusalem,[3] points to the Church of
Zion as the place where the outpouring of the Holy Spirit
took place ; and Jerome represents the pilgrim Paula as
ascending Mount Zion, and there visiting the place where the
Holy Ghost was poured forth into the hearts of the 120
believers.   The edifice in which this tradition places the
miracle of Pentecost was thus yet standing in the days of the
before-mentioned Fathers, and was a Jewish building which
had outlived the fall of the city ; but at the same time also a
crypt, because " the mother of the churches " was the prototype
of the Christian churches of the first century, which were all
of them crypts.   Such structure is the subterranean building
under the Aska Mosque at the south side of the temple area.
That these celebrated substructures were the Holy Church of
Zion will be shown in the Appendix, No. 19.

XI.—Critical Review of the History of the Resurrection.

Sec. 199. The most striking difference between John and
the Synoptists is, that these last seem to be acquainted with
only a single manifestation of the Risen One, whereas he
describes a series of such manifestations.   The Synoptists,
moreover, differ from each other, inasmuch as the two first
place the scene of the manifestation in Galilee, while Luke
places it in Jerusalem.   Matthew finally differs from Mark,
in that the former speaks of " a mountain " as the scene of
the appearing ; Mark, on the other hand, places it in a house.
But if the Gospel of Luke leaves upon us the impression that
the apostles had seen the Risen One only once, this impression
is weakened by the statement of Acts i. 3, that Jesus had
shown Himself alive after His Passion by many evident signs [4]
during forty days.   Now, it is possible that by the " many

---

[1] Acts ii. 2.   [2] Acts i. 15.
[3] Born A.D. 315.   [4] ἐν πολλοῖς τεκμηρίοις.

proofs" Luke would speak of only a single manifestation; but it is also equally possible that he combined the quintessence of the "many" in a single one. This latter seems to us the true state of the matter. The main purport of the apostolic ministry was the testifying of the Lord, the proclaiming to men of that which they had seen and heard. The first form of preaching was narration. By the frequent repetition of the same fact there must necessarily be formed a stock of narrative consisting of a series of cycles, which was for the most part presented in a purely chronological order, and in the same words. This form of communication led to a blending of single facts, separated by time and place, into one connected image. Such mode of proceeding is especially observable in the first Gospel, and has often been pointed out in that which we have already said. This must, however, from the nature of the case, reveal itself most of all in the history of the resurrection. The manifestations of the Risen One were sporadic, brief, without local connection the one with the other, now granted to a single individual, now to an assembly of disciples. Such an account of disconnected events must in the oral relations—divested of the mention of place and time, and of the individual beholders—assume the form in which the Synoptists have related them to us; and thus with Luke the many proofs during the forty days have seemingly blended into a single one, perhaps on the last of these days. Luke had certainly—the account of the Acts shows this—the consciousness of such blending; on this account we must pre-suppose it also in Matthew and Mark. If we are right in what has hitherto been said, then we have also the means at hand for establishing a harmony of the Gospels in this history, in the manner in which we have above sought to effect it.

Sec. 200. The apostles and evangelists who testify of the resurrection of Christ from the dead present this truth, not as one revealed to them in an extraordinary way, but as a fact of experience. They testify that they have seen it—have perceived it with their senses. If the resurrection of Christ had been a revealed truth, it would have been incumbent indeed on Christians to believe it; the believer would have had, in reliance upon the truth of that which was manifested by the Spirit of God, the blessing of the gifts of hope, consolation, and power contained in that resurrection. But the resurrection of Jesus would then remain exclusively a private possession of the believing Church, a mystery disclosed only to Christians, of which no apologetic or missionary use were possible; the Christian would accept the resurrection, because he believes in Christ. But the apostles make a missionary use of it; Christ has been manifested to them as the Son of God by the fact of the resurrection from the dead;[1] they seek to convince men of this fact by their testimony, and only upon this assurance (certainty) do they rear up the edifice of repentance and faith. John says:[2] "We proclaim unto you that which we have seen with our eyes, which our hands have touched of the Word of Life." Paul, who, where this is necessary, appeals also to revelations, does not make such appeal where he will lay the foundation of faith in the resurrection of Jesus, but cites witnesses, and appeals to that which others and he himself have seen.[3] From this very circumstance it arises that all the different evangelists do not report the same appearances of the newly-risen Lord, but each one only that which is attested by himself personally, or by the eye-witness on whose authority his Gospel is penned. As a pure fact of experience they present each of their histories. The account, too, in Matt. xxviii. 2–4 must be so regarded; for if the women themselves were not witnesses of the event, it may have transpired through the guards.

Sec. 201. But if the resurrection is presented, not as a revelation, but as a fact of experience, on which the faith of the believer is to be based, we have also to judge of it according to the ordinary laws of evidence, by which we judge of other facts of experience; only we protest against the importation of principles drawn from metaphysical reasoning, which formulate that which is historically possible, in such wise as to exclude à priori that which is supernatural and miraculous. The possible is not the criterion of the actual, but the converse is the case.

Sec. 202. It is certain that the evangelists present the resurrection as a fact of experience. What they testify to

---

[1] Rom. i. 4; Acts ii. 32.   [2] 1 John i. 1–3.   [3] 1 Cor. xv. 5–8.

having experienced is therefore either objectively real and true, or the narrators have deceived themselves, or else have intentionally spoken untruth. The hypothesis of a design to deceive cannot, in the presence of the moral character of these witnesses, be for a moment entertained; this is testified by the universal outburst of indignation with which M. Renan's presentation of the resurrection of Lazarus was received. Men shrank from it as an historical scandal. On the other hand, the hypothesis of unintentional self-deception has found acceptance on many sides; it must therefore be subjected to a closer examination.

Sec. 203. If it is asserted that the witnesses of the resurrection of Jesus deceived themselves, nothing else can be meant by this than that in a condition of excessive spiritual tension and hallucination they fancied they saw something, although no object sensuously perceptible presented itself to their senses. Such conditions indisputably exist. In our waking condition, the nerves of our senses play the part of the keys of a musical instrument; the external world, with its impressions, is the hand which plays on these keys, and in the soul resound the emotions awakened by this playing. In the life of sleep the case is reversed: passive conditions of the organism deprived of voluntary activity—an interruption in the flow of the blood or in the action of respiration, etc., awakens in the soul emotions and tones, bear a resemblance to the emotions which, in the waking condition of the life of day, are called forth by the impressions of external objects. It has perhaps happened that a dangerous, raging beast has inspired us with such sudden terror, that the blood ceased to flow, and we experienced a cold trickling about the spinal cord. If now in sleep, by any physical perturbation, by an attack of fever or something of the sort, the same sensation is produced, that the blood is arrested, and a cold trickling is produced about the spinal cord, the imagination conjures up before us this raging beast as the cause of our sensation. This is a dream. The sensation originates in the nerves of the senses, imagination creates the hand which touches the keys. The sensation is real, the hand which plays on the keys is imaginary. A like physical condition may, however, steal upon us in a waking state. The emotions of joy, of anguish, or of longing stirred up in the soul, may become so intense that for a moment they arrest the activity of the senses—the pupils of the eyes, *e.g.*, may become so greatly dilated that actual seeing becomes impossible. In a condition like this, the imaginative power may attain to such a degree of energy that the eye imagines it sees, the ear that it hears, and the senses in general seem to receive an impression of that which occasions the emotion in the soul. If this condition is produced by a morbid affection of our organism, it is called hallucination ; if, however, an objective spiritual power is active in the production of it—a power which will inspire into the soul a spiritual revelation—the condition is called vision. In one respect, therefore, there is an important difference between hallucination and vision ; in another respect they are, as a psychological act, identical—namely, a perception by the senses, without the presence of an object sensuously perceptible.

Sec. 204. Of what nature, then, was the beholding of the Risen One ? Was it, strictly speaking, the seeing of a real object ? or a purely inner vision without the presence of an object perceptible to the senses ? Visions as the medium of revelation are, in the New Testament, well-known phenomena, as well those given in sleep as those which present themselves while in a waking condition. As regards those experiences by night in the dream-life, these are always distinguished from actual seeing and hearing, and are represented as a dream. To these belong Matt. i. 20, 24, ii. 13, etc. But even the visions and trances (ἐκστάσεις) which fall upon one in a waking condition, as Acts x. 10 ff., 2 Cor. xii. 2 ff., Matt. xvii. 1-3,[1] are definitely distinguished from *seeing* in the strict sense of the term. Of a vision,[2] *e.g.*, Paul says, " Whether in the body, I cannot tell ; or whether .out of the body, I cannot tell." If any have wished to represent the seeing of the Risen One by the apostles as a vision or ecstasy, —as an inner beholding,—the ground of this judgment does not at any rate lie in the nature of the accounts, which testify to an actual seeing ; but in a metaphysical motive, in the

---

[1] Cf. sec. 125.   [2] [Here, however, there was an actual ἁρπάζειν, *rapture*.]

endeavour to set aside the miraculous and supernatural altogether. Where this endeavour does not obtain, it must be acknowledged that the reporters maintain that what they saw were not visions, but an actual beholding of Jesus. Were they perhaps deceived, and led to regard something that was only a vision as an actual beholding? Something of the kind would be conceivable, if the beholding of the Lord had been a fleeting one, one quickly passing, and granted only to single individuals. But the beholding of the Risen One, on the contrary, is presented by the evangelists as continuing for a lengthened period, and as being shared simultaneously by several hundreds of persons. The Lord is described as holding prolonged discourses, expounding texts, uttering doctrines, commands, promises; He eats and drinks, suffers Himself to be touched. In all this, no self-deception was possible; unless it was manifest fraud, it was a real beholding.

Sec. 205. Those critics who explain the beholding of the Risen One as visions, appeal principally to the presentation of that which was experienced by the Apostle Paul on the way to Damascus, which is regarded by them as a vision. But was this event really a vision? And if it was, must that which is related by the evangelists necessarily be so too?

The account of that event comes down to us in three relations. According to the first—Acts ix. 3–8—a light suddenly shone round Saul; he fell to the ground, and heard a voice, which said to him, " Saul, Saul, why persecutest thou me? " . . . The men who were journeying with him stood speechless, hearing indeed the voice, but beholding no one. In the second—Acts xxii. 6–11—Paul speaks again of a sudden light, which beamed around him. He fell to the ground, heard a voice speaking to him, . . . " and they that were with me beheld indeed the light, but the voice of Him that was speaking to me heard they not." Finally, Acts xxvi. 12–18 does not treat of the experiences of those accompanying him. If we combine these texts, we learn that Saul beheld a dazzling light, by which he was blinded; heard a voice, and received words which were spoken to him. Those who accompanied him saw the light, but no person; heard a voice ($\tau\hat{\eta}s$ $\phi\omega\nu\hat{\eta}s$), but understood not the words ($\tau\grave{\eta}\nu$ $\phi\omega\nu\acute{\eta}\nu$). Since those who accompanied him had like perceptions as Saul, it was not a vision in the strict application of the term. On the contrary, the senses were affected by an external object. At most, one could only assert that it was a real perception by the senses, accompanied by a visionary tension, since Saul heard more intensely than those who accompanied him. Paul says, 1 Cor. ix. 1, xv. 8, that he has seen the Risen One, and makes use of this fact as a proof of the reality of the resurrection. The great significance of this revelation for the apostle was, next to the conversion wrought by it, his calling to the office of apostle of the Gentiles.[1] The narrative does not indeed speak of this in the two first accounts which are given of the great event on the way to Damascus; but it does in the third, xxvi. 16–18. From this it follows with certainty that the apostle, when he speaks in the Epistles of having seen the Lord, refers to this event on the way to Damascus. In favour of this view pleads also 1 Cor. xv. 8, where Paul says that this manifestation was vouchsafed to him, while he was yet an ἔκτρωμα—an unripe fœtus, not yet born to the new life—that is, an unbeliever;[2] whilst the other apostles saw the Lord as men already born again. If Paul, when he saw the Lord, was as yet unconverted, this revelation cannot have been experienced by him later than the event on the way to Damascus, with which it must indeed be identical. It is true, according to the three accounts, he did not actually see the Lord, and, because blinded, *could* not see, but heard. It is, however, well known that " seeing" is often used for *any* perception by the senses.[3]

If, however, that which was experienced by Paul was really —what, nevertheless, we cannot admit—purely and merely an inner [subjective] vision, it cannot be concluded from this that the facts related in the Gospels were visions too; these are not

---

[1] Rom. i. 5.

[2] [The force of the argument will remain the same, if we understand by this expression, " One born out of the ordinary course (of the apostleship),'' which was by the call of the Lord *in the days of His flesh.*]

[3] [The apostle declares in Acts xxvi. 19, that he actually *saw* the glory that smote him—the οὐράνιος ὀπτασία, by the splendour of which, according to chap. xxii. 11, he was blinded. A comparison with Gal. i. 16 shows, nevertheless, that the subjective element was that which *predominated* in this manifestation.]

to be judged of by that which was experienced by Paul, but to be accepted as that which they claim to be, real and true perceptions by the senses. There is, in any case, the great difference in the experience of Paul and that of the other apostles, that Paul saw the Lord after His exaltation to heaven, and thus after the ordinary manifestations had ceased. It is comprehensible that in this latter case something visionary accompanied the real perception. In the case of the rest of the apostles, on the other hand, it was a real, objective beholding.

APPENDIX.

——◆——

THE TOPOGRAPHY OF JERUSALEM.

1. In the New Testament history we meet with the following topographical references to localities in Jerusalem :—

Siloah, the *Pool*, John ix. 7 ; and the *Tower*, Luke xiii. 4.
The Sheep Gate, and near it
Tho Pool of Bethesda, John v. 2.
The Prætorium (Gabbatha), John xviii. 28, xix. 13.
The Temple, ὁ ναός, Matt. xxvii. 51 ; Mark xv. 38 ; Luke xxiii. 45, etc.[1]
The Sanctuary, or *Temple-enclosure*, τὸ ἱερόν, Matt. xxi. 12 ; John ii. 14, and frequently elsewhere.
The Pinnacle of the Sanctuary, Matt. iv. 5 ; Luke iv. 9.
The Beautiful Gate of the Sanctuary, Acts iii. 2, 10.
The Stoa of Solomon, John x. 23 ; Acts iii. 11, v. 12.
Golgotha, Matt. xxvii. 33 ; John xix. 17 ; and near this
The Sepulchre of Jesus, John xix. 41.
The Sepulchre of David, Acts ii. 29.

The determination of these localities is possible, only if the general archæological topography of the Holy City is scientifically proved, and set free from its traditional errors. This subject, however, is one unfortunately still left in obscurity up to the present time. No further justification therefore is required for here making the attempt to settle the topography of Ancient Jerusalem.

2. **El-Kuds,** as Jerusalem is now called, is situated upon a

[1] [Compare the use made of ναός, Luke i. 21, with that of ἱερόν, chap. ii. 27.]

PLAN OF MODERN JERUSALEM,

With the remains of the ancient city.

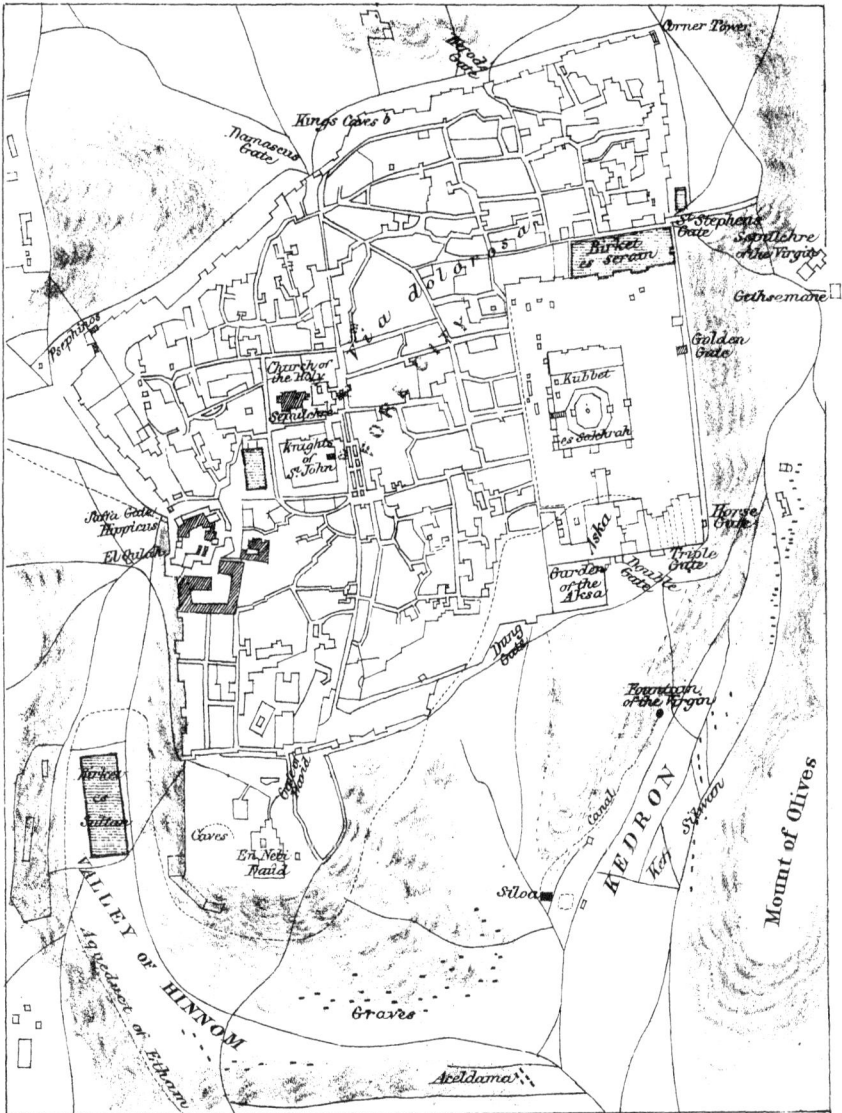

The second wall

a.a.a *Remains of the wall*
by the Hospice of the Knights
of St. John, before the Church
of the Holy Sepulchre, and on
the Via Dolorosa.

tongue of land, which on the western side is connected
by an isthmus of about 800 paces [about 700 yards] wide
with the uplands of Judea, but is on every other side shut
off by valleys. One of these valleys, the valley of the Kidron
or Jehoshaphat, closes up the northern side. Shallow at its
beginning, it runs from west to east, and then suddenly
taking a southerly direction it bounds the isthmus on the
eastern side, and separates it from the Mount of Olives. The
second valley, called Ben-Hinnom, takes its origin on the
southern side of the isthmus, and pursues its course at first in
a southerly direction, then turning to the east unites with the
valley of Jehoshaphat, where the latter descends as the Wady
en-Nâr to the Dead Sea. The city does not enclose the whole
plain of the tongue, but only its southern half. El-Kuds has
the form of an irregular square, the sides of which nearly
enough correspond to the four points of the compass. The
city has seven gates, of which the *northern* wall contains two.
One of these, Bâb el-Amûd, called also Damascus gate,
occupies the middle of the wall. In the middle of the
eastern half of the wall lies Bâb es-Sahari, or Herod's gate ;
it is at present blocked up. The *eastern* wall is divided by
two gates into three pretty equal parts. The northernmost
of these is called Bâb Sitti-Mariam, and by the Christians St.
Stephen's gate ; the southernmost lies in the east wall of the
Haram, and is an ancient double gate, now blocked up. It is
called by the Mahommedans Bâb ed-Daherîyeh, and by the
Christians the Golden gate [*Porta aurea*]. In the *southern*
wall there are also two gates. The first, at the east end, is
called Bâb el-Moghârbeh, and by the Christians the Dung
gate ; it is always closed. The second opens not far from the
west end of the southern wall, and is called Bâb en-Neby
Daûd, and also Zion gate. In the *western* wall, finally, there
opens only one, Bâb el-Chalîl, *i.e.* Hebron gate. Called also
Jaffa (*Yáfa*) gate.

3. The ground of the present Jerusalem is pretty much a
plain, sloping from west to east. This was not, however, the
conformation of the original soil, which, on the contrary, was
intersected by valleys now filled up with masses of *débris* in
parts of great depth. Of these depressions the one most

R

clearly marked is that which extends from the Damascus gate to the Dung gate. It is known as el-Wâd, is continued to the south beyond the city in the form of a deep ravine, called the Tyropœon, and opens into the valley of Jehoshaphat at the point of union between this latter and the Kidron. El-Wâd divides the city into two halves. The more easterly of these is separated into two quarters by a depression, partly artificial, which proceeds from west to east, and runs out at the one end into El-Wâd, and at the other sinks down perpendicularly into the Kidron. It is represented by the lower half of the so-called *Via Dolorosa*. The southern of these eastern quarters forms the Haram—the former temple area, with the addition of a small portion of the town adjoining its west side ; the northern consists of a hill, which Josephus calls Bezetha. The half, too, which lies to the west of el-Wâd divides itself into two quarters, which were formerly separated by a valley extending from the Jaffa gate towards the southern part of the Haram. This is now indeed obliterated by masses of rubbish ; but from the citadel [el-Kula'ah] there extends along the street of David, as far as the Mekhmeh,[1] an immense cloaca, which, without ever needing cleansing, carries off all the filth of the city.[2] This clearly marks out the course of the former valley. The northern of these two west-quarters contains the Church of the Holy Sepulchre. It is situated upon the isthmus which connects the tongue of land with the Judean uplands, and is not a hill, properly so called, but the continuation of the uplands in their gradual sloping down from west to east. The southern of the two west-quarters is on the other hand a hill, at the north-west corner of which is the citadel el-Kula'ah, and on the ridge of which is situated the Armenian Church of St. James. Later Christian tradition calls this hill—without justice, as we shall see—Mount Zion.

The object of the archæological topography is to trace out again upon this ground the form of the ancient Jerusalem.

---

[1] [The Council House at the west wall of the Haram, Ritter, iv. 101, of English translation.]

[2] Rosen. "Topographisches aus Jerus." in the *Zeitschr. der Deutsch. Morgenl. Gesellsch.*, 1860, ii. 610.

4. Josephus says:[1] " The city was fortified by three walls, except where it was surrounded by inaccessible valleys [φάραγξιν] ; for there it had but one wall." The valleys or ravines here intended are Ben Hinnom and Kidron, which, running south from the citadel, protect the west side, and after that the whole southern and eastern side. And again:[2] " The oldest wall was inaccessible by reason of the ravines, and the hill which was overhanging them, upon which the wall was built. . . . The north side of this wall began at the tower named Hippicus, and stretching to the place known as *Xystus*, then touched the Council House (τῇ *Βουλῇ*), and ended at the western stoa of the sanctuary." As to the general direction of this wall, there can be no doubt. The tower of Hippicus was at any rate situated in the citadel, at the N.W. corner of which M. de Saulcy[3] discovered the foundations of an ancient tower, which perfectly corresponded to the dimensions given by Josephus, *de Bell.* v. 4, sec. 3. From this tower the wall ran in an easterly direction along the northern brow of the south-west hill, and abutted on the western wall of the Haram, after having passed by the Xystus. The site of this public place is perfectly determinable. In *de Bello*, vi. 6, sec. 2, it is said that a bridge which connected the sanctuary with the Upper City led over the Xystus — ὑπὲρ τὸν Ξυστόν. Considerable remains of this bridge are still to be found at the west wall of the Haram, 39 English feet north from the S.W. corner of it.[4] The Xystus was thus the broad levelled valley-bed of the Tyropœon, which extends south from the Moors' quarter to the Dung gate. Such a situation in the hollow is also predicated of the Xystus by Josephus, *de Bello*, iv. 9, sec. 12; vi. 8, sec. 1. Josephus continues : " On the other side, towards the west, the wall began at the same tower—Hippicus, namely,—proceeding through the place called Bethso, to the gate of the Essenes ; then taking a southerly direction above the fountain Siloam, and thence again inclining eastwards to Solomon's Pool, it extended as far

[1] *De Bello*, v. 4, sec. 1.
[2] *De Bello*, v. 4, sec. 2.
[3] *Voyage en Terre Sainte*, ii. 40.
[4] Robinson, *Pal.* i. 288.

as the place which is called *Ophla*, where it abutted on the eastern stoa of the sanctuary." Robinson,[1] and with him many others, translate otherwise. The words of Josephus [2] are by him rendered : "Thence it kept along on the south to a point over Siloam ; and thence on the east was carried along by Solomon's Pool, and Ophla (Ophel), till it terminated at the eastern portico of the temple." But πρὸς νότον . . . ἐπιστρέφον does not mean a lying *towards* the south, but the turning of a course *to* the south, and designates, not a southern wall, but the western wall of the southern Moriah, which runs in a southerly direction. Equally does ἐκκλῖνον πρὸς ἀνατολήν designate a tending or continuation of the wall towards the east, from Siloah to the Pool of Solomon ; thus— not an east wall, but—a southern wall running in an easterly direction. If Robinson's translation were correct, it must be supposed that the southern wall was carried across the Tyropœon along the extreme verge of the south-west hill at Siloah. But it is certain that the city wall on Moriah was to such an extent separated from the city wall on the south-west hill, that this latter still continued a fortress complete in itself, when the former was already in the hand of the enemy. In this way a dividing wall must have existed along the whole southern Tyropœon, of which, however, there is nowhere found any trace. A translation which leads to such results cannot be accepted. The western wall ran from Hippicus to the place Bethso,[3] which seems to correspond to the site of the English school-house ; thence it was continued to the gate of the Essenes, which can only be the Mogharbeh gate ; because from that point the wall was carried (along the west side of Moriah) *south* to Siloah. From this fountain to the Pool of Solomon the southern wall of Moriah stretched eastwards, and thence finally the eastern

---

[1] Robinson, *Pal.* i. 279.

[2] Καὶ ἔπειτα πρὸς νότον ὑπὲρ τὴν Σιλωὰμ ἐπιστρίφον πηγὴν, ἔνθεν τι πάλιν ἐκκλῖνον πρὸς ἀνατολὴν ἐπὶ τὴν Σολομῶνος κολυμβήθραν. . . .

[3] Vitringa explains this name as = בֵּית צוֹאָה, "house of dung ;" but it is better to derive it from בֵּית שׁוֹא, "house of destruction, or perdition," a name which has reference to the idolatry of the valley of Ben Hinnom. There is, at any rate, no connection between *Bethso* and *Shaar ha-Shephoth*, the Dung gate of Nehemiah. (Later note of author.)

wall extended to the south-east corner of the Haram. The southern part of Moriah, as well as of the south-west hill, which now lie without the city wall, were within the enclosure of the ancient Jerusalem. For Josephus says, that on the other side of the valleys the city was unassailable, and the history of the sieges of Jerusalem proves the truth of this statement; for never was so much as an attempt made by the enemy to assail the walls on the south or east side. But had the city walls of the ancient Jerusalem occupied the site of the present ones, the attack on the south side would have been easily possible by means of the instruments of siege employed by the ancients, since both hills present in the present day a free, open plain beyond the walls. At the time of the Crusaders the walls had already their present course; for this reason the city was assailed also on its south-west hill,[1] a thing which had never taken place in antiquity.[2] We have consequently to suppose that the walls extended in such wise as to enclose the Mosque En-Neby Daûd on the south-west hill, and to make the ridge of the *Moria extra muros* as far as the Pool of Siloah, also part of the city; but yet in such wise that the bottom of the Tyropœon, at present excluded, was excluded at that time too, and that the gate of the Essenes stood on the site of the present Bâb el-Mogharbeh.

5. " **The second wall** had its beginning at the gate called *Gennath*, which belonged to the first wall; and encircling only the tract to the north, it extended up to Antonia." The gate Gennath belonged to the first wall, which extended from the Hippicus to the Xystus, and consequently lay to the east of Hippicus. The extreme point of this wall was Antonia, *i.e.* the north-west corner of the temple area or Haram. This wall was a comparatively small one, since it was crowned with only fourteen towers, whilst the third wall mounted ninety.[3] That it took its course, starting from the first wall towards the north, along the Damascus street, is indicated by the ancient remains of a wall which have been discovered in the domain of the Knights of St.

[1] *Gesta Dei*, i. pp. 74, 175, 750.   [2] *De Bello*, v. 4, sec. 2.
[3] *De Bello*, v. 1, sec. 3.

John.[1]   From the *Porta Judiciaria* it must then have taken
its course eastward, along the *Via Dolorosa*.

6. " **The third wall** began at the tower *Hippicus*, whence,
striking northwards, it extended to the Psephinus tower ;
then, passing in front of the monument of Helena, it was
continued through the midst of the Kings' Caves[2] to the
corner tower, where it swept round past what is called the
Fuller's Monument, and, joining the ancient wall, ended in
the valley of the Kidron.   This wall Agrippa placed around
the part added to the city ; since this was before entirely
unfortified (γυμνά).   For the city, being over-populated, had
gradually crept beyond the walls, so that north of the sanctuary the building was considerably extended, and thus the
fourth hill, called Bezetha, was covered with houses.   This
hill lies over against the Antonia, from which it is cut off by
a deep trench artificially constructed.   By the inhabitants the
place is called Bezetha—a name which signifies *New-town*." [3]
The Antonia was situated at the north-west corner of the
Haram.   Immediately to the north of this lay the hill
Bezetha, which is consequently the hill on which lies the
Dervish mosque.   The course of the third wall is defined by
a series of certain points, which show that it was identical
with that of the present city wall.   The third wall began at
the Hippicus, *i.e.* at the north-west corner of the citadel, and
extended to the north as far as the Psephinus tower (flint-
stone tower).   Considerable remains of this tower, composed
of flint-stones or pebbles, firmly cemented together, were discovered by Krafft[4] in Kasr Jalûd (*Goliath's Castle*), at the
north-west corner of the town, and the discovery has been
fully confirmed by de Saulcy.[5]   From this tower, which, at
Josephus' time, as now, formed the north-west corner of the
city, the wall ran eastwards and intersected the King's Caves.
Now the city wall to the east of the Damascus gate rests
upon a bed of rock, the side of which has been hewn into a
perpendicular form, showing that here the Bezetha hill was

---

[1] De Saulcy, *ll.*, Plan of Jerus., sub litt. vv.
[2] διὰ σπηλαίων βασιλικῶν.   [3] *De Bello*, v. 4, sec. 2.
[4] *Topogr.* 40. [Ritter, iv. 68 ff. of Engl. trans. ; Robinson, i. 318, iii. 193.]
[5] *Voyage*, ii. 128.

cut through and lowered. Opposite to this wall of rock lies the grotto of Jeremiah, in a wall of rock corresponding to this. Now in the rock under the city wall there is the entrance to a very considerable cave, penetrating under the city, towards the south.[1] It is thus evident that Agrippa had constructed at this place magnificent subterranean quarries, of which the grotto of Jeremiah and the one just mentioned are the northern and southern remains. These are the King's Caves. In the Damascus gate itself there are found considerable remains of a tower, of Jewish structure, which belonged with the rest to the third wall. If now, from this point to the corner tower, and thence to the eastern wall of the Haram, no remains of walls have been found, as to the antiquity of which we can be certain; yet, on the other hand, there is to be found about the north-east corner of the city such an enormous city-moat hewn in the solid rock—a Jewish work of colossal dimensions—as thoroughly establishes the course of the wall.[2]

7. Many topographers are of opinion that the ancient Jerusalem occupied a considerably larger space than the modern, by virtue of an extension not only to the south, but also to the north. According to them, the present northern wall of the city corresponds more or less to the second wall of Josephus, and they seek the third on the northern extremity of the tongue of land, where it is bounded by the Kidron in its eastward course, the present Wady el-Jos. The following passage of Josephus, understood aright, may assist in the decision of this question :—" The walls," he says,[3] " were mounted with towers, of which each one was 20 cubits broad. The number of these upon the third wall amounted to ninety ; they were distant from each other 200 cubits. The middle (second) wall had fourteen of them, the old wall was parted nto sixty (εἰς ἑξήκοντα μεμέρίστο). The whole circuit of the city embraced 33 stades." Here, unfortunately, a numerical error has crept in. A stadium contains 400 cubits. The third wall, with its ninety towers,

---

[1] Tobler, dritte Wanderung, 256 ff. [Tristram, p. 190.]
[2] [Cf. Ritter, iv. 97, Engl. translation.]
[3] De Bello, v. 4, sec. 3.

each at a distance of 200 cubits—or a half stadium—from the next, had thus in itself alone a length of 45 stades, and yet the compass of the whole city was only 33 stades ! The error evidently lies in the distance of the towers, which is given at 200 cubits. We will endeavour by another method to attain to the correct number. Since Josephus defines the fortifications of Jerusalem in such wise that the third wall contains ninety towers, the second fourteen,[1] and the first sixty, the total enclosure, τῆς πόλεως ὁ πᾶς κύκλος, must be the sum of the three towers, and not merely the exposed front of the fortifications. The towers amounted in all to $90 + 14 + 60 = 164$. If we divide by this number the 33 stades, or 33×400 cubits $= 13,200$ cubits, it results in a distance from tower to tower of 87, or, in round numbers, 90 cubits. The number 90, however, is expressed by the sign ϛ´ (κόππα), and the number 200 by σ´. It is easily conceivable that a copyist should have substituted the latter sign for the former; and the more so, in that immediately before the number of towers was given at ninety, and he might thus regard the repetition of the same numeral as an error, which he corrected into σ´. But since Josephus determines the whole sum of the three walls at 33 stades, we find the outer extent of the city wall, if from this sum we subtract the length of the inner walls. The inner walls were, of the first or oldest wall, the part lying between the Hippicus and the Xystus,— amounting to about 3 stades,—and then the whole of the second wall, amounting to 14×90 cubits, or about $3\frac{1}{2}$ stades —together $6\frac{1}{2}$ stades ; which, being deducted from 33 stades, gives $26\frac{1}{2}$ stades as the length of the line of fortifications which encompassed Jerusalem. The modern Jerusalem has, according to Richardson, 4630 paces, or 2315 Roman double paces. [Robinson[2] gives, from actual measurement, 12,978 feet English, which is equal to 2703 Roman double paces, since one of these was equal to $4\frac{4}{5}$ feet English.] The $26\frac{1}{2}$ stades give 3312 passus : whence it follows that the ancient Jerusalem counted about 1000 paces [according to Robinson's measurement, 600] more in circumference than the modern.

---

[1] [Τισσαρισκαίδικα, not *forty*, as given by Whiston.]

[2] Robinson, i. p. 268.

This difference is to be explained from the form of the southern wall, which did not, like the modern, describe a straight line.

8. The description Josephus gives of Jerusalem shows most clearly that at his time—before the destruction by Titus—the town was divided into five quarters or districts, of which each one was separated from the rest by a wall, and formed a fortress complete in itself. These were:

First quarter—**The Sanctuary,** which was enclosed on every side by walls, in such wise that the enemy who had made himself master of all the rest of the city, did not, on that account, obtain possession of the Temple Mountain, but on the contrary, must undertake a formal siege of it, as is evident from the history of the conquest of Jerusalem by Herod. In addition to this general enclosure of the Temple Mountain, there were also two separate works of fortification, namely, the Antonia, which occupied the north-west corner of the temple area, and formed a strong citadel; and the inner court, which was separated from the outer by a fortified wall drawn all around it.

Second quarter—**Bezetha,** or the New City, which was covered on the outer sides by the third wall, and on the inner was cut off from the rest of the city by the second wall and the northern wall of the Temple Mountain. This was the most northerly part of the Holy City.

Third quarter—**The Suburb,** or Fore City, τὸ προάστειον;[1] probably identical with the part of the city called *Parphar*, פרבר, mentioned 1 Chron. xxvi. 18. It was that part shut off from the rest of the city on the north and west by the second wall, on the east by the west wall of the Temple Mountain, on the south by the wall extending from the Hippicus tower to the Xystus.

Fourth quarter—**The Upper City.** Such was the name of that part of the city which was situated upon the south-west hill, which modern tradition falsely calls Zion. It was protected by the oldest or first wall on every side except that over against the sanctuary; on which side it was defended by the high rock, hewn into a perpendicular, which formed the

[1] *Antiq.* xv. 11, sec. 5.

western skirt of the Tyropœon or Xystus.   When Titus had
reduced the New City, the Old City, the Sanctuary, and the
Lower City, and only the Upper City remained in the hands
of the Jews, a parley was held between the Romans and the
Jews: " Titus stood upon the western side of the outer
Sanctuary, where was an arch provided with gates [*Robinson's
Bridge*], connecting the Upper City with the Sanctuary—γέφυρα
συνάπτουσα τῷ ἱερῷ τὴν Ἄνω πόλιν ; this bridge divided
Titus from the tyrants (patriots)."[1]   This account is sufficient
to justify the position we have assigned to the Upper City.
That this part of Jerusalem constituted a fortress in itself, is
shown by the formal siege which Titus had to lay to it, after
he had made himself master of all the rest of the town.

Fifth quarter—**The Lower City.**   This made up, with the
Sanctuary and the Upper City, the Old City properly so called.
It, too, was enclosed within the oldest or first wall ; but was
situated upon the eastern hill, the Moriah, south from the
Sanctuary.   This quarter is in the present day entirely *extra
muros;* only the garden of the Aksa, which formed part of it,
now belongs to El-Kuds.   This determination of the Lower
City calls for a thorough proof, since topographers are pretty
generally of another opinion.

9. Josephus says:[2] "The city, ἡ πόλις, was fortified by three
walls, except on the side of the inaccessible ravines, for there
there was only one wall.   The city was built, one part facing
another, upon two hills.   These hills were separated by an intervening valley, down to the edge of which the houses extended
on either side.   One of these hills, that which had the Upper
City, was considerably higher and straighter [steeper ?] throughout its length.   It was thus, on account of its strength, called
by David *Phrurion* (φρούριον = strong place, fortress) . . . among
us it is known as the Upper Market.   The other hill, which
sustained the Lower City, was called *Acra.*   It was crescent-
shaped (ἀμφίκυρτος).   Over against this was a third hill, by
nature lower than Acra, from which it was formerly divided
by another shallow ravine.   But afterwards, in the time of
the Asmonæans, they filled up this ravine, with a view to
bringing the city into connection with the Sanctuary ; and

---

[1] *De Bello*, vi. 6, sec. 2.   [2] *De Bello*, v. 4, sec. 1.

levelling the top of the Acra, they made it lower than the
Sanctuary, in order that the latter might tower above it.   But
the valley called the *Tyropœon*, which, as we have said, separated the hill of the Upper City from the lower hill, extends
as far as Siloam : for so we call that sweet and abundant
fountain. But on the outer side, the two hills of the city were
encompassed by deep ravines ; so that, on account of the cliffs
on either side, approach was impossible." By means of this
description of Josephus, topographers determine the site of the
Lower City simply as follows :—Jerusalem, say they, is here
divided into the Upper and Lower City—the Upper City is the
south-west hill; all the rest of Jerusalem is thus the Lower City.
This reasoning would be sound, if by " the city," ἡ πόλις,
Josephus meant all Jerusalem. But this is not the case.   On
the contrary, it is seen on closer examination that he understands
by this term not the whole of Jerusalem, but only the original
Old City, which was enclosed within the first wall.   For he says
that the πόλις was built upon two hills ; but of the New City,
he says,[1] that it occupied the *fourth* hill—τέταρτον λόφον.
Bezetha thus did not belong to the City of the *Two* Hills, and
in particular did not form part of the Lower City, which,
indeed, was situated on the second hill ; πόλις thus denotes in
this place Jerusalem, with the exception of the New City.
This mode of expression is, moreover, entirely in keeping with
ancient usage, according to which the term πόλις often excludes the suburbs and outskirts, and is applied by way of
distinction to the original fortified place or Old Town.   For the
rest, it is evident that not of all Jerusalem, but only of the
Old City, could it be said that it was fortified with *three* walls ;
for the Suburb, προάστειον, was covered only by *two*, the New
City only by *one*. From this we should be justified in concluding that not only is not the New City covered by the
third wall, but not even is the Suburb covered by the second
to be reckoned as forming part of the Lower City, and thus as
belonging to the πόλις. Yet this amount of proof does not
content us ; we shall below furnish a more thorough demonstration. Concerning the hill of the Acra or Lower City,
Josephus says that formerly it was confronted by a third hill ;

[1] *De Bello*, v. 4, sec. 2.   See above, sec. 6.

and the context shows clearly that by this third hill the
Temple Mount was intended. Why then were there formerly
three of them, and now only two ? What has become of the
third ? If the valley separating the two hills has been filled
up, and one of them has been considerably lowered, the two
hills henceforth form only one single hill. It would therefore
be folly in the Jerusalem of the present day to seek for a hill
of Acra, separate from the Temple hill, since Acra has in fact
become part and parcel of the Temple Mountain. The "*Moria
extra muros*" fulfils all the conditions of the text; it is one with
the Temple hill, and lower than the Haram. The garden of
the Aksa is a levelled soil, which in its northern part may well
be a filled up valley. This hill of the Lower City is separated
from the Upper City by a valley, namely, the lower El-Wâd.
The name *Tyropœon, i.e.* " Cheesemakers' Valley," was manifestly borne only by that part of the valley which was outside
the city, since the cheesemakers could there ply their craft.

10. The determining of the position of the *Lower City* just
given by us, receives confirmation from the history of the
siege and conquest of Jerusalem by Titus. Josephus relates [1]
that the Romans from the north carried the third wall by
storm, and thereby became masters of the entire New City ;
of the Lower City there is on this occasion no trace of
mention, from which it follows that this name was not applied
to the New City. *De Bello,* v. 8, sec. 1, we have an account
of the capture of the second wall, whereby the Suburb (Fore
City) fell into the hands of the Romans. But the name of
" Lower City " is not given to this part of the city either.
De Bello, vi. 1–5, gives an account of the taking of the
Sanctuary and the destruction of the temple. After this
conquest the Romans had consequently everything in their
hands that was comprised within the third and second walls,
together with the Sanctuary. To the Jews there then
remained nothing but the Old City, contained behind the
first wall. At this juncture of affairs was held the parley
before alluded to between Titus and the heads of the Jews.
Their deliberations were without result. Therefore Titus gave
orders for the plundering and burning of the city. " On the

[1] *De Bello,* v. 7, sec. 2.

next day," it is said, *de Bello*, vi. 7, sec. 2, "the Romans drove the robbers (patriots) out of the Lower City—τρεψάμενοι τοὺς λῃστὰς ἐκ τῆς Κάτω πόλεως—they burnt everything down to Siloam . . . but the rebels carried off all the spoil, and retired into the Upper City."[1] Here we have the first reference to the Lower City during the whole history of the siege. The place from which the Romans expelled the Jews belonged necessarily to the Old City ; for from the New City as well as from the Suburb they had long been driven. When, then, the Jews had evacuated the Lower City too, the Romans burnt everything—naturally in this Lower City—down to Siloam, to which point the Lower City thus reached. To the Jews there remained nothing but the Upper City, which formed a citadel in itself. If now we take away from the Old City—which here too is again called ἡ πόλις—the Upper City, that which remains must be the Lower City. But yet, since many topographers, for reasons hereafter to be spoken of, seek to discover the Lower City in various parts of Jerusalem, just as it suits them, it will contribute to the end in view if we adduce additional passages confirmatory of the proof. We have already seen that Josephus, *de Bello*, v. 4, sec. 1, states that the Acra hill bore the Lower City. Hence it comes to pass that these two names are used interchangeably as exact synonyms. *De Bello*, v. 6, sec. 1, it reads, "Acra, which is the Lower City : " τὴν Ἄκραν, αὕτη δ᾽ ἦν ἡ Κάτω πόλις. Now in this passage it is said that when Titus began the siege of Jerusalem, this city was torn with factions. The head of one of these factions, " Simon, had under his power the Upper City, the great wall as far as the Kidron, and that part of the old wall which stretches eastward from Siloam, and extends to the palace of Monobazus. He possessed also the fountain (namely, Siloah), and the Acra, which was the Lower City, and all as far as the palace of Helena." Thus here, too, the Lower City is brought into

---

[1] There was in any case a gate at the southern extremity of the Lower Town, " the Fountain gate " of Nehemiah. They would retire by this gate, and enter the Upper City by the Gea gate (*Valley gate*) of Nehemiah, corresponding to the Bâb en-Neby Daûd. There must, besides, have been means of effecting their retreat into the Upper City from the Tyropœon itself ; since there were in the walls of Jerusalem numerous little hidden gates.

connection with Siloah. We return further to the discussion of the passage already cited, *de Bello*, vi. 6, sec. 3. After the negotiations with the Jews at the Xystus, Titus gave orders for the plundering and burning of the city. By this he could not intend Bezetha and the Suburb, which had already been long in the power of the Romans, and had been plundered till there was nothing left, and indeed had been reduced to ashes. Nor did he mean the Sanctuary, which was destroyed; nor yet the Upper City, which was inaccessible to him, and still in the possession of the Jews. But the southern Moriah was accessible to him; because he had under his power the double gate which led to it from the precincts of the Sanctuary. The order for destruction was executed, and "the Romans burnt the *Archeion*, Acra, the Council House, and the place called Ophla; and the fire spread as far as the palace of Helena, which was situated in the midst of Acra." These buildings were all of them situated in the eastern Old City. Of these the Council House was manifestly the most northerly; because at this structure, as we have seen, the northern first wall impinged upon the outer sanctuary. Now the Council House was built on the side of the Xystus, south from the quarter of the Barbaresques (Hâret el-Mughâribeh). The other buildings were situated farther to the south. In a text earlier cited we found that the Lower City extended as far as Siloah: here we become acquainted with the fact that it began at the Council House, and extended to Ophla— which latter place must necessarily be sought on the eastern side of the southern Moriah. If, finally, we add the boundary valley Tyropœon, we have all the desired landmarks for determining the extent of the Lower City. Our text calls forth the observation that Josephus—here, as often elsewhere —used the term Acra at one time in the narrower acceptation for the Syrian fortress, at another in the wider for the whole Lower City; for only thus can this name be understood, as it occurs twice within the same clause. Further, it is said, *de Bello*, iv. 9, sec. 12, that when Simon was besieging the zealots in the Sanctuary, these latter—in order to be able from a higher position to combat their assailants—erected four great towers—the first at the north-east corner of the temple area, the second above the Xystus, the third at another corner, facing the Lower City, and the last upon the parapet of the Pastophoria.[1] Now the temple area had four corners: at the north-east corner stood the first tower; at the north-west corner stood the mighty Antonia, tower enough in itself, where thus, at any rate, none was erected. There remain now only the south-east and south-west corners: at one or the other of these " the tower at the other corner " must have been raised. It is here a matter of indifference at which of them the tower was erected, since the one and the other lay over against *Moria extra muros.* There, consequently, was situated the Lower City; for "they built the third tower at a corner over against the Lower City."

11. **The Acra.**—The Lower City was called also Acra. This name it received from the stronghold of the Syrians, which plays so important a part in the history of the Asmonæans. In *Antiq.* xii. 5, sec. 4, Josephus says that Antiochus Epiphanes came to Jerusalem, threw down the walls, and erected *the Acra in the Lower City:* τὴν ἐν τῇ Κάτω πόλει ᾠκοδόμησεν Ἄκραν; because this was high, and *overlooked the Sanctuary*—ὑπερκειμένη τὸ ἱερόν. In *Antiq.* xii. 9, sec. 3, he says: At this time the garrison of the Acra greatly distressed the Jews by slaying in unexpected sorties those who were going up to the temple to sacrifice; *for the Acra was adjacent to the Sanctuary:* ἐπέκειτο γὰρ τῷ ἱερῷ ἡ Ἄκρα. Finally, Simon the Maccabean succeeded in wrenching this stronghold out of the hands of the Syrians.[2] He razed it to the ground, and *lowered the Acra hill,* which before was higher than the Sanctuary; so that henceforth the latter was higher than the former. In this work of lowering, all the inhabitants of Jerusalem toiled zealously day and night for three years, and brought down the hill level with the ground, and made of it an even plain—καὶ κατήγαγον εἰς ἔδαφος καὶ πεδινὴν λειότητα. These facts Josephus sums up in his description of Jerusalem,[3] and there speaks, moreover, of a broad valley between

---

[1] *Pastophoria* is the Greek term for לשכות, the chambers of the priests, which were ordinarily placed in the tower surmounting the gates. The place mentioned by Josephus should be found above the double gate. (Later note of author.)

[2] *Antiq.* xiii. 6, sec. 7.   [3] See above, sec. 9.

Acra and the temple area, which was filled up, so that the two hills were fused into one, and the Sanctuary was visible above the Acra—ὡς ὑπερφαίνοιτο καὶ ταύτης τὸ ἱερόν. The effect of the carrying away and filling up was, that the Sanctuary was placed in connection with the city—συνάψαι βουλόμενοι τῷ ἱερῷ τὴν πόλιν. We shall hereafter attempt more nearly to define the site of Acra : suffice it for the present to say, that its site must have been somewhere on the southern Moriah, since there alone was the Lower City. See Note at end of Preliminary Observations, p. xxvii.

12. **The City of David.**—In 2 Sam. v. 6–9 it is said, "David and his men went to Jerusalem . . . and he took the stronghold of Zion . . . and dwelt in the stronghold, and called it the City of David." What was the situation of this Jebusite fort, the City of David ? In 1 Macc. i. 33 it reads : Antiochus Epiphanes and the Syrians "fortified the city of David with a great and strong wall, and it became their Acra" ᾠκοδόμησαν τὴν πόλιν Δαυΐδ . . . καὶ ἐγένετο αὐτοῖς εἰς Ἄκραν. Josephus relates, *Antiq.* vii. 3, secs. 1, 2, that "David took the lower city ; but as he had not yet possession of Acra, τῆς Ἄκρας λειπομένης, he promised the chief command in his army to the warrior who should climb from the intervening valleys and penetrate into the Acra—ἐπὶ τὴν Ἄκραν ἀναβάντι. The undertaking was carried out by Joab . . . David expelled the Jebusites from Acra, fortified anew Jerusalem, τὰ Ἱεροσόλυμα, and called it αὐτήν (namely, τὴν Ἄκραν) City of David—πόλιν αὐτὴν (sc. Ἄκραν) Δαυΐδου προσηγόρευσε—and dwelt there." [1] Thus, according to Josephus, as according to the First Book of Maccabees, is Acra the City of David. This fact is confirmed by a third witness. In the old Jewish festival calendar, *Megillath Taanith,* ii., we read, "On the 23d Ijar the sons of the Acra, בני חקרא, lost Jerusalem. It is written,[2] 'David took the citadel of Zion, that is the City of David.' This place, זה היא מקום, the Acrians חקרים, had possessed. In those days these oppressed the sons of Jerusalem, and the Israelites could no longer go in and out by day, but only by night.

---

[1] [Or we may translate, "the city itself," *sc.* τὴν κάτω, as opposed to the rest of Jerusalem.] [2] 2 Sam. v. 7.

But when the house of the Hashmonæans waxed strong, they drove those out, and the day of their expulsion became a day of good omen, יום טוב." With these three witnesses there is associated, finally, a fourth, the Targum, in which the עיר דוד, the City of David, is constantly translated by חקרא, Acra: thus, e.g. 2 Sam. v. 7; 1 Kings viii. 1. No topographical fact, indeed, concerning Jerusalem can be adduced, which is supported in so many ways and so definitely by certain, credible witnesses, as the fact that Acra is identical with the City of David. Of these four witnesses the topographers have hitherto, for some unaccountable reason, allowed only one to make its voice heard, namely, 1 Macc. i. 33. But, since this testimony was disagreeable to them,—inasmuch as it gave a formal contradiction to their preconceived opinion, that the City of David was to be found in the Upper City,—they have sought to weaken its force, either by declaring it to be an error on the part of the author of the First Book of Maccabees, or else, as Von Raumer,[1] have sought to evade the difficulty by understanding " City of David " in this place in a general sense, as a synonym for " Jerusalem." But this hypothesis falls before the statement of Josephus, and especially before that of the feast calendar, which evidently explain the " City of David "—which they identify with the Acra—in the limited sense, as equivalent to the fortress of the Jebusites : זה היא מקום, no other than the place which, according to 2 Sam. v. 7, David had subdued. It might occur to any one, in connection with the passage cited from Josephus—where manifestly " City of David " is taken in the narrower sense-—to take the expression *Acra* in the general sense of " fortress." But the other witnesses show that it is the Syrian fort which is intended. The favourite objection that in this very place Josephus locates the " City of David " in the Upper City, inasmuch as he says that the Lower City was already captured, while the fort was still holding out, proves nothing. For Josephus might equally well intend to say that the Lower City was already captured, but that the height round which it lay, the fortress of the said Lower City, did not yield. And this is actually what he does say. If it appears surprising

[1] *Palest.* p. 419 ff.

S

that this historian on the present occasion makes no mention whatever of the Upper City, the matter is explained very simply, by the fact that the Upper City—among the population of which there was a mixture of Israelites [1]—without making any resistance, voluntarily threw open its gates to David. And in fact Josephus says [2] that David came up from Hebron, not as *against* Jerusalem, but *into* the city—ἦκεν εἰς Ἱεροσόλυμα. We have no fear that any one in the present day will seek to weaken the force of the extract from *Megillath Taanith*, by the assertion that the reference there is not to the warriors of the Acra, but to the Karæans or Karaites, as was fabled by the earlier archæologists ; for the date of the 23d Ijar, at which the expulsion of the Hacrites is there said to have taken place, is the same as is given 1 Macc. xiii. 51. There it is said that Simon entered the Acra on the 23d day of the second month of the 171st year. The month following Nisan is Ijar, thus the second of the Jewish year. The City of David is a local name, and cannot designate Jerusalem in general. Equally is Acra in Jerusalem itself a proper name of a definite locality, and can just as little signify another citadel of this town as it was allowable in Paris to call the first palace we might meet with—*e.g.* the Tuileries—simply the Palais-Royal. If anything is established with regard to the topography of Jerusalem, it is the identity of the city of David with the Syrian *Acra* of the Lower City. This does not prevent our adducing yet another important witness.

13. Nehemiah, in order to inspect the condition of the gates and walls of Jerusalem, rode forth from the Valley gate, past the dragon spring, to the Dung port, and to the Fountain (Siloah), then up the Nahal (Kidron); and returned, and entered again by the Valley gate into Jerusalem.[3] Thereupon the restoration of the gates and walls was determined on, and carried out.[4] The dedication was celebrated with praise by two choirs appointed thereto, whose route is described xii. 31–43. These three accounts introduce thrice, in regular succession, the gates of Jerusalem, and afford us a topo-

[1] Judg. i. 21.
[2] *Antiq.* vii. 2, sec. 2.
[3] Neh. ii. 11-15.
[4] Neh. iii. 1-12.

graphical treasure which is without an equal. We must abandon the thought of explaining the whole description, and confine ourselves to that which is most indispensable—the determining of the position of the City of David. The starting-point for our examination is—

The Pool of Siloah. — In Neh. iii. 15 we read : " Shallum restored the Fountain gate, שַׁעַר הָעַיִן, . . . and the wall at the Pool of Siloah, בְּרֵכַת שֶׁלַח, by the king's garden." From this we perceive that Jerusalem, as represented by Josephus, extended to the Pool and the Fountain of Siloah ; and that beside the Fountain and the Pool there was a gate, which was called *Ain, i.e.* Fountain gate, from Ain Shiloach, the Fountain, which also was called simply Aïn, as it is in Josephus, *de Bello,* v. 6, sec. 1, ἡ πηγή.

The Dung gate, שַׁעַר הָשְׁפוֹת.—This gate was situated immediately before the last mentioned. When Nehemiah made his first examination he rode down the valley of Hinnom, and then up a portion of the Kidron, and thus took a direction in which he had Jerusalem on his left hand. Pursuing this direction, he came first upon the Dung gate, and then upon the Fountain gate.[1] The same direction is followed in the description of the Restoration, in which likewise mention is made first of the Dung gate, and then of the Fountain gate.[2] The first choir of those giving thanks pursued this route, and confirms the same order of succession.[3] The Dung gate is consequently the gate which immediately precedes the Valley gate—*i.e.* the *Bâb el-Mogharbeh*, the gate of the Essenes of Josephus.

The Valley gate, שַׁעַר הַגַּיְא.—It was, according to Neh. ii. 13, situated before, *i.e.* to the *west* of, the Dung gate. The wall lying between these two gates had a length of 1000 cubits,[4] *i.e.* 1500 feet, or 300 double paces. Now Richardson relates that from Bâb el-Mogharbeh to Bâb en-Neby Daûd there are 605 paces—that is, 302 double paces. [Robinson finds it 1700 feet.] The correspondence is so striking, that the supposition of the identity of the Bâb el-Neby Daûd with the Valley gate, and the inference that the wall described by

---

[1] Neh. ii. 13, 14.   [2] Neh. iii. 14, 15.
[3] Neh. xii. 31, 37.   [4] Neh. iii. 13.

Nehemiah upon the south-west hill has the same course as the present one, is almost unavoidable. But we have seen above, that in all probability the ancient wall enclosed within the city the site of the Mosque of David. Here, then, comes into account the remarkable fact that from Bâb en-Neby Daûd two paths run towards the south-east, and unite again at a point which, according to de Saulcy's plan, is likewise distant 300 double paces, or 1000 cubits, from the Dung gate. Paths in mountain districts are never the work of caprice, but are always determined by the nature of the ground. The said two paths correspond, therefore, to two former streets of the Upper City, and their place of union is the site of the Valley gate. This Valley or Gaïa gate points to the valley of Hinnom, which is just as regularly termed גי or גיא as the Kidron is נחל. In the description of the journey of the choirs of praise this gate is not mentioned, just because it was the common starting-point of both choirs, as is distinctly evident upon a comparison of xii. 31 with iii. 13, and of xii. 38 with iii. 11.

Thus in Nehemiah's account the Valley gate represents the gate of David, but lies farther to the south ; the Dung gate corresponds to the Bâb el-Mogharbeh, of which it occupies the site ; and then the Fountain or Siloah gate is to be looked for south of the Mogharbeh gate, in the wall of the Lower City, at the end of the Tyropœon.

The City of David.—In Neh. iii. 15 we read : " Shallum restored the wall at the Pool Siloah, by the king's garden, as far as the steps which come down from the City of David." Where were these steps ? At the west, or the east side of the lower Tyropœon ? To this Nehemiah gives answer, chap. xii. 37 : " They, the choir, went from the Dung gate to the Fountain gate—thus from north to south, on the east side of the Tyropœon ; then they went נגדם, *beside*, or *over against*, themselves, *i.e.* parallel with the course hitherto pursued, but in the opposite direction, from south to north, and went up the steps that lead to the City of David, at the ascent in the wall, above the house of David to the Water gate eastward." The Water gate lay on the south side of the Court of the Women. From the Fountain gate the choir thus entered into

the Sanctuary, where it met the counter-choir.[1] But in order
to reach the Sanctuary in coming from Siloah, the choir must
first ascend the hill of Moriah ; the ascent to the *house* of
David,—which was situated, as is admitted by all, in the City
of David,—and consequently also the ascent to the *City* of
David, led thus from the Fountain Siloah up the Moriah hill.
There, accordingly, was the City of David situated. Nehemiah's
account thus perfectly tallies with that of the First Book of
Maccabees, with Josephus, and with Jewish tradition.   If
topographers have not been able to understand the description
given by Nehemiah, the ground thereof lies only and alone in
the baseless supposition that the City of David belongs to the
Upper City.

Here we might break off our argument, since our main
object—that of defining the position of the City of David—is
attained.   But since we are here pleading for a view which is
in direct contradiction with that hitherto accepted, it becomes
us to support it on every side by confirmatory testimony. For
this the narrative supplied by Nehemiah affords us the most
favourable occasion.   If this report, so clear in itself, has
hitherto occasioned such great difficulties to the interpreters,
the cause of this failure to understand it is to be sought only
in the hypothesis accepted by the topographers, that the City
of David was situated in the Upper City.   So soon as this
hypothesis is dismissed, and the true position is assigned to
the City of David on the southern Moriah, all difficulties
vanish, and a series of topographical points becomes perfectly
clear.   We proceed to furnish some illustrations.

The city, the house, and the sepulchres of David manifestly go together.   When David had captured the Jebusite
fortress, " he called it the City of David, and dwelt there."
David's house or palace was consequently within the fortress,
upon South Moriah.   So, too, we find it in Neh. xii. 37, where
it is said that " they went up from the Fountain gate over
against themselves"—that is to say, parallel with the route
previously taken from the Dung gate to the Fountain gate, but
in the opposite direction—" upon the steps of the City of
David, up the ascent of the wall to the house of David, to

[1] Neh. xii. 40.

the Water gate on the east." In the same locality, too, are the sepulchres of David shown to us.[1] We have already observed that the description of the restoration of the walls follows such direction as always to have Jerusalem on the left. The description of the southern wall advances thus from west to east. Now Nehemiah says that after Shallum—who built from the Fountain or Siloah gate to the ascent to the City of David — a Nehemiah Ben Asbuq built over against the sepulchres of David. It is self-evident that here, eastward from Siloah, the expression "over against the sepulchres of David" cannot mean "over against the Mosque En-Neby Daûd," the locality assigned by tradition to the said sepulchres, but points to Moriah itself, at the southern end of which the labour took place. And in point of fact the sepulchres of David *can* only be sought for in the City of David.[2]

The Horse gate.—We read, Neh. iii. 28, "The priests repaired above the Horse-gate, each before his house." The fact that the priests were building there shows that the place was within the precincts of the Sanctuary. The groups of labourers enumerated after Nehemiah Ben Asbuq bring us up to the east side of Moriah, as far as the eastern wall of the Temple Mount. There, in fact, must the Horse gate be sought, since it is called, Jer. xxxi. 40, "The Horse gate eastwards." It derived its name from the proximity of the royal stables. The entrance to this stabling was the triple gateway, discovered by de Saulcy,[3] which lies to the east of the double gate, and leads to the renowned subterranean edifices in which were the king's stables. So Felix Fabri terms them in the year 1495.[4] Benjamin a Tudelis says of them: "There, even at Jerusalem, in the house which was Solomon's, are the stables, ארוות הסוסים, which Solomon built; a solid edifice, of which the stones are very large, the like of which exists no longer on earth." A gate, of which the traces are still distinctly visible, led out of these stables and subterranean edifices at the south-east corner of the Haram, into the valley of the Kidron, and this is no other than the Horse gate. The discovery of this gate was made by Gadow, who regarded its projection as the

---

[1] Neh. iii. 16.

[2] 1 Kings ii. 10, and elsewhere.

[3] *Mer Morte*, ii. 202.

[4] Vol. ii. 125, 252.

arc of an ancient bridge.[1] De Saulcy more closely investigated
the matter.   At first he took it for the remains of a balcony ;
but later he became convinced it was a gate, the traces of
which appear not only outside the eastern wall of the Haram,
but also within in the substructures.[2] This Horse gate played
a part in Athaliah's tragic end.   In 2 Kings xi. 16 it is said
that they cast the queen forth from the Sanctuary, laid hands
on her, and made her go by the way which the horses of the
king go ; and slew her there.   The same fact is thus related :
" They laid hands on her ; and they went by the way of the
Horse gate of the king's house, and there they slew her." [3]
Josephus, _Antiq._ ix. 7, sec. 3, relates the history in this wise :
Jehoiada commanded to bring Athaliah into the valley of the
Kidron, that she might there be slain.   They thus laid hands
on her, and led her to the gate of the king's mules, and slew
her there.   Since the locality is now known to us, this history
is explained to us with dramatic force.   Athaliah was cast
through the double gate out of the Sanctuary—not, however,
into the palace lying right before her, but was led round by
the left, through the triple gate into the stables, and out from
them through the Horse gate into the valley of the Kidron.

Ophel.—In Neh. iii. 27 the wall of Ophel is mentioned
immediately before the Horse gate ; the place thus lay upon
the eastern declivity of southern Moriah, and probably drew
its water supply from the Fountain of the Virgin.   There
dwelt the Nethinim or slaves of the sanctuary, iii. 26.   The
place seems—as was usual in the case of slave quarters—to
have been encompassed with a wall, and to have been shut
off from the Lower City proper.   This place is probably the
one intended in Joseph. _de Bello_, vi. 6, sec. 3, where it is said,
that with the Lower City were burnt " the lanes, στενωποί,
and the houses which were filled with the corpses of those
who had died from famine."

13*b*. That which has been already said serves to show
that _Moria extra muros_ was formerly one of the quarters of
the city, namely the Lower City ; and that in ancient time a
peculiar importance attached to this part, notwithstanding the

---

[1] Ritter, _Palestine_, iv. 46 of Engl. trans.   [2] _Voyage en Terre Sainte_, i. 130.
[3] 2 Chron. xxiii. 15.

smallness of its extent. Whilst the Upper City and the
Suburb (Fore City) constituted the civil city, the Lower City
was the city of the kings. For in this was, before the exile,
the royal fortress, the royal palace, the arsenal, the barracks,
and the royal tombs. Of all these monuments the name,
cleaving to the locality, had preserved itself until the time of
Nehemiah.[1] At the time of Josephus there was in this quarter
the Council House, the Archeion, the palace of Helena and
that of her son Monobazus, and a row of houses facing the
Upper City. For all these does the southern Moriah afford
the necessary space—but not for more. It is a long, narrow
extent of rock, flat at the top, but falling precipitously on the
sides, the east especially, whose ridge descends rapidly towards
the south, in terrace-like platforms. The length of it from
the south wall of the Aksa Garden to the Siloah Fountain
amounts, according to Robinson,[2] to 1550 feet; the width
from brow to brow, taken in the middle of the ridge, to 290
feet. From the south wall of the Aksa Garden to the temple
area there are, according to de Saulcy, 90 mètres = about
300 feet English; the upper terrace, the garden of the Aksa
included, is about 600 feet wide. The whole area of southern
Moriah thus amounts to about 107,500 square mètres ($= 10\frac{3}{4}$
hectares), or $26\frac{1}{2}$ acres English. The southern Moriah thus
affords the space necessary for the edifices of the Lower City.

14. We have until now been occupied in showing that the
Lower City was situated on the southern part of Moriah; that
upon the rocky ridge thereof once rose the Syrian Acra, which
Antiochus Epiphanes had built in place of the City of David.
With regard to all this we are in contradiction with most
topographers, who, with the exception of the Upper City,
regard the whole remainder of Jerusalem, with the Fore City
and New City, as the Lower City; place the City of David in
the Upper City, and seek the Acra in any spot that may commend itself to them in their hypothetical Lower City.

The reason why, in opposition to all the texts, they place
the City of David in the Upper City, is twofold. First, they

[1] Neh. iii. 16 sqq., xii. 37 sqq.
[2] Robinson, i. 267. [The southern end of the ridge is "a rocky bluff, forty or
fifty feet above the Pool of Siloam." *Idem.* Cf. Ritter, iv. 47, 48.]

assume without proof the identity of the south - west hill, called by modern tradition Zion, with the Mount Zion of the Old Testament; but since it is said in the Old Testament that Zion is the City of David, they place the latter upon this south-west hill. We shall presently subject this matter to a critical examination. It must at any rate be admitted that a tradition is to be rejected when it conflicts with definite texts, like those above adduced. Then, secondly, they appeal to Josephus, de Bello, v. 4, sec. 1, where it is said of the hill of the Upper City, " on account of its strength it was called by David, Phrurion," φρούριον μὲν ὑπὸ Δαβίδου τοῦ βασιλέως ἐκαλεῖτο. They explain these words as though it were written φρούριον Δαβίδου, Phrurion of David, i.e. City of David. In opposition to this, however, it is to be observed, first, that Josephus means to say the Upper City was called before the exile, from the time of David downwards, simply " Phrurion ; " but after the exile was called the " Upper Market." Further, he himself calls the City of David πόλις Δαβίδ,[1] and he would certainly have made use of the same expression here, and not have called the place φρούριον, if he had intended to speak of the City of David. We have seen that Josephus elsewhere identifies the City of David with the Acra, and places the Acra in the Lower City. From this fundamental error—the separation of the City of David from the Acra— is alone to be explained the topographical curiosity, that the Acra, like the wandering Jew, can nowhere find a permanent abode. There is not a corner in Jerusalem to which some topographer or another has not sought to bring down the Acra ; and always has it been found possible to adduce sufficient reasons for again removing it, and declaring the place to be impossible. We sum up at this point the conditions a place must fulfil, in order that it may bear the name of Acra.

Acra is identical with the City of David.

It was situated in the Old City, enclosed by the first and oldest wall ; because the Jebusite fortress is to be sought not in a Fore City or New City, which had sprung up in later time, but in the original Jerusalem.

---

[1] Antiq. vii. 3, sec. 2.

It was situated near to the Sanctuary.

The place on which it stood must, in the present day, form with the Temple Mountain one connected hill, and must be lower than the Sanctuary.

It must be divided from the Upper City by a valley—Tyropœon.

To these conditions the southern Moriah alone corresponds. All other proposed sites lie either outside of the Old City, or else higher than the temple area, or at least as high as it.

15. **Zion.**[1] Topographers, relying on the authority of tradition, are unanimous in calling the south-west hill or Upper City—as well the part enclosed within the present walls, as the part lying outside the same—"Mount Zion." This opinion is now to be critically examined.

In the historical books of the Old Testament the name of Zion occurs only twice—2 Sam. v. 7, where it is said, "David took the stronghold of Zion, which is the City of David;" and 1 Kings viii. 1 (2 Chron. v. 2), where it is said that the Ark of the Covenant was brought into the newly-erected temple, "out of the City of David, which is Zion." In each of these passages Zion is identical with the City of David: in the latter it is definitely distinguished from the temple. In the First Book of the Maccabees, on the other hand, Zion is formally distinguished from the City of David or the Acra; for while the Syrians garrisoned the Acra, i.e. the City of David,[2] the Jews held possession of Zion.[3] The name Zion seems thus, in the course of time, to have been transferred to another locality; and for this reason, if for no other, topographers should have avoided employing this term, after the example of Josephus, who entirely ignores it. In so far, then, as Zion is synonymous with the City of David, it belongs manifestly to the southern hill of Moriah, and by no means to the Upper City. But where was the Zion of the Maccabees, distinguished from the City of David? In 1 Macc. vi. 61, 62 we read, Antiochus entered into Mount Zion, and saw the

---

[1] See also the author's article, "Zion und die Akra," in *Theol. Studien und Kritiken*, 1864, ii. 309 ff.

[2] 1 Macc. i. 33, and elsewhere.   [3] 1 Macc. iv. 37, vi. 48.

fortifications of the place; then he broke his oath, and commanded to pull down the walls round about.   Josephus, who
relates the same history of the Maccabees in language of often
verbal agreement, says:[1] "The Jews received the oath and
evacuated the Sanctuary (τὸ ἱερόν), and Antiochus went into the
same (εἰς αὐτὸ, sc. τὸ ἱερόν); but when he saw how strong the
place was, he broke the oath, and commanded tŏ demolish the
walls to the ground." That which is said, 1 Macc. vi. 62, of
Zion, Josephus says of the Sanctuary.—In 1 Macc. vii. 33 it
is said that Nicanor went up to Mount Zion, where the priests
showed him the sacrifices which they were offering for the
king.   According to Josephus,[2] Nicanor came down from the
Acra into the Sanctuary, where the offerings for the king
were shown him.   It is self-evident that the Book of Maccabees understands by Zion the fortified Sanctuary, for only
in the Sanctuary could sacrifices be shown.   That at that
time the Sanctuary was a fortress garrisoned by the Jews, is
said not only in Josephus, but also 1 Macc. vi. 26, ὅτι τὸ
ἀγίασμα ... ὠχύρωσαν.   If, then, Zion had been distinguished
from the Sanctuary, the Jews would—according to the Book
of the Maccabees—have possessed two fortresses at Jerusalem,
namely, Zion *and* the Sanctuary.   This, however, is not only
in the highest degree improbable, the Jews then being so
greatly depressed; but it would also be purely inexplicable
that Josephus should know nothing of it, and yet more
inexplicable that he should transfer to the Sanctuary that
which the other says of Zion.   Zion and Sanctuary cannot
possibly in this history be distinguished the one from the
other: in the Book of the Maccabees the two names are
synonymous.   At the time of the Jebusites, Zion was the
name of the whole of Moriah; a definite point, a towering
peak of rock, was called "Fortress of Zion."   When this
fortress received the new name of City of David, the name
Zion was exclusively confined to the northern part of the
Moriah ridge—the Sanctuary.   In this way the whole problem is solved.   It is well known that in the Psalms and
Prophets the name Zion signifies the Sanctuary.   "Jehovah
dwelleth in Zion."[3]   "Jehovah hath chosen Zion, desired it

[1] *Antiq.* xii. 9, sec. 7.   [2] *Antiq.* xii. 10, sec. 5.   [3] Joel iii. 21.

for His habitation : ' This is my rest for ever.' "[1]   In all such
places Zion is specially the Sanctuary ; and if in the case of
some few others—*e.g.* Ps. lxix. 35, lxxvi. 2 ; Isa. xlix. 14 ;
Jer. xxxi. 12—this name seems to designate the whole of
Jerusalem, it is nevertheless always with the accessory idea
of the Holy City, the City of God or the Church, of which
the centre was precisely the House of God upon the literal
Zion.

16. Since we have now discovered the true site of the
O. T. Zion, a multitude of passages admit of an explanation,
—passages which have hitherto been a source of acknowledged perplexity to interpreters.   We mention the most
important of these, because they strongly confirm the conclusion we have reached with regard to the position of Zion.
In Isa. xiv. 13 the king of Babylon is represented as saying,
" I will dwell upon the Mount of the Assembly, on the side of
the north," צפון בירכתי.   The signification of these words is
explained in ver. 14, where the king of Babylon adds : " I
shall be like the Most High."   The meaning of the words is,
he would seat himself in the temple in the place of God.   As
victorious over the king of Judah, he had the right to dwell
in the City of David, in the royal palace ; this lay upon the
south side of the Mount of the Assembly ; but inasmuch as
he will dwell upon the north side of this mountain, he con-
templates treating not only the king of Judah, but also
Jehovah Himself, as vanquished.   This passage of the prophet
affords the key to the right understanding of Ps. xlviii. 1, 2.
There it is said : " Great is Jehovah, and greatly to be praised ;
in the city of our God, in the mountain of His holiness.   Fair
towers aloft, the joy of the whole earth, Mount Zion, on the
north side of the city of the mighty King," קרית צפון ירכתי ציון הר
רב מלך.   The city of the great King is the City of David, which
lay upon the south side of the mountain ; the north side of this
Mount Zion, and the north side of the City of David, is the
Sanctuary of Jehovah.   All this is in perfect harmony with
the topographical position of both places.   But, since this
grammatically accurate translation could not be reconciled

---

[1] Ps. cxxxii. 13, 14.   Cf. Ps. xx. 2, 3, lxv. 1, lxxxiv. 7, l. 2, [Jer. xxxi. 6],
and other places.

with the received opinion as to the position of the above-
mentioned localities, it was proposed to read: " Mount Zion,
whose north side is the city of the great King." We maintain
our translation, however, in favour of which we can adduce
philologists like Aben-Ezra, Lightfoot, Winer (*Real Wörter-
buch, s.v.* " Zion ").—In Ezek. xl. 2 it is related that the prophet,
in a vision, was set upon a high mountain,—according to ver.
3, it was the mountain of the Sanctuary,—upon it was " as it
were a frame (structure) of a city on the south." From this
it follows that south from the Sanctuary, upon the part of
Moriah now lying outside the walls, was a city—namely, the
city *par excellence, i.e.* the City of David. But one of the most
important passages is Ezek. xliii. 7–9, in which it is said :
" My holy name shall the house of Israel no more defile, they
nor their kings, by their whoredom, by the carcases of their
kings, their high places, *in that they set their threshold to my
threshold, and their door to my door, so that only a wall is
between me and them.*" Thus God's sanctuary and the palace
of the kings had threshold to threshold, door to door ; only a
wall was between them. This corresponds perfectly to our
topographical presentation, and can by no means be made to
harmonize with the supposition of a Zion and a City of David
upon the hill of the Upper City.

17. Until now we have concerned ourselves only with the
Biblical texts, without taking great notice of the Christian
tradition prevailing in the present day. We have now to
turn our attention to this latter.

Modern topographers are unanimous in regarding the hill
of the Upper City as Mount Zion and the City of David, and
rest their view upon the support of Church tradition. A high
degree of antiquity cannot be denied to this latter, but to the
primitive age of Christianity it does not extend. We have
subjected this matter to a thorough, detailed examination, and
are in a position to prove that in Christian antiquity Zion
was, in accordance with the Biblical representation, the
southern hill of the Moriah.—There was situated the Holy
Zion Church, which was no other than the magnificent ancient
substructures of the Aksa Mosque, behind the double gate—
buildings belonging in part to the age of Solomon. When, in

the year A.D. 637, the Mahommedans captured Jerusalem, they took possession of the temple area, which they occupied exclusively for their purposes of worship. That which is to be found within this area in the present day consists mainly of two sanctuaries—namely, the Mosque es-Sukhrah, a magnificent circular building standing in the midst of the sacred enclosure, and covering the sacred rock; and the Mosque el-Aksa at the south end of the area, built over the Salomonic substructures which stand in close connection with the double gate. The earlier topographers, Robinson and others, regarded the Mosque es-Sukhrah—which they also call the Mosque of Omar—as a Saracenic edifice, and the Aksa as originally a Christian church. More recent investigations, however, have thoroughly proved that the converse is the case. The Aksa is by no means a Christian, but a purely Saracenic edifice ; and the circular structure of the Mosque es-Sukhrah is the celebrated Basilica of the Theotokos, erected by the Emperor Justinian.[1] The edifice of the Zion Church, which for five centuries consisted of the substructures of the temple area, as well as the sumptuous temple of Justinian, which probably, as the parish church, took the place of the other, were wrenched from the Christians by the Moslem ; the circular building became a mosque, and the substructures were built over by the Aksa Mosque, with which they have been incorporated as a crypt, and remain so even to the present day. The Zion congregation, deprived of its church, fixed its abode on the hill of the Upper City *extra muros*, either building there the church which is now the en-Neby Daûd, or else taking possession of this structure already to hand. With the congregation the name, too, of Church of Zion and Mount Zion passed over to this place and the south-west hill, where it has preserved itself to the present day.[2] It is possible that even earlier than this, almost at the beginning of the second century, from the time of Hadrian, the name of Zion, which certainly

---

[1] Comp. on this subject, Sepp, *Neue architechton. Studien*, p. 25 ff., 45 ff. ; De Saulcy, *Voyage*, etc.

[2] Such migrations of names in Jerusalem are not rare. St. Stephen's gate was once the Damascus gate, and is now the Bâb Sitti Mariam. San Salvator was once in the Upper City, and is now near the Holy Sepulchre. The *Via Dolorosa* once ran from the tower of David, now from Antonia ! (Later note of author.)

belonged to the southern hill of Moriah, was also given to the hill of the Upper City *extra muros*—in other words, that the Christians called all the ground of the ancient Jerusalem which was cut off on the south side by the walls of Hadrian, as by the present walls, Zion. Any kind of proof for this hypothesis is, nevertheless, wanting to us. One might perhaps understand in this sense that which Eusebius says of Golgotha in the *Onomasticon*, that this, the place of the crucifixion of the Lord, was to the north of Mount Zion—Γολγοθᾶ . . . πρὸς τοῖς βορείοις τοῦ Σιὼν ὄρους ; but Eusebius determines the position of a locality exclusively according to the four cardinal points, and could not thus indicate the position of the garden of the Aksa, to the S.S.E., otherwise than he has here done.

18. From the time when the Mahommedans first took possession of the Temple Mountain, the south-west hill has been constantly known, in agreement with modern tradition, as Mount Zion. The earliest Christian pilgrim of this period is, if we mistake not, Arculf, who visited the Holy City about A.D. 670, thus nearly 50 years after the capture of Jerusalem by the Saracens. This pilgrim says of the *Porta David*, by which name he means the modern Jaffa gate, that it lies on the west side of Mount Zion.[1] It is remarkable that Willibald, who journeyed to the Holy City about the year 728 expressly and frequently says of the Church of Zion that it was situated in the midst of Jerusalem.[2] But though the name Zion had already at that period forsaken its original locality, and migrated to the western hill, yet the Church of Zion upon this hill does not seem to have been always the same. At the time of the Crusades all wavering in this respect comes to an end. William of Tyre says :[3] "Horum (montium) alter, ab occidente Syon appellatur, alter vero, qui ab oriente, Moria appellatur." With like distinctness speaks Saewulf, who was in Jerusalem about 1103. Of the Church of the Holy Sepulchre, and even of all Jerusalem, he says that

[1] Porta David, ad occidentalem partem montis Sion.

[2] *Cap.* 18 . . . ad illam ecclesiam, quæ vocatur Sion ; illa stat in medio Hierusalem ; and *cap.* 19, S. Maria in illo loco in medio Hierusalem exivit de hoc sæculo, qui nominatur sancta Sion.

[3] *Gesta Dei*, i. 747.

they are situated on the northern slope of Zion;[1] and of the Church of the Holy Ghost, that it is outside the city, a dart's throw from the southern wall,[2] by which, beyond doubt, en-Neby Daûd is intended. Thus the matter has remained until the present day, with this difference, that in the course of time tradition has gradually enriched this new Zion with the single objects of veneration which belonged to the genuine Zion. Arculf pointed out, in his Church of the Holy Spirit, the place where the Lord instituted the Supper, where the Holy Ghost descended upon the apostles, where Mary died, and where was the column at which the Lord was scourged. At the time of the Crusades there was added the grave of David, the house of Pilate, and the place where the Risen One first appeared to His disciples, which place was called by them Galilæa. It is further to be observed that the Crusaders attached to the Mosque es-Sukhrah the name *Templum Domini*, and to the Aksa Mosque, with its substructures, the name *Templum* or *Palatium Salomonis*. Tradition has not, however, entirely forgotten the originally Christian character of the substructures at the south side of the Haram, since even to this day the cradle of Christ is shown in the subterranean chamber of the south-east corner.

19. Let us now see what the Church fathers and pilgrims of the pre-Saracen period have to relate touching Mount Zion. Jerome says, on *Matth.* x., " ad radices montis Moria, in quibus Siloë fluit ;" and on *Isa.* viii. 6, "Siloë fontem esse ad radices montis Sion dubitare non possumus, nos præsertim, qui in hac habitamus provincia." If, according to this Father, Siloa issues from Moriah and Zion, Moriah and Zion must be one and the same mountain. According to Jerome, the hill from which Siloah springs is Zion. But this fountain comes by a subterranean canal from the Fountain of the Virgin on the eastern hill ;[3] this eastern hill is therefore the Zion of Jerome, as of the Old Testament. Had Jerome understood by Zion, in the place cited, the hill of the Upper City, he would have

---

[1] Ista ecclesia, scil. s. Sepulchri, est in declivio montis Syon, sicut civitas.

[2] Ecclesia Spiritus sancti in monti Syon extra murum ad austrum, quantum potest projici sagitta.

[3] [Cf. Isa. viii. 6, where the meaning is well given by Andrew Bonar : " waters of Siloah, that flow *unperceived*." *Narrative*, p. 155.]

been guilty of a glaring inaccuracy in placing the fountain in this locality, and that precisely where he vouches for the correctness of his datum on the ground of his special acquaintance with the district—dubitare non possumus, præsertim nos, qui in hac habitamus provincia. The Siloah flows indeed into the Tyropœon, but not from the foot of the hill of the Upper City. Of the greater *Piscina Siloë*, he might certainly have said, that it lies at the foot of the hill of the Upper City ; but not of the fountain. The same Father says, *Ep.* 30, *de Assumtione*, that the *Sepulchrum* of the Holy Virgin Mary is " in vallis Jesaphat medio, inter montem Sion et montem Olivetum." But the tomb of the Virgin lies close to Gethsemane, between the Mount of Olives and the Temple Mountain ; this latter therefore is called by Jerome " Mount Zion." The same Church Father says of Paula : Unde (sepulchro resurrectionis) egrediens, ascendit Sion, quæ in arcem vel speluncam vertitur. *Hanc* urbem quondam expugnavit et reædificavit David. De expugnata scribitur, " Væ tibi Ariël, id est leo Dei, et quondam fortissima, quam expugnavit David."[1] Et de ea, quæ ædificata est, dictum est, "Fundamenta ejus in montibus sanctis, diligit Dominus portas Sion super omnia tabernacula Jacob."[2] . . . Ostenditur illic columna ecclesiæ porticum sustinens, infecta cruore Domini, ad quam vinctus dicitur flagellatus. Monstratur locus, ubi super CXX. credentium animas Spiritus sanctus descendisset. The rendering of the word Zion by " Fortress or Cave," implies that Zion presents both : a fortress, the city of David, and a cave—the Church of Zion, in the substructures of the Haram under El-Aksa, behind the double gate. Here the celebrated *Columna porticum sustinens ecclesiæ* is still found in the present day. The " foundations of Zion upon the holy mountains " point to Moriah, and not to the hill of the Upper City. Ariel is both the City of David[3] and the altar of burnt-offering ;[4] both which characteristics must therefore belong to the same hill. Everything points to Moriah, and nothing to the hill of the Upper City. What, again, did Paula find on Zion ? She saw there, supporting the portico of a church, a pillar, on which

[1] Isa. xxix. 1.   [2] Ps. lxxxvii. 1, 2.
[3] Isa. xxix. 1.   [4] Ezek. xliii. 15 (margin).

T

the Lord is said to have been scourged; she saw, moreover, the place of the outpouring of the Holy Ghost. But this was, as we shall presently see, the Church of Zion, so greatly celebrated in Christian antiquity. Whoever so acquainted with Jerome's archæological learning and love of truth, will acknowledge that he allowed himself to become the channel of such traditions, only when he was fully assured that pillar, portico, and church were not the handiwork of Christians, but indisputable remains of a Jewish structure, which had survived the destruction of Jerusalem. He could have before his eye only the purely Jewish substructures of the Aksa Mosque, with their mighty pillar—behind the double gate— which supports the portico ; and not the manifestly Christian structure of the Mosque en-Neby Daûd upon the S.W. hill, which is wanting in any trace of remote antiquity.

The Pilgrim of Bordeaux, who visited Jerusalem in the year 333, thus fifty years before Jerome, speaks of the statues of Hadrian on the site of the old Jewish temple, and afterwards says, " est et non longe de statuis lapis pertusus, ad quem veniunt Judæi singulis annis ut unguent eum et lamentant se cum genitu et vestimenta sua scindunt, et sic redeunt. Est *ibi* et domus Ezechiæ regis Judæ." That this perforated stone, *lapis pertusus*, is not the rocky cave under the temple, but the present wailing place of the Jews, is evident from the fact that the *lapis pertusus*, if not far removed from the site of the temple, was yet at any rate at some distance from it—*est non longe de Statuis*. The wailing place of the Jews, situated down in the Tyropœon valley, in the Haram wall near to the S.W. corner, presents several niches in the old Salomonic wall, of which one is about four feet high. This is the *lapis pertusus*, the object of the special veneration of the Jews. " Lapis " never denotes a natural rock rooted to the soil, but a detached stone ; a natural rock with a cave in it of magnificent proportions is never, even in the worst ecclesiastical Latin, called a " perforated stone," *lapis pertusus*. The Pilgrim had consequently descended through a gate in the Haram, from the site of the statues, into the Tyropœon—the present as well as the former wailing place of the Jews—and stood thus within the Dung gate. His account immediately after continues thus : " Item exeuntibus Hierusalem,[1] ut ascendas Sion, in parte sinistra et deorsum in valle juxta murum est piscina, quæ dicitur Silua.   Habet quadriporticum, et alia piscina grandis foras.   Hæc fons sex diebus atque noctibus currit; septima vero die est sabbatum, in totum nec nocte nec die currit." The rendering of this barbarous Latin turns on the meaning given to the words *exeuntibus Hierusalem.* The translation, according to the text here adopted, would be : In going out of Jerusalem, in order to ascend Zion, there is on the left hand and down in the valley by the wall, a pool called Siloah, etc.   The Pilgrim was, as we have seen, at the wailing place of the Jews, and by Hezekiah's palace (El-Mekmeh ?) within the Dung gate.   In order to reach Siloah, he must thus go out of the city.   And that the Pilgrim in reality went out is manifest from the succession of the *piscinæ*, since he came first to the smaller one—the fountain basin itself—and then farther on (*foras*) to the greater one [*En-Rogel*] ; for in this order do the two pools succeed each other from north to south.   If the Pilgrim had come up the valley of the Tyropœon from the south, he would have had the hill of the Upper City, and consequently his Zion, on the left ; if he came out of the city and down the Tyropœon, he had Moriah on his left, and this was his Zion.   Let us see now what he found on Zion.   " In eadem (sc. fonte ; he writes immediately before : hæc fons) ascenditur Sion, et paret ubi fuit Domus Caïfæ sacerdotis, et columna adhuc ibi est, in qua Christum flagellis ceciderunt.   Intus autem intra murum Sion paret locus ubi palatium habuit David, et septem Synagogæ quæ illic fuerunt, una tandem remansit, reliquæ autem arantur et seminantur, sicut Jesajas propheta dixit." [2]   If we suppose now, with most topographers, that the Pilgrim, starting from Siloah, climbed the hill of the Upper City, it is at once surprising that he should say " in eadem, sc. fonte, ascenditur Sion ; " for the fountain would all the while be lying on the opposite side of the valley.   He next came to the place where the palace of

---

[1] We follow the text of the oldest MS., belonging to the eighth century, printed in the *Revue Archéologique*, 1864, Juillet, p. 98 sqq.   The reading of the ordinary editions—exeuntibus *in* Hierusalem—yields no intelligible sense.

[2] [The reference here is to Mic. iii. 12, as cited by Jeremiah, chap. xxvi. 18.]

the high priest Caiaphas once stood. This is again surprising; for the palace of the high priest was near to the Sanctuary, upon the eastern hill or Moriah.[1] He found, moreover, near or in the house of Caiaphas the pillar at which the Lord was scourged, yet standing—consequently the remains of an old Jewish building, of which neither in En-Neby Daûd, nor in the so-called house of Caiaphas, on the S.W. hill *extra muros*, a trace is to be found. All this, it is to be observed, Caiaphas' house and the pillar, existed according to our Pilgrim, outside the city wall. He now mentions what was to be found within the city wall. He found there nothing but an old synagogue; the rest was ploughed fields! Thus upon the hill of the Upper City, within the city wall—intus, intra murum—where is now one of the most populous quarters, there was anno 333 nothing but an old synagogue? Not even the tower of David? It must after all be confessed that the Pilgrim of Bordeaux did not mean the western hill in thus speaking of Zion.—Let us now suppose that, coming from the city, he went down the Tyropœon; he found there, as the text asserts, on the left hand, down in the valley, Siloah; he went up the slope of Moriah, by the route still frequented, which passes near to the fountain, " in eadem fonte ascenditur Sion;" came next to the place where, according to Neh. iii. 21, stood the house of the high priest; saw, within the substructures of the Haram, behind the double gate, the gigantic pillar; on his left was the ancient well of the garden of the Aksa Mosque, which is just the wall of Zion or the City of David; there he found an old synagogue, which seems now to have disappeared; the rest within these bounds was tilled land then, as in the present day. From this it follows that the Pilgrim of Bordeaux, like Jerome, regarded the upper terrace of southern Moriah as Zion. In like manner, too, does Eusebius of Cæsarea say, on Isa. xxii. 1, that the temple was built upon Zion (Σιών . . . ἐφ' οὗ ὁ Νεὼς τοῦ Θεοῦ ᾠκοδόμητο), and so also Athanasius on Psalm lxxxvii.

Aurelius Prudentius Clemens wrote in the year 394:

> Excidio templi veteris stat pinna superstes :
> Structus enim *lapide ex illo* manet *angulus*, usque

---

[1] Neh. iii. 21.

In sæcula Sæculi, *quem sprerunt ædificantes.*
Nunc caput est Templi et laterum compago duorum.

The stone thus, which the builders had rejected, and which is become the corner-stone, existed, according to early Christian tradition, in a corner of the wall belonging to the Sanctuary, which had survived the destruction. There is nothing unwarranted in the supposition that the south-east corner of the Haram is intended, in which enormous stones form the foundation. Of this stone, which had become the corner-stone, the Pilgrim of Bordeaux also gives an account. He, too, places it within the precincts of the temple, and, moreover, brings it into connection with the pinnacle of the temple upon which the tempter had placed Him. After he had described the Pool of Bethesda,[1] he says: " Est ibi et crypta, ubi Salomon Dæmones torquebat. Ibi est angulus turris excelsissimæ, ubi dominus ascendit ; . . . Ibi est lapis angularis magnus, de quo dictum : 'lapidem quem reprobaverunt ædificantes.' Item ad caput angeli [2] et sub pinna turris ipsius sunt cubicula plurima, ubi Salomon palatium habebat ; ibi etiam constat cubiculus, in quo sedit et sapientiam descripsit, ipse vero cubiculus uno lapide est tectus ; sunt ibi et excepturia magna aquæ subterraneæ et piscinæ magno opere ædificatæ, et in æde ipsa ubi templum fuit quod Salomon ædificavit, etc. . . . Sunt ibi statuæ duæ Adriani ; est et non longe de statuis lapis pertusus." The text then continues in the form in which we have treated of it in the preceding section. That the passage adduced places us in the area of the Sanctuary does not admit of doubt. That the palace of Solomon and the cubicula plurima are the substructures in the south-east corner must in like manner be admitted. Thus the pinnacle of the south-east corner is regarded as the place of temptation ; and in its basis is seen the *lapis angularis,* as is the case with Prudentius. That which has been hitherto related could be seen and visited by the Pilgrim without forsaking the Haram, since a subterranean passage with stairs leads down to those substructures. The approach to the vaulted chamber, which is connected with the double gate, was, however, at that time—probably from

---

[1] He writes this name, Vetaida.   [2] *Read* anguli.

strategetical considerations—blocked up from above. The
Pilgrim was obliged, therefore, in order to enter upon the
Zion *extra muros*, to quit the Haram, to enter the Tyropœon
at the house of Hezekiah, and to pass out through the Dung
gate. Here, then, he relates, as we have seen in the preceding paragraph, the "exeuntibus Hierusalem, ut ascendas Sion,
in parte sinistra," and here met with that which we have seen
above.—Antoninus Martyr visited Jerusalem in the sixth
century. After speaking of the Turris David, he continues :
Deinde venimus *in Basilicam Sion*, ubi sunt mirabilia multa,
inter quæ est quod legitur *de lapide angulari* . . . Ingresso
Domino in ipsam ecclesiam, quæ fuit domus Jacobi, invenit
lapidem istum deformem in medio jacentem, tenuit eum et
posuit in angulum. . . . In ipsa ecclesia est *columna*, ubi
Dominus flagellatus est ; . . . ibi est monasterium puellarum.
De Sion usque ad basilicam Sanctæ Mariæ, ubi est congre-
gatio magna monachorum ac mulierum innumerabilis, lecta
languentium plus quinque (? quoque) millia ad minus tria.
Et oravimus in prætorio, etc. This text does not enable us
to discover which of the two hills Antoninus regarded as
Zion. That which immediately precedes the account of the
tower of David, would lead us to conclude it was the Upper
City ; that which immediately follows, on the other hand,
places us in the area of the temple, for the Basilica S. Mariæ
with its Xenodochium is unquestionably Justinian's temple of
the Θεοτόκος and the thereto appertaining Ξενῶνες. Antoninus' account must therefore be explained from the previous
accounts of Jerome, of the Burdigalensis, and of Prudentius,
who place the mirabilia here treated of, and in particular the
lapis angularis, upon Mount Moriah. That, moreover, the
Zion of Antoninus was the Temple Mountain, is evident from
the following datum : *Vallis Gethsemani inter montem Sion
et montem Oliveti posita.* Epiphanius of Eleutheropolis, who
belongs to the end of the fourth century, writes in his work
adv. Hœres.,[1] "The Acra, which was formerly upon Zion, but
is now removed, was then higher than Golgotha." Here thus
we find in a Church Father the assimilation of Zion with

---

[1] *Adv. Hœres.* 1. i. t. iii. ; *Hœres. Tatian*, 5 : ἡ Ἄκρα ἡ ποτὶ ὑπάρχουσα ἐν
Σιὼν, νῦν δὲ τμηθεῖσα, καὶ αὐτὴ ὑψηλοτέρα ὑπῆρχε τοῦ τόπου (Γολγοθᾶ).

Acra, the Lower City,[1] as already takes place in the First Book of Maccabees. The Zion of Epiphanius, therefore, cannot possibly be the hill of the Upper City.

In harmony, consequently, with the Old Testament, does the earliest Christian tradition place the City of David and Zion upon the Moriah *extra muros.* The tradition which places Zion upon the hill of the Upper City is thus of later origin.

20. **The Church of Zion.**—Among all Christian churches the Basilica upon Zion is unquestionably the oldest. Cyril of Jerusalem—about the year 330—relates (*Cateches.* xvi.): "We know that the Holy Ghost on the day of Pentecost, here at Jerusalem, in the *Upper Church of the Apostles,* descended upon the apostles." Epiphanius, who belongs to the end of the fourth century, writes :[2] " The Emperor Hadrian found the city of Jerusalem destroyed, the temple desolated and trodden under foot, with the exception of a few buildings and the *little church of God,* which existed at the place whither the disciples repaired after the Ascension of the Lord from the Mount of Olives, and went up into the upper room (τὸ ὑπερῷον). It stood upon that part of Zion which, with a few side buildings, and the seven synagogues—which stood upon the same hill like shepherds' tents—was all that remained of the city. One of these synagogues had continued standing till the time of Bishop Maximonas and of Constantine, 'as a hut in a vineyard.' " The congregation of this church had its burying-place, at the time of the Greeks, in the valley of Hinnom, where the inscription is often found upon sepulchral caves : † *THC AΓIAC CIΩN.* This church upon Zion is known also to Jerome.[3] He says : Ostenditur illic columna ecclesiæ porticum sustinens, infecta cruore Domini ; . . . monstratur locus, ubi super CXX. credentium animas Spiritus Sanctus descendisset. If men like Cyril, Jerome, and Epiphanius make themselves responsible for a tradition marking out in their day a certain church as that which the Lord Himself had entered, and in which the Pentecostal miracle had been witnessed, it must at any rate be admitted that the house so designated was an ancient

---

[1] See above, Appendix, No. 12.   [2] *De Ponderibus et Mensuris,* xiv.
[3] See above, No. 19.

Jewish structure, which could be shown to have survived the destruction of the city. These men, therefore, could not have before their mind En-Neby Daûd, upon the hill of the Upper City *extra muros*—a mosque which is evidently a church erected by the Christians, and not a Jewish structure. En-Neby Daûd, too, is a very large church, and, according to the authority last cited, the Church of the Apostles upon Zion was small. Jerusalem has three places of special sanctity for the Christians : the Holy Sepulchre, the scene of the Ascension, and the scene of the outpouring of the Holy Ghost. Constantine provided the two first places with sumptuous buildings, why not the third ? Manifestly because he did not presume to lay hands upon the sacred walls of the yet existing building. Now it is well known that the Church of the Holy Sepulchre and that of the Ascension have been several times destroyed and rebuilt. History records the destruction and rebuilding even of churches and chapels of lesser rank ; but nowhere is there an account of this kind concerning the Church of Zion. If this had been destroyed, history would have related it ; since it has not done so, we are perfectly justified in concluding that it is standing to the present day. It exists still in reality, in the substructures of the Haram under the Aksa Mosque upon the true Zion, that is to say, upon *Moria extra muros*.

21. In the southern wall of the Haram, which is—at least so far as its basement is concerned—confessedly of ancient Jewish origin, there is found somewhere about the middle an ancient double gate, now built up. It is partly concealed by the city wall from the south, which abuts upon it, and to the west of it encloses the garden of the Aksa. A grated window fitted in beneath the arch of the gate affords a glance into the vault behind. In the vicinity of the window one perceives a flight of eight stairs, leading from within to the double gate. A *colossal circular pillar*, of which the capital is adorned with palm leaves, supports, along with the pillars somewhat projecting on either side, the little cupola of the gate.[1] On the north front of the Aksa Mosque, which extends to a length of 280 English feet, there leads out from the inner

[1] Krafft, *Topogr.* 72.

area of the Haram a doubly vaulted passage, proceeding from north to south, under the said mosque, and ending at the double gate. Thick square pillars separate this passage from the parallel side corridor ; the latter maintaining a horizontal course, while the former continues to descend until it leads to a square chamber, in the midst of which rises majestically the monolith pillar, of which the capital is of remarkable formation, and strikingly reminds of the Egyptian style. Hebrew inscriptions—partly, alas ! plastered over—which are to be seen on the pillars and walls, prove beyond question the ancient Jewish origin of these structures.[1] This subterranean passage, 280 feet in length and 50 feet in width, is undoubtedly the connecting route formed by King Solomon between the City of David and the Sanctuary ; " the ascent which led up to the house of Jehovah," which the Queen of Sheba so greatly admired ; " the going up in the wall above the house of David." [2] On the eastern side of this corridor is found a door, at present walled up : this door leads to the mighty substructures at the south-east corner of the Haram. These substructures are vaults, resting upon fifteen rows of square pillars, composed of bevelled stones. They are about 300 feet broad from east to west, and extend from 1 to 300 feet from the south wall towards the north. These are the stables of Solomon, which had their outlet into the valley of the Kidron, at the " Horse gate " in the eastern wall, near to the south-east corner. Somewhere about midway between the south-east corner and the double gate is a triple gate, discovered by de Saulcy [3]—likewise of ancient origin—which seems by one of its openings to have led into the stables, while the two other doors led, and still lead, to the area of the temple.[4] The porch, supported by the colossal pillar, existing immediately behind the double gate, was the Church of the Apostles.

22. **The Portico of Solomon.**—" Now there came the

---

[1] Cf. de Saulcy, *Voyage*, ii. 327.   [2] 2 Chron. ix. 4 ; Neh. xii. 37.

[3] Josephus seems to presuppose the existence of these gates—the double and the triple gate—τὸ πρὸς μισημβρίαν (μέτωπον) εἶχι μὲν καὶ αὐτὸ πύλας κατὰ μέσον (*Antiq.* xv. 11, sec. 5).

[4] See on this question de Saulcy, *Voy.* i. 123 ff., and comp. Ritter, *Pal.* iv. 42, 43 (translation) ; Robinson, i. 302–306 ; Tristram, 183, 184.

Encœnia (feast of Dedication) in Jerusalem. It was winter; and Jesus walked in the Sanctuary, in the portico of Solomon."[1] We read in Acts iii. 11, that in consequence of the healing of the lame man at the Beautiful gate of the Sanctuary all the people ran together to Peter and John, as they walked in the portico of Solomon. And, Acts v. 12, we read: " By the hands of the apostles were wrought signs and wonders, many in number, among the people, and they (the Christians) were all with one accord in the portico of Solomon; but of the rest durst no man join himself to them." Where was this portico of Solomon? Josephus[2] speaks of the eastern portico of the outer Sanctuary, ἀνατολικὴ στοά, which rose above the deep (Kidron) valley, and had 400 cubits of wall. This does not mean, as it is ordinarily interpreted, that it was 400 cubits high, but 400 cubits—or one stadium—long, a length which Josephus gives to each side of the Sanctuary. "The wall was of white squared stones, which were 20 cubits long, and 6 high; it was the work of King Solomon, the first founder of the temple." Because Josephus here ascribes the eastern wall of the temple area to King Solomon, this name has been erroneously transferred to the portico which rises above it, and it has been asserted that this eastern stoa was the portico of Solomon mentioned in the N. T. The topographers forgot that Josephus does not say of the portico, that it is the work of Solomon, but of the wall. Had the portico borne that name, we may be sure Josephus would not have passed it over in silence; yet he calls it simply the eastern stoa. It is certain that in Josephus' day there no longer existed any such portico dating from the age of Solomon. That, however, which really was Solomon's work, and which has been preserved until that time, and even to the present day, is to be found in the substructures under the Aksa; the subterranean passage, especially, which led from the City of David into the Sanctuary; the corridor with the double gate. This we regard as the portico of Solomon: there Jesus walked in winter; because the cold did not penetrate into this crypt, and this must naturally be a frequented place of resort during

---

[1] John x. 22, 23.   [2] Josephus, *Antiq.* xx. 9, sec. 7.

the winter season. According to the Acts of the Apostles, they selected this place for holding their meetings ; this place we have accordingly to look upon as the scene of the outpouring of the Holy Ghost, as indeed early tradition asserts it was. The portico of Solomon became for later Christians the Church of Zion. We know not how to explain the origin of the tradition which represents this as the pillar of the scourging. The evangelists mention only the scourging in the prætorium. Does the tradition perhaps imply that the Lord was also scourged by the high priest, whose house was close at hand ? The *prætorium* is to be sought nowhere else than in the Antonia. This is evident from the indications of the Pilgrim of Bordeaux, who says : Inde, ut eas foris de Sion euntibus ad Portam Neapolitanam *ad partem dextram, deorsum in valle* sunt parietes ubi domus fuit sive *Prætorium Pontii Pilati ;* ibi Dominus auditus est antequam pateretur ; a sinistra autem parte est monticulus Golgotha, ubi Dominus crucifixus est ; inde quasi ad lapidis missum est cripta, ubi corpus ejus positum fuit. From Zion the Pilgrim entered the Tyropœon valley *intra muros*, went northwards towards the Neapolitan [Nablûs] or Damascus gate, and had below him in the valley,—*i.e.* at all events, in El-Wâd,—at a given point, the prætorium on the right, and Golgotha on the left. He had accordingly, passing along the western wall of the Haram, reached the north-west corner of the same—the site on which Antonia formerly stood. Those topographers who seek the prætorium in the Upper City must either leave this most important text entirely out of consideration, or do violence to it ; for the bearings on the right and left, and the *deorsum in valle*, do not agree with the position of the Upper City. Thus we recognise in the corridor under El-Aksa the Holy Church of Zion, the place of the outpouring of the Holy Ghost, the place where the Lord walked in Solomon's porch.

23. **Moria extra muros.**—That which has been already said sufficiently proves the archæological importance of the southern part of Moriah—a locality the topographers pass over in almost entire silence, or at best attach an historical significance to it only under the name of Ophel. It becomes necessary here, finally, to describe the place more nearly.

The southern wall of the Haram, which runs from east to west over the hill of Moriah, has a length of 840 feet. The south-east and south-west corners of the Haram wall confessedly present in the immense rough square stones, bevelled at the edges, the indisputable characteristics of the early Jewish style of building. The south wall which unites them bears the same stamp of antiquity. We do not hesitate therefore, with archæologists of note, such as M. de Saulcy and others, to regard it—at least in its foundation—as of Salomonic origin. In this wall there is to be found, 230 feet from its south-east corner, the triple gate above mentioned, which was discovered by de Saulcy. This gate, now built up, formerly led on the one hand into the Haram, and on the other into the royal stables. 500 feet west from this same east corner the present city wall impinges at right angles upon the wall of the Haram, and partly covers the double gate existing in the same at this point. Westwards from this gate, and the city wall abutting upon it, the Haram wall is continued in undeviating line to the south-west corner, near to which are found in the western wall the remains of the ancient bridge. In this southern wall not only are the lowest tiers of rectangular stones, but also the foundation of the gates, of decidedly early date. The upper parts are of a more or less recent origin—Roman or Saracenic. That part of the city wall which from the south abuts on the double gate is of later origin. It runs in a southerly direction from the Haram wall, but retreats in two sections to the west; after the second section, 85 feet south from the double gate, it runs again towards the south; and then—again turning west at a distance of 240 feet from the double gate—pursues a straight course to the Dung gate. The last portion of this wall running south, as well as part of that which is prolonged to the Dung gate, is again of ancient origin. Robinson[1] calculates the height of this wall at 60 feet; inasmuch as there are 8 courses of stones having an average thickness of at least 3 feet, and above these 24 courses each of 1 foot to $1\frac{1}{2}$ in thickness. From the double gate to the south-east corner of the garden wall and city wall, the ground of the plateau of Moriah sinks about 50 feet. Within the

[1] *Pal.* i. 285.

garden itself this depression does not take place, but the soil
there is perfectly level. It is at the lowest corner 50 feet
higher than the external ground. Robinson thinks this ground
has been artificially raised. But a filling up to a depth of
50 feet on this spot would be a surprising performance.
That such really was the case is for us in the highest degree
doubtful. On the contrary, we are convinced that excavations
will bring to light the natural rock at but a short distance
beneath the suface of the cultivated soil. For here, in this
garden of the Aksa,[1] must have been situated the Acra, the
hill of which was levelled by Simon Maccabæus, until it was
20 feet lower than the temple area. The zigzag-formed
modern fragment of wall, between this ancient wall at the
south of the garden and the double gate, marks the place of
the filled up valley, which probably had its upper commencement immediately to the west of this gate, and ran down
beside the Haram wall into the Tyropœon. The whole
garden, as well as the land contiguous to it on the west, is
almost a perfect plain—a plain reminding of the words of
Josephus, *de Bello*, v. 4, sec. 1 : "They filled up the valley,
with a view to bringing the (Upper) City into connection
with the Sanctuary ; " for from the Xystus one may reach the
double gate by a level route.[2] The summit of the Acra or
City of David, of which there remains now only a filling up
of 50 feet in depth within the ancient garden wall, may have
risen at one time yet 50 feet above the level of the garden.
If, as is probable, it was surrounded on the four sides by a
wall, of which the south-east corner of the garden wall may
be the remains, it presented a tower or fortress of about 100
feet high, with a basis of 150 feet square, which was unassailable for the instruments of siege known to the ancients,[3]
since at the most accessible point—in the vicinity of the
double gate—it rose to a sheer elevation of 60 feet. Such a

---

[1] This garden is still, according to Wilson, called *Hakûrat* el-Khatûniye—a
title in which is to be recognised an echo of the old name *Acra*. Even though
"Hakûra" might signify "ruin," this signification does not apply in the
case of the Aksa Garden, where the ruin is wanting.

[2] Captain Warren's excavations, moreover, prove the existence, at the south-
west end of the Haram, of a mass of refuse of about 50 feet in thickness. (Later
note of author.)   [3] 2 Sam. v. 6-8.

position of the Acra explains how perilous a hostile garrison
might become to the Jews entering the Temple through the
double gate; because the Acra was situated so near at hand,
and towered above the Sanctuary. Such a rocky fortress had
in any case but one entrance; it required, therefore, only a
little piece of wall to close up the egress of the garrison, and
to reduce them by famine. This Simon really did: " he built
through the midst of the city a wall, in order to cut off from
those in the Acra the market or supply of provisions." [1]

The sepulchres of the Davidic kings were in the rock of the
City of David upon Zion-Moriah; [2] when the rock was lowered
they necessarily disappeared. Without any mention of the
fact on the part of the historian, we may infer with certainty
that the sarcophagi and bodies were deposited in another
grave; that the newly-erected monument was raised outside
the city, follows from Ezek. xliii. 7–9; that it was prepared
with royal splendour is only what was to be expected. Now
there is to the north of Jerusalem a monument worthy of the
kings of Judah—the Tombs of the Kings, with their twenty-
six sepulchral chambers. A sarcophagus from the same was
brought by M. de Saulcy to Paris, and placed in the Museum
of the Louvre. It bears, in Samaritan (ancient Jewish)
characters, the inscription צרה מלכה or צדה,—and not, as de
Saulcy would read, מלכתה,—and underneath, scratched in
Hebrew letters, צרה מלכתה. This shows that at the time of
the removal of the coffins in the Maccabæan age the names
were added in later Hebrew characters for the guidance of the
labourers ignorant of the ancient Hebrew writing. That at
the time of Hyrcanus the Tombs of David were no longer in
the City of David, but outside of Jerusalem, follows to a
certainty, from the fact that, according to *Antiq.* xiii. 8, secs. 3,
4, Hyrcanus did not at once take out of the Tomb of David
the ransom price promised to Antiochus, who was laying siege
to him, but must first await the departure of the enemy before
he could obtain access to the treasure contained in the sepulchre.
The Tombs of the Kings, north of Jerusalem, are thus in
reality the posthumous graves of the Davidic kings, from the
time of the levelling of the Acra rock.

[1] *Antiq.* xiii. 5, sec. 11. [2] Neh. iii. 16.

Thus, too, we are in a position to explain the course of the aqueduct of Hezekiah. We read, 2 Chron. xxxii. 30, " This same Hezekiah stopped the upper water-spring of Gihon, and conducted it straight, by the west side, to the City of David." Now Antoninus Martyr says of the Church of the Holy Sepulchre : Juxta ipsum altare est crypta, ubi ponis aurem et audis flumina aquarum, et jacta pomum et vadis ad Siloa fontem ubi illud recipies. Inter Siloa et Golgotha credo esse milliarium. Similar reports are afloat in the present day, to the effect that if you put your ear to the earth in the vicinity of the Damascus gate, you will hear the sound of water. Not long ago in El-Wâd, in digging for a foundation, there was opened an arched roof, which covers a well-supplied channel of water. The water-course along the west side of the Haram, which feeds Turkish baths, has long been known,[1] and it has been shown that the water has the same sweetish salt taste as that of the Fountain of Siloah. The water-course seems in the present day to be conducted through, under the Haram, to the Fountain of the Virgin, because it is no longer needed on South Moriah. Hezekiah conducted it on the west side of the Temple Mountain to the City of David, i.e. into the garden of the Aksa, whence it flowed away to the Fountain of the Virgin. The Gihon Fountain would appear to be somewhere near to the Holy Sepulchre. That this Gihon is to be sought in the upper valley of Hinnom, is one of those errors of topographers which has its origin in the false position assigned to Zion. It is further to be observed that de Saulcy, in connection with excavations in front of the triple door, discovered several canals and subterraneous water-courses, which may be connected with Hezekiah's works. (*Voyage*, ii. 9.[2])

---

[1] Cf. Ritter, iv. 87.

[2] Renewed investigations with regard to this part of the geography of Jerusalem have led me to the conviction, that *the palace of Solomon was in the Haram itself, on the south side thereof.* The construction of the Beth ha-Melech is described, 1 Kings vii. sqq.; 2 Chron. vii. 11 sqq. Where was this palace situated ? The groups of workmen, Neh. iii. 15-28, proceed from the south towards the north-east, in the following order : Pool of Siloah—Steps of the City of David—Tombs of David—Angle and Corner—Upper King's House in Hazar ha-Mattara —Water gate eastward. Since this Water gate eastward was situated within the Sanctuary—Neh. xii. 37, 40—the King's House and Mattara were consequently

24. Golgotha.—" Jesus *went forth* (ἐξῆλθεν) to the place called place of a skull, in Hebrew, Golgotha; there they crucified also in the Haram. In Ezek. xliii. 7, 8, the charge is made that the kings placed "their threshold against my threshold, and their posts beside my posts ; so that only a wall was between me and them." That which should be no more in the future, thus existed in the past : threshold to threshold, post to post, only a partition wall (not even an outside wall) between palace and Sanctuary. The palace was thus situated upon the Haram. Athaliah was led out from the Beth-Jehovah by the way of the going of the horses from Beth ha-Melech, and there slain, 2 Kings xi. 16. (So also 2 Chron. xxiii. 15 : " Way of the Horse gate of the King's House.") Further, according to 2 Kings xi. 20, "they slew Athaliah in Beth ha-Melech." Josephus says, *Antiq.* ix. 7, sec. 3, " Gotholja was led forth out of the Sanctuary into the valley of Kidron, in order to be slain there ; so they led her to the gate of the king's mules, and there put her to death." The Horse gate, which Jeremiah (xxxi. 40) places by the Kidron, at a corner on the east side, thus belonged to the King's House ; and, according to Neh. iii. 28, assuredly to the Haram. Remains of the Horse gate are to be found even to the present day, under the form of an ancient cornice, in the eastern wall of the Haram, near to the S.E. corner. At the time of the Crusaders the Aksa and its surroundings were known as the *Palatium Salomonis ;* and the substructures were called, and still are called, the Stables of Solomon, in accordance with a tradition thoroughly well-founded.—On the other hand, it has been observed that it is not conceivable the kings should presume to dwell on the same area with Jehovah. To this we reply : The fact that they *did* so venture stands recorded in Ezek. xliii. 8. Royalty was, before the Captivity, a theocratic institution, and was permitted to occupy theocratic soil ; as, moreover, it had its tombs in the Holy City. If, after the exile, a profane Baris, the palace of the Asmonæans, and later the Antonia, could exist without offence on the north side of the Haram, why should the King's House on the south side of the same be a thing unheard of ? To the proofs already given we add that, according to 2 Kings xi. 5, 6, three watches were set in the Sanctuary upon Beth ha-Melech, which consequently was bordering on the Sanctuary.—By the Hazar ha-Mattara, which was situated near to the King's House, Jer. xxxii. 2, there was a gate, in which the second dedication choir remained standing, and which was consequently in the Sanctuary, Neh. xii. 39, 40.—Further, we read, 1 Kings vii. 1–12, the description of the erection of the King's House, ending with the following words : "And the great court round about was of three rows of Gasith, etc.,—and so also the inner court of Beth-Jehovah." Whence arose this mention of the outer and inner court, in the account of the building of the King's House, unless the great court belonged alike to the King's House and to the house of God, and these two houses formed architecturally one whole?—Josephus says, *Antiq.* viii. 5, sec. 2, that in the palace of Solomon there were subterranean chambers (οἰκήματα ὑπόγαια καὶ ἀφανῆ) ; are not these the substructures in the Haram ? So also the LXX., Jer. xxxviii. 11, are acquainted with a subterranean house of the king— τὴν οἰκίαν τοῦ βασιλέως τὴν ὑπόγαιον. The triple portico on the south side of the Sanctuary was called the *royal portico*, βασιλικὴ στοά, that is, Beth ha-Melech. The people, however, called it by a more definite title : the portico of Solomon. The Millo,—*i.e.* "that which is *filled in*,"—of which the construction occupied so long a time, is the pile of walls which support the Haram ; and on this account a part of the palace was called Beth-Millo, 2 Kings xii. 20 ; cf. 2 Chron.

Him : the place where Jesus was crucified was *near to the city*." [1]
Near to Jerusalem therefore, but outside the city, was Jesus
crucified ; or, as it is said in Heb. xiii. 12, Jesus "suffered
without the gate." [2] As concerns the site of the Lord's grave,
it is written, John xix. 41, 42 : " Now in the place, ἐν τῷ
τόπῳ, where He was crucified there was a garden ; and in the
garden a new sepulchre, wherein was never man yet laid :
there then, on account of the preparation day of the Jews,
because the sepulchre was nigh, they laid Jesus." Where was
Golgotha, and the sepulchre ? Eusebius, *Vita Constantini*,
iii. 25–40, relates that after the proceedings connected with
the Council of Nicæa the desire arose in the mind of Constantine to accomplish a laudable work in Palestine, by adorn-
ing and consecrating the place of the resurrection of our Lord.
For until then, wicked men, or rather the whole race of

xxiv. 25. [Millo is thrice rendered by the LXX. Ἄκρα ; viz. 2 Sam. v. 9 ;
1 Kings ix. 15 (x. 22 of the Sept.), and xi. 27.] It becomes a question worthy
of consideration, whether the מִסָּד of 1 Kings vii. 9, 10 does not denote the
substructures ; for one does not make use of "precious hewn stones" as a
foundation. De Saulcy (*Voyage*, ii. p. 17) supplies an inscription which he
found on the inner side of the triple gate. The ancient Hebrew characters are
difficult to decipher ; but it is quite certain that the first word reads בלבנן.
Does not this imply that this gate led to Solomon's "Forest of Lebanon"? The
same traveller communicates an old Hebrew inscription from the portico of the
double gate, in which the name of ישו, *Jesus*, twice distinctly occurs—*and there
we have already recognised the Church of Zion*.

Yet a word as to our opinion with regard to the antiquity of the south wall.
We regard it as Salomonic in its foundation : (1) Because the S.W. and S.E.
corners thereof are decidedly the most ancient structures in Jerusalem.
(2) Because Captain Warren discovered at the foundations of the S.E. corner
Phœnician writing, which can point only to the age of Solomon. (3) The
structure cannot belong to the time of Herod ; because Josephus credits this
king with an enlargement of the area on the north, but not on the south.
(4) Still less can the south wall have been erected by Hadrian or Justinian after
the destruction of Jerusalem ; for at that time, when access to the temple was
denied to the Jews, the old Jewish inscriptions could not possibly have arisen,
as they nevertheless exist in the porticos of the double and triple gates.

The history of the southern Haram seems thus to be as follows. Solomon
built his palace upon this rocky height, Millo ; this was destroyed by Nebu-
chadnezzar, and there was consequently left a vacant broad space, which from
this time belonged to the Sanctuary, Ezra x. 9 ; Neh. viii. 1, 16. Here
Herod afterwards built the royal portico. In this the Christians had their
ὑπερῷον, and in the double gate their Church of Zion ; which they held until they
were expelled therefrom by the Mahommedans. (Later note of author.)

[1] John xix. 17, 20. [2] Cf. Matt. xxvii. 32.

dæmons through them, had put forth their utmost efforts to consign to oblivion this glorious monument of immortality. They had covered up the cave with earth brought from elsewhere, and had raised upon it a temple of Venus, there to celebrate the impure worship of this goddess and her unhallowed rites. Thereupon he gave commands to erect upon and around the sepulchre a sumptuous temple. This church was completed in the thirtieth year of the reign of Constantine, A.D. 335. On this occasion there was summoned by the Emperor a great Council of bishops out of all provinces of the empire, first in Tyre, and then in Jerusalem. Among them was also Eusebius.[1] Thus much must at once be admitted, that by the Church of the Holy Sepulchre erected by Constantine the place regarded as the site of Golgotha and the Holy Sepulchre was determined; and that from that time to the present day the same place has been regarded, without intermission, as the scene of the crucifixion and resurrection; and that the present Church of the Holy Sepulchre stands on the site of Constantine's edifice. It consequently remains for us only to test the question whether the cave, which Constantine regarded as such, is the genuine grave of the Lord; for with the answer to this question stands or falls the claim of this locality to be regarded as the scene of the resurrection. How did Constantine learn that the place built over by him was really the Holy Sepulchre? Robinson supposes, Because the place was revealed to him by a miracle,— that is to say, by an act of pious fraud,—and appeals in proof to a letter of this Emperor to the patriarch Macarius, preserved in Eusebius.[2] Constantine speaks in this letter of the gladdening discovery of "the sign of the most sacred passion of the Redeemer, which had been so long buried beneath the earth," and regards this discovery as miraculous. But the sign of the passion, τὸ γνώρισμα τοῦ πάθους, is not the grave, but the cross; Constantine does not here speak at all of the discovery of the Holy Sepulchre, but of that of the cross, of which the genuineness could of course be made manifest only by miracle. How the sepulchre was discovered we are told neither by Constantine nor Eusebius, because

[1] Cf. Robinson, i. 372 ff.   [2] *Vita Const.* iii. 30.

there was no room for speaking of any discovery whatever:
on the contrary, it is presupposed that the place is well
known; the Christians knew that it was marked out by the
temple of Venus; it was a question, therefore, simply of
removing the temple and the rubbish. But when three crosses
were found therein, only a miracle could decide which of these
was the cross of Christ.[1] With the account of Eusebius, it is
true, Jerome is in conflict.[2] He says that from the time of
Hadrian to that of Constantine, a period of about a hundred
and eighty years, there was worshipped in the place of the
resurrection an image of Jupiter; upon the rock of the cross,
a marble statue of Venus. But that here an error obtains, is
evident from another passage of the same Jerome,[3] where he
says, that on the site of the Holy Sepulchre there was a
temple of Venus. That, however, the tradition followed by
Constantine really pointed out the true sepulchre, follows
from the main argument directed against the genuineness of
the Holy Sepulchre, which consists in the following deduc-
tion: " According to the Gospels, Jesus was crucified and
buried without the city; but the Church of the Sepulchre lies
in the midst of Jerusalem; it cannot therefore indicate the
true spot." But in Constantine's day, too, they were acquainted
with the Gospels, as well as with the statement of Heb.
xiii. 12; if, nevertheless, they accepted a spot lying within the
city as the site of the grave, the improbability of this being
the true site must have been counterbalanced by a trustworthy and primitive tradition. If at the time of Constantine
the place had been no longer known, but had first to be sought
out, it could not possibly have been sought in the city itself,
but must have been looked for without it. The place is
therefore genuine, because improbable.

25. If the place is from the nature of the case possible, it
must be the true position, because improbable; that is to say,
because it would not be looked for in the city. This possibility
in the nature of the case we have now to show. The third
wall of Jerusalem was built by Agrippa I., ten years after

---

[1] Rufin. i. (xi.) 7, 8.   Theodoret., *Hist. Eccles.* i. 17.

[2] *Epist. ad Paulin.*, 49.   Tom. iv. 564, edit. Mart.

[3] *Contra Jovian.* Opp. iv. 2, 16.

the crucifixion of Christ. At the time of Christ, the city had
only two walls. If, then, that part of the city which was
enclosed by the third wall, and incorporated with Jerusalem,
comprehends the site of the Church of the Holy Sepulchre,
the same would lie, at the time of the crucifixion, without the
city, that is to say, without the second wall. That the present
wall corresponds on the western, northern, and eastern sides
to the course of the third wall, we have already shown above,
sec. 6. It now devolves upon us to prove that the second wall
did not enclose the site of the Holy Sepulchre, but passed to
the east of the same. About a hundred paces to the east of
Mount Calvary, at the north-east corner of the crossing of the
Damascus Street with the *Via Dolorosa*, excavations were
made under Pierotti's direction, with the view of preparing
for the erection (not carried out) of a Russian consulate : these
excavations laid bare a fragment of ancient wall, which beyond
doubt belonged to the second city wall. Similar ancient
fragments of a wall are to be found on the eastern side of the
demesne of the Knights of St. John, and between the Damascus
Street and the Church of the Holy Sepulchre. It is true that
the Fore City, enclosed within the second wall, appears to be a
moderately insignificant little space, if the second wall had the
course indicated by these ancient remains. But the manner
in which Josephus speaks of this Fore City, and especially
the comparatively insignificant number of fourteen towers
which he ascribes to this wall, confirm the conclusion as to the
narrow space of this quarter. Many topographers object that
in this case, as indeed is true, the Pool of the Patriarchs, or
Birket Hammam, was *extra muros*, if it was not dug by Agrippa
for the use of the New City.[1] But the most important, Siloa,
Mamilla, Es-Sultan, etc., lie without the city. It is inconceivable
that the Christians, who were never banished during a whole
generation from Jerusalem, should not have preserved in hallowed memory the site of the crucifixion and the resurrection.
The tradition unquestionably reaches back to the apostolic
age, and vouches for the genuineness of the Holy Sepulchre.

[1] [On this pool, which bears also the name *Pool of Hezekiah*, cf. Ritter,
iv. 72-75 ; and, on the fragments of an ancient wall discovered near to it,
Robinson, i. 329, 330.]

INDEXES.

I.—GENERAL INDEX.

II.—INDEX TO THE SYNOPTICAL ARRANGEMENT OF THE GOSPEL HISTORY.

III.—CHRONOLOGICAL TABLES.

(To find the year B.C., subtract the year U.C. from 754.   To find the year A.D.,
subtract 753 from the year U.C.)